THE COMPLETE GUIDE TO MODERN CABINETMAKING

Jim Christ

PRENTICE HALL, Englewood Cliffs, New Jersey 07632

Library of Congress Cataloging-in-Publication Data

Christ, Jim
    The complete guide to modern cabinetmaking.

    Includes index.
    1. Cabinet-work—Amateurs' manuals. 2. Built-in
furniture—Amateurs' manuals. I. Title.
TT197.C55   1988   684.1′6   87-1269
ISBN 0-13-160177-6

Editorial/production supervision and
   interior design: *Erica Orloff* and *Kathryn Pavelec*
Manufacturing buyer: *Lorraine Fumoso*

© 1988 by Prentice Hall
A Division of Simon & Schuster
Englewood Cliffs, New Jersey 07632

Printed in the United States of America

10 9 8 7 6 5 4 3 2

ISBN 0-13-160177-6 025

PRENTICE-HALL INTERNATIONAL (UK) LIMITED, *London*
PRENTICE-HALL OF AUSTRALIA PTY. LIMITED, *Sydney*
PRENTICE-HALL CANADA INC., *Toronto*
PRENTICE-HALL HISPANOAMERICANA, S.A., *Mexico*
PRENTICE-HALL OF INDIA PRIVATE LIMITED, *New Delhi*
PRENTICE-HALL OF JAPAN, INC., *Tokyo*
SIMON & SCHUSTER ASIA PTE. LTD., *Singapore*
EDITORA PRENTICE-HALL DO BRASIL, LTDA., *Rio de Janeiro*

For Ernest Jobst Christoph Christ:

"...Friends, I owe more tears
To this dead man than you shall see me pay.
I shall find time ...."

-W. Shakespeare

CONTENTS

PREFACE

This book was written, as a complete introduction to cabinetmaking. It is intended to provide the reader with ways of solving woodworking problems and saving time while maintaining high standards for workmanship and the sense of pride which comes along with those standards. The book does not deal extensively with the multitude of detailed instructions that are necessary to begin using and caring for hand tools, although mastery of these skills is vital to all woodworkers. It is presumed that the reader of this book has already learned a good deal about these techniques and is ready to make more practical applications of them in an environment such as a cabinet shop, in a home workshop, or even in an industrial arts classroom. For example, the novice woodworker who does not know the differences between crosscut saws and ripsaws will not be ready to use the information presented in this book. *The Complete Guide to Modern Cabinetmaking* has been written for use in cabinet shops that are seeking long-term knowledgeable employees. Home woodworkers with some background in working with wood and with only a reasonably well-equipped home workshop will find the material valuable, especially if they are growing tired of simple projects such as repairing a drawer for their next door neighbor and would like to try something a bit more challenging, such as remodeling their own kitchens without spending more than the cost of materials and electricity.

Teachers of vocational woodworking may easily utilize the book as a text for students who want to use cabinetmaking tools and skills in a trade or profession. The words "to use" are key words, for it is presumed that readers will want to spend more time in the building of cabinets than they spend in reading about woodworking. Therefore, it was my intention to present as much information as necessary to produce high-quality cabinets for almost any purpose, while purposely failing to include information that belongs in a woodworking "primer."

This book presents instructions for several methods of cabinet design and construction, and as you read each section, you should be prepared to make choices as to which designs are best for you as a cabinetmaker in your own situation. Cabinetmaking is obviously a series of processes that lead to the achievement of very particular goals, and choices made in each phase of cabinet construction must be based on which methods will attain the goals that have been set. As an example, if you are going to remodel your own kitchen and your family likes the notion of a corner sink, you may choose to leave the toekick off until the cabinet is inside the kitchen, simply because you only have a 32-in. doorway into the room. Or perhaps you have a cash-paying customer who likes the appearance of European style cabinetry, and you will be forced into building a unit with no face frame and fully concealed hinges. Perhaps it should simply be said that it is always necessary to *plan ahead*!

It has been my intention to write *The Complete Guide to Modern Cabinetmaking* as a useful book, with a great deal of pertinent information and "no fat." Because we live in a world in which time is perhaps the most important commodity, I have strived to make the book helpful to the cabinetmaker who prefers to work with machines whenever possible. Yet not everyone has a brad gun and air compressor, or a doweling machine, or perhaps not even a saber saw. When I began working independently for my own customers, my only power tools were a belt sander and an oscillating sander. Consequently, this book presents viable hand-tool options for many of the procedures described.

Finally, I urge you to be critical as you read this book. No cabinetmaker can write a book without revealing his own construction preferences—his "cabinetmaking philosophy." Whether you are a student who plans to seek a job in woodworking or an in-home cabinetmaker, now is the time to begin deciding the sort of craftsman or craftswoman you intend to be. If you have it in mind that there is something about using a hand scraper that makes the process somehow better than using a belt sander or a flush-cutting bit in a router, even though the results are virtually identical, then put this book down promptly. On the other hand, if you are product oriented and believe as I do that great cabinetmakers like Thomas Chippendale would have given almost anything to have been able to utilize the methods and materials we have today, then I urge you to read on.

JIM CHRIST

ACKNOWLEDGMENTS

My first experiences as a cabinetmaker were at the age of 12. It was the first summer of operation for E. Jay Cee Cabinet Shop, my father's business. What I learned first was a healthy respect for sandpaper. On Labor Day that summer, I learned how to mount hinges, using a hinge template jig and a spiral ratchet screwdriver. They were paint grade hinges with slotted screws. Even then, I wished for a faster way. I knew nothing about Phillips-head screws or variable-speed drills, but I thought there must be a less tedious way of working. However, I started the eighth grade the next day, glad to have learned what I had learned, and glad to be making a dollar an hour. My apprenticeship continued on Saturdays and school vacations, and during every summer. I stayed on the door-and-drawer table for a long time (forever, it seemed), but that is where I learned the importance of meticulously-made doors and drawers in creating an attractive finished cabinet. I was doing installation and assembly when I was 16, detail work when I was 21, and layout (the stick method) when I was 22, and since that time I have also been involved in the management of several shops.

I have worked as a history teacher, as a basketball coach, and as a carpenter, and I currently teach English at the junior high level; but it is impossible to stop being a cabinetmaker.

My father sold his business in 1973, but up to the day he died in 1980, he showed me ways of solving cabinetmaking problems. That is what custom cabinetmaking often is, after all: a problem-solving process. As a man, my father taught me what it means to love and to be responsible; in the shop, he taught me the skills of a practical modern cabinetmaker. My hope is that this book will help others to solve their cabinetmaking problems. I know that my dad is proud of me for this, my first book, but I am thankful for the things he gave me while he was alive, and I only hope that the book does him justice.

* * *

Most of the drawings in the text were prepared by Gary A. Williams, and most of the photographs were taken by William Fong. They have my deepest thanks.

Several Tucson businesses were quite helpful to me in writing this book as well. Names of those firms are as follows:

Custom Counter Top Co.

Oakotillo, Inc.

Tuscon Builders Hardware

Woodcrafters Cabinet Co., Inc. (especially Joe Burke)

I would also like to thank all the manufacturers named within this book for the help and consideration they gave me.

ONE

THOROUGH PRECISION: CABINET MEASUREMENT

GENERAL PROCEDURES

Before the cabinet designer makes a cutting list, before the cutter ever runs a board over the jointer, and perhaps even before the estimator figures a price, someone must acquire certain cabinet dimensions. Since it is the first step in the production of custom cabinetry, all future phases of production will hinge on measurement that is both thorough and precise. Nothing is more costly than a perfectly built and finished product which is unusable because it is either too large or too small. Furthermore, the demand for custom cabinets continues to exist mostly because they are wooden "individuals" fabricated for particular spaces and purposes. One incorrect measurement may result in the loss of a good deal of time and money invested in materials and production time. The failure to get one important dimension can halt the progress of an entire job before it is even begun. The cabinetmaker can ensure that he or she has measured both completely and exactly enough by remembering always that the cabinets will fulfill a particular purpose or function. The principle of "function first" will suggest which measurements are necessary to take and how precise they must be.

Since good measurements are vital to any cabinet job, it is surprising how little attention measuring gets as a cabinetmaking skill. It is often presumed that anyone who can read the numbers and divisions on a tape measure will be able to derive on-site measurements for cabinet production. This is not necessarily true. On the other hand, measurement requires the mastery of only a few skills, and most people who exercise a little care and foresight will be successful measurers.

Nearly all custom cabinets are built from measurements taken at the actual site where the cabinets will be installed. Naturally, the vital tool for measuring is a tape rule such as the Stanley Powerlock or the Lufkin Ultralok. The wider rules (1 in.) are preferred for job-site measuring because they remain rigid to greater lengths without support than do the narrower rules. Lengths of 20 ft or more are preferable to the shorter rules since room dimensions are frequently greater than 12 or 16 ft. It is most convenient to write down measurements directly on a floor plan, but if this is not possible, almost any piece of paper will do. A level and a framing square can also be helpful.

The experienced measurer quickly recognizes which dimensions are pertinent to the cabinet project. This skill is neither magic nor a special talent from the heavens; it is simply a learned skill. In general, proper measuring is performed by first situating the floor plan in the same way as the room to be measured, next finding features of the room that will dictate cabinet arrangements (windows, sink pipes, outlets, etc.), then visualizing where such features will be positioned, and finally taking and noting down all the dimensions that might be helpful. We will look at several situations that should prepare most students and home woodworkers for measuring and laying out their first relatively major jobs. We will examine built-in cabinets first since built-ins usually must fit particular ceilings, walls, and floors. Then we will give attention to some common furniture designs as problems in measurement. Regardless of the situation, the cabinetmaker remembers that function is first even in the measurement phase.

BATHROOM CABINETRY

Bathroom Cabinetry usually consists of a sink base (a base cabinet rests on the floor) that is shorter and shallower than a kitchen base cabinet and accessory cabinetry. This base cabinet is often called a "vanity" regardless of whether it includes a dressing area or not. The height of this cabinet is usually 32 in., and the depth 22 in. These are trade standards. Therefore, we need only measure for cabinet length and sink location unless there is a reason to modify the standards.

To arrive at the correct length for the vanity, we arrange our floor plan in the same way as the room, with wall designations on the plan parallel to the actual corresponding walls. If we do not have a floor plan, we may draw one of our own with straight lines for walls. It is important to jot down building materials present in the room. This is vital in determining cabinet length because measurements are often taken before walls have been finished, and it is necessary to account for materials that have yet to be added, such as plaster or drywall.

If the cabinet is to fill the entire space between two walls, a careful measurement is simply taken between them, usually at floor level. Because of the way a steel tape measure bends in a corner, many cabinetmakers like to measure from both walls to a point in the middle and add the two figures together. For example, we can measure from the

right wall and place a mark on the wall or floor at some convenient, easy-to-add spot such as 40 in. Then we would measure from the left wall to this point and add the two measurements. (See Figure 1-1.)

Since most of today's cabinetry employs scribe moldings to cover gaps between straight-edged cabinets and irregular walls, this single measurement is usually adequate for determining cabinet length. However, if plans call for "scribing" the face of the cabinets themselves to walls or floors, it is better to measure wall to wall in more than one location. Still, a cabinet which is to be scribed between walls will generally be designed with a facing that is larger than the opening, and measuring more than necessary is a waste of effort. We can arrive at a very accurate measurement across the front of the cabinet location using two sticks. The sticks should be longer than half the length of the space but shorter than the full length. Suppose that the desired dimension is at the top and front of the future cabinet. We would first find the correct points on the opposing walls by measuring out the correct depth from the rear corners (usually 22 in.), and up from the floor to the future cabinet height (often 32 in.). Marking these two points as the upper front corners of the future cabinet, it is necessary only to situate one end of each of the two sticks on either point. Placing the two sticks together, it is possible to mark the place where they meet, giving quite an accurate measurement. (See Figure 1-2.)

Another situation often encountered for a vanity cabinet is a plan calling for a finished end on either the right or the left side of the cabinet. The length of the installed cabinet is usually determined by allowing for the necessary clearances to adjacent fixtures. Cabinetry can be mounted fairly close to a tub or shower, but a finished end must be a sufficient distance from the toilet to allow its convenient use. We must therefore measure the location of the tub or the center of the toilet. In new-home construction, a drain pipe in the floor will indicate the location of the toilet. When the vanity is being laid out, we can simply allow an 18-in. space between the end of the cabinet and the center

FIGURE 1-1 Measuring by addition can give very accurate results. We measure from one wall, place a mark, and then measure to the mark from the other wall.

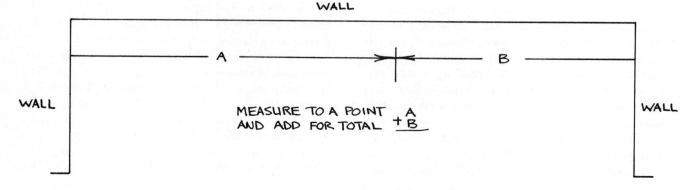

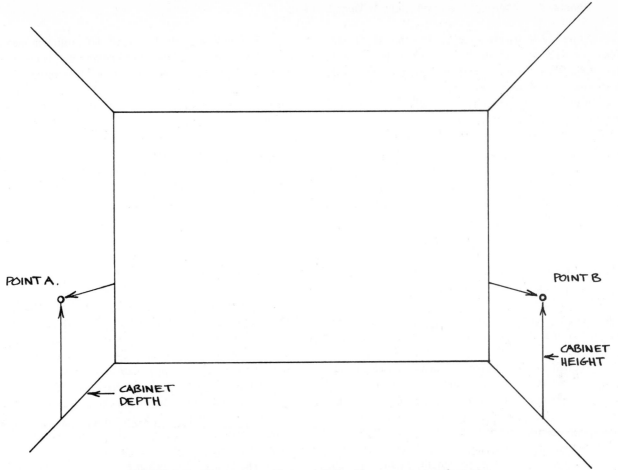

POINT A.

POINT B

CABINET
HEIGHT

CABINET
DEPTH

FIGURE 1-2 Measuring with two sticks. If we want a perfect measurement at the future location of a cabinet's top rail, we first determine its location by measuring out from the rear wall and up from the floor. Then we place a straight stick at either end (points A and B), join them together, and measure.

of this pipe. Sometimes the measurer will encounter a room where the cabinet must be built with both ends finished. Then it is important to determine clearance on both sides of the future cabinet.

Since almost all vanity cabinets will have sinks mounted in them, it is also vital to measure the position of pipes for the sink. Looking ahead, we want to ensure that the plumber will not find a water tube on the wrong side of a cabinet partition or so close to it that the finished plumbing will be a more difficult job than it should be. If the vanity is to be mounted against a wall on one side or both sides, measurements are taken from these walls to the location of the pipes. It is not necessary to get perfect dimensions of the location of these three pipes (hot water, cold water, and drain); there is almost always a good deal of clearance. We measure and note down the distances from the wall to the first pipe and to the last pipe. Since the sink section of the vanity usually has no shelves or drawers, we just need to verify a height measurement that places the pipes above the cabinet bottom, which is usually close to 5 in. (See Figure 1-3.)

Finally, it is important to make sure that the cabinet

FIGURE 1-3 Measuring pipe location.

will fit correctly in its given depth. In some small bathrooms, the wall on one side of the vanity is less than the 23 in. needed for a vanity top. This usually completes the measurement operation for a vanity cabinet. Notice that we must always think ahead to how the cabinet will function when taking measurements.

In general, we measure for a vanity by doing the following:

1. Situate or sketch the floor plan.
2. Identify walls, fixtures, and pipes that must be considered in designing the cabinet.
3. Visualize the location of wall ends, finished ends, and other cabinet features.
4. Measure for cabinet length and depth, and pipe location.

Accessory cabinets for which we must sometimes measure include medicine cabinets and linen cabinets or fronts.

Although most homes incorporate prefabricated metal medicine cabinets with mirror fronts, many plans call for incorporating wood into this common bathroom fixture. The measurements to take are the length, width, and depth of the rough opening in the wall.

Linen cabinets are usually built to fit into an opening in the wall also, and checking the length, width, and depth of the opening is usually adequate information for designing this unit. If the linen cabinet must have a finished end, it is also necessary to check for clearance of bathroom fixtures as we did for the vanity.

Measuring the height or elevation for this type of cabinet, or for any cabinet that must fit under a ceiling, is performed most accurately by using the adding technique. The measurer places a mark on the wall to show a point 20 or 30 in. from the ceiling or soffit, measures from the floor to this point, and adds the two figures together. Sometimes the cabinetmaker will be asked to build only a linen front—a face frame with doors—that must overlay an opening with shelves already installed by a carpenter. In this case it is necessary to check the height of the shelf closest to the middle so that one of the rails of the face frame will line up with it. The other shelves will have no rail to cover them; they will simply be edged.

In today's building trades, cabinetry which fills an entire opening is usually designed so that the entire cabinet product will slide back into the space, *except for the face frame*. The face frame will cover the opening so that neither molding nor scribing is necessary. Therefore, it becomes important to measure the distance from the wall opening to any wall or fixture that might be nearby. This limits the size of the overlay on the face frame. (See Figure 1-4.)

Before leaving the bathroom, the proficient measurer will check the size of the door opening that leads into the bathroom. The narrowest dimension of the future cabinets must be smaller than this doorway. He or she should also check the arrangement of any hallway to be sure that cabinetry will make the necessary turn into the room. The reason for this is obvious, but the number of times that an installer stands scratching his or her head over a beautiful cabinet that cannot go into a room is surprising. Again the importance of planning ahead and "function first" is emphasized.

KITCHEN CABINETRY

To measure for kitchen cabinets, we utilize similar methods to those employed in the bathroom. Most cabinetry in the kitchen may be classified as one of three types: base cabinets, which are generally 24 in. deep and 36 in. high with the countertop; upper cabinets (often referred to as wall cabinets), which are generally 12 in. deep and vary in height; and floor-to-ceiling cabinets such as those built to house an oven, which are most often 25 in. deep. Again, cabinet design will be largely decided by wall lengths, together with the position of appliances.

The best way to measure for kitchen cabinets is one wall or length at a time. If a blueprint is available, it may contain frontal views or elevations that will help the measurer isolate sections of cabinetry. Each of these is called a view. On the floor plan, there will be a letter or number shown together with an arrow that points at a single top view of cabinetry. This letter or number will correspond to a particular elevation of cabinetry. (See Figure 1-5.) If no print is available, all the necessary dimensions can be shown on a floor plan that the measurer sketches on the job site.

The first task is to situate or sketch the floor plan and identify the locations that will require cabinets to be installed. To avoid confusion, the proficient measurer will arrange the floor plan in the same way as the room. The types of building materials present should be noted down for each wall as mentioned earlier in the discussion of bathroom measurement.

The man or woman who does the measuring should next identify the kitchen features around which the cabinetry will function. As in the bathroom, we are usually concerned primarily with determining lengths, and the first factors to determine are the dimensions and locations of door openings and windows. When cabinets are to be constructed along one wall only, the single wall is measured much as it was described for the vanity. If the kitchen has a corner where cabinets will come together or "return,"

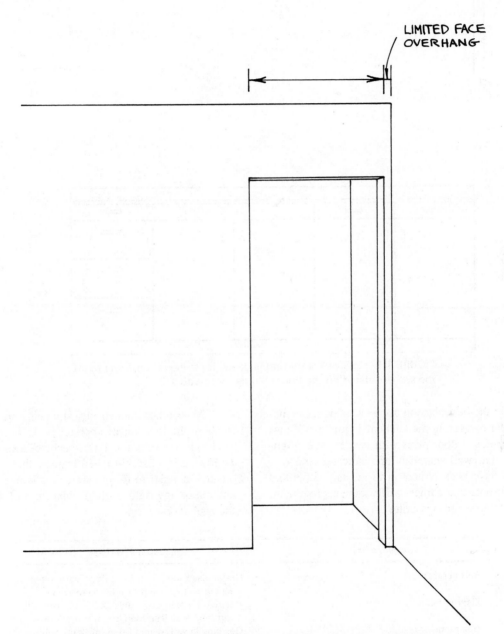

FIGURE 1-4 The amount of overlaid face frame width is limited here by the return wall on the right.

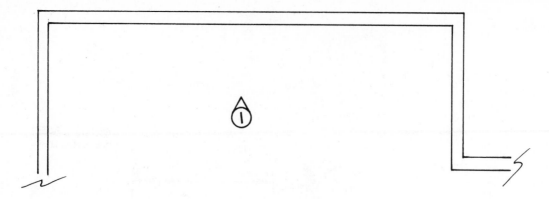

FIGURE 1-5   The cabinetry that is called for in elevation 1 will fit into the space defined on the floor plan as ''arrowed 1.''

this is probably the best place to use as a reference or beginning point in measuring the kitchen. Figure 1-6 shows two roughly sketched floor plans with very basic configurations. Note that wall materials are indicated and that measurements have been written in to indicate doors and windows. Also note that corners where cabinets return are used as the reference for measuring.

Most other kitchen measurements are written down to show the location of appliances. If we know how the kitchen is to be equipped, this becomes a simple operation. Following is a list of kitchen features that usually must be located in order to design well-functioning cabinets. The column on the right explains what to look for in locating the appliances.

Appliance or feature	*Located at or near:*
Refrigerator	Outlet less than 72 in. from floor; sometimes a single water tube protrudes from wall
Electric range or cooktop	Heavy-duty electrical cable (220-volt) protruding from wall less than 36 in. from floor
Gas range or cooktop	Gas pipe in wall within 36 in. of floor, outlet
Self-venting hood	110-volt cable protruding from wall approximately 70 in. from floor
Vented hood	Cable as above and a sheet metal duct in wall or soffit
Down-venting range (e.g., Jenn-Air)	Sheet metal duct in floor or wall below 36 in.
Built-in oven	Heavy-duty electrical cable protruding from wall
Dishwasher	Electrical outlet to right or left of sink area
Sink	Two water pipes and a drain, often below a window

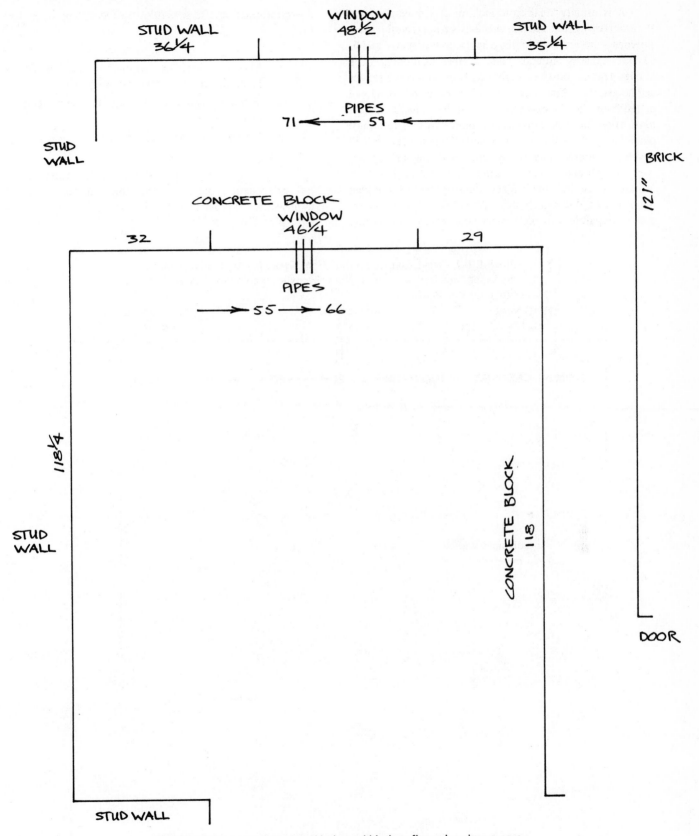

FIGURE 1-6 L-shaped and a U-shaped kitchen floor plan drawn carefully by a measurer. Note that we only draw and measure those walls and features which will affect cabinetry.

It is usually clear from looking at a floor plan and from surveying the kitchen whether or not careful measurements are required to place appliances properly and to design cabinetry around them. If the positioning of a kitchen feature must be nearly exact, as with some ranges and hoods, the cabinetmaker should measure and note down on the floor plan the exact locations of the features present, most often only the horizontal distance from a reference point, but perhaps the height as well. Some measurers will develop a simple notation system for distinguishing between length and height measurements. One such system is merely to encircle the height dimensions on the floor plan or sketch to distinguish them from horizontal measurements. Regardless of the system you develop for writing

down information, the best rules for measuring are as follows:

1. Make sure that the measurements and notations taken down are understandable.
2. When in doubt about whether to take a measurement, take it.
3. Do not trust your memory.

Figure 1-7 shows the L-shaped kitchen from Figure 1-6 with locations for appliances noted. It was presumed in measuring this kitchen that the range and the hood had to be placed exactly.

FIGURE 1-7 The L-shaped kitchen from Figure 1-6 with approximate appliance locations indicated. Note the exact measurements written down for the hood.

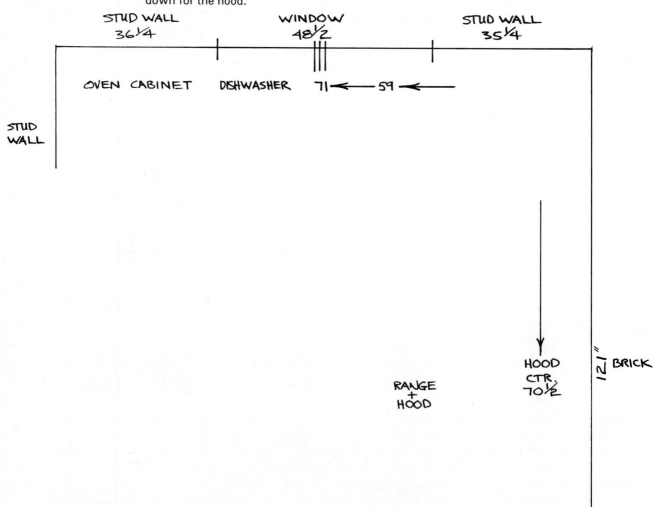

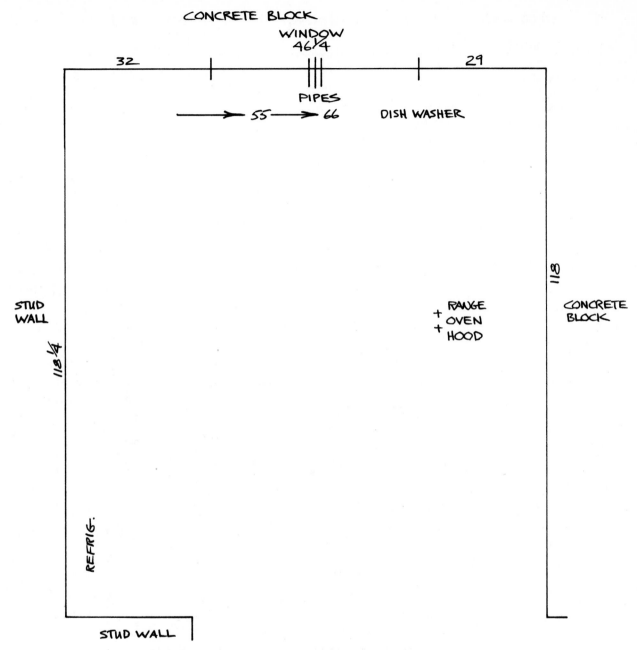

FIGURE 1-8 In this U-shaped kitchen, only approximations of appliance location were necessary.

Most of the time, it is enough to write down only the general position of appliances in a kitchen. An example of this sort of notation can be found in Figure 1-8. This is the same U-shaped kitchen as that in Figure 1-6, with general appliance notations added.

Height measurements are also integral in designing the kitchen. With modern construction, upper cabinets most often will be mounted with tops against a soffit or a ceiling which has been furred down to a height somewhere near 84 in. from the finished flooring. The measurement between the floor and ceiling or soffit is most efficiently taken with the adding technique, measuring a distance from the ceiling and then measuring to the same point from the floor. This dimension is most important in building cabinets that extend from floor to ceiling, such as the cabinet for a built-in oven or a pantry unit.

The length of a soffit can also be the determining factor for the linear dimension of both base and upper cabinets. This is because we generally desire to have the ends of bases and uppers plumb or "in line" with each other.

In some homes, the tops of kitchen cabinets will extend to an 8-ft ceiling, or they will not extend to the ceiling

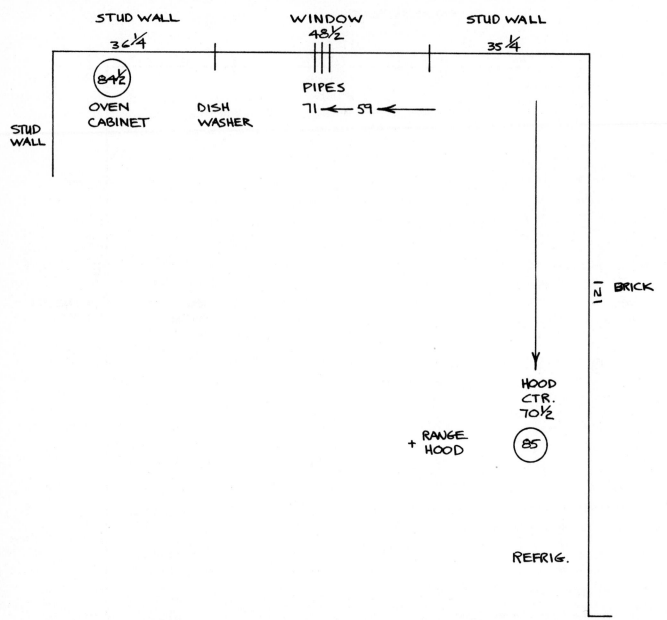

FIGURE 1-9 The L-shaped kitchen again, now with heights indicated.

at all. Still, the vertical dimension will be important in designing kitchen cabinets. Figure 1-9 shows the previously mentioned L-shaped kitchen floor plan, now with the height or elevation dimensions noted.

Following are some other important considerations in measuring the kitchen:

1. Most upper cabinets are 12 in. deep and soffits should therefore be at least 13 in. deep.

2. All cabinets, especially base cabinets, require minimum depth on walls where cabinet ends are located (usually 25 in., minimum).

3. Countertops often require 1 in. more clearance

in depth than the base cabinets on which they are mounted.

4. Workstations (sink, range, etc.) should be located as far as possible from doorways and traffic areas.

5. Switches and wall-mounted outlets for countertop appliances must be above countertops and backsplashes, below upper cabinets, and to the right or left of tall units.

6. Kitchen traffic should flow easily—allowing a minimum width (at least 36 in.) for such traffic in the kitchen will often determine cabinet sizes.

It is a good idea to visualize the kitchen as it will look with appliances and cabinets in place. This will often indicate the need to take some measurements that otherwise might be overlooked. It is easy now to take the dimensions of the kitchen necessary to begin the layout.

In summary, measuring the kitchen for cabinetry requires the following:

1. Situate or sketch the floor plan.
2. Identify walls, windows, doorways, and ceiling or soffit that will dictate cabinet design—identify the future location of sink and kitchen appliances by finding the gas, power, or plumbing feature that indicates where the appliance will be hooked up.
3. Visualize the kitchen as it will look when cabinetry and appliances are installed.
4. Carefully measure and note down the dimensions suggested as necessary by the previous stages.

OTHER BUILT-IN CABINETRY

Other built-in cabinetry may include sewing centers, "desk" areas, room dividers, bars, or those cabinets which are today referred to as "wall units." The only limitation on uses and designs for today's built-in cabinetry is the imagination of the designer. As measurement problems, each piece designed may require unique considerations, but such problems become easily solvable when the cabinetmaker can employ what he or she has learned from experiences in the kitchen and the bathroom. It cannot be stressed enough that the intended function or use of a piece will often dictate its design, and that this design will almost always define for the measurer which dimensions are necessary for completing the project. Before considering some special situations that the cabinetmaker may encounter, we will look at wall unit measurement as another practical application of this principle.

Wall units may vary substantially in function and design. In fact, wall units are not a type of cabinet at all, but rather, several types of cabinetry. They may vary in dimension, for example, from a 5- or 6-in.-deep shelving unit for the storage of paperback books to a 28-in.-deep electronics entertainment center. It is clear, then, that the design of the system and the measurements to be taken will depend on its intended purpose. We will obtain length and height dimensions following the techniques that we employed in the kitchen and bathroom. It is important to determine a measuring reference point for the walls to be measured and to indicate this on our floor plan. For electronics-housing cabinetry, it is necessary to identify the position of electrical and telephone outlets. It is even a good idea to take down exact measurements of cover-plate lo-

cations when measuring for this type of cabinetry. These measurements will allow us to keep electrical modifications to a minimum while providing easy access to wiring for the intended equipment. Built-in desks, sewing centers, and bookcases may also call for such careful procedures. For a bar sink to be incorporated into a wall system, we will only need pipe locations as we did in the kitchen and the bathroom, but bar sinks are generally much smaller than basins for the other rooms. A closer tolerance may be called for there.

SPECIAL SITUATIONS

Special situations will occasionally be encountered when taking measurements for the residential cabinetry we have been discussing. Walls may meet at angles which are not 90°, or a floor plan may even call for cabinetry on curved walls. In these circumstances, there are a number of ways to proceed.

Template making is a frequently used and extremely reliable method for determining both angles and arcs. The cabinetmaker may make a template from any convenient material. Many cabinetmakers use cardboard because it is fairly rigid, yet lightweight, inexpensive, and easy to cut with a knife. Some prefer to use 1/8-in. hardboard, although it is heavier than cardboard and requires a saw for shaping into the desired pattern. The advantage of hardboard is its strength and ability to hold intricacies of shape.

To transfer the angle of two straight walls, we need only a relatively small piece of template or scribing material—perhaps the depth of the future cabinet itself or an inch larger. One straight edge of our cardboard or hardboard is placed against one of the walls, as close to the corner as can be positioned. A line is then made on the template, parallel to the wall with which the template is not in full contact. When we remove the material outside this line, the template should fit into the corner nearly perfectly, now fully contacting both walls.

Transfer of arcs and curves requires an operation much like scribing. We begin with a piece of hardboard or cardboard of enough depth so that a fairly firm piece will be left after all the excess material is removed, and of sufficient length for the entire curve to be transferred. Using a scribing tool such as a compass (or trammel points for deep arcs), we mark a line on the template that is the same distance from the wall for its entire length. This is done by holding one point of the scribing tool against the wall and the pencil or marking end in contact with the template material. The tool is then drawn along both the contour of the wall and the surface of our template, taking care to keep it at the same angle at all times. Cutting along the line with a saw or a knife will yield the desired template. One fairly accurate cut will usually be enough for layout and construction to proceed, but more perfect fitting can be accomplished through further shaping with saw, plane, knife, or sandpaper. It will also be helpful to mark directly on the template the location of other significant features, such as windows, pipes, and outlets. (See Figure 1-10 for an illustration of the template-making techniques.)

"Difference measurement" is a much simpler method for determining the intersecting angle of two walls in a cabinet location. This operation requires only a framing square and a flexible steel tape. The framing square is placed so that one of its edges fully contacts one of the two intersecting walls as close to the corner as possible. If the angle is obtuse, the heel of the square will contact both walls and we need only measure the distance between the uncontacted wall and the toe of the square at some convenient

depth such as 18 in. (See Figure 1-11.) If the wall angle is acute, the end of the toe will touch the intersecting wall and we must get the measurement in the back corner from the edge of the square to the point at which the two walls meet. This dimension, together with the depth of the blade of the square, will give us the length of both legs of the triangle which will define the walls' angle. (See Figure 1-12.)

FURNITURE

Dimensions for custom-made furniture are frequently not derived from measurement at all, but rather from drawings or sketches. Today's cabinetmakers are often asked to pro-

FIGURE 1-10 Pattern or template making. When following a curve, we mark the cutting line with a compass or trammel point set.

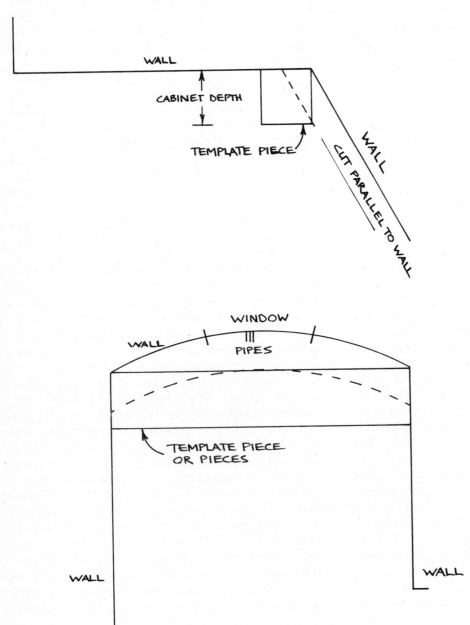

FIGURE 1-11 Difference measurement with a square. We measure the "arrowed distance."

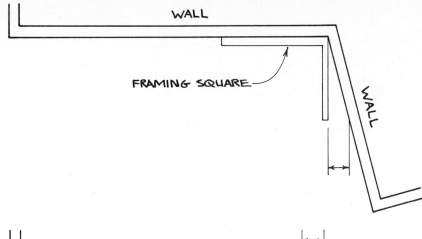

FIGURE 1-12 Difference measuring in an acute angle.

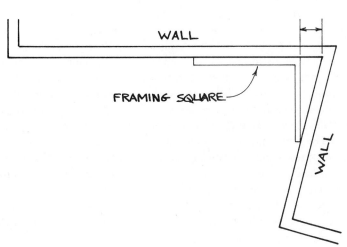

duce these sketches or "shop drawings" for a customer, or the cabinetmaker may want to develop such a drawing for his or her reference while building. The techniques for shop drawing and for reference sketching will be discussed in Chapter 3, but the drawings themselves can also be used as measuring tools. Such drawings should be used for notation regarding the many details that must be considered in designing furniture. Verbal notations will often be too lengthy and complicated to be useful. For example, building an armoire such as that shown in Figure 1-13 would require a great deal of specific information, from the dimensions for drawers, to the overall height, to the molding configurations. The determination of such matters on a piece such as this once again requires function as the first consideration. If the armoire is for an unusually tall person, we may want to plan for a higher top surface. Drawers intended for sweater storage may need to be of particular size and materials. If the piece is to match existing cabinetry, molding designs are predetermined. All of these notations are used more easily when recorded on a sketch or drawing.

All furniture pieces share certain dimensioning prerequisites. The most important of these are as follows:

1. The piece should be large enough to fulfill its function but should not be large enough to impede convenient movement in common-sized rooms.

FIGURE 1-13 With a piece such as this, a sketch (or even a photograph) is a measuring tool.

2. If the piece is designed for a particular place, it should fit with no wasted space and yet be easy to set in place and remove.

3. Even if the piece is designed for a specific location, it should be built as if it may one day be moved elsewhere. It should be light enough, compact enough, and strong enough for fairly easy movement.

CHAPTER SUMMARY OF CABINETMAKING SKILLS

To be both thorough and precise in taking measurements for the production of cabinetry, the woodworker must develop knowledge and techniques beyond the simple ability to read a tape. Most of these skills are based on a good understanding of how the proposed cabinetry will function in a particular room or space, especially in conjunction with appliances and other fixtures. Measuring well requires familiarity with certain trade standards, such as the usual heights and depths of kitchen cabinetry, as well as the abilities to read or to sketch floor plans and to locate appliances by the presence of unfinished construction features. The cabinetmaker should also know what degree of precision is required for each measurement. If great accuracy is required, as with some height measurements, the measurer should be able to use the adding technique and the two-stick measurement system to acquire these dimensions. When job sites have curved walls or walls that do not meet at a right angle, the ability to make a template and to perform difference measurement with a framing square will be important. The able measurer will recognize appropriate reference points to use in measuring, such as walls where cabinets meet or "return." He or she will also know the types of materials to be used in construction of both the proposed cabinets and that of the house or building itself. Trusting nothing to memory or chance, the measurer must write down all significant dimensions carefully and must check to be sure that units produced off-site will be easy to set in place and install.

TWO

Function First - Part I:

DECISIONS IN CABINET DESIGN

THE PRINCIPLE OF FUNCTION FIRST

No step of cabinetry is more basic than layout and design. Proficiency in this phase requires an understanding of all the subsequent phases of cabinetmaking. The designer must take into account all the available specifications, dimensions, and style factors and develop from these a shop drawing or a layout stick that will generate a cutting list and answer possible questions for the cutter, the assembler, and the installer. Yet most cabinetmakers can develop plans for kitchens, bathrooms, and other residential rooms with only a few instructions. It is suggested that you attain some mastery over the ideas in the later chapters of this book before attempting layout of complicated projects, but do not be apprehensive over trying layouts for basic cabinetry. Layout is simply a problem-solving task, and your goal should be to get your project moving, not merely to avoid errors in design.

There are two methods of cabinet layout: the shop drawing method and the stick method. Most cabinet shops today employ the shop drawing system because it is faster and more portable than using layout sticks. A few cabinetmakers trust the stick system because it allows full-scale measurements during each phase of production.

Regardless of which method you choose, it is almost always best to consider the function of each project feature first when making layout decisions. To illustrate this principle, let us consider a particular kitchen configuration. (See Figure 2-1.)

Notice that the plan calls for a workstation—the range and hood—to be on a wall between an interior doorway and a door that leads outside. There are two functions to consider. First, it is convenient to have counter space on both sides of the range or cooktop. Second, the cooking station faces a traffic area. There is a problem here because we want the cook to have a convenient work area with counter space on both sides of the range, but we do not want him or her to be run over by anyone who might need to use the exterior door. We may wish to question the architect who would develop such a design, but instead we will simply solve the problem for both the architect and the cook.

In this case, the concerns of safety and reasonable traffic flow clearly override the inclusion of convenience, and since the plan calls for a built-in oven to the right of the range, we will surely design the cabinets so that the range is as far from the outside door as possible. It is obvious that the functioning of the kitchen range must take precedence over the symmetry of the cabinets that surround it. If the oven is not a double oven, we might suggest including a slide-out work surface in the soffit-high oven cabinet, to provide the much-needed counter space to the right of the cooktop. The elevation or shop drawing of cabinets

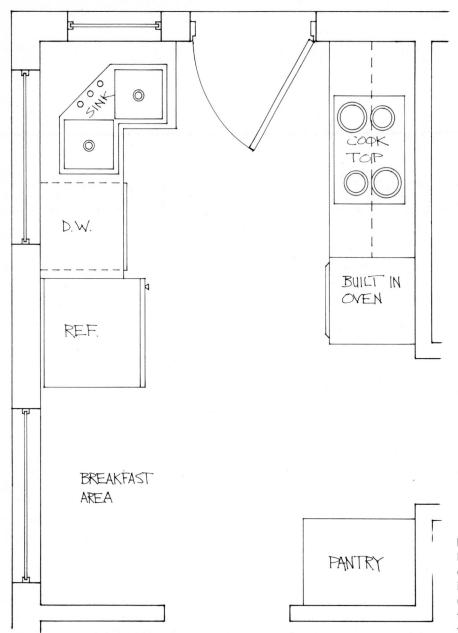

FIGURE 2-1 Imperfect floor plan. Note that to stand at the range, the cook will be in a traffic area. This is not only inconvenient but also unsafe. Note also that the unit built to house the built-in oven is deeper than the base cabinet next to it.

for this wall should be the one at the bottom of Figure 2-2 rather than the one originally drawn (Figure 2-2, top).

Layout can be defined as the development of a construction plan that will be understood by all personnel involved in the fabrication and installation of the cabinet. This plan should be detailed enough for a cutting list to be developed and should indicate all the facets of construction that must be incorporated: dimension of material, finished end location, distance between shelves, and so on. Before any drawing can begin, however, the cabinetmaker must make a commitment to a particular cabinet structure and then determine overall cabinet sizes and configurations. After the actual drawing or layout stick is completed, the

designer must still make a cutting list before production can begin. Thus layout is a four-step operation. As in any process, these operations or stages may overlap. For example, you may decide to change the width of cabinet stiles from 2 in. to (1¾ in. while writing out the cutting list, but the four stages of layout are best explained step by step.

DETERMINING CABINET STRUCTURE

Determining cabinet structure requires consideration of both the preferences of the cabinetmaker and the design features required by the specific characteristics of the job.

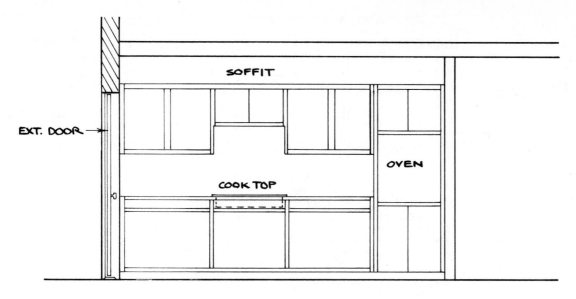

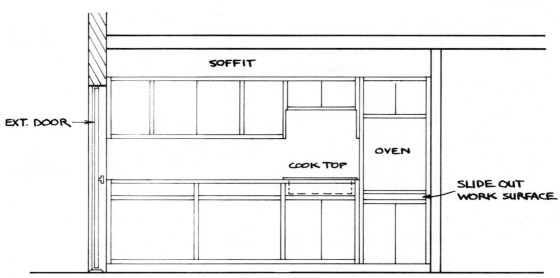

FIGURE 2-2 The elevation below will locate the cook farther from traffic to the outside. Note that a work surface may be installed in the oven cabinet.

The designer will have to make decisions based on construction features in three general areas: (1) box or case design, (2) facing design, and (3) accessory design (doors, drawers, etc.).

Box Design

The box or case consists of every piece of the cabinet behind the face. (See Figure 2-3 for reference in the discussion.) A finished end is the vertical portion of a case which is open to view. In a base or vanity cabinet it will contact the countertop at the top and will usually rest directly on the floor. This ensures the best support for countertops and appliances, but some cabinetmakers like to end this piece above the floor, even with the bottom edge of the face frame. (See Figure 2-4.) Since the top-to-floor design is stronger, the best uses for the other type of design are to provide toe space on a finished end, such as at the end of

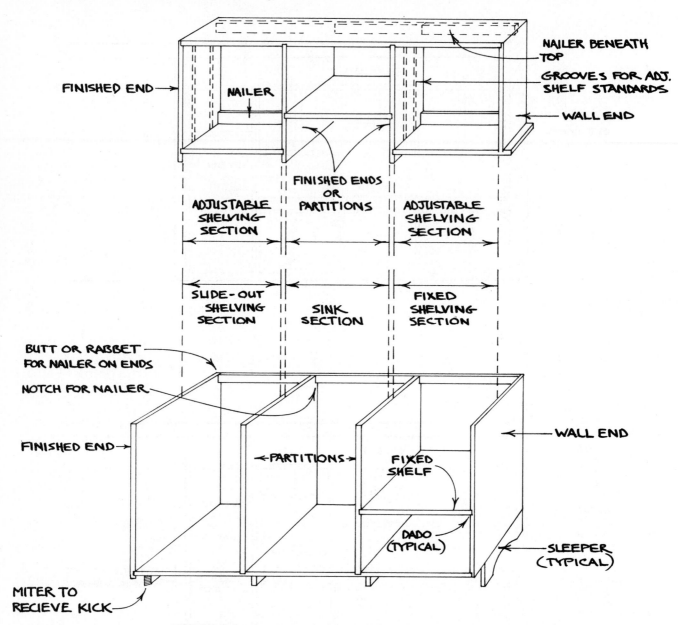

FINISHED END →

NAILER

NAILER BENEATH TOP

GROOVES FOR ADJ. SHELF STANDARDS

— WALL END

FINISHED ENDS OR PARTITIONS

ADJUSTABLE SHELVING SECTION

ADJUSTABLE SHELVING SECTION

SLIDE-OUT SHELVING SECTION

SINK SECTION

FIXED SHELVING SECTION

BUTT OR RABBET FOR NAILER ON ENDS

NOTCH FOR NAILER

FINISHED END →

← PARTITIONS →

FIXED SHELF

WALL END

DADO (TYPICAL)

SLEEPER (TYPICAL)

MITER TO RECIEVE KICK

FIGURE 2-3 Common assembly details for bases and uppers.

an island, or to cut down on splintering with cabinets that are not permanently mounted in place. The top-to-floor finished end on a base unit will also be mitered to receive several inches of the toekick, which usually runs along the bottom front edge of most base cabinets. This is because both the finished end and the toekick are made of plywood, and a miter is the simplest and most complete way of hiding the ply edges. The finished end will usually be dadoed to receive the bottom and any fixed shelves within the unit. The stringer or nailer that runs horizontally across the back of the unit is usually affixed to the finished end with glue and nails in a surface joint, although builders with more time may want to provide a rabbet for the nailer too, so that the nails may be driven in from the rear and hidden

from view. The front edge of the finished end must be flat and straight in order to receive the facing. Since moldings usually cover the spaces between a straight-backed cabinet and an irregularly contoured wall, there is usually no need to rabbet the back edge of a finished end for a back (molding will cover the raw edge of the back as well), but if the additional time required is not a consideration, you may decide to do so. In fact, a finished end may be rabbeted to a depth of $7/8$ in. or more so that the nailer can be hidden behind the cabinet back. Such a rabbet may also be deep enough to allow for scribing when ''molding-less'' installation is required. Finished ends for upper cabinets are similar, except of course there will be no toekick for which to miter, and the designer will usually want to include a top which must be dadoed in. If adjustable shelves are called for, as is common with upper cabinets, the finished end should be dadoed or "grooved" to accept adjustable shelf standard. The depth of this groove will influence shelf length. The best material for finished ends is ¾-in. plywood of a suitable grade. Half-inch plywood generally possesses only very thin veneer, and thinner materials are simply not strong enough.

Partitions are vertical members of a box that help support the top and divide a cabinet into different sections according to function. With Figure 2-3 the two partitions separate the sink section of cabinetry from two others—one with a fixed shelf and one to receive slide-out shelves. Partitions are naturally dadoed to support fixed shelves, and they are usually dadoed into the bottom for additional strength and ease of assembly. They are usually notched in the rear to receive nailers. As with finished ends, upper partitions may need to be dadoed for shelf standard. There are a number of materials that may be used for partitions, each with its own advantages. If there are no doors on the cabinet and the partitions are exposed to view, the designer will want to use the same material that he or she chose for the finished ends, but with most kitchen and bathroom cabinetry the partitions are only in view upon the opening of a door. Therefore, the material for partitions (and other unexposed pieces as well) is usually fir plywood or medium-density fiberboard (MDF). The advantage of fir plywood and other plywoods lies in their appearance. Many woodworkers and customers prize the beauty of real wood grain, even behind doors. It is also lighter in weight than medium-density fiberboard or any other particleboards, and in that sense is easier to work with. Although MDF is a particleboard and is possessed of no grain appearance, it does have advantages for the cabinetmaker and the customer also. In production, it is superior to fir plywood because of its surface texture, which never requires filling and barely requires sanding to yield a smoother surface than almost any plywood. There is never a void below the surface of MDF, there is less waste than with ply material, and it is easier to lacquer or paint. Most modern customers

will prefer the ease with which MDF can be wiped and cleaned as well. The thickness of partition material is probably ideal at ⅝ in. because ½-in. material is a bit too flexible and ¾-in. material is too heavy. Woods visible only after opening a door are called "secondary woods."

A wall end is the vertical member of a cabinet box which will not be seen at all on one side because it is situated next to a wall. Like the finished end, it supports the countertop on a base cabinet and is dadoed to receive fixed shelves. On the base cabinet, it may be dadoed to receive the cabinet bottom also and may even extend to the floor, but in a wall or upper cabinet the bottom edge of a wall end is almost always received by a dado in the upper cabinet's bottom. (Again, see Figure 2-3. Also see Figure 2-9.) It may be dadoed vertically for the mounting of shelf standard. A wall end should be fabricated of the same material as a partition.

The function and location of a cabinet bottom are obvious. The bottom of a base cabinet is most often a continuous piece, received by dadoes in both ends and dadoed to secure partitions. Since it does not contact the floor, it is supported by a toekick and supports called "sleepers" which are attached beneath the bottom every 18 in. The sleeper is usually milled in such a way that it will contact the floor only near the front and the back of the cabinet. (See Figure 2-4.) This design ultimately allows easier installation over irregular floors. The bottom of a base cabinet is usually located a sufficient distance from the floor to allow a workable toe space (3 to 5 in.). Base cabinet bottoms should be made of the same material as partitions.

Many upper cabinets do have a continuous bottom, but many do not. The height of upper cabinets is often shortened for a section to accommodate certain appliances, especially in the kitchen. The bottom of an upper cabinet is affixed to finished ends in a dado joint, but it should be designed to have wall ends dadoed into it just like partitions. This is so that the bottom will contact the wall of the building in which the cabinet is installed. Since the bottom of such a cabinet is not in plain view, it is usually acceptable to fabricate it from the same material as partitions, but

FIGURE 2-4 Detail of a finished end that does not contact the floor.

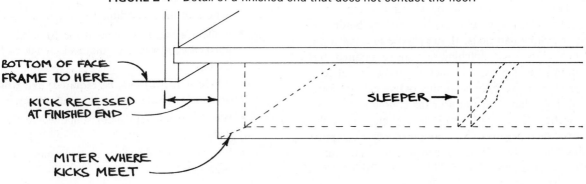

BOTTOM OF FACE FRAME TO HERE

KICK RECESSED AT FINISHED END

SLEEPER →

MITER WHERE KICKS MEET

some builders prefer to use the same grade of plywood as they use for finished ends because the underside of an upper is partially in sight, especially from nearby seating.

Fixed shelves are usually designed to be supported on both ends in dado joints that are cut into ends and partitions, although occasionally it may be necessary to mount them with cleats for some reason. These pieces will generally be edged with the same type of material as the facing, usually after the face frame is in place. In base cabinets, shelving should be at least 5/8 in. thick and of the same material as partitions and bottoms. In designing upper units, the cabinetmaker may want to use 3/4-in. material for shelves, especially if a section of shelves must span spaces of approximately 36 in. or more, but the type of material should be the same as that chosen for partitions.

Adjustable shelves most often appear in upper cabinets, but some base units may employ them as well. These are supported on each end by clips and shelf standard in most cases (although there are also hole and peg systems that might be employed), and they are usually edged with the same wood as that used on the face frame.

Tops in an upper cabinet are similar to the bottom of base cabinets: continuous, supported on both ends by dado joints, and dadoed to receive the ends of partitions. The top should be made of the same material as the shelves.

Backs for most residential cabinetry will be fabricated from sheets of 1/4-in. plywood or 1/8-in. hardboard. Backs are essential in most cabinetry for strength, especially in cabinets of the European look (with a thin facing only and no face frame). Even 1/8-in. materials add great rigidity to bases and upper units alike. Further, since the irregularity of construction in many buildings sometimes requires installation of many units in less than perfect contact with walls, backs prevent the need for fitting or trimming cabinet interiors to such walls. The appearance of the back should be as similar as possible to that of the cabinet interiors. Therefore, the designer will probably choose hardboard for backs in cabinets with MDF interiors and plywood backs to match interiors of other pieces.

Nailers or stringers are the pieces built into the cabinet for the purpose of attaching the unit to a wall in the rear. Nailers should be both straight and strong, most often fabricated of an inexpensive solid material such as pine which is free of large knots. Almost all cabinets must have a top nailer, which is most easily attached by butting to ends and notching partitions. If you choose to conceal the nailers behind the back, notching will not be required, but the partitions, wall ends, and shelving must be cut to a narrower width to accommodate this design. Upper cabinets should also have a nailer near the bottom of the case in each section. These will usually be mounted below the lowest fixed shelf or joined to the bottom of a case equipped with adjustable shelves. Base cabinets may have other nailers also, mounted either horizontally or vertically for ad-

ditional strength or merely as an aid in drawer mounting. Nailers should be at least 2 in. wide, cut either from solid pine or 3/4-in. plywood.

Most base cabinets are covered with plastic-laminate tops made by gluing pieces of plastic down to a plywood or particleboard bed or "substrate." These should be held in place with screws installed from below, through a "hold-down" attached horizontally to ends and partitions. (See Figure 2-5.) The countertop substrate material should not be nailed in place for at least two important reasons: first, like the cabinets, the plastic-laminate top is most easily fabricated off-site and then simply set into place and installed, and we obviously cannot do this if the substrate material is nailed into place at the job site; second, over time some nails may work their way upward, causing a bulge or even a hole in the plastic laminate. Hold-downs may be cut from any 3/4-in. plywood or solid material. As the cabinetmaker, you may prefer to mount the hold-downs along the front of the top nailer and along the rear top edge of the face frame. This is a superior way of attaching the hold-downs because they may then also serve the purpose of holding the face frame more rigid and straight. (See Figure 2-5.)

So far, our discussion of the nature of cabinet box design has had to do only with standard bases and uppers. The design of most other residential cabinetry, such as oven cabinets, pantries, and wall systems, should be relatively easy to determine from the previous discussion. In a book of this length it is impossible to discuss the design factors of every type of cabinetry and furniture. Nevertheless, most of the decisions made prior to drawing a kitchen layout plan are the same sorts of decisions made before planning any woodworking project. Mastery of basic cabinetmaking design is vital in producing any complex project. The furniture-design modifications that must be made in common cabinetmaking practices are discussed in Chapter 13.

Since most cabinets and furniture consist of some sort of box covered with a facing and with certain accessories attached, the planning of any woodworking project should proceed only after answers have been given to the following box-design questions:

- Will finished ends contact the floor or stop at the bottom of the face frame to yield a toe space?
- Is there a reason to rabbett the back edge of the finished end to receive the back or the nailer and the back?
- Where will partitions be required, and what controls their distance from ends and other partitions?
- Which joints require dadoes, and where else would dado joints be helpful?
- Where will fixed shelves and adjustable shelves be necessary?

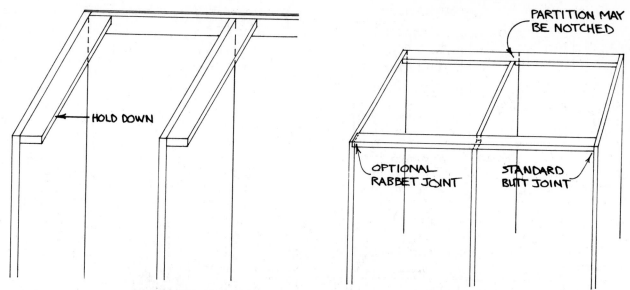

FIGURE 2-5 A hold-down may be attached to ends or partitions in butt joints with glue and nails. Hold-downs may also be attached along the front and back of the cabinet. The counter top may then be attached by screwing upward through the hold-down.

- Will there be doors, or must the cabinet interior be constructed of primary wood?
- What thicknesses, types, and grades of material will be used for each cabinet part?
- In general, where and how will nailers be attached? Will the nailers be in front of the back or behind it?
- What types of countertops will be used, and how will they be fastened in place?

Facings

The facing of a cabinet may be either a "face frame" or a relatively thin edging. A face frame is constructed as a single piece, independently. It is then laid over the cabinet box and fastened to it. This type of construction gives the cabinet great strength, allows for a wide variety of door-and-drawer mountings, and presents a beautiful front to anyone who will be seeing the cabinet.

The face frame is nearly always made of solid material of the same type as the veneer on all the finished ends. For example, an "ash kitchen" would be fabricated from ash-veneer plywood for finished ends and a face frame of solid ash hardwood. The finished thickness of the face frame is usually ¾ in. The cabinetmaker may use either surfaced or unsurfaced four-quarter (4/4) hardwood. Using surfaced hardwood eliminates the need for thickness planing, but some pieces of hardwood will be too warped or twisted for good face frame material. You may prefer to

purchase unsurfaced hardwood and surface it yourself with a wide jointer and a planer.

Face frames consist of three types of pieces. Stiles are the vertical end pieces of a frame. Their length is the full height of the face frame. Rails are the horizontal pieces of the frame. Mullions are the vertical pieces of frames which divide the face frame into sections. (See Figure 2-6.) If the cabinetmaker has decided to employ face frames on his or her cabinetry, decisions must be made regarding the widths of stiles, rails, and mullions as well as what type of joint is to be used in assembling these pieces.

All the pieces in a face frame should be wide enough to provide structural strength, but they should not be so wide that they limit access to the cabinet interior. Naturally, narrower stock is also less expensive. For most cabinets, stiles should be a minimum of 1¾ in. wide. A 2-in. width is also very common. Where two cabinets meet in a corner or return, stiles must usually be at least 3 in. wide to allow the proper functioning of doors and drawers, together with the attached hardware. Mullions may be as narrow as 2 in., but sometimes the size of door overlap or a particular hinge design will require a mullion width of 2½ in. or more.

The width of rails is dictated by several factors. Again, we want rails wide enough for strength and support and narrow enough to permit easy access to the box within. The overlap of doors and drawers and the proper functioning of hinges must of course be considered. In addition, the width of a top rail on a base cabinet is controlled by the weight of the countertop which it must help support and

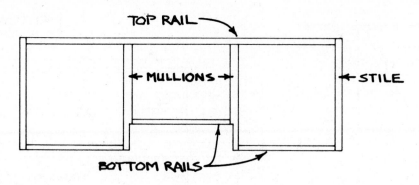

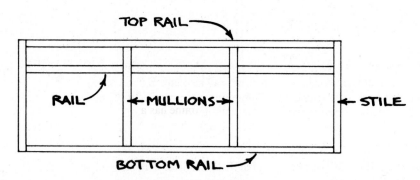

FIGURE 2-6 Face frame stiles, rails, and mullions.

the size of the countertop overhang. The top rail of a base cabinet is usually between 2 and 2½ in. The top rail for an upper cabinet will be partially hidden by molding and should be at least 2 in. wide. Some cabinetmakers prefer to build face frames without a bottom rail, but a bottom rail obviously helps to make the cabinet stronger and helps to make it square. It is fairly simple to make the top edge of this rail flush with the cabinet bottom. For the purpose of strength, bottom rails should be at least 1¼ in. wide.

Most other rails are present to separate drawers from other sections of the cabinet and to support them. These rails should be at least 1½ in. wide, but certainly no wider than 2 in.

The most common face frame joining systems are as follows: the butt joint supported with screws, the butt joint supported by dowels, and the mortise-and-tenon joint. (See Figure 2-7.) The great advantage of the mortises and tenons is that they provide an extremely strong joint. When

FIGURE 2-7 Common face frame joining methods.

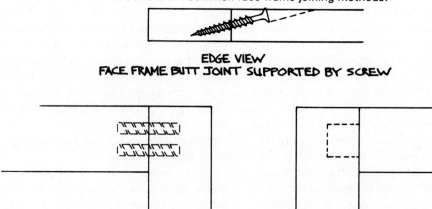

the stiles and rails are fit carefully and glued under the pressure of clamps, the frame will be rigid and secure. The principal disadvantage of building all the frames in this way is that the process is quite time consuming. Some shops, large or small, will possess a mortiser and a tenoner to perform these operations, but many shops cannot afford the expense of such machinery. Unless you have either the machinery or a customer who does not mind paying for your additional time, this type of joint may be somewhat impractical, especially since other joining systems are faster and may be nearly as strong.

Many large-scale cabinetmaking firms have converted to a face frame machining and assembly system which is basically sound and very rapid. Butt joints are employed, secured by either a wood screw or a drywall screw that is driven in and countersunk at an angle from the rear face of the frame. Some expensive equipment may be required for this operation, however. Since a good drilling setup is required, a machine is required that will hold each stock firmly and drill clearance and countersink holes at the same time and at exactly the correct angle and depth. Since screws driven at an angle ("toe screwing") will tend to pull individual pieces off line, we also need a large, perfectly flat table and clamp-down system to use in assembling frames. (More information on this system is developed in Chapter 7.) Toe-screwed joints may or may not be as strong as other face frame joints, depending on who is making the comparison. It is good to remember, that the strength of the joints will be limited by the wood's working hardness—screws can pull out of soft wood fibers fairly easily. Still, this type of joint has been proven to be strong enough for most face frames, and it is much faster to make than a dowel or worked joint.

Doweling remains a preferred frame assembly system with many cabinetmakers. As with the screwing systems, we make butt joints, but these are easy to make flush because the only pressure applied is directly across the joint. A machine that will drill dowel holes is much less expensive than the machinery for mortising, tenoning, or toe screwing. Accurate homemade dowelers are also fairly easy to construct. Gluing with dowels under the pressure applied by clamps is quick and yields a very strong face frame. In effect, a dowel becomes a round tenon that fits snugly into a round mortise.

Before moving to a discussion of frameless cabinetry, it is important to consider the method that is to be used in joining the face frame to the cabinet box. Where there is a finished end, the best appearance will be achieved by making the stile of the frame flush to the outside surface of the plywood, filling the seam if necessary, and sanding the entire side. Less attractive alternatives are to V-groove the seam with a specially designed router bit or to allow the face frame to overhang the plywood a small amount in order to avoid some sanding. (See Figure 2-8.)

If the frame has a bottom rail, it should be made flush to the cabinet bottom. V-grooving would create a dust collector, and we certainly do not want the edge of the bottom rail to protrude above the surface of the cabinet bottom.

Stiles that are fastened to wall ends should *not* be mounted flush to them. At the wall, we want an overhanging face or scribe that will allow ease of installation. Scribe width should be at least ⅜ in. (See Figure 2-8.)

Stiles that join to a return cabinet (cabinets that meet in an L-shape are said to "return") may contact neither an end nor a partition. These should be mounted securely to any fixed shelves, to a hold-down at the top of a base cab-

FIGURE 2-8 Top views for three types of face-to-finished end mounting, and face-to-wall end mounting.

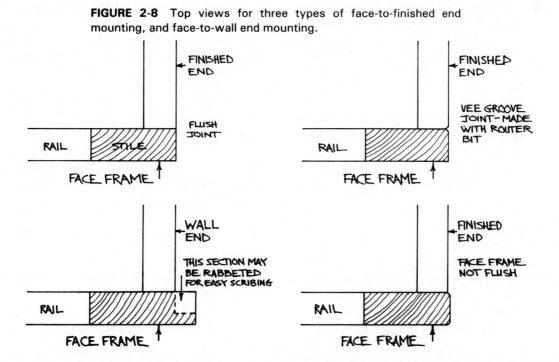

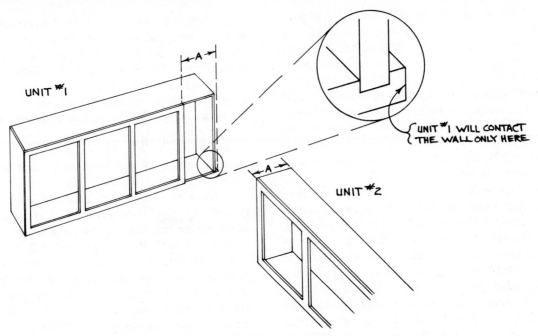

FIGURE 2-9 Two upper cabinets to be joined in a return. Note that the right-hand stile of unit 1 is positioned far enough from where the unit contacts the wall to accept the entire depth of unit 2 (dimension A). Also note that the wall end of unit 1 is dadoed into the cabinet bottom in such a way that it will not contact the wall.

inet, and to the top itself in an upper cabinet. The position of this stile must be a sufficient distance from the cabinet end to allow for the depth of the return cabinet. On the return cabinet itself, the stile should be exactly even with the end of the case itself. (See Figure 2-9.)

Mullions are usually centered over partitions of the case. On base cabinets, care should be taken to allow enough space for drawer-mounting material where needed. Some mullions are used simply to divide a space that is too large for a pair of doors. In this case, the mullion will be fastened only to fixed shelves that may be present. The structure of a face frame is strong enough to support this configuration. (See Figure 2-10.)

An upper cabinet's top rail will be secured to the top of the case, usually flush at the top edge. If moldingless installation is planned, the designer will want to hold the top of the box below the top edge of the face frame so that the cabinet may be scribed directly to a soffit or ceiling. (See Figure 2-10.)

Most of the other rails of a cabinet are present to support drawers. Other than in some furniture designs, these will be secured only to other members of the face frame. (Furniture drawer rails are discussed in Chapter 13.)

When a thin edging is used for a facing rather than a frame, it is to create a "European" look or because the cost of hardwood prohibits using a face frame. This sort of cabinetry originated in Europe, where solid stocks are in

short supply. Because these facings are so thin and narrow (often ¼ in. thick and whatever width is needed to cover the thickness of plywood used for the box or case), little solid stock is required for a cabinet. Some of the disadvantages of this system are obvious—there is no face frame for strength at the front of the cabinet, and there is no frame to be used in squaring up the cabinet. Furthermore, hinge choices can be limited, and some European-style hinges may cost $5 per pair or more. Still, European-style cabinetry is growing in popularity, and the difficulties can be overcome.

Cabinets in this style are easy to fabricate. The width of ends, partitions, and shelves must be wider to achieve the desired cabinet depth, and we may want to design the cabinets with enough scribe material so that they may be installed without molding, but the chief difference between this type of cabinetry and face frame cabinetry is that facings are mounted prior to assembling the box. This allows ease of machining and sanding.

Before proceeding with layout, then, the face-design questions that must be answered are as follows:

- Will the proposed cabinets have a frame or only a thin facing?
- Will the face be cut from surfaced lumber or milled from unsurfaced lumber? (Remember that you need

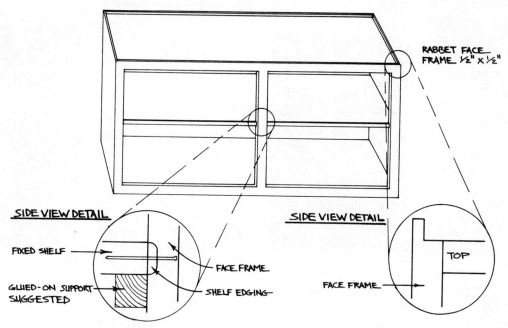

FIGURE 2-10 Upper cabinet to be scribed to a soffit at the top. A mullion is used to divide a wide door opening. The "glue block" gives additional support for the fixed shelf, and the top edge of the face frame is rabbeted for ease in scribing.

both a wide jointer and a thickness planer to prepare unsurfaced material.)

- How will the components of the face frame be joined together? (Consider the equipment available.)
- In general, what will be the widths of stiles, mullions, and rails?

Accessories

Accessories are all those items added to a cabinet, either inside the case or attached to its front, after the facing has been attached to the box and the whole unit has been sanded. These include doors, drawers, slide-out shelves, lazy susans, and a few other components. Here we are concerned primarily with structural features such as the materials employed, common joints, and systems for attaching the accessory to the cabinet. However, the appearance of accessories such as doors and drawers is often a major factor to be considered in determining their proper functioning.

Doors. We discuss this first in connection with doors. It is obvious that flush-mounted doors should not have a detail along the edge that is to align with the facing. Flush doors are used to give the cabinet a flat, simple appearance, and edge details detract from this appearance. The size of door openings may also be influenced by door

appearance; doors with decorative arches cannot be fabricated in narrow widths without destroying the integrity of the arch. With this type of door, we may want to make adjustments during layout to ensure that no single door openings are narrower than 10 or 12 in. and that no paired door openings are narrower than 20 to 24 in. Several door designs are shown in Figure 2-11. Different appearances in doors may be gained by a combination of factors: the method of fabricating the door itself, hinging, and hardware or finger pull for opening the door.

Doors may be fabricated in a number of ways. Flat or single-surface doors may be constructed either from solid materials or from plywood. Ply doors are the simplest to make. They are merely cut to the necessary size, perhaps detailed in some way (a lip, bevel, or finger pull on its edge or decorative routing or molding on its surface), sanded, and hung on the cabinet. In today's cabinet trade, this door material may be ply core, lumber core, or single core (MDF or particleboard core) sheets. The single-core material is heavier but generally requires less void filling and edge sanding. Some cabinetmakers like to cover raw ply edges of these doors with veneer or solid edging. The dimension of this edging must naturally be accounted for during layout. Plank doors, doors made by gluing pieces of solid wood together, are also usually flat doors. Most commonly consisting only of vertical pieces, these doors may also be assembled in other configurations to yield eye-catching appearances. (See Figure 2-11.) Doors constructed entirely of hardwoods are generally heavier than plywood doors,

(1) (2) (3) (4)

(5) (6) (7) (8)

(9) (10) (11)

FIGURE 2-11 Sampling of door designs: (1) laminated vertical planks; (2) horizontal planks within a frame; (3) plain flush door with drawer front; (4) plywood door with random plank appearance; (5) flush overlay door with drawer front; (6) raised inset panel; (7) arch-top, raised inset panel; (8) flat inset panel; (9) arch-top with back panel; (10) Back panel doors with long-curve rails; (11) back panel door with plant-on.

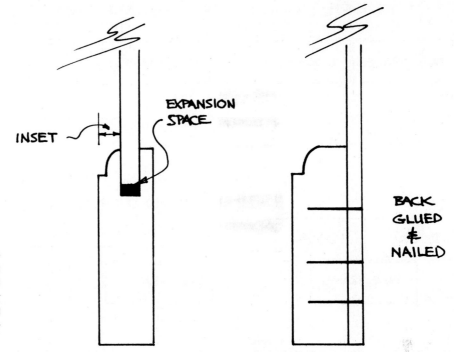

FIGURE 2-12 Inset panel doors may be used with any mounting design; if the inset panel is solid material, room must be allowed for expansion. Doors with overlaid panels are seldom used as overlay type doors.

and the larger sizes such as those which are used on pantries may require extra hinges or heavier-duty hinges. Solid hardwood doors will also be more expensive and time consuming to build than most ply doors.

Frame doors can be constructed when a more decorative appearance is desired on the cabinetry. These doors consist of stiles and rails, a frame similar to a face frame, with a panel that is either fit into slots in the stiles and rails, or attached as an overlay to the back of the frame with glue and brads or staples. (See Figure 2-12.) An inset panel may fit tightly into the slots designed to hold them if it is plywood or a material that does not shrink and expand much. If the inset is of solid stock, such as with most raised-panel doors, it must not fit too tightly into the slots or its expansion will break or crack the door frame. The layout person must be aware of these factors in order to be able to develop the cutting list. Back panels, panels attached as overlays to the back of the door frame, are almost always made from ¼-in. plywood. They are seldom used on slab overlay doors but rather on lipped doors or reverse bevel doors. These edge details help to conceal the raw edge of the plywood back. The back panel is generally cut to the same size as the overall dimensions of the frame and attached. The backs may be glued into position without any brads or staples if the cabinetmaker has a press or the time to clamp a set of doors, but builders with a pneumatic staple or brad gun will prefer to use these tools and simply fill the backs of the doors with a good filler paste. Cabinetmakers with good shaping equipment will usually make frame doors with an inset panel rather than a panel overlaying the back of the frame. The panel of the door is as-

sembled into the body of the door when the frame itself is put together. Assembly is a one-step rather than a two-step operation since we do not have to assemble a frame and then attach a back. There are also no visible ply edges or staple holes to deal with.

In terms of door appearance, then, the layout person is interested as to how the looks of the door will affect its assembly and how these assembly procedures dictate the making of the cutting list. Arch-top and curved-rail doors obviously require wider rails than do simpler square-frame doors. The dimensions of door parts will also be a factor in choosing door frame joining method. Most door frames that are to receive overlaid backs will be glued as dowel-strengthened butt joints; the length of rails is simply the overall width of the door minus the width of the two stiles. With doors that are put together using shaper-cut details, the joint will be similar to a mortise-and-tenon joint. The length of rails depends on the additional length needed to provide for this tenon. Laying out and listing depends on knowledge of exactly how the doors are to be detailed and assembled.

Plywood doors are usually made from ¾-in. ply. Plank doors, the stiles and rails for frame doors, and raised panels are all made from surfaced four-quarter (4/4) solid stock. The true thickness of this material is usually slightly more than ¾ in. Flat inset panels and overlaid backs are most often ¼-in. plywood.

Another important factor in door design is the way in which the door will fill its cabinet opening. Usually, this is designed in one of three ways: flush, lip, or overlay. (See Figure 2-13.)

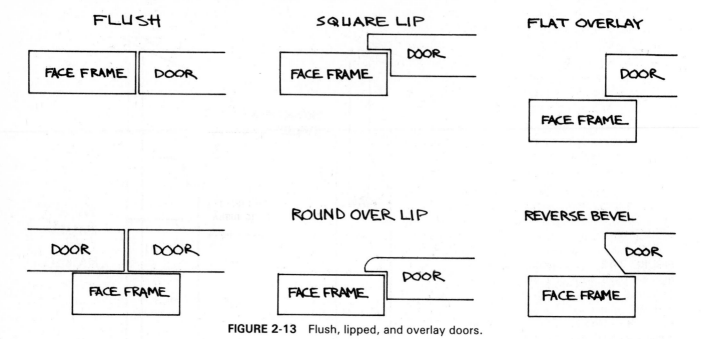

FIGURE 2-13 Flush, lipped, and overlay doors.

The size of a flush door is simply the size of the opening in the face frame where it will be mounted, less a small amount for hinge swing and clearance (³/₃₂ in. or more) along each edge and end of the door. For example, a cabinet opening that is 12 in. × 20 in. will require a flush door with finished dimensions of 11¹³/₁₆ in. × 19¹³/₁₆ in. If pairs are required, the designer will want to allow at least another ¹/₁₆-in. clearance for where the two doors meet. If an opening is 34 in. × 20 in., there will be two doors, each 16⁷/₈ in. × 19¹³/₁₆ in. [This is the total width minus all three clearances, with the result divided by 2 (34 − ³/₃₂ − ³/₃₂ − ¹/₁₆)/2]. Some cabinetmakers prefer to subtract less clearance size and to trim away material that rubs against other cabinet parts by sanding, but if face frames are as square as they are supposed to be, such a procedure is unnecessarily time consuming. Hinges for flush doors are usually either strap hinges or butt hinges. (See Figure 2-14.)

Whereas flush doors are almost always flat plywood, lipped doors (or inset doors) may have just about any appearance design. The lip is a rabbet along all the edges of a single door, and along the top, bottom, and the hinged side of a pair door. The size of this rabbet is often close to ³/₈ in. × ³/₈ in. However, since this type of door is almost always mounted on the face frame with a semiconcealed lip hinge (Figure 2-14), the exact machining of the lip should conform to this hinge.

Sizes for lipped doors are extremely easy to determine, partially because they do not have to conform to the opening in the face as perfectly as do flush doors, and partially because they almost always have the same size of lip. Ideally, this sort of door will cover its opening with a ¼-in. overlap on all four sides. To determine the finished door size, we have only to add ½ in. to the opening width and height. This allows room for the hinge and for clearance, while still covering the opening nicely. Thus the finished door size for an opening of 12 in. × 20 in. will be 12½ in. × 20½ in. No additional clearance is usually needed for pair doors; we simply add ½ in. to the overall width of the opening and divide the total by 2. A 34-in. width should yield doors that are 17¼ in. wide. A wide variety of styles is available in the semiconcealed lip hinge—some of which are screwed to the front of the face frame, some of which are screwed to the hidden edge of the frame, and demountable hinges which are put in place using a router. In addition, there are a few strap-type hinges available for round-over lip doors.

As with lip doors, overlay doors (sometimes called slab doors or lap doors) may be fabricated to yield almost any appearance. They may often be mounted without pulls

FIGURE 2-14 Hinge types. *Top (L-R):* Pin, butt, European; *bottom (L-R):* Demountable, semiconcealed, "knuckle."

or knobs because their full thickness extends in front of the facing, and they can easily be detailed with a reverse bevel or a cove to be used as a finger pull. Flush doors and lipped doors may also be mounted without pulls and knobs, but usually this requires installing some type of pressure latch. Fully concealed hinges are designed primarily for overlay doors, and the hinging for this type of door almost always swings the door entirely clear of the door opening. This allows freest access to interior accessories such as slide-out shelves. The overlay door also allows for some error in mounting since it does not have to clear any portion of the facing to function. For all these reasons, it is probably the most commonly used type of door today.

Since the overlay door simply laps over its opening by some particular dimension, its finished size is very easy to determine. The overlay dimensions are simply added to the sizes of the door openings. Some hinges, particularly the fully concealed variety, will require the use of certain overlay amounts. With many other hinges, exact overlays are not specified, but it is important to determine the minimum overlay that will allow the hinge to function. The overlap is most often at least ½ in. and usually greater. Doors with reverse bevels or those with a cove detailed as a finger pull must possess at least a ⅝-in. overlay. A flush overlay arrangement can also be created by using pin hinges and allowing the overlay doors to come within ³⁄₃₂ in. of each other on each mullion. (See Figures 2-13 and 2-14.) Since there is so much flexibility in the overlay chosen, it is important for the designer to allow room for the specified overlay and the specified hinges on all face frame stiles and mullions. If machined finger pulls are planned for instead of knobs or pulls, the cabinetmaker should also allow sufficient space between doors and drawer faces for fingers to reach the pulls. The minimum for this should be ¾ in. between edges.

If a door opening is 12 in. × 20 in. and the cabinetmaker is planning for a ⅝-in. overlay, the door for this space should be 13¼ in. × 21¼ in. Each door of a pair designed to cover a 34-in. opening width should be 17⅝ in. wide.

There is a wide variety of hinges available: semiconcealed, fully concealed or European, demountable, pin, and even specially contoured hinges for reverse bevel doors. (Again, see Figure 2-14.)

Drawers. When planning the cabinet job, the cabinetmaker must already know much about the drawers to be used. Just as with the doors, no specific layout can take place until the designer has made several decisions regarding drawers. He or she must know something about the appearance of the drawer front—usually how its appearance will be related to the look of doors on the same cabinet job. Decisions must also be made concerning the way in which the drawer front will fit its opening, the method to

be used in assembling the drawer box, and the system of drawer guiding to be employed.

In general, the choice of a particular door style will automatically suggest the appearance of the drawer front. Outer edge forms will be the same, for example. Plywood doors will mean plywood drawer fronts of the same material. Although the grain runs vertically on most plywood doors, most cabinetmakers choose to display horizontal grain on the fronts of drawers. One exception to this is when a flush overlay arrangement is used. (See Figure 2-11.) Since there is only a small gap between all doors and drawers on this type of cabinet, we usually want the grain to match wherever possible. All the grain is vertical, and we make sure that a drawer mounted directly above a door is cut from the same piece of plywood. In fact, a few cabinetmakers used to fabricate face frames and flush mount doors from the same pieces of plywood so that all the grain matched. This is seldom done today. If the plywood doors on a cabinet have decorative routing, there is usually not enough room on the drawer front for this decoration, and most cabinetmakers simply keep the surface of the drawer front free of detail. Occasionally, the detail can be modified in some way for the drawer front, as with provincial molding or routing. With plank or frame doors the drawer front is most often a single piece of solid material with the grain running horizontally. Drawer fronts are almost always ¾ in. in thickness, and they will usually have the same edge detail as doors on the job. This is true even when the doors are lipped doors with overlaid backs that protrude only ⅝ in. from the cabinet face. If the doors have such backs and are used as overlay doors, the designer may want to plan for drawer fronts that have a thickness of 1 in.

The drawer front usually fits its designated cabinet opening in the same way as doors on the same job. Drawers may be flush mounted, lipped, or overlaid. The only exception is the lipped door with an overlaid back discussed above.

The front of a drawer may either be assembled as part of the drawer box, or it may be attached to a separately built drawer box, using countersunk screws. (See Figure 2-15.) There are many advantages to building a separate drawer box, and this is the way that most drawers are con-

FIGURE 2-15 Drawer front mounting with and without a subfront.

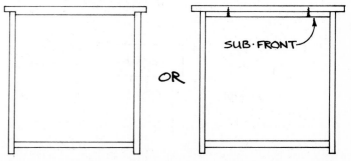

structed today except when drawer fronts are lipped. One advantage is that there is less detailing to do with separate drawer boxes—the drawer front needs no rabbeting or other machining to make it accept the drawer sides and bottom. The subfront in a separate box design can be milled in much the same way as the back and sides. In addition, drawer fronts can be adjusted to fit a cabinet opening without altering the position of the box or guides. This can be a tremendous advantage in fitting flush drawers and in other situations.

There are several common joints and fastening sys-tems which can be employed to assemble drawers. (Refer to Figure 2-16 in the discussion.) Drawer fronts or sub-fronts may meet drawer sides in several ways. Least time consuming is a butt joint held together by gluing and either nailing or stapling. This is a very common joining system in today's trade, even though it is not as strong as inter-locking joints that can be made. Most drawer guides in modern use function with wheels or ball bearings that greatly reduce friction as the drawer slides in and out, and there is much less stress on drawer joints than there would be in using wooden guiding systems. In addition, glues are

FIGURE 2-16   Drawer joining details. Note the side view of the dove-tail joint.

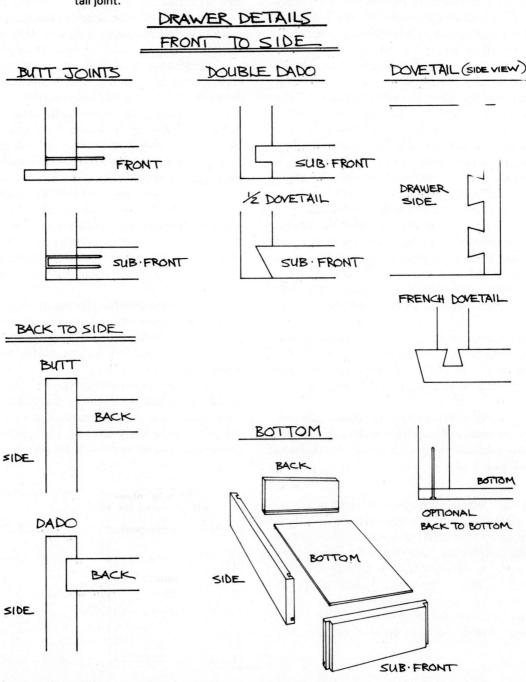

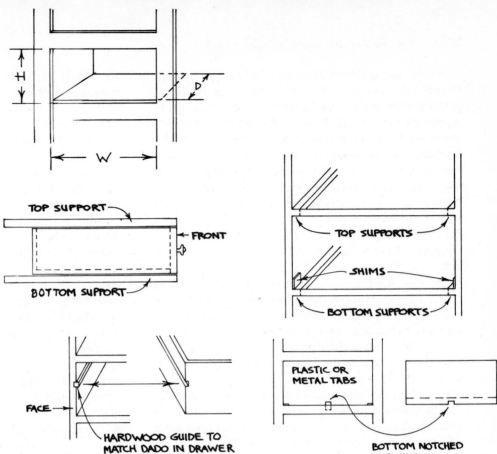

FIGURE 2-17 Drawer dimensioning. Box width is a factor of opening height and designed clearance. Naturally, box width and depth are controlled by width and depth of opening. (See Tables 2-1 and 2-2.)

stronger now than they ever were before, and pneumatic-driven staples have great holding power. For all but heavy-duty applications, this is a quite satisfactory joining system, especially in small shops with limitations upon equipment. The half-dovetail joint is somewhat stronger, and the necessary detailing may be performed with only one setup of the router, shaper, or table saw. During layout, the cabinetmaker has to determine the additional length needed to perform this type of milling on the subfront. Stronger still is the double dado joint, which requires two more milling operations than the butt joint. The French dovetail (sometimes called the dovetail dado) is a very strong interlocking joint. The slanted dado itself is run vertically in the rear face of the drawer front (a subfront is not easily applied to this type of joint) and beveled rabbets are machined on the mated edges of the drawer sides. Most time consuming is the dovetail in which interlocking pins and tails must be milled or hand cut. The French dovetail and the dovetail joints are very strong but can be costly in time. They are best applied in furniture and in heavy-duty drawers such as file drawers.

Drawer backs are usually joined to drawer sides with nailing or stapling and glue in one of two ways—either a simple butt joint or a dado joint. Generally, if the cabinetmaker has chosen butt joints for the front-to-side connection, he or she will also employ same joints for joining the back to the sides. Choosing one of the more complex joints for the front and sides will usually be a signal to employ a dado for the rear joints.

The simplest way, and probably the strongest, to build in the bottom of the drawer is to run dadoes near the bottom edge of the front or subfront, the sides, and the back. Some builders prefer to dado only the front and the two sides and to position the back on top of the rear edge of the drawer bottom and nail it in place. The all-dado or all-slot system requires no additional machine setups, is more quickly assembled, and is stronger. (Again, see Figure 2-16.)

The designer must also determine drawer part dimensions as part of the layout process. Subfronts and sides should be the same thickness, especially for ease of machining when interlocking or semi-interlocking joints are used. This thickness should be a minimum of ½ in., and may be ⅝ in. Drawer backs may be as thin as ½ in. but are more commonly ¾ in. Plywood is often used for subfronts, sides, and backs because it can be purchased in the desired thicknesses, but many people prefer to mill solid stock such as pine to this thickness with a planer. Bottoms are cut from either ¼-in. plywood or from hardboard. The cabinetmaker is choosing here between the grain of plywood and the smaller expense and less waste of hardboard.

There are many ways to guide a drawer's operation. (See Figure 2-17.) Wooden guides are an option even in building furniture. With some furniture, especially old or antique furniture, the bottom edges of the drawer sides are the drawer guides, sliding directly on hardwood supports installed below the drawer box. Similar supports installed above the drawer keep the drawer from tipping as it is

31

drawn out, and spacers or shims limit its lateral movement. Drawer sides may also be dadoed to fit around hardwood guides that project into the drawer opening far enough to support the drawer. The drawer may also ride on a center-mount rail beneath the drawer. A back that has been dadoed to accept the drawer bottom can easily be notched to ride along this center guide, or the bottom may be fitted with a plastic glide specifically made for this purpose. Some drawers intended for this sort of mounting will be fitted with a dadoed strip that extends the full length of the drawer. This type of drawer mounting will also require a top guide or rail to keep the drawer from tipping as it is drawn out. With wooden guides, plastic or metal tabs may be inserted into the bottom corners of the face frame to reduce friction. Wooden guiding systems are inexpensive and simple to make, but they are seldom used today for high-quality guiding, except in furniture. Modern customers and cabinetmakers prefer smoother-gliding hardware that is available for drawer mounting. When using wood guides, however, the layout man or woman is using almost all the available space of the cabinet opening. Sides may be as long as the depth of the cabinet, minus the thickness of nailers, back, and that portion of drawer front depth which is concealed behind the face frame. The depth of the bottom will be the length of the sides minus the depth of the subfront and back and plus the depth of the dadoes run to support the bottom. The subfront will be as long as the width of the drawer opening, less the thickness of the drawer sides and any clearance desired, and plus any additional length needed for nonbutt joints (double dado, dovetail, etc.). The back will be as long as the width of the cabinet opening, less any clearance desired and the thickness of the two sides, and plus the additional length needed

for nonbutt joining to the sides. The length of the bottom is the distance between the two drawer sides plus the depth of the dadoes (usually ¼ in.) which support it in the sides. The width of sides, back, and subfront is the same as the height of the cabinet opening less any clearances desired. (See Figure 2-17 and Tables 2-1 and 2-2.)

One common hardware guide available consists of a single metal track, a rear rolling bracket, and a pair of rollers for eliminating friction between the drawer side and the face frame. The center track is usually mounted beneath the drawer box, screwed or stapled to a rail of the face frame in front and to a nailer in the rear. Roller-type frame slides are mounted in each lower corner of the face frame opening. The back of the drawer box is fitted with a single-roller bracket which is guided by the metal track. (See Figure 2-18.) For light-duty applications such as most kitchen drawers, this is a satisfactory guide. It is probably just as inexpensive to use as most wood guide systems because it requires no machining in addition to that already done for box assembly. The roller frame slides will require the designer to allow at least a ⅜-in. total clearance between the height of the drawer opening and the width of drawer sides, subfront, and back. These same slides need a small amount of the opening width to function properly also. The width of the assembled drawer box should be at least ¼ in. less than the width of the opening in the face frame. The depth of the drawer is also limited because the rear roller bracket requires at least 2 in. between the back of the drawer and the front of the nailer to which the metal rail is mounted.

Most popular in the cabinet trade today are side-mounted drawer slides consisting of two drawer members and two cabinet members. (See Figure 2-19.) Each member has a roller and a metal track. The tracks and rollers

TABLE 2-1

Drawer box dimensions

To Derive:	Use:	Deduct for:
Depth	Depth of case between front of face and front of nailer or back	Thickness of flush drawer front if used Clearance of rear mounting bracket and rear roller bracket if center, steel rail drawer guide if used
Width	Width of the face frame opening	Shims and side clearance if wood guides are used (usually ³⁄₁₆ in. total) Frame slides, roller or plastic friction type (usually ¼ in. total) Side-mounted guides (usually 1 in. total)
Height	Height of face frame opening	Vertical clearance with wood guides (usually ³⁄₃₂ in. at top of drawer) Clearance of roller frame slides if center steel drawer guide is used (usually ⅜ in. total) "Frictionless" clearance with side-mounted guides (usually ¼ in. total)

TABLE 2-2

Drawer part dimensions

To Determine:	*Use:*	*Then:*
Width of sides, subfront, back	Height of box	If not dadoing bottom into back, subtract distance from bottom of box to top of dado (usually ½ in.). This is the width of the back.
Subfront length	Width of box less thickness of both drawer sides	Add for dovetail or other interlock system if used.
Back length	Same as subfront	Add for dado into sides or other interlock system if used.
Side length	Depth of box	Add depth of French dovetail if used (no subfront).
		If using an interlock and no subfront, consider the front as part of the box and subtract the depth of the front not detailed as part of the interlock.
		If using a lipped or inset drawer front, consider the inset portion of the front to be part of the drawer box.
Depth of drawer bottom	Depth of box	Subtract undadoed depth of back unless the bottom is to be secured to the back by nails.
		Subtract any distance allowed for clearance between the rear edge of the side and the rear of the back (as with backs dadoed into sides).
		If a subfront is used, subtract undadoed depth of subfront.
		If no subfront is used, consider the front to be part of the drawer box and subtract any of its undadoed depth.
Width or length of bottom	Box width less undadoed depth of sides	

Note: This chart is not as complex as it looks. A cabinetmaker generally finds the system that works for him or her and becomes used to it. The designer may have to make several decisions and do some careful calculating the first time he or she plans a kitchen, but those are probably the last such decisions and careful calculating to be done for kitchen cabinetry in that shop. Look at the following example:

> *Example:* Sue has decided to remodel her kitchen. She chooses to use standard-depth bases (24 in.), but she wants nailers concealed behind the ¼-in. backs. Allowing ½ in. clearance behind the drawer box and using an overlay drawer front with a subfront gives her a box depth of 22½ in. She likes to slam drawers when she is angry, and she determines to build them with ⅝-in. sides joined to ⅝-in. subfronts with a $\frac{5}{16}$-in. $\times$ $\frac{5}{16}$-in. double dado and joined by dado to ¾-in. backs. There will be ½ in. between the rear edge of the drawer side and the rear of the drawer back to make the back joint a dado and not a rabbet. She will be using steel side guides which require ½ in. on each side of the box. Part of the drawer section of her cutting list looks like this:

Opening Size	Double-Dado Subfronts (⅝ in.)	Dadoed-In Backs (¾ in)	Sides (⅝ in)	Bottoms (¼ in)
2 ea 4 × 16	2 ea 3¾ × 14⅜	2 ea 3¾ × 14¼	4 ea 3¾ × 22½	5 ea 14¼ × 21⅛
3 ea 6 × 16	3 ea 5¾ × 14⅜	3 ea 5¾ × 14¼	6 ea 5¾ × 22½	(listed ˆ)

The overall box dimensions for each unit were easy to calculate. Sue allowed ¼ in. vertical clearance and 1 in. for her side guides. The box dimensions for the drawer listed first were 3¾ in. high, 22½ in. deep, and 15 in. wide. To obtain the length of her subfront, Sue subtracted the thickness of the two sides (1¼ in.) from the box width and then added back the depth of her interlock system on each side (⅝ in. total). The sides are to be dadoed to a depth of ¼ in. to accept the back, and Sue just subtracted 1¼ in. from the box width and then added back ½ in. for the length of the back. The sides obviously need to be the same dimension as the depth of the box. With the bottom dadoed into all four sides to a depth of ¼ in., its width was the same as the length of the back. The depth of the bottom worked out as the depth of the box (22½ in.) minus the length of side behind the dadoed back (½ in.) minus the depth of undadoed back (½ in.) and minus the depth of undadoed subfront (⅜ in.).

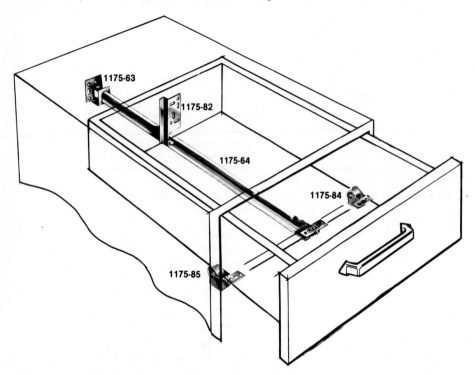

1175-63
1175-82
1175-64
1175-84
1175-85

FIGURE 2-18 Drawer guide with center steel guide and three rollers. (Courtesy of Knape & Vogt Mfg. Co.)

mate so that the drawer glides in and out almost effortlessly, even when heavily loaded. Many manufacturers produce this type of guide, and they are available in different duty ratings up to 150 pounds and more. Other, more complex side-mounted slides of this general type also allow full extension of the drawer box. With these guides, the designer should allow approximately ¼ in. vertical clearance for the assembled drawer box. Most of these guides require exactly ½ in. width on each side of the drawer. The assembled drawer box is therefore 1 in. narrower than the opening into which it fits. The only limitation upon the depth of the drawer is the depth of the cabinet. When properly installed, side-mounted slides give smooth, reliable service for virtually a lifetime. The person

who performs cabinet layout determines overall box dimensions from the width, height, and depth of the drawer opening and from the requirements of the drawer guiding system. He or she can then determine dimensions of drawer box components from knowledge of the joints to be used in assembling the drawer. Factors that dictate overall box dimensions are listed in Table 2-1. For dimensioning drawer parts from overall box dimensions, see Table 2-2.

Slide-Out Shelves. Slide-out shelves are a third common accessory that may be used to build convenience into many cabinets. They are of great advantage in the kitchen because they can bring items stored in the rear of the base cabinet into easy reach near the front of the cabi-

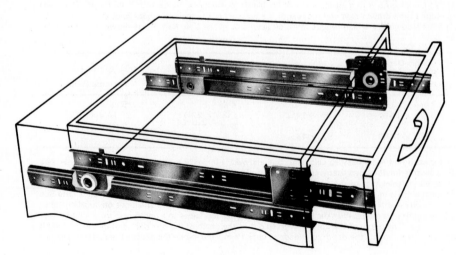

FIGURE 2-19 Side-mounted hardware drawer guides. (Courtesy of Knape & Vogt Mfg. Co.)

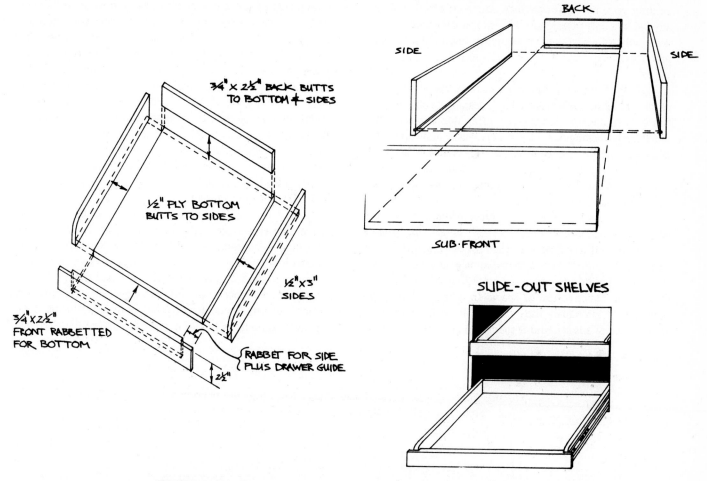

FIGURE 2-20   Slide-out shelves. Contrast to drawer box construction at upper right.

net. (See Figure 2-20.) In many ways, the slide-out shelf is simply a type of drawer that is mounted behind doors, but there are some differences.

To assemble the slide-out, we may employ any of the joints used in drawer assembly, but since the bottom of the slide-out shelf is usually ½-in. plywood, it is possible to use glue and nails for attaching the bottom to front, sides, and back. Therefore, it is most common to use butt joints for this unit except that the front is often rabbeted to accept sides and bottom. (See Figure 2-20 for a suggested design for the slide-out.)

The front of the slide-out shelf has several functions. It serves as a handle or pull for operating the slide-out feature, and it covers the front of the guiding system. It is often made of the same hardwood as the face frame in order to present an attractive facing. The rabbet along the bottom edge and those along the two ends allow for the face to be free of nails. The front should be made of material that is ¾ in. thick to accommodate rabbeting, and a minimum of 2½ in. wide to provide a functional handle. Length is governed by the width of the opening less any clearance needed to avoid contact with the face frame and doors that do not

entirely clear the opening (all doors except overlay). The rabbett along the bottom is usually ⅜ in. deep and just wide enough to fit the bottom. The rabbetts on the ends of the front are ⅜ in. deep and wide enough to cover sides and side guides (usually 1 in.).

Sides must be at least ½ in. thick. Their minimum 3-in. width allows coverage of the raw edge of the shelf bottom and sufficient height for the mounting of side-mounted guides.

The back has at least two purposes: to prohibit stored items from falling off the back of the shelf and for the general strength of the unit. It should be at least ½ in. thick, and its width should bring its top edge flush with the top edge of the sides. In this design, the length of the back is the same as the length of the inset (unrabbeted) portion of the front.

The bottom, as noted earlier, should be at least ½ in. thick. In this design, its depth is the same as the length of the sides, and its length is the same as the length of the back.

The all-butt-joint design greatly simplifies designing, listing, and machining. With side-mounted steel and roller guiding systems, it is more than strong enough for almost any kitchen duty. Designers who choose other joining systems will, of course, have to modify their dimensioning practices.

Lazy Susans. Another accessory that is frequently employed in the kitchen is the lazy susan or revolving shelf. Since these are rounded shelves fitting into cabinetry that is basically rectangular, lazy susans waste some space but add convenience. As we shall see, a lazy susan can be almost necessary in some cabinet situations. In base cabinets, susans usually have two shelves, and in uppers, they most often have three.

In general, there are three types of lazy susan: full-round, pie-shaped, and "dead-corner" susans. (See Figure 2-21.) The full-round susan is used for convenience in corners where cabinets meet with two joints that are each 135°. This configuration is frequently employed with upper cabinets in an effective use of space. In a base cabinet, this arrangement obviously uses up more floor space than the other types of susans, and it should be used only in rooms with plenty of space in which to walk and work. A cabinet designer should also consider two other aspects of the full-round susan before he or she elects to use it. Since the cabinets in this arrangement do not return at a right angle, it is impossible to mount two drawers above the susan. The designer may call for a single drawer mounted above the susan in the angled section of cabinet or eliminate drawers in this area altogether and perhaps call for a third shelf in the base cabinet susan. Also, the center on which this type of susan rotates is farther from the door opening than with the other types of susan, and the designer should be sure to provide a large enough door opening for easy access into this portion of the cabinet.

The pie-shaped susan got its name because it looks something like a pie with one piece removed. It is used where cabinets return at a 90° angle in either a base or an upper. It is possible to mount two small drawers above the susan, one on each leg of the L-shape that makes the return. With the piece of pie cut out to meet the configuration of the cabinet, the center of rotation is closer to the door opening. In fact, as this unit rotates, some of the shelving

FIGURE 2-21 Three types of lazy susan. Note that the blind-corner susan can be used effectively in returns located next to appliances.

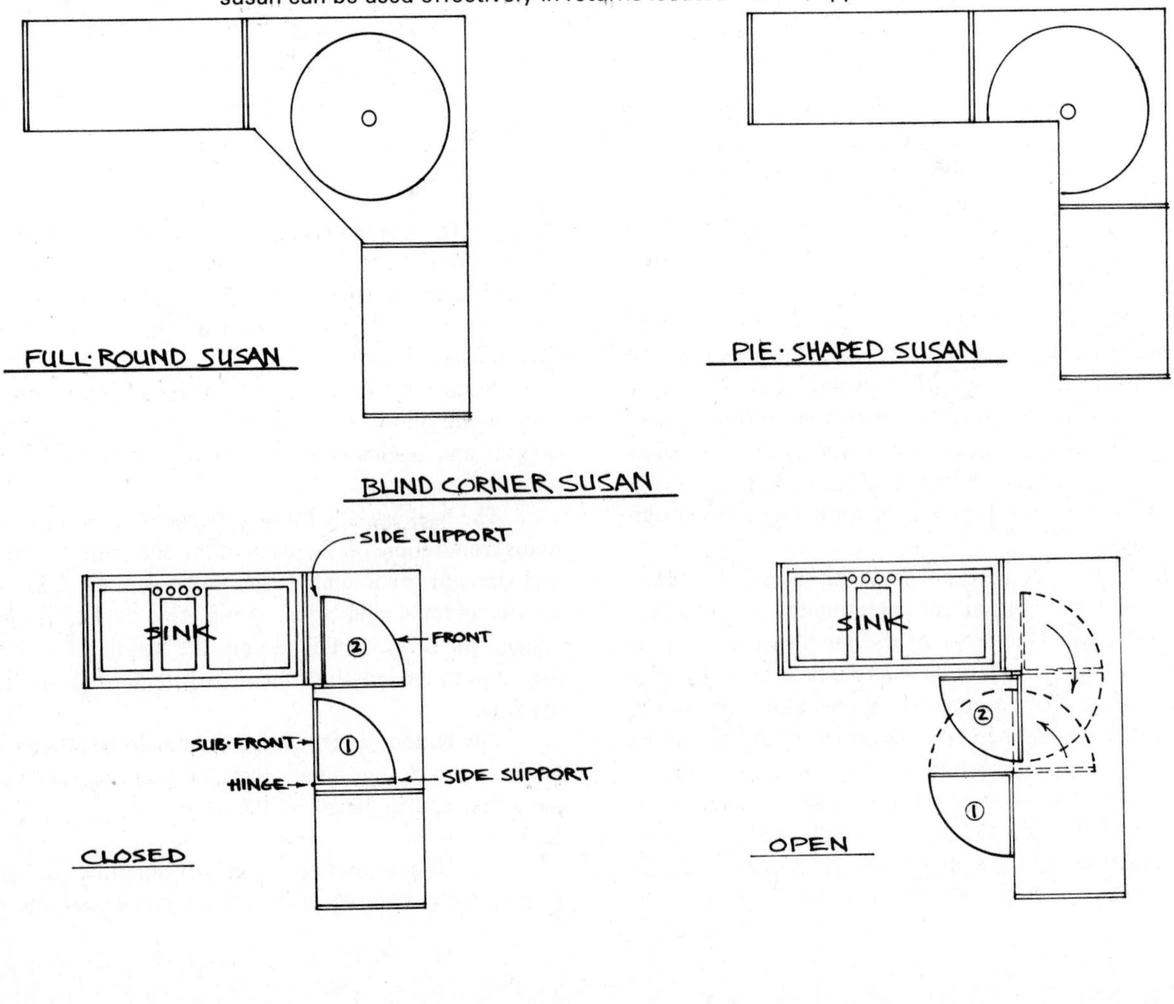

actually moves outside the cabinet. All in all, stored items are within easy reach. Doors to cover the right-angle opening may be in either of two arrangements. There can obviously be no stiles or mullions where the faces of these cabinets meet, and it is therefore necessary to plan for doors that meet in the corner. They may be hinged together in the corner where they meet. This is often done with lipped and overlay doors. One of the doors is then hinged in the standard way to the face frame so that the entire door assembly will swing clear of the corner and the shelf rotation. With flush doors, the two doors are frequently mounted directly against the straight edges in the wedge-shaped cutout of the shelves, and the doors simply turn with the entire susan assembly.

Both the full-round and the pie-shaped susan are available as prefabricated units, complete with metal or plastic shelves, a rotation assembly that looks like a length of pipe with wheels, and mounting brackets and screws. The cabinetmaker may also build the shelves out of wood and purchase only the hardware needed to rotate the shelf.

The prefabricated susans vary in diameter from 18 to 28 in. Designers should make sure that they choose an appropriate size and that as little space as possible is wasted. Each diameter of susan may require its own minimum door width for access. The cabinet planner must program this into the cabinet job from the very beginning, whether the susan shelves are prefabricated or made "from scratch." Manufacturers generally provide such information with their susan sets. With susans of different sizes, a full-scale layout may have to be performed to determine the exact placement of cabinet partitions, doors, and susan. Full-scale layout is explained in Chapters 3 and 9.

Blind-corner susans are not common in today's cabinetry. Such susans cannot be found as prefabricated units and will usually require careful full-scale designing if the maximum amount of cabinet space is to be utilized. Nevertheless, some situations still seem to call for this type of system, particularly in small kitchens. A floor plan often calls for an appliance to be placed so close to a cabinet return that access to the deepest reaches of the shelving in such a cabinet is limited to one door opening. This opening is so far from the rear corner of the shelving that only a person with elastic arms can use the storage. Many of today's cabinetmakers simply give up on this problem and make a dead corner. This is a valid solution in at least one respect—the use of any curved shelving system automatically is a sacrifice of storage space, and we are therefore giving back some of the space we are trying to salvage. On the other hand, small kitchens probably need every bit of storage space that can be made available, and a blind corner susan not only saves space but also rotates that space into very easy reach. In this susan system, the curved shelving units should be made as large as possible. This calls for a wide door opening in the face frame. The first

shelf unit is built independently like a drawer box with a subfront and mounted to the inside of the door that covers this opening. Most doors mounted in a corner are hinged on the stile of the face frame so that the door swings toward the return cabinet. In this system, however, hinging must be reversed so that the first shelving may clear the entire door opening for the operation of the second shelf unit. The first shelf unit should be constructed of ½-in. plywood or similar material for the side support, subfront, and shelves. The second shelf assembly is hinged on a vertical member installed inside the face frame for this purpose. Since this inside shelf assembly has no subfront, its front should be maade of ¾-in. plywood. A rabbet should be run in the front or subfront to accept the side support, and all shelves should be supported by dado joints. The open, curved edges of all shelves should be edged with a material flexible enough to be attached and wide enough to project above the surface of the shelf and serve as a retainer for stored items.

Other Accessories. The types of accessories that may be used with cabinetry are almost endless. See Table 2-3 for a short list of other common accessories together with usual fabrication materials and joining techniques. The designer must have answers to the following accessory-related questions before developing a drawing or layout plan:

- What will be the appearance of doors, and how will this affect their construction and mounting?
- What materials will be used to fabricate the doors, and how will these materials be detailed and assembled?
- Will the doors fit the facing as flush, lip, or overlay?
- How will the doors be hinged to the cabinet, and how does this affect their size?
- How will drawer fronts be made, and how will their appearance be "related to" nearby doors?
- Will a subfront be employed, or will the front be detailed to accept sides and bottom?
- What types of joints will be used to assemble the drawer boxes?
- What type of guiding system will be employed, and how will this affect the overall size of the box?
- Does any cabinet arrangement in the job call for slide-out shelving, lazy susans, or another accessory?
- What materials will be used in making miscellaneous accessories, and how will each accessory be assembled?
- How will the overall cabinet structure help to determine the sizes of all accessories?

TABLE 2-3

Accessory design factors

Accessory	Common Materials	Usual Joints, Mounting
Spice racks (approx. 1½ to 2 in. deep)	*Sides:* ⅜-in. solid *Shelves:* ⅜- to ½-in. ply or solid *Retainer strips:* ⅛-in. min. solid, ply, or hardboard *Back (if used):* ¼-in. ply *Nailers (if used):* ½- × 1½-in. solid	Dado sides for shelves Rabbet sides for back or butt nailers to side Overlay retainers on sides, high enough to secure spices, low enough to place spices on rack Secure to back of door near range with screws Entire unit must be narrow enough to clear opening
Door-mounted rack for rear of door (oversized spice rack—approx. 4 in. deep—used for convenience in a pantry—can also serve to keep long doors from warping)	*Sides:* ¾-in. solid *Shelves:* ¾-in. ply *Retainer strips:* ⅛-in. min. solid, ply, or hardboard	Dado sides for shelves Overlay shelves and sides with retainers; these should be wide enough to hold items on shelf and brace the rack square Mount to back of door with counterbored screws through sides Entire unit must be narrow enough to clear opening
Swing-out pantry shelving (often 8 to 9 in. deep—may be two-sided with center divider—used for convenience in deep pantries)	*Sides, top, and bottom:* ¾-in. solid stocks *Shelves:* ¾-in. ply *Back or center divider:* ½-in. plywood *Retainer strips:* ⅛-in. min. solid, ply, or hardboard	Dado sides for bottom, shelves, and top Rabbet sides, bottom, and top for back, or dado these pieces for a center divider, or prepare to butt the divider to these pieces Overlay retainers on sides, shelves, and bottom Mount unit independently with piano hinge and catch Unit must be narrow enough to clear door, shelves, and other accessories as it swings open
Tray dividers (divides widths of cabinetry into narrow storage spaces, allowing trays and other shallow items to be stored without stacking)	*Divider:* ¼-in. ply or hardboard *Top mount:* ¾- × min 1½-in. solid *Bottom mount:* may be ¼-in. undadoed material or thicker material with dadoes	Dividers should be removable Groove top mount to receive top edge of divider Dividing opening width equally, fasten ¼-in. bottom mounts in place with enough space for bottom edge of divider, or dado thicker bottom support for edges of dividers and fasten in place
Cutting boards (slide-out)	*Board:* ¾-in. solid birch or maple *Facing:* ¾-in. min. × 1-in. minimum solid material to match wood used for doors *Side mounts:* ¾-in. hardwood	Modify face frame to accept bread board above drawer Laminate board together from 1½ in. or narrower solid stock, using waterproof glue Detail facing with finger pull and attach to board by mortise, French dovetail, or doweling Run dado in side mounts for supporting the board and attach to face frame and rear nailer
Sliding doors (especially useful where door swings are limited)	*Doors:* plywood *Guides:* usually prefabricated hardware	Cut doors wide enough to overlap in middle Find door height from guides (e.g., plastic top and bottom track)
Swing-out-and-hideaway doors (often used if vision from an angle is important as when doors conceal a television)	*Doors:* often ¾-in. ply, flush type; many door styles will work *Guides:* hardwood as for cutting board with hardwood sliding brace, or steel and roller hardware guides	For easiest installation, door edges should not be lipped or detailed—this is why flush doors are easiest to mount in this way.

TABLE 2-3, *Continued*

Accessory design factors

Accessory	Common Materials	Usual Joints, Mounting
		With wood guiding, miter top edge of door and front edge of sliding brace—join by hinging—door can be lifted from bottom and slid back into dadoed hardwood side guides—when open, the underside of the door is supported by rollers
		With hardware guiding, follow unit directions
		Paired doors may be similarly mounted for operation to sides
Tambour doors	*Doors:* wood strips joined by canvas backing usually purchased ready to install	Rout curved groove in bottom and top guides for door material to ride in—corners of groove must be curved enough to allow members of tambour to make the turn
	Bottom guide: cabinet bottom	
	Top guide: similar to cabinet bottom	Install partitions if desired to hide canvas backing
Roll tops	Similar to tambour	Similar to tambour
File drawers	Same as with other drawers	Use interlocked joints
	Bottom: if weight of files is to rest on bottom, use ½-in. ply	Drawer size determined by size of files, use or nonuse of interior hanger frames, use of nonuse of hanger-type files, and frontal or lateral file arrangement

CHAPTER SUMMARY OF CABINETMAKING SKILLS

Design and layout can be viewed as a four-step problem-solving task, but before determining cabinet configurations, drawing a plan, or making the cutting list, the cabinetmaker must first make commitments to particular cabinet structures. As the cabinetmaker gains experience, this step—of choosing among the various construction systems—becomes almost automatic, but designers must possess familiarity with all the cabinet components and how these will function together effectively.

Planning a cabinet project requires selection of types and thicknesses of material to be used, joints and fasteners to be employed, and the styles and mountings for accessories. Each selection is based on tools available as well as the personal preferences of each cabinetmaker. He or she must know how ends, bottoms, partitions, and shelves will be fit together, how the face will be assembled as well as how it will be attached to the case, and how each door and drawer is to be built and mounted.

THREE

Function First - Part II:

CABINET CONFIGURATIONS AND LAYOUT

DESIGNING CABINET CONFIGURATIONS

Once a cabinetmaker has decided on the general box, facing, and accessory designs that best suit the job, he or she is ready to carry on with planning the job by determining the cabinet configurations called for, drawing the actual plan, and making a cutting list. Experienced designers are used to working again and again with the same construction details, and they can simply launch into these phases of layout, barely giving a conscious thought to the techniques which they rely on to fabricate most cabinetry. If you are inexperienced with cabinet layout and unfamiliar with the wide variety of building methods that are possible, it is best to give some thought to the options discussed in Chapter 2. On the other hand, a cabinet designer does not need to know *all* the options available, there is probably no one craftsman who knows everything there is to know about good woodworking. This is because the process of cabinetmaking continues to change as materials and techniques improve. In addition, custom cabinet work is by definition the building of cabinetry to fit individual needs and to solve specific problems. Every cabinet that we make can be unique, and there are obviously problems to be solved which we have not yet faced and which we cannot foresee. Once again, then, do not be reluctant to carry out basic cabinet design and layout—if you already know something

about the assembly methods you are going to employ on a job, get the project moving.

Designing cabinet configurations is a bit like solving a math-oriented puzzle; we are given all the necessary measurements and general cabinet locations. We simply solve the puzzle or problem by employing what we know about cabinetmaking in an organized way.

Every cabinetmaker naturally develops his or her own designing system to follow, but all designers probably adhere to the following principles of the configuration designing process:

1. Getting Organized. All the "given" information should be available for easy reference. It is clearly best to post floor plans, elevations, sketches, measurements, and notes on a bulletin board or wall if possible. This keeps reference material in view while freeing the designer from paper shuffling and other confusions. Drawing or layout tools should all be readily available.

2. Gaining an Overview. The designer must look over all the reference materials and get an idea of the job as a whole. It is important to survey all the measurements, notes, and drawings, focusing on the specifications and particularly taking mental note of anything that is out of the ordinary (e.g., an out-of-the-ordinary drawer guide or cabinets of nonstandard height). If there is a floor plan, it should be in general agreement with on-site measurements.

3. Isolating a Single View.   The designer should look at one wall of cabinetry at a time, even if there are returns as in L-shaped or U-shaped kitchens. There may be bases, uppers, floor-to-ceiling cabinets, or a combination of these in a single view, but these should still be looked at as a unit; the whole influences each part.

4. Determining Overall Length.   For each single wall of cabinetry, the next step is to arrive at an overall length, from where the cabinets should begin to where they must end.

The first factor to consider is whether the on-site measurements provided are finished measurements, taken after drywall board and plaster was in place, or rough-in measurements, taken when only studs, block walls, and furring was in place. If the measurements are rough measurements, it is important to deduct the thicknesses of materials that will be added to finish the walls. Since these thicknesses vary from building to building, it is the responsibility of the cabinet designer to find out which materials are to be used. Some thickness dimensions are listed in Table 3-1 for building materials commonly used. Suppose that the cabinetmaker is called on to build and install a standard base cabinet between two walls. The rough-in measurement indicates a 70-in. space between the two walls. One of these walls is an exterior block wall to be finished with 1-in. furring, ½-in. drywall, and a plaster coat that will be ⅛ in. thick. The other wall is a stud wall that will be finished with the same drywall and plaster. The finished wall-to-wall dimension is therefore 67¾ in.

Clearances and scribe materials are also vital to account for, especially where a cabinet must fit wall to wall. If a trim or molding is to be used to cover gaps between the vertical end pieces of a cabinet (the stile of a face frame) and a wall, the designer should deduct a small amount (often ½ in. from the finished wall-to-wall dimension for clearance. A 60-in. finished opening size will yield a cab-

TABLE 3-1

Thicknesses of wall finishing materials

Wall Material	Thickness (in.)
Furring for block walls	¾ to 1
Stud wall behind block (for insulation)	3½
Drywall	½ or ⅝
Lath and plaster	⅝ to 1
Plaster	⅛ to ¼
Texture	⅛

inet facing of 59½ in., whether a face frame or a European style is used. If the measurer has provided more than one dimension between walls, it means that at least one of the walls is so crooked or out of plumb that the same measurement was not accurate for the entire height of the opening. For molding-type installation, the designer should use the smallest opening measurement provided and then subtract the desired clearance. If the cabinet facings are intended to be scribed into position, the facing should be longer than the largest provided dimension for the width of opening.

Window and door openings are the next concern. The finished ends of cabinets must be placed a certain distance away from a door or window. The length of wall exposed between a finished end and a door or window opening is "reveal." The size of a reveal is usually left to the preferences of the cabinetmaker, but this distance is often 2 or 3 in. A tall cabinet such as a unit for a built-in oven or a linen cabinet must sometimes be held farther from a doorway if the reveal space must accommodate a wall-mounted light switch. Further, when only rough-in dimensions are provided, the designer must determine the size of casing and trim or drywall and plaster that is used to finish rough door and window openings. Because they are added to the inside of rough openings, casings, drywall, and plaster add to the finished cabinet measurement, whereas trim will deduct from the finished size. Suppose that an upper cabinet is called for where a rough-in dimension between a stud wall and a window opening is 50 in. The stud wall is to receive ½-in. drywall and ⅛-in. plaster. The window opening is to be finished with 1-in. furring and the same drywall and plaster. The finished distance between wall and window will therefore be 51 in. If the cabinetmaker allows for a 3-in. reveal, the length of the upper cabinet will be 48 in.

Sometimes, especially between kitchens and dining areas, sections of cabinetry are used to separate rooms. Such a cabinet may be called an island or peninsula cabinet. In a kitchen, the island may be a base cabinet or both a base and upper cabinet. Elsewhere it is simply referred to as a room divider. In these circumstances, the location of the island helps to define the length of any cabinets that return from it. (See Figure 3-1.) In locating the island cabinets, the designer should first look for any construction feature that would limit its placement. There may be a soffit, for example, or a dropped ceiling in the kitchen area that would logically define the placement of an island upper. The designer should allow for molding and a small reveal along the edge of a soffit for positioning the finished back of the island. There may also be ductwork or wiring in the floor which must be covered by the island base. With reference to Figure 3-1, the designer may want to consider the size of a dining table and the easy flow of traffic around it for placing the island, or it may be necessary to confer

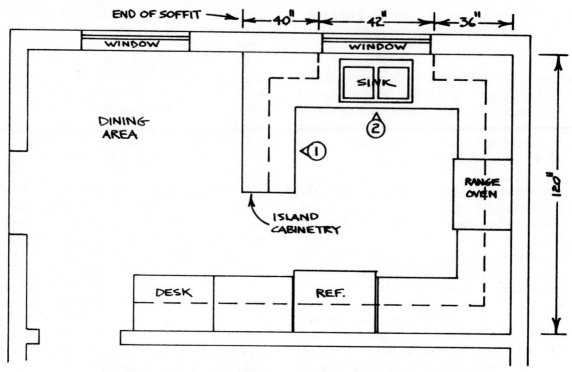

FIGURE 3-1 Floor plan for an island base and upper used to separate a kitchen and dining area. Note that the location of the back side of the island helps to define the length of cabinets that return from it, those mounted on the wall where the sink will be located (view 2).

with the general contractor or homeowner to make this important decision. Once an island has been positioned, the length of its returns has been defined.

The length of the island cabinetry itself is based almost entirely on concerns for movement around it. There should be at least 36 in. for walkways between any two fixed features, and designers must not neglect to consider countertop overhangs as part of their cabinetry. A countertop will usually project 1 in. beyond the base cabinet on which it sits unless a seating overhang is needed. In Figure 3-1, the countertop for the island should be a minimum of 36 in. from the refrigerator. If the finished north-south dimension is 120 in. and the refrigerator is 30 in. deep, the island cabinets should be 89 in. in length, from the north wall to the finished end.

Cabinet length is sometimes a factor of the size of fixtures or of a minimum space required between some fixture and a cabinet. The most common type of cabinet used in the laundry room is an upper cabinet that is mounted directly above the washer and dryer. These appliances usually sit side by side in the laundry room with a small space between them for ease of hookup and removal. A single-view configuration is easy to visualize since we need one cabinet on one wall. It is desirable for the upper cabinet's finished ends to line up with the sides of the two appli-

ances. Therefore, the overall length of this cabinet will be equal to the width of the two appliances added together plus any clearance desired between them. This length is often close to 60 in. In many bathrooms, a vanity is called for between a wall and a toilet fixture. If possible, the designer will allow 18 in. between the center of the stool and the finished end of the cabinet.

One situation that requires a slightly different approach is when plans call for shelving or cabinetry to fill the recess in a wall, as with some linen cabinets. (See Figure 3-2). The woodwork called for may either fit entirely into the space as with any wall-to-wall situation, or the face frame may overlay the entire opening. When the face of such a unit is to overlay the walls that make the opening, the overall length is longer than the width of the finished opening. Each stile should overlap the finished opening by approximately 1 in. so that it will be easy to drive a screw or nail through the frame directly into studs or wall anchors. If such a shelving unit is built as a single cabinet and then simply slid into place, the cabinet box should be narrower than the finished opening by approximately ½ in. One circumstance in which it is better to install the shelving and then cover with a linen front is a narrow doorway or any wall configuration that does not permit bringing a large unit into the room. In this case, homebuilders usually

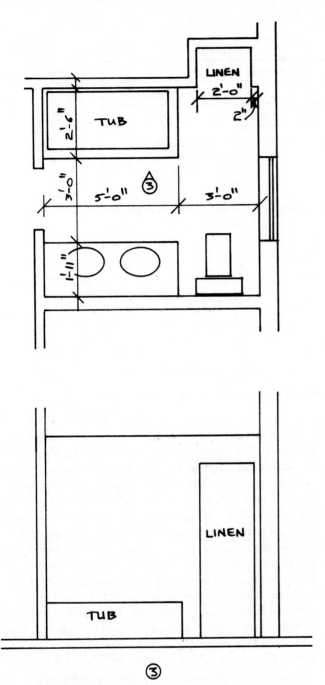

③

FIGURE 3-2 Floor plan and elevation for a room with a wall recess for use as a linen cabinet. The face of the linen may be installed inside the recess as in any wall-to-wall situation, or it may overlay the opening.

call for carpenters to install the shelves, and the cabinetmaker provides only the linen front. It is better for the cabinetmaker to do both tasks, however, so that shelves and face frame edges may be planned to meet perfectly. Shelf size is the same as the width and depth of the finished opening, or a bit less (perhaps ⅛ in.). The shelves should

not project beyond the wall where the face frame fits because this will cause a gap between the back edge of the face and the wall to which it is mounted. Naturally, if time is of no concern, the shelves may each be scribed into place for a perfect fit. Cleats—strips of wood that are fastened to the walls of the linen space and on which the shelves rest—must be planned for. These should be ¾ in. thick and at least 1¼ in. wide. Since a linen front usually has no toe space, the bottom rail should be as wide as the planned-for height of the bottom shelf (e.g., if the storage surface of the bottom shelf is to be 2 in. above the floor, a 2-in. bottom rail is used).

5. Modularizing. With prefabricated or factory cabinets, units are built to certain standard lengths, and these units are placed to fill cabinet spaces which are approximately the same size as the cabinet. Wood pieces called fillers are used to enclose spaces where the presized units do not conform well to room sizes and configurations. Such cabinets can be referred to as modular. Custom cabinets are constructed to fit particular spaces in particular buildings. With custom cabinetry, modularizing is simply determining where a single view of cabinetry must be broken into separate pieces because of appliance location or other factors. Whenever possible, custom cabinetmakers build single walls or views as long as required to fill each space. However, some considerations call for breaking a length of cabinetry into segments.

Probably the most obvious reason to modularize is a difference in cabinet depths along the same wall. Table 3-2 indicates the usual or standard depths of several common cabinet types. Wherever cabinets of different depths meet, it is convenient and often necessary to fabricate separate units.

Oven and pantry units which are part of the same single cabinet view as bases and uppers should be built independently. These units, or any taller piece placed next to a base unit, is usually 1 in. deeper than base cabinets so that countertops will not project beyond the face of the oven or pantry cabinet (as with the oven cabinet in Figure 2-1).

Some wall units and desks are designed as base cabinets and countertops, with shallower shelving or upper units that rest on them. (See Figure 3-3.) Here again the base section and the upper section are built separately and joined at the job site. Because there is really no bottom in the upper or shelving unit, cabinetmakers frequently run dadoes in the base unit's countertop to receive the upper's finished ends and partitions.

Desk or "knee-under" sections are frequently designed to be shallower than base cabinetry to which they are attached. This makes for an easy-to-make and perfect-looking joint where the desk section is joined to other cabinet sections. Even if such a desk section is designed to be the same depth as other cabinetry on the same wall, it is most often built as a single unit. (Again see Figure 3-3.)

TABLE 3-2

Cabinet dimension standards

| | Total Finished Dimensions | |
Cabinet Type	Height (in.)	Depth (in.)
Vanity	32	22
Kitchen base	36	24
Bar (for stools)	42	Varies with function
Table	29 to 30	Varies with function
Desk	29 to 30	Varies with function
Typing well	27	Varies
Pantry or oven cabinet	84 (to soffit)	25
Knee-space cabinet	4½ to 6 (mounting usually at desk height)	Varies according to nearby base cabinets
Upper		
Standard	30	12
Over hood	18	12
Over sink, no window	24	12
Over island or peninsula base cabinet	24	12
Over refrigerator	Varies with refrigerator, often 12 to 15	12
Bookcases		4 to 12, varies with type of book

In many of today's kitchens, the upper cabinet which is mounted above the refrigerator is built deeper than standard upper cabinetry (usually 24 in.). This is so that the cabinet doors are easy to reach and open. In this situation also, the cabinet is built as an independent unit.

A second place for separation of cabinets into independent units is in each corner where a return is located. Unless the length of a return is very short, the designer will call for straight sections of cabinetry only (no single-unit L-shapes). Where the two pieces meet, the face stile of one cabinet is positioned far enough from the end of the case to accept the entire depth of the other segment of the "L." (See Figure 3-4.) It can be important to determine which cabinet will "run through" and accept the other leg of the "L." In general, the cabinet with the shorter face frame should run through so that length and weight are more manageable for the installer. Obviously, if one leg of the return is an island with a finished back, it should run through to the rear corner so that the finished back will not have to be pieced together on the job site.

Some appliances also require separation of a single view into separate cabinet units, especially with base units. Continuous cabinetry must be interrupted for built-in dishwashers and trash compactors as well as free-standing ranges and refrigerators. Wall ends may be placed next to each of these appliances except for the refrigerator.

There are two other reasons for separating continuous sections of cabinet. First, if a single unit is impossible to get into its installation location, building it in separate joinable sections will often allow easy placement and installation. One instance of this is the floor-to-ceiling cabinet which may be possible to get into its room but which will not stand up. Employing a separate toekick design usually solves this problem. Sometimes a joint in the face will be necessary. In most cases it is acceptable to build such cabinets as two independent units with narrow face frame stiles which can be joined tightly with screws on the job site. (See Figure 3-5.) Second, cabinets that are feasible to build as a single piece are sometimes built in two pieces to make them shorter and lighter, for ease of transport and installation. For example, the cabinetmaker will sometimes encounter a kitchen in which a single wall is to be fitted with a continuous upper cabinet. There may be no reason to interrupt cabinetry on this wall for 15 ft or more, but some designers may call for fabricating separate units that are easier to build and move. Some cabinetmakers will prefer to build and move cabinets that are even longer, simply to avoid making the joint at the job site.

6. Sectioning. This is the step of the layout process in which a designer specifies exact locations for every cabinet component and feature. In general, it is best to define the ends of the single view of cabinetry, locate the specific features which are to be built into the cabinetry (such as lazy susans) and those which must function around it (such as appliances), and then to seek as much symmetry as possible in dividing lengths of cabinet into door and drawer sections. The designer has undoubtedly begun to

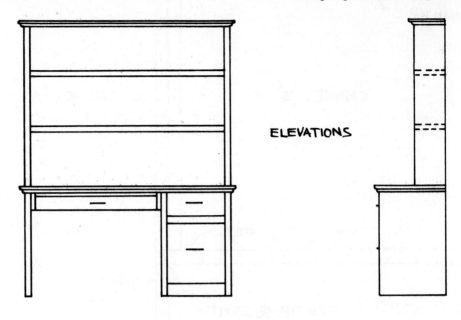

ELEVATIONS

PLAN VIEW OF BASE CAB. UNIT

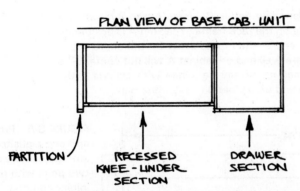

PARTITION   RECESSED   DRAWER
                   KNEE - UNDER   SECTION
                   SECTION

FIGURE 3-3 Front and side elevations of a desk unit with overhang-ing countertop and a shelving unit that rests on it. These would be modularized (built separately). Note the top or plan view of the base cabinet, which shows a recessed desk section. This piece, the drawer section, and the partition may be easily fabricated as three separate pieces and then simply screwed together. Vanity dressing sections may be similarly designed.

draw his or her plan while doing this, and the step becomes a series of subtractions from and divisions of the lengths specified by the measurer.

Dividing a cabinet into convenient sections requires consideration of at least three factors: unsupported shelf length, hinged door swing, and symmetry. Neither fixed nor adjustable shelves should be longer than 30 to 40 in. or they will bend from the weight of items stored on them. Shelves up to about 30 in. may need to be ⅝ in. thick with only a veneer for an edging if they are standard upper depth or less and they will not be used for the storage of heavy items such as books. Shelves for heavier duty may be built somewhat longer if constructed for greater strength. This is done by using ¾-in. material for the shelving and per-haps by attaching wider (often ¾ in. × 1½ in.) hardwood edging material to the front of the shelf. Partitions should be located so that the length of shelves is not too great for adequate support.

No door should be so wide that it interferes with movements in the room as it swings open; a person should not have to back up to open a cabinet door. This means that the designer should try to control the width of door openings. The width of a door should seldom be over 20 in. and somewhat narrower if possible. Paired doors (doors that meet at the center of an opening with no mullion to separate them) are usually not employed for openings

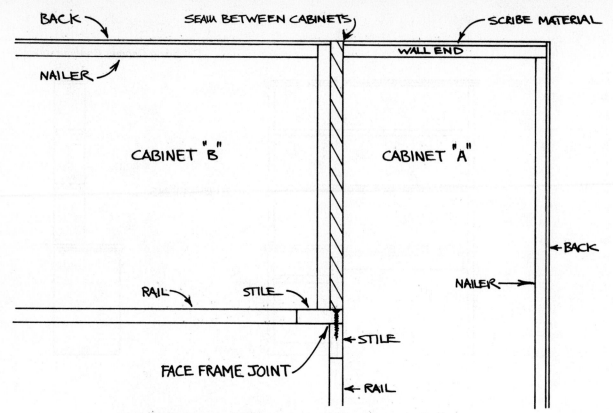

BACK

SEAM BETWEEN CABINETS

SCRIBE MATERIAL

NAILER

WALL END

CABINET "B"

CABINET "A"

BACK

NAILER

RAIL

STILE

STILE

FACE FRAME JOINT

RAIL

FIGURE FIGURE 3-4 Plan view detail. Cabinets A and B return in a corner. The left-hand stile on the face frame of cabinet A is positioned far enough from the left end of the box to allow for the entire depth of cabinet B. Note that the wall end of cabinet A will not contact the wall. The two face frames can easily be joined with screws if the optional partition or wall end of cabinet B is not in the way.

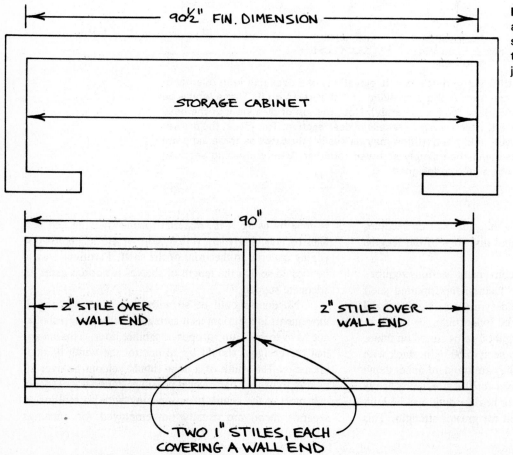

90½" FIN. DIMENSION

STORAGE CABINET

90"

2" STILE OVER WALL END

2" STILE OVER WALL END

TWO 1" STILES, EACH COVERING A WALL END

FIGURE 3-5 Problem floor plan and one plausible solution. The storage cabinet may be built as two units with narrow stiles for joining together.

greater than 38 in. Cabinet door openings up to 40 in. wide are best suited to having two equal-sized doors. These may be a pair or, for slightly smaller and easier-to-fit doors, two singles with a mullion of the face in between. Cabinets with an opening width between 50 and 76 in. should be divided into two sections, separated by a mullion and a partition. Each section may then be fitted with a pair of doors. In-between sizes might have the face frame divided in such a way that it will accept three doors, either all singles or a pair with a single door. (See Figure 3-6.) The faces of longer cabinets may be sectioned similarly, by considering desirable door size, keeping door widths as close as possible to the same size, and making sure that all shelving is adequately supported. Naturally, these dimensions are given as approximate guidelines, and you will find and use door size maximums and minimums that are convenient and manageable for you.

Example: After seeing the nice job that Sue did remodeling her kitchen, Herman hires her to build a laundry upper for his house. It is to be a purely functional cabinet, made to trade standards with face frame construction, simple overlay doors, and a molding-type installation. The wall-to-wall measurement is 60 in. The finished walls are existing, and Sue subtracts a ½ in. to get the overall cabinet size at 59½ in. She is using 2-in. stiles, which give the face frame an opening of 55½ in. This is obviously too wide for two doors and too long for unsupported shelves, and Sue plans for a partition and a 2½-in. mullion to divide the space exactly in half. Subtracting the width of the mullion (2½ in.) from the width of the opening (55½ in.) and dividing the result in half, Sue is ready to draw and make the cutting list for a cabinet with two pair-door openings which are each 26½ in. wide.

7. Standardizing. After lengths of cabinetry have been determined, the designer similarly considers and plans for cabinet heights and depths, especially if these are nonstandard. Most custom cabinetry is built to certain usual heights and depths (Table 3-2), but since custom cabinetry may have any height or depth to fulfill certain needs, it is often necessary to vary designs from the standards. Any wall of a building that is to have the end of a cabinet mounted against it must have sufficient depth to cover the entire wall end. Linen-type cabinets that are to slide into a wall opening entirely except for the face frame should have a box depth that is just a bit less than the finished depth of the recess (perhaps ⅛ in. less than the shallowest measurement provided). No irregularity at the back of the opening will then interfere with the installation of the slide-in unit. Tall units that must fit under a soffit or a ceiling

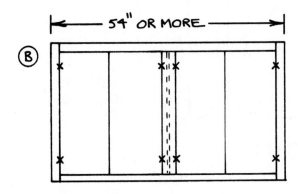

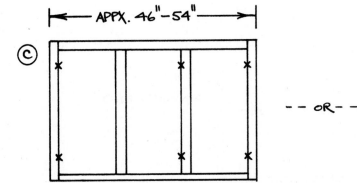

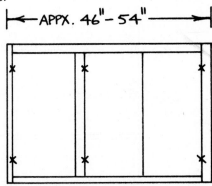

FIGURE 3-6 Feasible configurations for upper cabinets with a continuous height. Note hinging. Measurements are total cabinet lengths.

should have some clearance allowed in determining their height (like wall-to-wall clearance, this should be approximately ½ in. less than the finished opening).

Some of the terms we have just used are somewhat artificial. When we design a cabinet job, we do not say, for example, "Now I will modularize," or "It's time to perform sectioning." Designing is a process. The designer frequently makes decisions about length, height, depth, and accessory configuration at virtually the same time. Yet, with these seven steps and their general rules in mind, even inexperienced cabinetmakers can lay out jobs that will be machined, assembled, and installed without costly errors.

Since function is of primary importance in designing custom cabinets, it is best to look at design situations as they occur under actual job conditions. We will look then at the common cabinet-designing situations one at a time, presuming that we have all the necessary information spread before us in an organized way, that we have scanned the specifications, and that we are ready to isolate single views.

Throughout the discussion, we will also presume that the cabinetry called for conforms to trade standards. If your designing situation calls for other requirements, simply change the standards where necessary.

Laundry Room Configuration

The most frequently used laundry room cabinet is the laundry upper. It is usually slightly longer than the two appliances over which it is mounted. Since most washing machines and dryers are 36 in. high, and since 18 in. is sufficient clearance above these appliances for opening lids and for loading, a laundry upper may have the same height for its full length. It will have a continuous top and bottom. (See Figure 3-7.) There is no need to modularize unless the unit will not go into its space as one piece. If it is to have fixed shelves, the designer ought to specify at least one vertical space high enough to accommodate tall detergent boxes.

FIGURE 3-7 Common laundry upper configuration. This example shows a "finished-right" arrangement. (A) Face frame and door arrangement; the door openings are equal in size and will accommodate pained doors. (B) Box components and their dadoes; note the taller fixed shelf spacing on the washing machine side.

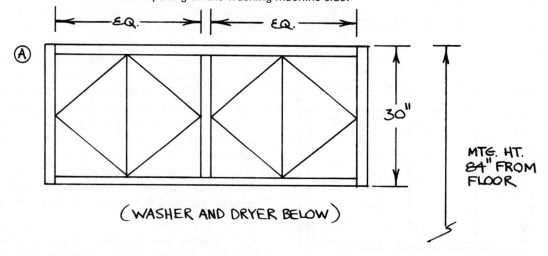

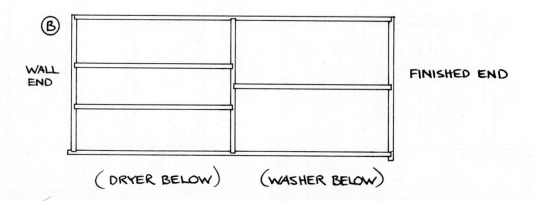

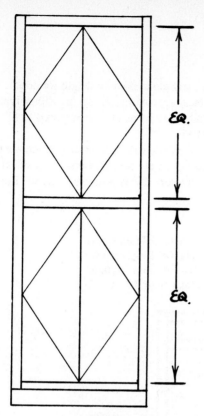 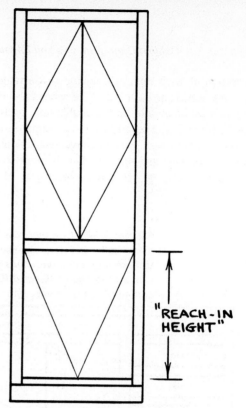

FIGURE 3-8 Two face frame and door configurations for tall linen cabinets, each with a toekick. *Left:* Vertical space divided exactly in half for doors and shelving; *right:* shorter height on the bottom for a hinged hamper.

The cabinet designer will usually call for construction of a linen storage unit with two equal-sized door openings in a top-and-bottom arrangement, whether plans call for an entire cabinet or cleat-mounted shelves covered with a linen front (face frame and doors). When a customer desires a hamper to be located in the tall linen unit, the opening on the bottom is made to the most convenient size for the hamper to operate and the remaining vertical space is used for a door opening to cover shelves. The height of the hamper opening should be limited to the length of an arm so that emptying the hamper is a relatively easy task. (See Figure 3-8.) There may or may not be a toekick with single-piece construction.

Bathroom Configurations

Bathroom sink cabinets, commonly referred to as vanities, may have a variety of different arrangements. In laying out vanities, the chief controlling factor is locating the sink section or sections. First, the vertical box members must be far enough apart to allow easy installation of the sink basin. Partitions or ends that enclose the sink section should be a minimum of 24 in. apart for the smaller basins. Designers should always verify the sink size and allow at least 1 in. on each side of the basin for locating vertical box members. If space is limited, shortened partitions will sometimes allow the sink basin to lap over slightly into another section of the unit. (See Figure 3-9.) Second,

whenever possible the sink should be located far enough from walls so that there is "elbow room" for people standing at and using the sink. Therefore, small vanities will not always have their sink basins mounted in the center of the cabinet.

The most common single unit vanities in today's trade are cabinets divided into three sections. There may either be a single sink section in the center with an auxiliary door

FIGURE 3-9 Box design with shortened partition to allow an unusual sink placement. The false front used to cover the sink would extend into the top portion of the drawer section. Notice that the sink is farther from the wall on the left than it is from the finished end on the right.

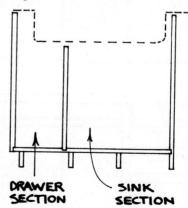

or drawer section on each side, or a double-sink arrangement with a sink section on each end of the cabinet and the auxiliary section in the middle. In the double-sink configuration, the designer should be reminded to place partitions a sufficient distance from wall ends for convenient sink use. (See Figure 3-10 for these and other vanity configurations.) Center-sink vanities may be constructed in lengths of at least 48 in., and the maximum length for double-basin vanity cabinets is approximately 58 in. Either type of three-section vanity may be as long as required to fill a space up to about 110 in.

Smaller vanity cabinets which can accommodate only one section (there are no partitions, only ends) should be fitted with drawers if it is possible to do so. Longer pieces

FIGURE 3-10   Common vanity configurations. Panels or false fronts cover sinks, and naturally they have no drawer pulls. (A) Single center sink arrangement with two auxiliary sections; (B) common double-sink arrangement; (C) and (D) used for lengths less than 48 in.; (E) configuration for a very long double sink.

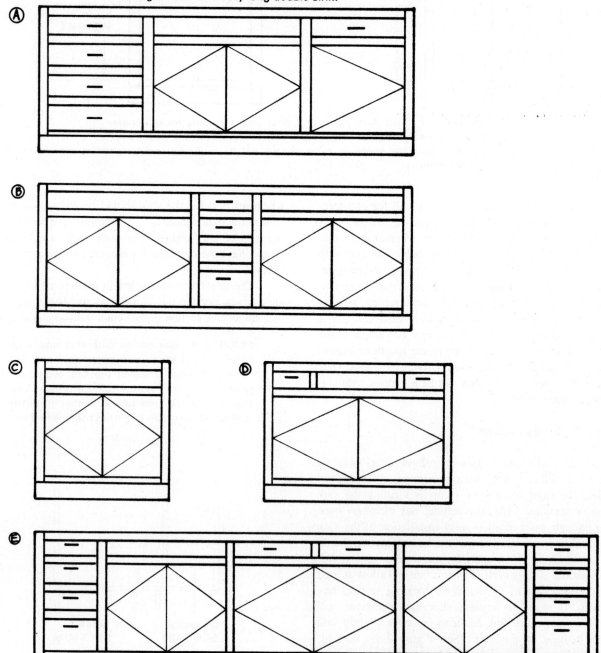

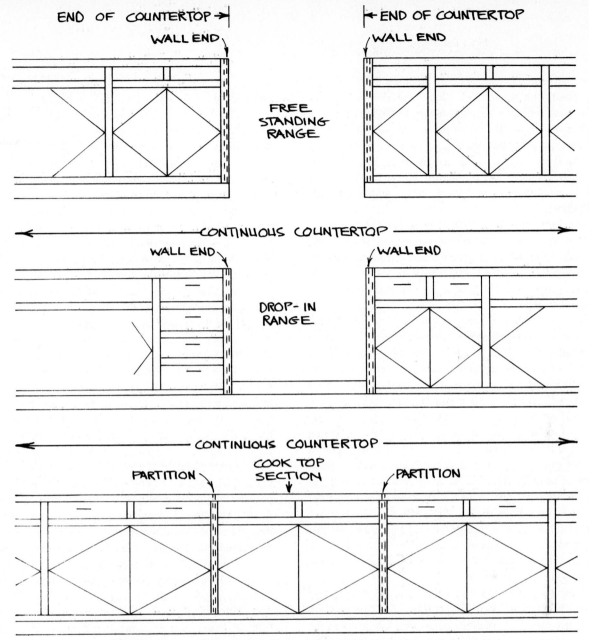

FIGURE 3-11 Three configurations for the cooking station. False fronts are generally used in front of a cooktop rather than drawers.

should be divided into more than three sections with mullions and partitions. (See Figure 3-10.)

The designer should also be aware that the longer vanity units will often have to be constructed as more than one piece, especially if they are wall-to-wall units. This is so because bathrooms are usually small rooms where it may be impossible to turn a large unit and position it properly.

Some bathrooms, particularly master bathrooms, are equiped with a knee-under section in the vanity cabinetry. Its function is convenience in making up and dressing in front of the large bath mirror. This piece is most often built independently as a small unit with one or two drawers for storing makeup. It is frequently mounted between two vanity base sections, even with their height and slightly re-

cessed behind their face, quite similar to the desk unit in Figure 3-3.

Kitchen Configurations

One of the three basic workstations in the kitchen is the range or cooktop. There are several basic types, and each requires a slightly different cabinet arrangement, but whenever possible the appliance should be positioned so that it has a minimum of 18 ins. of open countertop length on each side. Most often, the cooking station faces a wall and has a hood vent mounted in the upper cabinet above it. (See Figure 3-11 for range–cabinet configurations.)

The free-standing range is a gas- or electric-operated

unit that sits directly on the floor. Standing 36 in. high, it is equipped with a surface cooking unit that is approximately flush with the standard-height counters next to it and an oven below. It divides the single wall of the base cabinetry into separate pieces. The adjacent cabinet units have a wall end and stile arrangement where they meet the free-standing range. The countertop with its backsplash is likewise separated by the range. The cabinet designer should check for the exact size of the specified range, but most are slightly less than 30 in. The designer should allow this 30-in. space between base units along this single view. The space should be positioned where measurements indicate an electrical or gas connection in the wall of the kitchen so that no holes have to be cut in the cabinet to hook up the range.

A second kind of range–oven combination unit actually rests on the countertop of the base cabinet into which it is installed. This type of range is called a "drop-in" or "set-in" range. As far as the cabinet designer is concerned, it is somewhat like the free-standing range. That is, there will be a stile and a wall end next to the drop-in range. However, the two sections of cabinetry are usually joined by a continuous toekick and, very often, a bottom rail. There is usually insufficient room below this type of range for even a drawer, and so there is no need to put a bottom beneath it. Also, since the back and two sides of the appliance have a lip that sits directly on the countertop, the counter must be built as a single length and then have a section cut out of it to receive the range. The size for this appliance varies from one manufacturer to another, and the designer must determine the exact cabinet cutout size in order to complete the layout.

Very common in today's kitchens is the independent cooktop. It may have the cleanest look of all the cooking stations because it is mounted directly into a hole cut in the surface of the countertop and fastened there securely with machine screws. Except for a mounting ring similar to a sink rim, it appears perfectly flush with the countertop. The section of cabinetry below a cooktop will usually be fitted with a pair of doors mounted on two mullions. As with a sink, a false drawer front or panel is usually mounted to the face above this pair of doors, but some cooktops are so compact in height that drawers can be mounted instead. Employing a cooktop will not require separating a single wall of base cabinetry. The cooktop section is simply separated from adjoining sections with partitions and mullions. Such appliances are frequently 30 in. in length, but some are manufactured to larger and smaller sizes. The cabinet designer should take care to keep partitions far enough apart for easy mounting of the cooktop. Of course, the counter into which the cooktop is mounted must be built as a single length.

A hood and light appliance is almost always mounted above the range or cooktop. Hoods vary somewhat in size, but the most popular is 30 in. long. All hoods, unless equipped with a microwave, are less than 8 in. in height.

The upper cabinet to which a hood is mounted may be a standard depth of 12 in., but the cabinet height must be modified to allow sufficient vertical clearance between the hood and the cooking surface directly below it. The bottom of the hood-mounting cabinet should be approximately 30 in. above the range top. With custom cabinetry, this is *not* a separate cabinet unit. There is no need to separate a single view or wall of upper cabinetry into pieces to accommodate the hood. After placement of the hood along the wall has been determined, the designer simply shortens a section of the continuous upper unit to receive the hood. (See Figure 3-12.) A finished end and a mullion should be placed next to the hood. The piece of plywood that makes the finished side is actually dadoed into the top of the upper like a partition would be. In the door space above the hood, the mullion will often overhang this piece of plywood by $\frac{1}{4}$ in. or more so that the cabinetmaker does not have to finish a flush joint inside the door space. The mullion meets the top rail of the face frame like any mullion, but the bottom rail of the face frame is butted into it like a stile. Some cabinetmakers like to employ a wide piece for this mullion and then cut its width down for the hood portion of the cabinet so that there is no need to make flush the part of the finished end that is behind doors. Whenever possible, the hood should be centered over the range below it, and if the hood is vented outside, it is important to locate this section of the cabinet where the measurer has indicated the presence of the duct to be connected with the hood.

With one type of cooking appliance, an eye-level range, it is absolutely necessary for the hood space to be perfectly aligned with the range. The appliance is a single unit, with a range and oven to be incorporated into the base cabinets below and a combination hood, microwave oven, and light which must be fitted into the upper cabinet above. Since it is a single piece, the stiles of the base cabinets must align perfectly with the finished ends of the upper cabinet. Appliance height is also important for correct layout of upper cabinetry that will accommodate the hood–microwave. (The "cutout" for a typical eye-level range–oven is illustrated in Figure 12-14.)

Finally, one type of range needs no hood or vent above it. This appliance possesses a built-in fan and duct to vent away cooking exhausts from below through the base cabinet in which it is mounted. The cabinet configuration is like that for a standard cooktop, but shelves inside the base cabinet must usually be shallower to allow for the ducting in the rear. Useful accessories to incorporate into the cabinets near a range are slide-out shelving in the bases for storing pots and pans and spice racks mounted on the rear of upper doors.

If the kitchen is equipped with a cooktop rather than a combination range and oven, it will generally also require

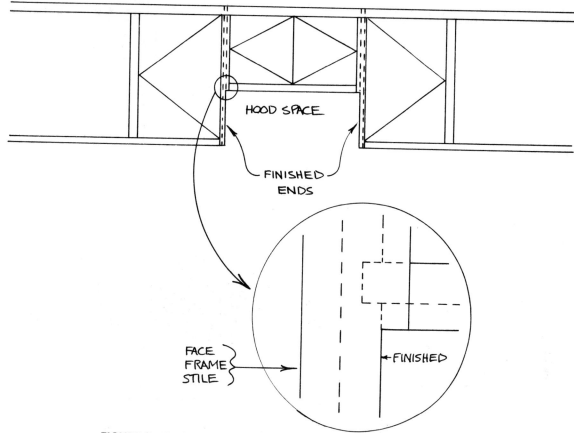

FIGURE 3-12 Sectioning of an upper cabinet to receive a hood. Note that the mullions may be detailed to avoid making a flush joint behind the doors above the hood. Also note that doors on either side of the hood should be hinged to swing away from the cooking station.

a special floor-to-ceiling cabinet in which to mount a built-in oven. Such a cabinet usually has a pair of doors above the oven and either a pair of doors or one or more drawers below the oven. There are no standard or usual sizes for the oven itself, and the designer must determine the exact height and width of the oven opening or cutout. Most oven manufacturers not only provide these dimensions, but also recommend a specific distance from the floor for oven placement. The depth of this cabinet is almost always 25 in., that is, 1 in. deeper than the base cabinet which is next to it. (See Figure 3-13.)

The designer should be careful not to place the oven cabinet over any light switch or outlet. A measurement showing the location of a 220-volt electrical cable in the kitchen will usually indicate approximately where to locate the cabinet, even if elevations are not provided. It is naturally appropriate to place a tray divider section within the oven cabinet or near the oven.

Another tall cabinet which is often designed into a single wall of kitchen cabinetry is a pantry unit. Inside, it may have adjustable shelves, swing-out shelving units, large susans, or door-mounted storage racks. Its exterior configuration is often simply two door spaces, a shorter one above a longer one. The rail that divides these door sections is best placed near eye level. (See Figure 3-14.)

The refrigerator requires an open space in the base cabinetry, of course. A cabinet end that is next to a refrigerator must be a finished end. The countertop for this base unit will overhang the finished end by approximately 1 in. In determining the amount of space necessary for a refrigerator, the cabinet designer must remember to allow for this overhang. Refrigerators are often 30 ins. wide, but they may be 34 in. or 36 in. or wider. Again, accurate layout will require knowing the exact size of the refrigerator to be used. Where the refrigerator space comes between two sections of base cabinetry, the distance between the two finished ends should be at least the width of the refrigerator plus 2 in. or the overhang of each section of countertop). Where the refrigerator is placed at the end of a single view of cabinetry (as when it is next to a doorway), the width of the space allowed for the refrigerator must be the width of the appliance plus 1 in. If one side of the appliance is

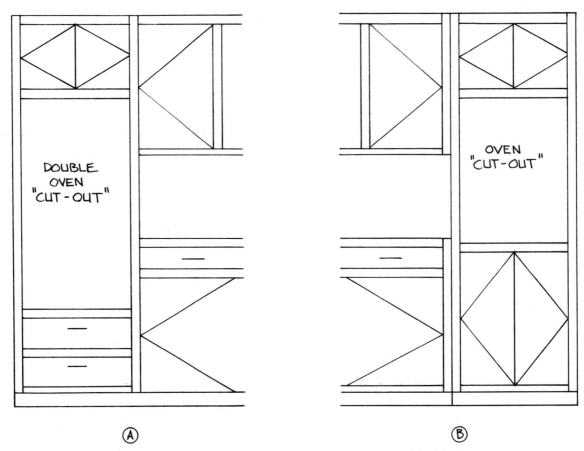

FIGURE 3-13 Face configurations for a double oven (A) with drawers beneath, and a single oven (B) with doors beneath.

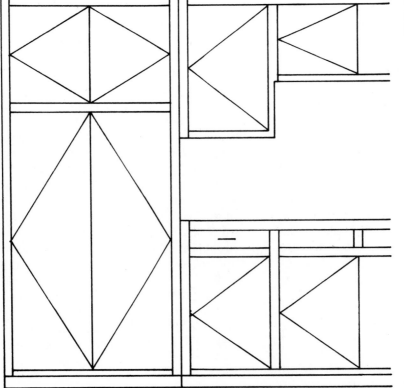

FIGURE 3-14 Typical arrangement for a pantry placed next to a base and upper cabinet.

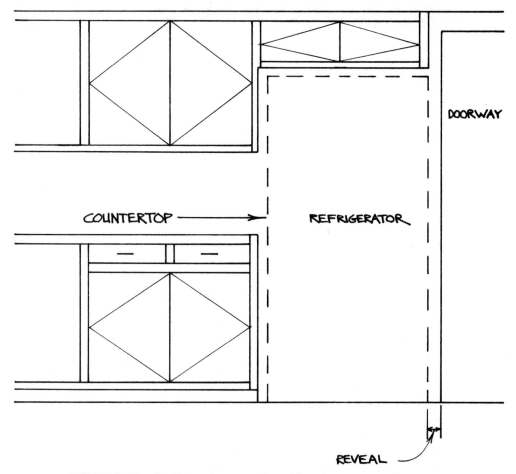

FIGURE 3-15 Configuration around a refrigerator next to a doorway. If the doorway were a return wall, the upper would extend to it and the reveal spacing would be maintained for clearance of the refrigerator door handle. Note that there is no need to build the refrigerator upper as a separate unit unless it is to be of a different depth than that of the rest of the uppers on the wall.

to be next to a wall of the house, an additional 2 to 3 ins. should be allowed for the handle of the refrigerator door so that this door will open at least a full 90°.

The upper above a refrigerator unit is often 12 to 15 in. in height, depending on the size of the appliance. Its length is the same size as the opening allowed in the base cabinetry below. Unless plans call for this section of upper to be deeper than the rest of the upper cabinetry on that wall, it is not built as an independent unit. It is sectioned and built similarly to the upper over a hood, as discussed earlier. (See Figure 3-15.)

The base cabinet into which a sink is mounted is designed quite similarly to a vanity cabinet except that a kitchen sink is generally larger than a bathroom sink (often 32 in. long). The face of this cabinet section is usually fixed with false fronts in the top portion where drawers normally would go and a pair of doors below. The sink

section of cabinetry has no shelf in it other than the cabinet bottom. This is because of the room required for plumbing connections to the sink.

A dishwasher is almost always called for directly next to the sink section. Wall ends may be employed next to a dishwasher. The cabinetmaker only needs to ensure that an appropriate space is provided between stiles for this appliance. Almost all dishwashers are 24 in. wide and slightly more than 34 in. in height. Also, the designer should be aware that proper mounting of a dishwasher will require at least a standard base cabinet depth. (The cabinet configuration around a trash compactor is the same as for a dishwasher, except for opening size.)

The countertop that covers a sink base and dishwasher is built as a single length and then has a hole cut for mounting of the sink. (For the most common sink and dishwasher cabinet arrangement, see Figure 3-16.) There

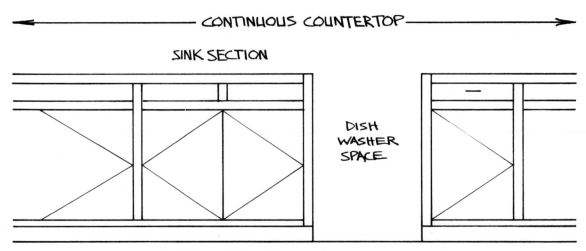

FIGURE 3-16   Kitchen sink and dishwasher arrangement.

should be 24 to 30 in. of countertop length on each side of the sink.

Since kitchen sinks are generally centered on a window, there is usually no upper cabinetry above a kitchen sink base. Sometimes a valance is used above a sink to connect the uppers located on each side of the window. The valance is simply a short framework that can be used to mount a light or to conceal a drapery rod. It should be built separately from other cabinetry and then fitted and mounted on the job site.

Where there is no window over the sink, plans will often call for a section of upper over the sink with a light mounted below. The bottom of such a section should be at least 24 in. above the countertop and somewhat longer than the width of the sink. This section should be constructed as part of the single wall of upper cabinetry just as was performed for the hood. The light may be hidden behind a wide bottom rail, or to maintain a consistent door line, a wide edging may be used behind the doors to conceal the light. The design may be employed in any upper to yield overcounter lighting. (See Figure 3-17.)

Another situation that may be encountered in design-

FIGURE 3-17   End view of uppers showing methods of concealing over-counter lighting.

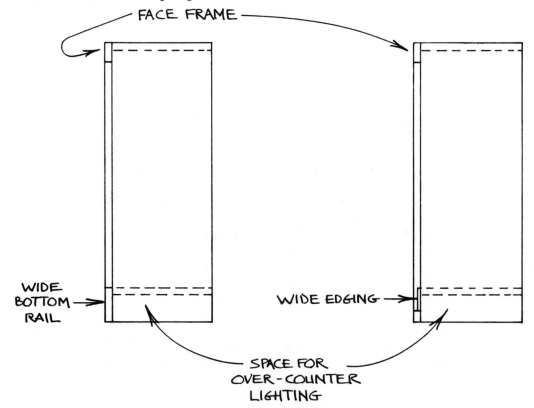

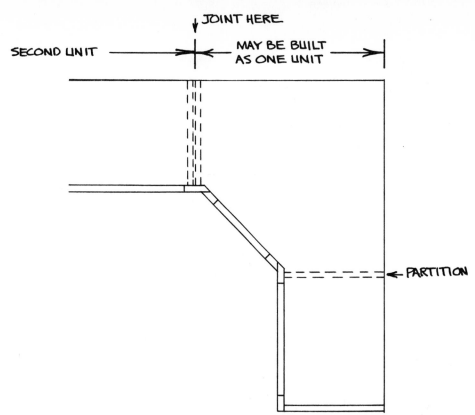

FIGURE 3-18 Top view showing joints in angled cabinetry. The mitered face frame for the corner should overlap the face of straight sections. If the return (second unit) is not long, the entire L shape might be built as a single piece.

ing the kitchen is the angled cabinet, particularly the 135° cabinetry used to house a full-round susan. Many cabinetmakers like to build this cabinet as a single unit to be joined to both straight sections on the job site. Others prefer to fabricate the angled section as part of one of these straight sections so that only one job-site joint has to be made. From the standpoint of making a more perfect joint, it is generally a better procedure to do as few job-site joints as necessary. The angled section of cabinet is most easily formed by mitering the assembled face frames and overlaying the stiles for the straight sections with the stiles for the angled section. Partitions are used to separate the section from others in the same cabinet. (See the top view in Figure 3-18.)

Kitchen floor plans for custom-built homes vary widely, but in general, home planners try to base the floor plan on the sink–range–refrigerator triangle. The cabinet designer is often required to place appliances and workstations according to an architect's plans. By simply combining the various configurations as necessary, it is possible to create a beautiful and functional kitchen. Further, the same general principles for sectioning and modularizing cabinetry in the kitchen can be easily applied throughout a house for built-in cabinetry. A wet bar, for example, is merely a base cabinet with a short distance between partitions for the small bar sink.

Configurations for Other "Built-ins"

Room dividers and wall systems may be built to almost any dimensions and for almost any purpose. Books are often stored on open shelves. These, of course, may be adjustable. Records, tapes, and other audio and video software are often stored on shelves behind doors to keep them free of dust. Stereos, televisions, and other electronic equipment may either be stored on shelves or built into custom-sized cabinet cutouts. The fold-up bed has made its return to use recently also, and the cabinetry which may be built around it may consist of shelving, drawers, slide-out or drop-leaf tops, and door-covered cabinetry. Room dividers are simply wall system cabinets that have cabinet facings on both sides. (See Figure 3-19 for two examples.)

Closets may be subdivided and organized with drawer and shelf units. A sewing center or built-in desk usually consists of a knee-under section and desk-height base sections with drawers. The top may be made to allow the sewing machine to fold down into the knee section when it is not in use.

Furniture Configurations

Much furniture can be constructed using the same basic construction details that are employed with residential built-in cabinets. A desk, for example may be constructed similarly to a sewing center configuration, with a knee-under section and one or two desk-height base cabinets with drawers. The separate units may be screwed together and then fitted with a continuous back and top. If plans call for legs to be used instead of having the finished ends, face, and back in contact with the floor, these legs may be rabbeted to fit into the corners of the base units. The legs may then be fixed to the inside of joints between the finished ends and face or back. It is probably superior, however, to incorporate full height legs, doweled to face and ends, in such a desk. (See Figure 3-20.)

Tables for dining and for conferring are usually made

Ⓐ

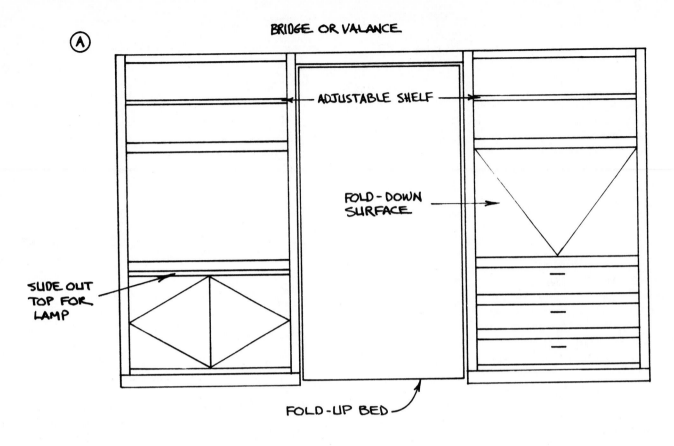

ADJUSTABLE SHELF

FOLD - DOWN
SURFACE

SLIDE OUT
TOP FOR
LAMP

FOLD - UP BED

Ⓑ

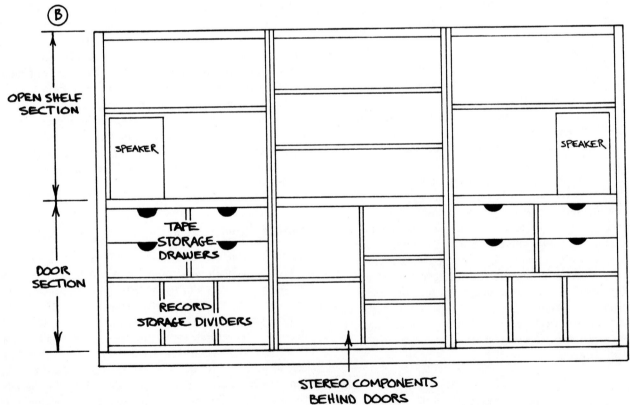

OPEN SHELF
SECTION

SPEAKER

SPEAKER

TAPE
STORAGE
DRAWERS

DOOR
SECTION

RECORD
STORAGE DIVIDERS

STEREO COMPONENTS
BEHIND DOORS

FIGURE 3-19 Two of an infinite variety of wall system configurations. (A) The bridge may contain a reading light; (B) stereo setup. If finished in the rear, such a unit may serve as a room divider. The large size suggests building this single view as three separate pieces.

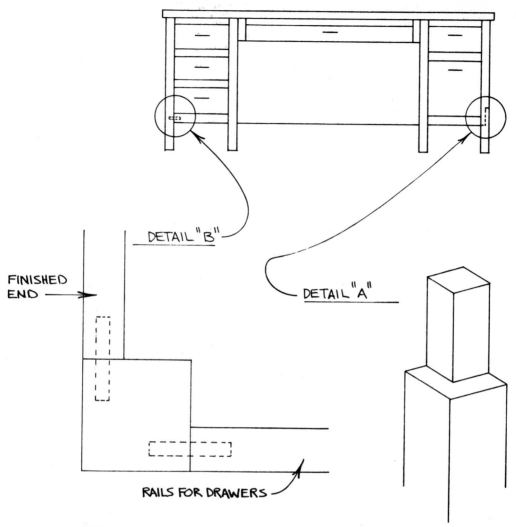

FINISHED
END

DETAIL "B"

DETAIL "A"

RAILS FOR DRAWERS

FIGURE 3-20 Desk configuration with legs. The legs are best made continuous, but detail A shows how to machine separate legs to use with stand and face and finished end construction. Detail B shows how continuous legs might be incorporated with dowel joints.

by building a leg-and-apron unit and then attaching the table top itself with screws from beneath. The joints between the table legs and the sections of the apron are usually made with dowels. The joints should be strengthened with a wood or metal corner bracket. (See Figure 3-21.)

Dressers or armoires are frequently made with standard box and face frame construction, but they can be constructed with continuous legs as in a desk or table. Frequently, no face frame is used, and drawer spaces are separated with narrow box members. (See Figure 13-20.) More detailed information on furniture building techniques is presented in Chapter 13.

FIGURE 3-21 Common leg and apron joining system for tables.

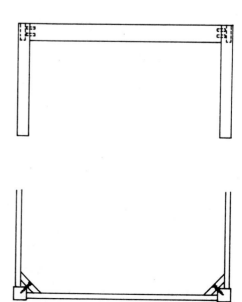

DRAWING THE LAYOUT PLAN

Drawing the layout plan, whether it is done on paper or on layout sticks, requires great concern with communication. Shop drawings are either "customer drawings," performed to let a cabinet customer know exactly how the completed cabinetry will look, or "production drawings," which tell detailers and assemblers where to locate joints and other important data. Since layout sticks probably have no meaning to customers, they are used only to communicate with other woodworkers.

Customer Drawings

Customer drawings are neat, careful two-dimensional representations of a single view of cabinetry. A customer will view the drawings and have a good idea of how proposed cabinetry will look when it is installed in the home or building. Therefore, such drawings must be rendered to a consistent scale. The designer will show not just one cabinet configuration, but an entire view—one wall with bases, uppers, and everything else that will be in sight when the woodwork is installed: appliances, windows and doorways, switches and outlets, and so on.

The tools required for customer drawing are common drafting tools: leads and lead holders or pencils as well as a pencil pointer or fine sandpaper pad for keeping the drawing instruments sharp, a drawing board, T-square, one or two triangles, and an architect's scale. Even though customer drawings must be neat and careful, the objective of this type of drawing is clearly not the same as with architecture or drafting, and the designer should not become so involved in creating such drawings that he or she is over-planning the cabinetry. Still, the designer may find uses for other architect's tools, such as gum eraser, erasing shield, compass, and protractor.

The cabinetmaker usually needs only to present a frontal view of each wall as it will look with the woodwork incorporated. This drawing may reflect door and molding details because these features relate to appearance, but it will usually exclude fabrication information such as exact partition location and arrangement of nailers and hold-downs. Since door and molding details give cabinetwork the character of its appearance, it is often the best practice to show actual sample doors and moldings to the customer rather than relying on drawings to convey the look and feel of these items.

A customer will often want a picture that shows an entire wall as it will appear with the cabinets in place, but it is sufficient to prepare a two-dimensional drawing of the cabinet facings. In fact, such views are similar to the type that architects draw when they present a particular cabinet arrangement in a building. These drawings are called elevations.

Drawing a "communication" picture for a customer should follow this general order:

1. Isolate each section or view of cabinetry.
2. Draw the outline of the entire wall to scale and all those features that will show after the cabinetry is in place, including windows, doorways, and wall fixtures.
3. Draw to scale the frontal view of the cabinetry as it will be arranged on the wall.
4. Draw or make notations regarding those features which will be of interest to the customer.

With a sheet of paper positioned on the drawing board and taped in place, the designer begins by drawing an outline of the entire wall or view that he or she has isolated. This is done using the dimensions yielded by on-site measurements. If only rough-in measurements are provided, the designer allows for the building materials which will be used to finish the walls. The cabinet artist will render the floor line, the ceiling and/or soffit lines, the line or return walls, the outline of windows, and the outlines of outlet and switch plates. As an example, suppose that the designer is working on view 2 of the floor plan in Figure 3-1. The wall outline should look something like that shown in Figure 3-22.

Before attempting to draw in the proposed cabinetry, the designer should pause to consider the configuration that he or she is drawing in, asking whether there are any potential problems to be solved. The designer might visualize the location of important features such as returns and appliances before proceeding. If standard cabinetry is to be used in the kitchen of Figure 3-22, a proficient designer will realize that allowing for 24-in. returns on each end will not allow a dishwasher to be placed on either side of a 32-in. sink centered beneath the window. The sink may be placed off-center, the length of base cabinets could be increased several inches beyond the end of the soffit into the dining area to accommodate the space required for the dishwasher, or the dishwasher may be moved around the corner into a location in one of the return cabinets. More radical solutions to this problem would be to have the home builder move the soffit farther into the dining area or to eliminate the dishwasher. The customer should make this decision.

When all decisions regarding the configuration have been resolved, the designer may draw cabinet features into the elevation in the following general order:

1. On each end, the return portions of the single view, which, of course, have no face

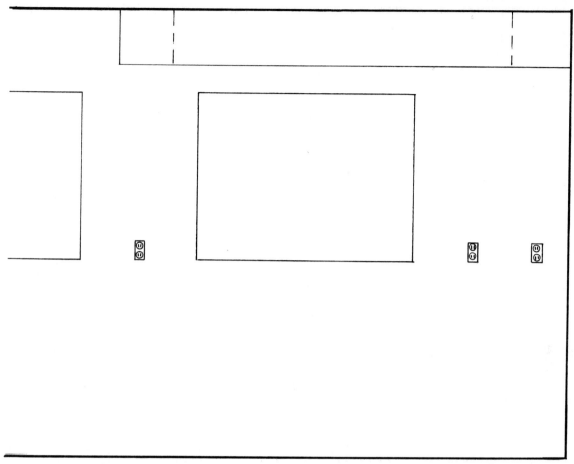

FIGURE 3-22 Single view 2 from Figure 3-1, showing soffit, windows, switch, and outlets, as well as floor, ceiling, and wall lines.

2. The toekick and countertop, which are continuous except for where free-standing appliances are located
3. The stiles on the ends of each face frame
4. Top and bottom rails
5. Mullions
6. Other rails
7. Appliances and other features

If the decision was to move the sink off center from the window in our example kitchen, the completed customer drawing would be as shown in Figure 3-23.

Production Drawings

There are several differences between drawings of this type and those done for a customer's approval. In the first place,

it is not nearly as important to render neat, carefully scaled representations of the cabinet. The layout person uses production drawings to communicate with other cabinetmakers, who can presumably visualize the details of a completed cabinet more easily than most customers. The objective here should be to communicate construction details rather than finished appearance. Second, production drawings are usually in two parts: a sketch of the face frame and a sketch of box components. These are on the same piece of paper, and an entire single view is usually not drawn. Rather, each drawing is of a single cabinet unit. Also, since these drawings are not frequently drawn to a careful scale, the designer usually notes on them measurements and other pertinent data that will be vital to the detailer and assemblers. The designer may use the same tools for production drawing as those used for customer drawing, but some cabinetmakers use only a pencil and a straightedge. Figure 3-24 shows a very simple production

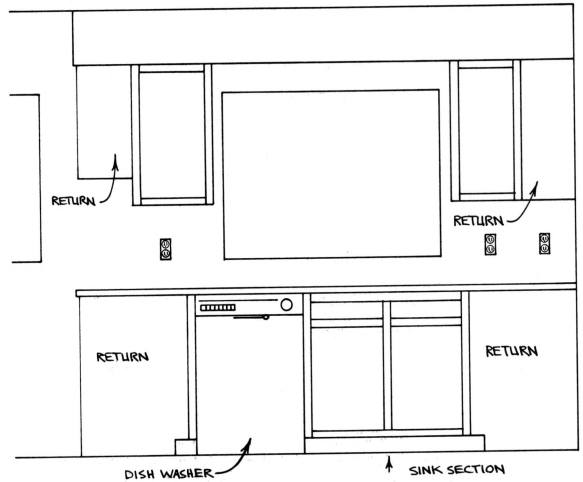

FIGURE 3-23 Completed elevation for view 2 from Figure 3-1. Note that the sink is not centered on the window. The stile to the left of the dishwasher might have to be wider so that the dishwasher door will open without interference from projecting hardware on one return cabinet.

drawing for the upper cabinet to the right of the window in Figures 3-1 and 3-23.

Layout sketches are produced in the following general order:

1. Isolate each individual case or cabinet and determine its overall size.
2. Determine the relationship of face to box, considering flush finished ends, scribe overhangs, and returns.
3. Sketch the face frame and indicate all the dimensions necessary to locate components and determine their sizes as they will be listed for the cutter.
4. Sketch the box components as they are to be assembled, indicating all the measurements to be used for listing parts and for locating dadoes.

5. Note onto the drawing anything that will be important to the assembler (do not trust your memory).

When performing production drawings, the designer draws the face frame by first determining its overall size, drawing the outside, and then drawing (in order) stiles, top and bottom rails, mullions, and other rails. The box is a bit more difficult to draw. It is probably best to begin by drawing an end and locating its dadoes. Top, bottom, and fixed shelves can then be drawn to meet these dadoes. Other ends and partitions are then drawn to meet dadoes in the top, bottom and fixed shelves. (*Note:* Trade standards usually call for dadoes that are ¼ in. deep.)

As a final note on drawing, remember that customer drawings are in wide use today. Many architects routinely call for "shop drawings" on blueprints. The ability to perform such drawing may be considered vital to the cabinet-

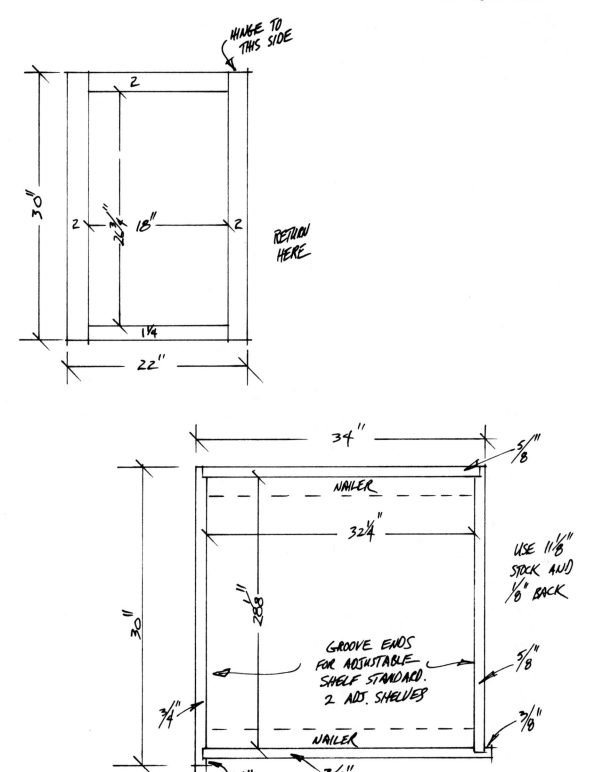

FIGURE 3-24 Production drawing for the upper cabinet to the right of the window in Figure 3-24. Note that 12 in. of the box is not covered with a face. This is where it accepts the full 12 in. depth of the return cabinet. Measurements are used by the designer to make the cutting list, by the detailer to perform doweling and dadoing, and by the assembler for verification.

making trade. On the other hand, there are still a number of cabinetmakers who have never done such a drawing. Builders and homeowners have become familiar with their work and never request such drawings from these people.

Layout Sticks

Cabinetmakers who use layout sticks do so because they allow full-scale designing. Rather than paper, the designer uses a strip of wood that is equal in length to the overall finished length of the single view of cabinetry being designed. Rather than an architect's scale, the designer uses a tape measure. Marks, as wide as the stock to be used, are made along the edge of the stick to represent stiles and mullions. Other marks represent the location of ends, partitions, and other features. An entire view of cabinetry may be represented on one stick with bases marked on the front edge and uppers marked on the rear edge.

The procedure for making a full-scale layout stick is usually in the following order:

1. Prepare a wood strip exactly as long as the overall length of finished cabinetry on one wall or view.

2. Make marks on the stick to indicate exact locations of windows, pipes, and other wall features.

3. Beginning at the ends and working toward the middle, measure out and mark stiles and mullions as dictated by wall reveals, returns, appliance location, and so on.

4. Mark exact thicknesses and exact locations of ends and partitions.

5. Similarly, create a separate stick showing location of rails, tops, bottoms, and fixed shelves if cabinets are nonstandard.

Perhaps the easiest way to understand stick layout is to follow the steps in creating a particular one. Here we will use as an illustration the same wall of cabinetry that we looked at for shop drawing—the sink wall of the kitchen shown in Figure 3-1.

We begin by making a stick to be 118 in. long. This is the finished measurement between the wall on the right and the end of the soffit on the left. Measuring from the right, we place lines on the stick at 36 and 78 in. to signify the location of the window. Pipes are similarly indicated on the stick so that we do not wind up with water and drain pipes behind the dishwasher.

Still measuring from the right, we make marks along the top edge of the stick to indicate the exact placement of upper stiles at these locations:

- One stile from 12 to 14 in. and one stile from 32 to 34 in. (These define the width of the face frame for the upper to the right of the window, allowing for a return upper and a 2-in. reveal next to the window.)

- One stile from 80 to 82 in. and one stile from 103 to 105 in. (These define the width of the face frame for the upper to the left of the window, allowing for a 1 in. reveal along the edge of the soffit, a return upper of standard depth, and the 2 in. reveal along the window.)

We now place marks to indicate the exact placement of the ends. There is one wall end to the view—on the extreme right—and three finished ends.

Supposing that we line up the backs of the two island cabinets, that we need 3-in. stiles in the corners where our base cabinets meet their returns, and that we squeeze the dishwasher in to the left of the sink, we would measure from the right and place our stiles for the base cabinets as follows:

- From 24 in and from 64 to 66 in. (These define the size of the sink cabinet face frame, allowing for a return of standard depth.)

- From 90 to 93 in. (This allows for a standard depth return and a dishwasher space. This stile on the extreme left may actually be mounted to the island return cabinet since its only function is to allow sufficient space for the dishwasher door to open. Sheet material such as plywood should be used to close off this island cabinet from the dishwasher space entirely.)

We may now mark the exact locations for the two wall ends that will be used in the sink base. (Figure 3-25 shows a portion of the completed layout stick.)

For the layout person, sticks have an advantage in listing. After the marks are correctly placed on the stick, the cutting list is made by measurement, not by math computations. The stick system is prone to very few errors in layout. The great disadvantage of using layout sticks is their sometimes cumbersome length. A long workbench is often necessary for this type of designing, rather than a smaller desk or drafting table. Also, the stick cannot be easily copied and taped onto a pile of wood for the detailer and the assembler.

Full-Scale Layout

Some circumstances call for full-scale layouts whether or not you decide to become a "stick designer." Curved walls, custom-made lazy susans, and some other situations may require this type of designing.

When the backs of cabinets are to be fitted to curved walls, it is best to perform the layout directly on the piece

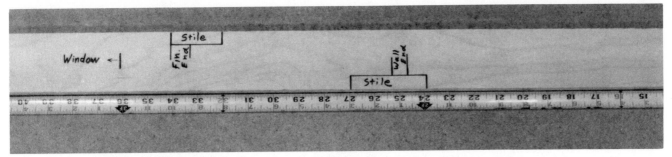

FIGURE 3-25 Portion of a completed layout stick. This is a portion of view 2 of the floor plan in Figure 3-1.

of plywood or MDF that will become the cabinet bottom. The measurer should have provided a template of the necessary curve or angle. This can be directly transferred to the cabinet bottom, cut to the required contour, and then locations of other cabinet components can be determined. For example, the designer may draw lines to indicate where a partition goes, and this becomes the location for a dado. Since the depth of a curved cabinet varies, the width of a partition is most easily determined after its location is fixed on the cabinet bottom. Its size can simply be measured.

Some accessories are most easily fabricated from full-scaled layout. These include some susans, spice racks, and hinged pantries. The entire plan view (top view) of the cabinet may be drawn out on inexpensive material such as hardboard. Using hinge points as reference, it is a simple matter to determine the arcs of these accessories as they open and close. These arcs will thus define the maximum allowable size of the accessory. (See Figure 3-26.)

Full-scale layouts are useful for any nonstandard cabinetry, but it is time consuming. Encountering a call for a shoe rack with angled shelving, some designers might perform a full-scale section drawing, while others would not. (See Figure 3-27.)

DEVELOPING THE CUTTING LIST

Developing a cutting list is the final phase of laying out the cabinet job. The exact dimensions of every piece of wood to be used in the cabinet job must be determined and written down in the clearest and easiest-to-read way. It is best to complete *all* the drawings or *all* the layout sticks before listing.

FIGURE 3-26 Full-scale layout of a quarter-round blind-corner susan.

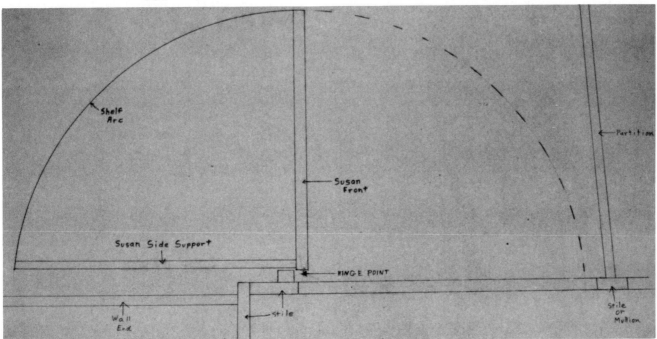

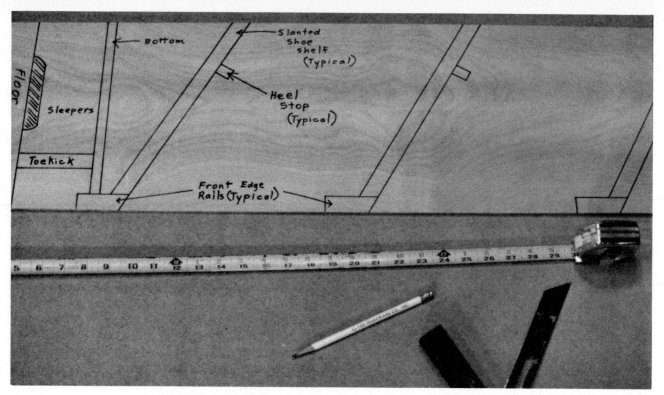

FIGURE 3-27 Full-scale layout of a slanted-shelf shoe rack. This is a "section" or side view.

A "drawing designer" bases the sizes of materials on math computations. This is why production sketches are covered with dimension notations. Once the designer has determined the overall size of an opening or the width of a stile, he or she will not want to repeat the computations. The length of stiles and finished ends is usually obvious from our drawing. For the length of rails, we must subtract the width of stiles and some mullions. The length of mullions is obtained by subtracting the width of rails. For mortise-and-tenon assembly, we must add for the length of tenons. To arrive at the sizes of box parts, the designer should first determine the distance between each component and then add or subtract as necessary for scribes, dado depth, and other assembly features. For example, to determine the length of the upper bottom in Figure 3-24, we begin with the distance between ends ($32\frac{1}{4}$ in.), add the depth of the dado in the finished end of the left ($\frac{1}{4}$ in.), add the thickness of the wall end ($\frac{5}{8}$ in.), and add the width of the scribe on the extreme right ($\frac{3}{8}$ in.). This piece should be listed with a length of $33\frac{1}{2}$ in.

The "stick designer" can derive all dimensions by measuring between marks on the layout stick. We would derive the same dimension for the cabinet bottom in the example above simply by measuring between the extreme right-hand end of the layout stick and the point where the bottom ends in the dado of the finished end.

Some designers who use production drawings will also list the dimensioned pieces directly on each cabinet drawing. This practice works well enough for small jobs—jobs with only one or two cabinet units, but it is generally better to organize the cutting list on separate paper. It is easier and much faster for the cutter to do his or her job when all the parts of one type are listed together. All the face frames might be listed on one sheet and all the box components on another. The individual parts that make up the doors and drawers should also be listed by themselves. Sheets with columns and lines can be employed to make work even easier. All 2-in.-width face frame stock might be listed in one column, all $1\frac{1}{4}$ in.-width stock in another, and so on. The cabinet units should have a number. All the face frame members for unit 1 should be listed first, then those for unit 2, and all others in order. This way, the cutter can mark each piece of a single unit with the same number, and the pieces can be kept together for easy machining and assembly. Figure 3-28 illustrates a well-ordered cutting list.

CHAPTER SUMMARY OF CABINETMAKING SKILLS

A cabinetmaker who is familiar with the construction details and standards of a job is ready to begin designing. Creating good cabinet designs is a matter of acquiring knowledge of how cabinets are positioned to function within a room as well as how each cabinet is assembled.

To determine cabinet configurations, the designer

E. Jay Cee Cabinet Shop Tucson, Arizona 85714			DATE	PLAN#	JOB# 4
PRODUCTION ORDER AND CUTTING LIST			CUSTOMER		Sheet / of /

Face# Case#	Solid Oak	Solid Oak	Solid Oak			
	Miscellaneous	$3/4 \times 2$	$3/4 \times 1\frac{3}{4}$			
Face #1	$1-\frac{3}{4} \times 4\frac{3}{4} \times 56$	$1-56$	$2-32\frac{1}{4}$			
		$4-17\frac{1}{4}$	$2-25\frac{1}{2}$			
Face #2		$1-11\frac{3}{4}$	$2-46\frac{1}{2}$			
Face #3		$1-11\frac{3}{4}$	$2-46\frac{1}{2}$			
Other:	$2-\frac{3}{4} \times 4 \times 87$ – trim					
	$1-\frac{3}{4} \times 4 \times 70$ – trim					
	$1-\frac{3}{4} \times \frac{1}{2} \times 63$ – edging					
Change — Change — Change — Change — Change — Change						
	$3/4$ Oak Ply	$5/8$ mdf	$5/8$ mdf	$3/4$ Pine	Miscellaneous	
	$3/4 \times 26\frac{3}{4}$	$5/8 \times 26\frac{3}{4}$	$5/8 \times 26\frac{3}{8}$	(nailers)	$1-\frac{1}{8} \times 28\frac{1}{8} \times 58\frac{3}{4}$ Back	
Case #1		$2-28\frac{1}{8}$	$1-18$		$1-\frac{1}{4} \times \frac{5}{8} \times 18$ Oak Edging	
		$2-27\frac{3}{4}$		$4-2 \times 25\frac{1}{2}$	$4-\frac{3}{4} \times 4\frac{1}{8} \times 26$ Sleepers	
		$1-58$				
Case #2	$1-46\frac{1}{2}$	$1-46$	$3-13\frac{1}{4}$	$1-2 \times 13\frac{1}{2}$	$1-\frac{1}{8} \times 14\frac{7}{8} \times 46$ Back	
		$1-14$		$1-1\frac{1}{4} \times 13\frac{1}{2}$	$3-\frac{1}{4} \times \frac{5}{8} \times 13\frac{1}{4}$ Oak Edging	
Case #3	$1-46\frac{1}{2}$	$1-46$	$3-13\frac{1}{4}$	$1-2 \times 13\frac{1}{2}$	$1-\frac{1}{8} \times 14\frac{7}{8} \times 46$ Back	
		$1-14$		$1-1\frac{1}{4} \times 13\frac{1}{2}$	$3-\frac{1}{4} \times \frac{5}{8} \times 13\frac{1}{4}$ Oak Edging	
Other:	$1-\frac{3}{4} \times 27\frac{3}{4} \times 60$ – Ply Top					
Change — Change — Change — Change — Change — Change						
Drawer Parts						
Fronts – Solid Oak	$\frac{1}{2}"$ Ply Subfronts	$\frac{3}{4}"$ Ply Backs	$\frac{1}{2}"$ Ply Sides	$\frac{1}{4}$ Hardboard Bottoms	
$2-\frac{3}{4} \times 12 \times 17\frac{1}{4}$	$2-10\frac{1}{4} \times 15\frac{1}{4}$	$2-10\frac{1}{4} \times 15\frac{1}{4}$	$4-10\frac{1}{4} \times 24$	$2-15\frac{3}{4} \times 23\frac{1}{8}$	
$1-\frac{3}{4} \times 5 \times 17\frac{1}{4}$	$1-3\frac{3}{4} \times 15\frac{1}{4}$	$1-3\frac{3}{4} \times 15\frac{1}{4}$	$2-3\frac{3}{4} \times 24$	$1-15\frac{3}{4} \times 23\frac{1}{8}$	
$2-\frac{3}{4} \times 6 \times 17\frac{1}{4}$	$2-4\frac{3}{4} \times 15\frac{1}{4}$	$2-4\frac{3}{4} \times 15\frac{1}{4}$	$4-4\frac{3}{4} \times 24$	$2-15\frac{3}{4} \times 23\frac{1}{8}$	
$1-\frac{3}{4} \times 6\frac{1}{2} \times 17\frac{1}{4}$	$1-5\frac{1}{4} \times 15\frac{1}{4}$	$1-5\frac{1}{4} \times 15\frac{1}{4}$	$2-5\frac{1}{4} \times 24$	$1-15\frac{3}{4} \times 23\frac{1}{8}$	

FIGURE 3-28 Well-organized cutting list.

should take pains to establish organization and to get a good overview of the requirements of the job. He or she must learn to isolate one view of cabinetry, accounting for wall-finishing materials, scribes, clearances, and reveals. Determining where one cabinet unit ends and another begins may be called modularizing. This requires knowledge of cabinet height and depth standards as well as the ability to position and allow for various appliances and fixtures. After locating these constants, individual cabinet units may be sectioned—divided into manageable door and drawer sections.

In choosing a designing system, some prefer the speed of production drawing, whereas others like the full-scale measuring capabilities of layout sticks. Quite careful, scaled drawing is sometimes necessary for communication with a customer.

Listing the sizes of various cabinet components should be made as organized as possible for ease of cutting. Sizes are derived by addition and subtraction in the drawing system, and by measurement under the stick system.

FOUR

MATERIAL SELECTION AND PURCHASING

WOOD SELECTION

With the wide variety that people have today in choosing woods, hardware, and other materials, it is best to look first at the considerations that limit these choices. As the cabinetmaker, you should consider three factors: job requirements, cost/availability, and your own limitations (tools, volume of purchasing, etc.) and preferences.

When taking on an individual job, the cabinetmaker will often ask his or her customer to select at least three materials. First, the customer will choose visible woods—the hardwoods and veneers that are to be used in fabricating the facings, finished ends, drawer fronts, and doors. In general, the customer simply specifies one wood, such as birch, ash, or red oak. In building most cabinetry, we do not want to slice or laminate our own veneers, and so we suggest to the customer those hardwoods that are available as plywoods. The most common of these are red or white birch, red or white oak, ask, knotty pine, hard maple, walnut, and the mahoganies. A customer usually also chooses visible hardware—door and drawer pulls or knobs. With new construction, blueprints often indicate both the primary (visible) wood and the hardware to be used as part of the specifications. Finally, customers almost always choose finishes—the color of stain when used and the sheen (se-migloss, flat, high gloss) of clear and protective finishes such as lacquer, varnish, or oil. Of course, a customer may also specify other cabinet factors in custom cabinetry. Some people come to custom builders because they want to have a voice in selecting cabinet interior materials, drawer guiding systems, and other materials. All these factors become job requirements.

Cost and availability are highly significant concerns for anyone who constructs wood products, and these are frequently factors of the volume of buying. Large shops and cabinet factories can often buy sheet goods in bunks or units containing 30 pieces or more. They can purchase solid stock in large quantity also—banded units of 1000 or more board feet of lumber. Large-volume buyers not only get better pricing but are able to order special items more easily than are smaller shops. As an example, architectural-grade plywood, which has a single-piece face on both sides, must be ordered from plywood mills and is available only in unit quantities. Small shop owners usually have neither the space nor the cash flow for this type of buying. To recover from this competitive disadvantage, they will have to find other ways to cut costs (at-home shops can be inexpensive to operate). They should be sure to build a superior product, and they must naturally do some shopping around. Owners of small shops soon discover that they can do volume buying for some items, such as hinges and drawer guides. Because of packaging costs, substantial breaks in price are usually offered for hardware items packed in bulk rather than in individual wrappings. The savings available are sometimes so great that it is less expensive to buy 100 pairs of hinges packed loose in a box than it is to buy 50 individual pairs. A 20% or greater reduction in price is often available when buying bulk-packed drawer guides. For a single job, you may only need six sets of 22-in. drawer guides, but it may make more sense to buy at least 10 sets, especially if this is a guide you can frequently use. Such items may even become the "standard" materials that you employ on profit-making cabinet jobs. It is obvious that the more cabinet materials purchased in bulk, the greater will be the savings, not only in cash expenses but also in labor, since we become more efficient using the same hinging and guiding systems again and again. On the other hand, the more standard items that a cabinetmaker uses, the less his or her work can be called "custom." Every craftsman must decide, then, where to draw the line between standardization and customizing. Perhaps a solution is to stock certain items, make customers aware of your standard items, and adjust pricing when someone calls for anything special.

Types of wood will also make a substantial difference in cost for producing a piece of cabinetry. The prices of these materials will vary greatly, depending on current popularity of a particular wood, the area of the country, and many other factors. Oak, for example, has enjoyed recent popularity in the cabinet trade (and an increase in price), whereas there have been times when it was used only as a secondary wood.

People often begin cabinetmaking not by opening a shop, but as a hobbyist or as a wage-earning employee. Their introduction to woodworking may have come in school or under the training of a parent or relative. But sooner or later, most cabinetmakers take on their first job; this leads to another, and before long they are acquiring tools for a shop. In a direct way, material selection is also a factor of the tools that a cabinetmaker has available. A thickness planer is not usually one of the first tools that a cabinetmaker buys, and he or she will thus buy surfaced facing materials. Those without a jointer may find dealers who sell lumber that is already dimensioned in standard face frame widths. Owners of low-horsepower table saws will sometimes avoid working in the hardest woods. Woodworkers without pneumatic nailing systems may also prefer working in the softer woods. After working with a variety of woods, most people develop particular tastes and preferences in all facets of material selection. In the next several sections of this chapter we discuss the attributes of common cabinetmaking materials, but obviously the best way to become familiar with the various woods and hardwares available is to work with them.

HARDWOODS AND SOFTWOODS

Hardwoods and softwoods are classifications for solid material used in the cabinet trade. These terms actually refer to the type of tree from which these woods are milled. Softwoods come from trees which have cones and which usually have needles. Most are evergreen. Softwood includes redwood, fir, and pine—materials not often used as primary woods in cabinets and furniture. Hardwoods are sawn from broad-leaved trees that are usually deciduous. These are the woods used as primary or visible in most cabinetry.

The "soft" and "hard" designations can also be thought of in terms of workability. Most softwoods are, in fact, light and easy to cut, shape, and nail through. The hardwoods are generally heavier and harder to work with. There are naturally exceptions—fir is a fairly dense and heavy wood which is often applied in home construction because it possesses great strength, whereas some mahoganies, although true hardwoods, are open-grained and easily scratched or dented.

Softwoods

Following is a list of the softwood lumbers frequently employed in the cabinetmaking trade, with a summary of properties and grades. (See Figure 4-1 for reference in the discussion.)

Pine. Pine, a softwood, is a yellow-to-white wood which is quite soft in terms of workability. Depending on its grade or quality, pine may have a number of brown knots which weaken each board and which the cutter must often cut out. This naturally increases the amount of waste. Unless a rustic look is desired, it is usually not used for cabinet faces, doors, or drawer fronts because it is easily marked and scratched. Still, there are pine plywoods available for box members behind a pine face. Its principal use in the cabinet trade is for nailers, countertop hold-downs, drawer box parts, drawer guides, and other secondary uses.

Pine is generally sold as "one-by-" dimension lumber. That is, it is available in a nominal thickness of 1 in, but it is actually surfaced to a thickness of ¾ in. Its nominal width may be 2, 4, 6, 8, 10, or 12 in. (as 1 × 2, 1 × 4, 1 × 6, 1 × 8, 1 × 10, or 1 × 12), but its actual width will be less. For example, a 1 × 12 will actually measure out at approximately 11¼ in. in width. The length of pine boards for sale will also vary, up to 20 ft or more.

The pines have a number of grades, based on appearance and workability. The best grade is "B and better," but even large cabinet shops find it difficult to acquire this grade of virtually perfect lumber because furniture mills buy nearly all of it. The grade called "C select" or "C and better," with only pin knots and very minor defects,

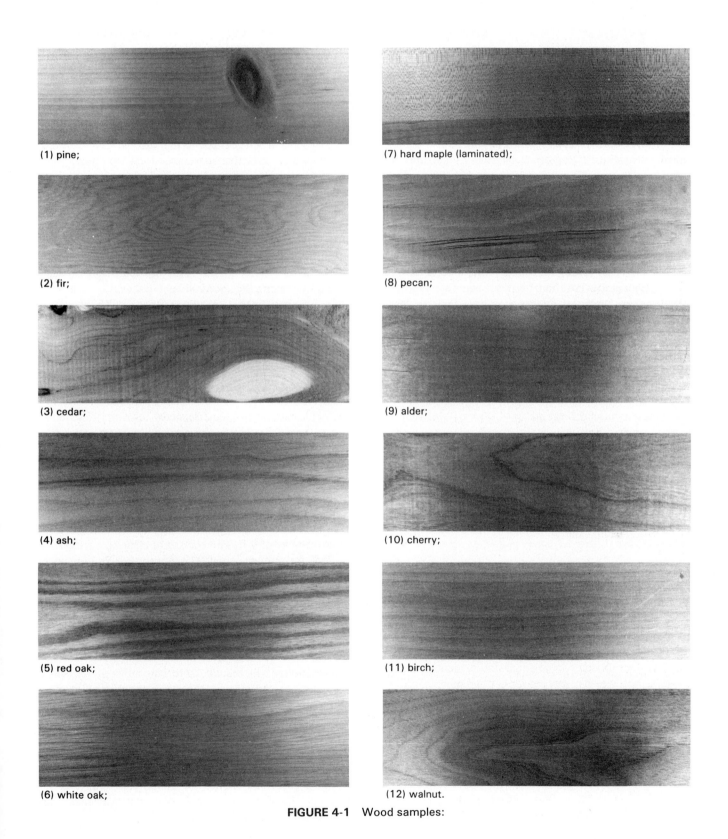

(1) pine;

(2) fir;

(3) cedar;

(4) ash;

(5) red oak;

(6) white oak;

(7) hard maple (laminated);

(8) pecan;

(9) alder;

(10) cherry;

(11) birch;

(12) walnut.

FIGURE 4-1 Wood samples:

is also generally unavailable to retail customers and cabinet shops.

The next grade, "D select," is available from lumberyards and other suppliers. It is straight, free of large knots, and all its knots must be tight in the wood fiber. Many woodworkers use D select to fabricate drawer box members. A similar grade to D select is "molding grade," a designation often used with sugar pine. But molding grade is based entirely on workability, not appearance.

Most of the remaining grades of pine lumber are signified by number. "Number 1 and better" is somewhat inferior to D select, but it is still usable for drawer parts. There will just be more waste in cutting these. Very little waste will result in cutting nailers, hold-downs, and drawer guiding material from this grade of lumber.

The "common" grades of pine are "number 2 and better," "number 3 and better," and "number 4." Number 2 is useful for cutting functional pieces such as nailers, but the other grades are almost useless to the cabinetmaker. Number 3 or number 4 lumber may have large or loose knots; it may be cupped, warped, or twisted.

Spruce.   Spruce, a softwood, has an appearance and texture like its pine relative, but is lighter and more flexible. It is graded quite similarly to pine, and can be used in much the same way. Since it marks easily, spruce should not be used for drawer sides or backs, however.

Cedar.   Cedar, also an evergreen softwood, is most readily available as an aromatic lining material for chests and storage cabinets. Cabinetmakers can sometimes find four-quarter (4/4) cedar lumber, but more available in lumberyards is the lining material—approximately ⅜ in. thick with a tongue-and-groove detail.

Fir.   Fir, a softwood, is denser and stronger than pine, but it is usually employed more for residential construction than for cabinetry. It may be sold as "one-by-" or "two-by-" dimension lumber with net thicknesses of ¾ or 1½ in., respectively. Fir plywood is available in almost any desired thickness, and lumber mills do provide a select grade of four-quarter (4/4) dimension fir lumber, but fir splinters rather easily, its open grain often requires filling, and many people do not like its appearance.

Redwood.   Redwood, a softwood, is a light porous wood with a brownish-red color and occasional yellow bands and streaks. Like fir it is available as dimension lumber. Its use for a cabinetmaker may only be in constructing outdoor furniture. Redwood is very easily dented and scratched, so it is almost never used for residential cabinetry, but it is extremely resistant to all adversities of weather.

Lumber Grades

Again, for most cabinet work, softwood lumber is generally employed in secondary applications. The most useful of the commonly available grades of pine are D-select and numbers 1 and 2 common.

Hardwoods are usually used as primary cabinet woods because most people consider them more attractive than pine and fir, and because most hardwoods are, in fact, hard woods. They are not easily marked and therefore maintain their attractive appearance for a long time.

Almost all hardwoods are graded in the same way. Grading is based on the width and length of a board and the percentage of the board with a clear face. Naturally, lumber with larger widths and lengths and higher percentages of clear face is most useful to the cabinetmaker since it will result in a small amount of waste. Except with the grade called "selects," the grade of each board is established by judging the poorer side.

The best boards are called "firsts." These have a minimum width of 6 in. and a minimum length of 8 ft. Firsts have a conversion factor (percentage of clear face) of 91⅔%. "Seconds" are boards with the same size requirements as firsts, but their conversion factor is somewhat less—81⅔%. Most lumber retailers and wholesalers make these two best grades available to customers as a single grade called "firsts and seconds" or simply "FAS."

"Selects" must be at least 4 in. in width and 6 ft in length. The conversion factor may be from 83⅓% to 91⅔%. Although this grade is a step down from firsts and seconds, it is the best grade available for some hardwoods, such as alder and soft maple.

Boards graded "number 1 common" and "number 2 common" must have minimum widths of 3 in. and minimum lengths of 4 ft. Percentages of clear face are 66⅔% to 75% for number 1 and 50% for number 2. Lumber in these grades will show more waning than first and seconds. (Waning is a defect in lumber—bark is present, or there is an absence of wood where bark used to be present.) Number 1 common lumber can be employed for cutting out cabinet facings if the cabinetmaker does not mind dealing with the costs of the additional waste. Wide pieces such as drawer fronts will require more laminating if fabricated from this grade of material. Most cabinetmakers altogether avoid lumber graded number 2 common.

There are two other grades of common lumber, "number 3A common" and "number 3B common," but these are generally used only for parts that are totally concealed. Furniture factories employ this grade of lumber in building hardwood frames for upholstered furniture, for example. Most material suppliers do not even make this type of lumber available to cabinetmakers.

"Sound wormy" is lumber quite similar to number 1 common grade, except that it also possesses wormholes.

In addition to these grades, some suppliers will use their own lumber designations, such as "prime" or "mill grade." Such terms really have no widely accepted meanings. Encountering such designations, the cabinetmaker must usually view and evaluate the lumber in person unless the supplier can clearly define the terms.

To make informed and wise lumber purchases, a cabinetmaker should be familiar not only with the characteristics of lumber grades, but also with some other lumber quality factors.

Moisture Content. The grade of an individual board is determined while it is green and rough. Moisture content is therefore not a factor in grading, and it is important to make sure that the solid woods to be used in a cabinet project are dry enough to work with efficiently. More than almost any other building material, wood is subject to variations in humidity conditions. There is nothing more important in the cabinetmaking trade than the limitation of moisture content in the wood we are using. Excessive moisture can cause the failure of glue joints and may even result in rotting.

Fortunately, it is not necessary to know all about the cell structure of wood fibers to be a good cabinetmaker. Only a few principles need to be remembered. First, the percentage of water within pieces of wood is based on weight. A board that has had all moisture removed is said to have a 0% moisture content, whereas a board whose wood fiber weight is equal to the weight of the water present is said to have a 100% moisture content. Most important, the ideal moisture content for woods used in the cabinet trade is greater than 5% but less than 10%. Dry regions require lower percentages, and more humid regions call for percentages closer to 10%. Second, drying and absorption of water causes swelling and shrinking of pieces of wood. This variance is negligible along the length of a board, but it is significant across the width of a board, sometimes resulting in twisting and cupping. Third, plain-sawn or flat-sawn boards (cut along the tangents of the tree growth rings) will be more susceptible to cupping than quarter-sawn or rift-sawn boards (boards cut through the growth rings toward the center of the tree). Lumber that has been air dried is usually not dry enough to employ in cabinet construction.

Adequate moisture control may be performed in one of two ways. We may either use a moisture meter, or we may simply stick to the purchase of kiln-dried lumber from our suppliers. Reputable lumber suppliers know how their materials have been dried, shipped, and stored, and they make no secret of this information. Carefully testing boards for moisture may be necessary in areas where there are great changes in humidity or when you suspect that lumber has been stored improperly, but purchasing kiln-dried products for a cabinet project is usually sufficient precaution in limiting moisture content.

Other Designations. Sellers of hardwood lumber use several other designations to assist customers in making suitable purchases, and cabinetmakers must be familiar with these terms and what they mean in terms of cabinet construction. Unlike softwood, most hardwood is sold in "random widths and lengths" (abbreviated "R/W&L"). The meaning of this term is obvious—the solid materials are not cut to standardized sizes as pine and fir are; instead, they are cut at the mill only to a standard thickness. When we buy 100 board feet of pine, we may receive ten 1×12 boards, each 10 ft long. If we purchase a similar amount of red oak, we generally get pieces as narrow as 6 in. and as wide as 12 in. or more, as short as 8 ft and as long as 14 ft or more. Lumber dealers will also tell us whether the material is rough or surfaced. Material that has been made smooth on both its faces is referred to as "surfaced two sides" or "S2S." As mentioned earlier, some craftsmen like to begin with rough hardwoods and prepare smooth flat surfaces with a wide jointer. They can make the material the same thickness with a planer. Others, especially those without these fairly expensive tools, know that S2S material is readily workable for most cabinet projects—the straightest boards are used for pieces that will have no reinforcement, such as door components. Boards that are not quite as flat may be used for face frames because these pieces will be glued and nailed in place. Finally, the thickness of hardwood is designated by its nominal thickness. Most of it is sold in "four-quarter" (4/4) thickness. This material will be approximately 1 in. thick if bought rough and about ¾ in. thick if purchased as surfaced lumber. Almost all hardwood lumber is similarly designated in "quarters" to indicate its nominal thickness—"six-quarter" (6/4), "eight-quarter" (8/4), and so on.

In sum, then, the cabinetmaker should purchase firsts and seconds in hardwoods that have been kiln dried and properly stored indoors. Choosing between rough and surfaced material depends on the availability of a wide bed jointer and thickness planer as well as on the preferences of the craftsman. Once the solid material has been purchased, it should be properly stored by the cabinetmaker—as flat as possible and not in contact with the floor, where it can pick up additional moisture.

Hardwoods

Following is a list of hardwoods commonly used in the cabinet trade today.

Birch. Birch is one of the best cabinet woods for a variety of reasons. Birch has a very light tan color with wide darker sections that are reddish brown. The grain appearance is fairly straight and regular when compared with many woods, but clear finishing brings out the grain contours rather than blending them together. Most people like the appearance of birch, although dark staining does cause the distinctiveness of its grain to disappear. Birch is a smooth, closed-grain wood that machines and finishes easily. It is hard enough to resist marking. Further, it is easy to find, birch plywoods are available for finished box parts, and birch is moderate in cost.

Hard Maple. Hard Maple is similar to birch in coloration, texture, and appearance, although its grain can follow much more irregular contours. Because of its smooth texture and the closed grain, it is easy to finish. It is harder than birch and resists marking very well, thus making it probably the best wood for the "cutting boards" used in so many kitchens as a surface for slicing bread, vegetables, or meat. Its price is in the same neighborhood as that of birch, varying somewhat with the region of the country. Maple is not as widely available as birch; in fact, maple veneer plywoods can be quite difficult to find in some areas. Also, because of the combination of hardness and irregular grain pattern in maple, it can be a troublesome wood to machine. Any tool with knives—jointers, shapers, planers—can tear chips out of the surface of a maple board. As with most cabinetmaking problems, there are solutions to these difficulties that maple presents—surfacing only with the grain instead of against it, taking small "bites" with a cutter, and using a table saw for surfacing, to name a few. It is not the purpose of this discussion to recommend against the use of maple, simply to point out the difficulties of working each of the common hardwoods, together with its advantages. (*Note:* Bird's-eye maple is a type of hard maple with distinctive circular grain markings called "bird's-eye." It is less readily available than other hard maples and is therefore much more expensive.)

Alder. Alder can be very similar to birch in color and grain pattern, but it is more porous, lighter, and softer. It is also substantially less expensive than birch. For these reasons, and because plywoods are not made with alder veneer facings, many cabinetmakers use alder for face frames, doors, and drawer fronts on cabinet boxes with birch plywood finished ends. The character of alder makes it superior to birch and similar woods in some ways and inferior in others. The virtue of lower cost is obvious, but alder is also much easier to work with than the birches and maples because it is so soft. Sharp blades and cutters will cut and shape alder with very little chipping, splintering, or burning. It is very easy to drive nails through alder facings, whereas cabinetmakers without pneumatic nailing equipment must often drill pilot holes through birch and maple face frames to attach them to their cabinet boxes. On the other hand, alder is more easily dented and scratched than the harder woods. It tends to absorb more stain than do most hardwoods, and the alder portions of a birch-and-alder cabinet may look darker than the birch sections. With

dark stains, the light and dark streaks that give alder its definition as a wood can blend together so much in color that the grain pattern tends to disappear. (Solutions to these problems—bleaching, shading, and so on—are discussed in Chapter 11.)

As pointed out earlier in the discussion, the best grade of alder lumber available is not FAS but select. Comparing the best grade of alder to the best grades of its birch and maple relatives, it is important not only to note cost per board foot, but also to look at waste factors, which are related to overall cost. Alder has more knots and larger knots, alder boards are generally narrower and shorter, and alder boards often require more material to be removed to achieve a straight edge. All these factors increase waste and therefore cost. Further, choosing alder over the harder woods will not decrease the cost of sheet goods on a job. The only savings will be on solid-stock parts such as face frames, drawer fronts, and door frames. To put this in perspective, consider the following example.

Example: Ernie has won a job which he has bid at $2000.00. If he does the job with solid-birch face frames, he will need 150 board feet of birch, but he determines that he would need 175 bd ft of alder to accomplish the same job. He can buy alder from his supplier for $1.20/bd ft (net cost = 175 × $1.20 = $210.00), or he could buy birch for $1.85/bd ft (net cost = 150 × $1.85 = $277.50). This would amount to a net savings of $67.50, which is certainly not an amount to be thrown away. On the other hand, the savings only amounts to slightly more than 3% of the total job cost, and Ernie may choose the harder birch if he believes the greater durability is important for his customer.

Alder is certainly a suitable cabinet wood. Its appearance lends it well to a comparison with birch and hard maple, and the cabinetmaker should consider its attributes as advantages or disadvantages in relation to these woods.

Cherry. Cherry is another wood which is appropriately compared to birch, possessing a very similar grain pattern to birch and often being just as hard. Cherry hardwood generally has more of a reddish tint to it than birch, and like alder, it is usually unavailable in firsts and seconds. Unlike alder, cherry plywoods can be purchased from some suppliers, although cherry plywood is much more expensive than birch. As workable as birch, cherry is often selected for building furniture.

Curly Soft Maple. Curly soft maple is a relatively rare and expensive wood which is used primarily for furniture, desks, and gunstocks. It is true maple with a grain pattern that takes a very irregular, "curly" course. It is not known what causes this type of growth pattern in some trees, but the appearance is highly prized. Whereas bird's-eye design is found only in the maple tree, the curly effect may be found in other types of wood. Curly maple is not only expensive, but also difficult to work with (even though it tends to be a bit softer than other maples), especially in situations where the cabinetmaker relies on knives.

Ash. Ash is a grayish-white wood that may have brown or dark gray streaks and bands. It is porous, yet very hard. The wavy grain pattern stands out distinctively whether it is stained or left natural—so distinctively that some people avoid ash as being "too busy." Despite this wavy grain pattern, ash can be cut and machined virtually without chipping or splintering. Ash plywoods are available, and ash can easily be used in both furniture and cabinetry. During the 1960s ash was a very popular wood for constructing kitchen cabinets, but its cost has gone up considerably since then and it is now used less frequently than either oak or birch in most areas.

Pecan. Pecan trees yield a wood that is quite similar to ash in grain pattern, and it should be considered in comparison to ash, especially since pecan plywoods can be difficult to locate. Pecan is slightly grayer than ash, and it may have wider sections of brown and dark gray. The best grade of pecan is usually select; thus pecan boards are narrower than ash, shorter, and possess more knots. Select pecan is less expensive than ash firsts and seconds, but it costs more than either red oak or birch. It is just as hard as ash, finishes just as nicely, and is about as easy to mill. In general, pecan solid stock can be used with ash plywoods to yield a quite desirable product.

Red Oak. Red oak has become perhaps the most popular of all cabinet woods in recent years. Its color is loosely in the red category—actually, more orange or pink than red—mixed with distinct elements of gray, brown, and yellow. Like ash, the oaks have a hard, yet porous quality which gives them a high visibility factor. Unlike ash, the oaks have narrow but very visible streaks, called medullary rays, which run lengthwise through the wood. Further, oak that is quarter sawn or rift sawn (cut into boards by cutting through rather than along the growth rings) will display wide ribbons or figures in the wood called "ray fleck" or "silver grain." Staining does not detract from this distinctive "grainy" appearance, but the wavy patterns of oak really require no added colors to define their grain textures. Red oak is extremely workable; it is easily straightened, cut, shaped and sanded, but it may require pilot-hole drilling for conventional nailing. Red oak plywoods are readily available in a variety of thicknesses. The price of red oak is about the same as that for birch.

White Oak. White oak is the most highly prized of all the oaks. Its color is fairly consistently a pale gray, while its grain appearance pattern is similar to that of red oak or ash. Like red oak, it is hard, yet porous; it presents no unusual problems in milling, sanding, or finishing. It is somewhat more expensive than red oak and a bit harder to find, but white oak plywoods are available.

Mahogany. Mahogany used to be a highly respected and sought-after wood for manufacturing both cabinets and furniture, but it is currently going through a period of lessened popularity. One reason for this is that the name "mahogany" is used not only for genuine mahogany woods, but also for lauan and other woods which have some similarity in appearance to true mahogany. Further, the term "genuine mahogany" may include wood from Honduras, which is relatively hard and which often yields a rich grain pattern or figure called ribbon, or it may refer to wood from the Philippines, which is much softer and has quite a straight grain pattern. It is obvious that mahogany may vary from soft to hard in density and from yellow-brown to dark brown or reddish brown in color. It may be quite expensive Honduran mahogany or relatively inexpensive lauan. When constructing mahogany cabinetry, the cabinetmaker must first know which "mahogany." Then it is possible to proceed. Mahogany sheet goods are available; it is extremely easy to surface, cut, shape, and nail; mahogany readily accepts stains and other finishes.

Walnut. Walnut is often considered the premier cabinet wood and has been for a very long time. Used in constructing fine furniture and built-in cabinetry, walnut is also an exquisite choice for paneling and gunstocks. The color of the walnut that we see most often is akin to the darkest mahoganies—a rich lavender-brown with some paler bands that look a bit like ash or pecan. Walnut has the approximate workability of ash. It is moderately hard and heavy, and it may possess bold grain patterns, but it is a wood that will surface smoothly and cut evenly. It is a pleasure to put a finish on walnut because it needs no stain—only oil or some other high-quality clear finish. There are two significant problems with producing walnut cabinetry, both related to its scarcity. First, walnut is very expensive. It may cost up to twice as much per board foot as solid birch. Furthermore, it is difficult to find walnut firsts and seconds, not because of the percentage of clear face, but due to a shortage of long walnut boards. Working with short stock means increased waste, and this further increases production cost. It is not too difficult to locate and purchase walnut plywood, but these sheet goods are also expensive.

In addition to these hardwoods, there are others which are occasionally used by the cabinetmaker, but it is not within the scope of this book to discuss the virtues of every wood variety that might be utilized to build a piece of fine cabinetry. Further, the wise craftsman naturally does not depend on a discussion such as the one just completed to guide material selection—he or she gains knowledge of cabinet woods through experience, examining colors, feeling textures, and ultimately, building cabinets.

Again, hardwoods are generally used as primary cabinet woods—those portions of a cabinet that are visible without opening a door or drawer. Hardwood solid stock is used mainly to fashion face frame members, drawer faces, and door frames. The choice of a hardwood should depend on factors of desired appearance, workability (not forgetting the restrictions of the tools and machines with which the craftsman will perform surfacing, cutting, and shaping), resistance to marking, and availability (including appropriate plywood) as well as price.

PLYWOODS AND OTHER SHEET GOODS

Plywoods and other sheet goods are an important part of today's cabinet trade, but there are still people who misunderstand the virtues of these materials. The modern cabinetmaker considers plywood to be a raw material of production, but a surprisingly large number of customers seem disappointed when we tell them that certain portions of their cabinetry will be fabricated from hardwood veneer plywood. Whenever possible, those of us in the trade should correct misconceptions about plywood and pressed wood products by pointing out how these products extend and promote the virtues of wood.

Plywood

Plywood is made of thin layers of wood or plies which are glued together under great pressure. To promote strength and to reduce shrinking and swelling, the grain direction

of each wood layer or ply is perpendicular to the grain direction of each layer or ply that contacts it. The outermost plies are called faces if they are to be seen and backs if they are not. The wood used to make the faces of plywood, referred to as veneer, is naturally selected for its beauty in color and grain figure. The interior plies are called a core. Some plywoods, called "lumber core," have as their core a relatively thick center layer of edge-glued lumber covered on each side by a thin, perpendicular-laid ply called a crossband. Still other plywoods are made simply by gluing veneer over a particleboard core. (See Figure 4-2.)

Hardwood plywoods are used to fabricate finished ends, upper bottoms, toekicks, unconcealed shelves, finished backs, and sometimes drawer box parts as well as some types of doors. Softwood plywoods are sometimes used by the cabinetmaker in secondary applications: wall ends, partitions, and shelves. Plywood is used for these cabinet parts rather than solid stock for several reasons which are significant to the craftsman and the customer alike. First, a sheet of plywood (or fiberboard) extends the width of the raw material beyond the limits of natural wood boards. To come up with a 24" finished end, the cabinetmaker has a choice: either find six or eight boards that more or less match in color and figure, cut them slightly oversize, use a jointer to get perfect edges for gluing, glue the boards together and clamp until the glue is set, scrape and plane and sand until the board is flat and smooth, and finally cut to the exact desired size—or take a piece of suitable plywood off the lumber rack and cut to the exact size. Most cabinetmakers prefer the latter choice for obvious reasons, and most customers will prefer it, too, if they understand that they have the choice between paying for 2 hours' work or 2 minutes' work.

A second major advantage to employing plywoods in the cabinet trade is that it shrinks and expands only a negligible amount. It may thus be used for wood countertops without fear of the miter joints on the hardwood edging eventually separating due to expansion. Further, if ply-

FIGURE 4-2 Plywood core. Note that grain direction is at right angles in adjacent layers.

wood is kept reasonably well protected from moisture, it will not warp. If some method is used to conceal the raw ply edges, it is a desirable material for fabricating certain types of cabinet door. (Some plywood sheets will come from the factory already possessing a slight bow, cup, or twist. Such pieces should naturally be avoided in cutting doors.)

Another major advantage of ply materials is that they do not split or crack along grain lines in the veneer. All wide pieces, such as finished ends, shelves, backs, and doors, are less likely to develop cracks in their faces if they are constructed from plywood rather than from solid stock. This is especially important where we want thin material incorporated, as with cabinet backs and drawer bottoms. Anyone who has done repairs or restorations of older cabinetry and furniture, such as antiques, knows that drawer bottoms are very likely to need repair or replacement due to cracking and twisting. In "wall systems," backs are most often finished on only one side, with the opposite side positioned against a wall. Since these backs are frequently rather wide and long, plywood is the best possible material for them. It will strengthen the rear of the cabinet and will not shrink, expand, or crack.

Finally, plywoods come in standardized sizes. Most is available in sheets 48 in. wide and 96 in. long. Common thicknesses range between ⅛ and ¾ in. in increments of ⅛ in. It is also possible to find plywood in greater thicknesses.

Plywood Grades. Plywoods have two classification systems, one for softwoods and one for hardwoods. Softwood plywood is most commonly available with Douglas fir veneers or faces, and this is probably the type used most frequently in the cabinet trade today. A variety of other species (pine, hemlock, spruce, redwood) is also employed in manufacturing softwood plywood. As discussed in Chapter 2, many cabinetmakers use fir plywood for secondary box components such as partitions, wall ends, and shelves which will only be seen when a door is opened.

Softwood plywood may be rated either interior or exterior. Exterior plywood has completely waterproof glue joints and is often employed for garage doors and other items that are exposed to the weather. Cabinetmakers seldom need this sort of plywood, although it is advisable to use exterior ply as decking for ceramic tile tops near sinks and other sources of moisture. Interior plywood makes use of glue that is highly resistant to moisture. Further, plywoods may be considered "engineered grade," which is rated for strength, or "appearance grade," which is naturally of greater interest to the builder of cabinets.

Each face of a sheet of plywood is rated for its quality. A letter indicates the rating for each face. N is the best rating, but plywood with this quality of veneer is generally not available except by special order. The veneer grades that are readily available are, from best to worst, A, B, C, C-plugged, and D. The meaning of these is as follows:

A	The veneer is free of open defects; knots have been cut out and filled with football-shaped plugs; seams are permissible; the grain figure of adjacent pieces of veneer must be matched for grain figure but not necessarily color; uneven textures of grain figure are sanded fairly smooth.
B	Similar to A-rated faces, but more seams are permissible, and adjacent pieces need not be similar in color or figure; fairly smoothly sanded.
C	Open defects are permitted; knots and knotholes may be present; sanded, but uneven textures caused by grain figure remain; exterior glue used to join layers of ply.
C plugged	Open defects such as knotholes have been filled with football-shaped plugs; exterior glue used.
D	Same as C-rated face, but this plywood is made with interior glue.

Since every sheet of plywood has two faces, it will usually have a two-letter rating, with one letter representing the quality of each face. If a craftsman selects a softwood plywood for secondary application on a cabinet job, he or she will choose A-A, A-B, or B-B for cabinet members to be semivisible on both sides. This may include partitions, shelves, and even drawer sides. If only one side of a piece will ever be seen, the cabinetmaker usually selects A-C or A-D plywood. Wall ends, partitions next to stacks of drawers, bottoms of base cabinets, tops of upper cabinets, cabinet backs, and drawer bottoms are regularly cut from these types of plywood.

Hardwood plywoods have a somewhat similar rating system to the softwoods. Naturally, hardwood veneers are judged for beauty in grain figure and color. The quality of sheets is designated by the ratings of the two veneer faces. The following list summarizes this rating system.

A	This is a premium face, often made from a single piece of veneer. Such pieces are usually rotary sliced—sliced from a log as it is turned. If there are seams or joints in the face, the pieces are carefully matched for color and grain figure. (See Figures 7-15 and 4-3.) Premium hardwood faces have no more than four veneer pieces to a single sheet. One exception to this is knotty pine, which is not only a softwood that gets rated under the hardwood rating system, but is also considered an "A" premium face for

RANDOM "MATCH"

FIGURE 4-3   Common methods for matching plywood veneers. (See also Figure 7-15.)

possessing more than four or five veneer pieces prized for expressing clear contrasts in color and figure.

Number 1   Only a slight step down from A-rated veneer, this may also be considered a premium face. Number one veneer generally will consist of several pieces to each face that may be relied upon to have no major contrasts in grain pattern or color.

Faces rated A and those rated number 1 are both desirable as fully exposed surfaces on furniture and cabinetry. It displays exactly the type of color and grain pattern that is preferred for the outside of finished ends and backs, door and drawer faces, and other highly visible finished surfaces.

Number 2   Often called sound grade, this grade of face is free of open defects, although a few minor flaws may be present. Up to nine or ten slices may be present on the number 2 face, and these do not necessarily match one another. It is sanded smooth and is acceptable in semiexposed locations such as the inside of finished ends, open shelving, and the interior side of doors and drawer fronts. Half-inch or ⅝-in. plywood that has a rating of

number 2 or better on both sides (2-2 plywood) is suitable for drawer sides.

Number 3   Permitted in this grade of face are a variety of defects, including discoloration and stains, tight knots, and some splitting of the wood fibers. It is sometimes called utility grade.

Number 4   Referred to as backing grade, number 4 is only required to be free of defects that affect the strength of the plywood sheet. Number 4 veneer is thus used only to lend strength to plywoods which have a superior grade of veneer on the opposite side. It is not even necessary for this backing to be of the same wood species as the better veneer on the opposite face.

Number 3 and 4 faces are not considered acceptable for exposed or semiexposed surfaces on cabinetry. Cabinetmakers generally consider both these grades of veneer face to be suitable only as backing to plywood with a premium face. It is common to find this quality of veneer on the back side of ¼-in. plywood pieces used for drawer bottoms and for cabinet backs.

As with the softwood plywoods, we find hardwood plywoods with two ratings, one for each face. It is very difficult to find plywood with an A-A rating. This is a special-order item, sometimes called "architectural grade." Fortunately, it is almost never necessary to use such plywood in constructing cabinetry. Most commonly used cabinet plywoods are as follows: A-2 and 1-2 are employed for finished ends, for finished backs where the poorer face of the material is visible upon opening a door, for flat (non-frame) cabinet doors and drawers, for inset panels in some frame doors, for shelves and partitions of open cabinetry, for wooden countertops, for bottoms of upper cabinets, and sometimes for drawer box parts; A-3 and 1-3 are employed for cabinet parts that will only be seen on the good side, especially for backs of open cabinetry designed to be mounted against a wall; 2-2 (a similar import is graded B-B) is suited well for fabricating drawer parts and some types of shelving, such as the parts of lazy susans and the bottoms of slide-out shelves.

It should be mentioned that in addition to the grades already discussed, both hardwood and softwood plywoods are available in a rather loosely defined grade called "shop." Sheets of shop plywood actually started through production as another grade (often A-2 in the hardwoods) but because of some error in manufacture, were downgraded to shop status. This error may be oversanding or a poor joint line between veneer slices or some defect in the core. The defect is frequently a minor one that can be eliminated in cutting or is not noticeable at all. It is manufactured only for interior applications, but it is always smoothly sanded on both sides. Shop-grade Douglas fir plywood is less expensive than A-B, and shop-grade hardwood plywoods are less expensive than either A-2 or 1-2. It often makes a great deal of sense to purchase this type of material for a cabinet job, but firsthand inspection of the sheets before buying is a good idea. The worst defect—ply separation—can make sheets useless.

Particleboard

"Particleboard" is made either from chips of wood that have been glued and compacted under pressure or from wood that has been broken down into its tiniest fibers and reconstructed into sheets by chemical bonding. Like plywood, particleboard is misunderstood by many people, and it is not always considered an acceptable cabinet-building material. Before coming to such a judgment yourself, make sure that you have an understanding of the real characteristics of the several types of particleboard. The density of particleboards varies somewhat. Naturally, the greater the density or compaction of the wood fibers, the greater is the sheet's strength and smoothness and the greater is its suitability for use in the cabinet trade.

One type of particleboard that is commonly available is called underlayment. Although this material is sometimes used for cabinetry, it is not recommended. Its surface is not suitable for high-quality finishing since it is fairly rough and composed of rather large flakes. The flakes near the center are even larger and looser, allowing for little fastening strength when nails are driven into the edge of the board (as when face frame is attached to partitions, wall ends, and other cabinet members). When used for its intended purpose—as a subflooring material—underlayment is a highly acceptable building material.

Industrial board is somewhat smoother and denser than underlayment and can be found in many factory-made cabinet units in the usual secondary wood locations as well as for drawer box parts and, when covered with plastic laminate, veneer, or an imitation wood, for finished ends. Custom cabinetmakers will often employ this type of particleboard as the base or substrate material in making plastic-laminate tops.

Medium-density fiberboard (MDF) is probably the best of the particleboards for constructing cabinets. Its fibers are tiny, densely packed, and well bonded. This gives it a regular, smooth surface that finishes nicely. Proper gluing and nailing into its edge yields a joint strong enough for most cabinetry. As discussed in Chaper 2, MDF is appropriate in most secondary or semivisible locations. It is naturally, more expensive than either underlayment or industrial board.

Particleboard is most often produced in thicknesses of ½, ⅝, and ¾ in., but other thicknesses can be located. Possibly the most suitable for use in building cabinets is the ⅝-in. thickness. It is strong enough for most applications but not overly heavy. Some cabinetmakers prefer to use the stronger ¾-in. thickness for adjustable shelves. Like plywood, particleboard sheets are usually found in 48- × 96-in. sheets, but larger sheets are sometimes available.

Hardboard

Hardboard is a composite wood product similar to particleboard, but it is much harder and denser. It is generally produced only in thicknesses of ⅛ and ¼ in. It may be smooth on both sides, or since it is frequently seen only on one side, it may possess a rough "screen" pattern on one surface. There are three densities or types of hardboard: service (generally considered too soft and weak for cabinet work), standard, and tempered. Standard hardboard is light-to-medium brown in color. In a ⅛-in. thickness, it is strong and rigid enough for cabinet backs and small drawer bottoms. For larger drawer bottoms, the cabinetmaker should employ the thicker ¼-in. material. Strongest and least flexible of the hardboards is the type called tempered. It is high-density standard hardboard that has been treated with resins and heat for greater hardness. Its color is darker than that of standard hardboard, and it may be employed in the same ways. With its greater stiffness, it can also be used in ways that the standard board cannot, such as for fabricating tray dividers. All the hardboards are less expensive per sheet than plywood. The most costly to use is naturally the tempered variety.

In addition to the composite materials just discussed, there are several types of sheet goods available which possess a hard, factory-applied finish. Produced in the same thicknesses as conventional particleboards, these usually have a particleboard core with the thin coating on either one face or on both faces. An example of this, made by Willamette Industries, is marketed under the name Kortron. As with all materials that we have discussed, it has both advantages and disadvantages. First, the coating on such sheet goods is to be praised for its durability and smoothness. For the customer, this means long wear, beauty, and ease in care and cleaning. Naturally, the cabinetmaker does not have to sand or finish such materials when they are incorporated into the cabinet box. On the other hand, sheets of this material are substantially more costly than other sheet goods that might be employed for cabinet interiors. Further, when the material is cut with a conventional saw blade, the coating tends to chip along the sawn edge. It is wise to invest in circular saw blades designed specifically for cutting this material. The drawback can also be overcome by cutting the pieces oversized and trimming to the proper size with a jointer. Cabinet backs and drawer bottoms may need to be finished with matching paint before assembly, and the raw edges of drawer sides and shelves must either be carefully trimmed or painted. Working with these materials can be time consuming and expensive, but the results are beautiful, easy-to-care-for cabinet interiors.

The trend toward using plywoods and composite woods will, in all probability, not only continue but accelerate. Forests are a renewable but limited resource, and whatever practices can extend the use of wood products should be followed. In today's cabinet trade, this means using good-quality plywoods and composition wood products where feasible as well as keeping our minds open to new developments in wood usage.

HARDWARE

Hardware includes all nonwood cabinet components. There are various systems for hinging doors, for guiding drawers, for mounting adjustable shelves, and for incorporating other cabinet accessories. In addition, there is a huge selection, always changing, of knobs and pulls used as handles to open and close cabinet doors and drawers. Choosing among the various options is often a customer decision, but cabinetmakers naturally develop preferences of their own, and these preferences will often shape the choices of their customers.

Hinges

Hinges can be purchased from a number of manufacturing companies. Although these may help to convey an assortment of different appearances, the function of all hinges is essentially the same. In Chapter 2 we looked at the ways in which hinge designs could affect cabinet designing, and there is no necessity of repeating this information. (See Figure 2-14 and the related discussion.)

Conventional hinges all consist of four parts: the frame wing, which is mounted to the face frame; the door wing, which is fastened to the door itself; the knuckle or the parts of the two wings that come together to form a hollow barrel; and the pin, which is inserted into the barrel to allow the two wings to turn. (See Figure 4-4.) Some fully concealed hinges may be more complicated, depending on the model. (See Figure 4-5.)

In general, the cabinetmaker determines the type of door to be used on a job, and then chooses an appropriate hinging system: for ⅜-in. inset doors, overlay, reverse bevel, or flush. Depending on the tools available, we can also select among diverse types of mounting. Most hinges are screwed into place; the frame wing is screwed to either the surface or the side of a face frame stile or mullion, and the door wing is mounted with screws to either the face or the back of the door. If the frame wing is designed to be mounted to the front of the face member, the visible parts of the hinge are the pin and knuckle assembly as well as all of the frame wing. With this sort of hinge, a huge

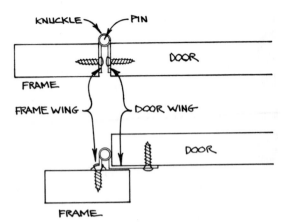

FIGURE 4-4 Door mounting with a butt hinge and a semiconcealed (overlay) hinge. Note the hinge terminology.

FIGURE 4-5 European, fully concealed hinging. (Courtesy of Julius Blum Inc., Cabinet and Furniture Hardware.)

variety of decorative styles are fabricated into the frame wing to dress up its appearance. If the frame wing has a section contoured to wrap around the face member and fasten to its side, only the knuckle and pin assembly will be visible when the door is closed. (See Figure 4-6.)

With some special machinery, the cabinetmaker may opt for the more expensive but easier-to-adjust demountable hinge system. These are mounted by routing a special hole into the face frame or into both face frame and door, inserting a specially designed part of the hinge into the hole(s), and tightening a single screw. (See Figure 4-7.)

With the fully concealed or European hinge, doors are usually mounted overlay fashion, but it is also possible

FIGURE 4-6 Door mounting with a wrap-around "knuckle"-type hinge.

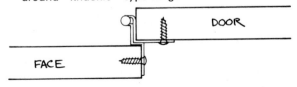

FIGURE 4-7 Double-demountable hinging system. (Courtesy of Amerock Corporation.)

to mount them as flush or inset. Such hinges consist of three sections: a mounting plate, which is fastened to the cabinet; a hinge arm which contains the actual mechanisms that allow the hinge to work; and the hinge cup, which must be countersunk and fastened into the rear side of the door. There are a number of options available within the European hinge systems. Most are manufactured for European-style cabinetry and the mounting plate can be fastened to a partition or end, but some are made specifically for use with face frame construction. These hinges may open as little as 95° or as much as 176°. Naturally, the hinges that open the widest are also the most costly. To countersink the hinge cup section of the hinge into the rear of the door, the woodworker needs a specially designed drill bit which will drill a very smooth, flat-bottomed hole [usually 35 millimeters (mm) in diameter]. The mounting plates and the hinge cups are fastened in place either with conventional screws or with press-in plastic fittings. Tooling a cabinet shop to do rapid mounting of European hinges can be quite expensive, but this style of hinging appears to be growing in popularity with Americans. Some cabinet shops are even specializing in European construction because it appeals to those who like a flat, hardwareless, contemporary decor. Those cabinetmakers who prefer building more conventional frame-type cabinetry, but who need to use European hinges for the occasional customer who requests them, will find that the only tools needed are a drill press and the previously mentioned 35-mm drill bit, in addition to conventional screwdrivers.

In the same way that the fully concealed hinge has risen in popularity, the knife hinge or pin hinge has fallen out of use somewhat in today's cabinet trade. Before the appearance of the European hinge, the pin hinge was often requested by customers who wanted a plain, hardware-free design. With pin hinges, the barrel and the pin of the hinge are still visible with the door closed, but this knuckle assembly is very small and projects through an angled slot that the cabinetmaker cuts into the door. The frame wing is fastened to the face of the cabinet, and the door wing is mounted directly to the back of the door. (See Figure 4-8.)

Another hinge option that should be considered is the

VARIABLE OVERLAY

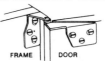

FIGURE 4-8 Mounting with a pin hinge.

presence of a self-closing mechanism. Whether a hinge is conventional, demountable, or European, there is usually an option to purchase it with or without a self-closing mechanism. When available and when the customer has no objection, self-closing hinges should be selected. They are slightly more expensive than those without the mechanism, but they save having to purchase, mount, and adjust a separate door catch or latch.

Probably the last hinge consideration is finish or color. It is wise to purchase hinges in bulk, using the same color and style of hinge again and again. This greatly reduces cost. On the other hand, we will often receive requests for a different color from that of our selected standard, and it is a fairly simple matter to figure this additional cost into the initial estimate. Finishes vary widely, from the brightest chrome to dull black. The best way to acquaint yourself with these is to browse through a hardware display board or several catalogs. As with all cabinetmaking decisions, it is wisest to consider function before appearance.

As a final note on hinges, remember that costs will vary with all the factors which we have discussed. In general, though, the least expensive hinges to buy are the conventional hinges, with the demountable type costing a bit more, and the European style costing the most. Labor cost is substantially less with demountable and European hinges *if* the shop uses the special hinging machinery that is available.

If the need for door catches arises, it is best to be acquainted with the several most common types. Magnetic catches, roller catches, and friction catches are generally used in conjunction with those hinges that do not possess self-closing mechanisms. Their purpose is simply to hold the doors closed. Magnetic catches consist of two parts: a magnet and its frame, which is mounted to the cabinet box, and a steel strike plate, which is fastened to the door. Roller and friction catches hold their doors somewhat more securely than magnets since they have two parts which interconnect by virtue of some sort of spring action. Elbow catches are often used on one half of a pair of doors when the other half of the pair is to be fitted with a lock. The elbow catch cannot be released unless the release button is pressed. Pressure catches or touch latches are often used where we want a flush door with no knob or pull. The touch latch holds the door closed by either friction or magnetic force until the surface of the door is pressed. The door is then released and sprung open.

Drawer Guides

Drawer guides, when not fabricated from wood by the craftsman, are available in a number of styles intended to fulfill specific needs that arise in the trade. In Chapter 2, we discussed the two most commonly found types of manufactured hardware for the guiding of drawers: the three-roller guide and the side guide. (See Figures 2-18 and 2-19 and the related discussion.)

There are several factors that influence the quality of drawer guide performance and cost. One of these is the weight rating. Since most guides puchased are in the 20-in. length or a size close to it, the weight ratings given by suppliers usually refer to this length. If a guide is rated at 50 pounds, it means that it is designed to carry a drawer which, with its contents, weighs 50 pounds or less. It will give long service under those conditions. A guide with such a rating is certainly sturdy enough for normal kitchen usage, and it will be relatively inexpensive. Guides rated 150 pounds are strong enough to carry loads up to the specified weight, making them suitable for use in file cabinets and for storing other heavy articles. The lowest weight ratings are about 30 pounds; the highest rating of those guides readily available is 150 pounds. Naturally, the higher the rating, the higher is the cost of the guide. Many cabinetmakers use guides with a rating of 50 pounds or slightly less for kitchen drawers and guides rated at 60 to 75 pounds for slide-out shelves in the kitchen.

Another feature of prefabricated drawer guides that affects cost and performance is full extension. If a drawer must have ease of accessibility all the way to its rear, such as with many file drawers, the full extension guide is not a convenience but is a necessity. Full extension guides are available in all the weight ratings, and of course the full extension feature adds substantially to cost. Although they are no harder to install than other guides, most cabinetmakers find that they take a bit longer to mount simply because we use them less frequently than other guides.

Some drawer guides have self-closing capability, closing by virtue of the work of gravity. These guides possess roller channels which are inclined, allowing the weight

FIGURE 4-9 Adjustable shelves on standard and clips.

of the drawer itself to perform the closing. This option should always be left to the customer to decide. Many people prefer to have drawers remain open while using the contents, and the self-closing option requires one hand to hold the drawer open.

As with the purchase of hinges, drawer guides are least expensive when purchased in a bulk package. It is therefore wisest to employ one guide as a standard and to use other guides as the need arises.

Adjustable Shelf Hardware

Adjustable shelf hardware is of two basic types. In the more common system, metal standards are attached to the vertical members of cabinets. The standard is usually countersunk into a groove or dado, but a slightly different type of standard with flanges is available for surface mounting. Small metal clips may then be set into premachined holes in the standards to support shelving. (See Figure 4-9.) Standards and clips can be purchased in aluminum or steel and in several different finishes: bright brass, brown, nickel, and zinc. The aluminum is less expensive and easier to work with (standards can be cut with a side cutter instead of a hacksaw or special cutter), and it is easily strong enough for most applications. The other adjustable shelf system involves drilling a series of holes into which pegs will fit to yield the necessary support for shelving. This system costs less for materials but can require more time to utilize than the standard-and-clips system. The holes must be carefully aligned to match one another. Shops with a multiple-spindle drill press can overcome this difficulty with ease.

Knobs and Pulls

Knobs and pulls are usually mounted to the faces of doors and drawers so that they may be opened and closed. This is most often done by drilling one hole (for knobs) or two (for pulls) all the way through the door or drawer. A machine screw is inserted through the hole from the rear and into the threads of the knob or pull to hold it in place. There is more of a variety of shapes and finishes for knobs and pulls than for any other hardware item, and it is the policy of most shop owners to allow customers to choose these for each job. Some effort should be made to coordinate the style and finish of hinges with the knob or pull, but this is not always feasible. Hinges are made primarily to fulfill a function, not to convey an accent or style of cabinetry, especially since only some parts of the hinge are usually visible. Knobs and pulls, since their function is so easily performed and since they are in full view, are designed to convey a style. Manufacturers of hardware generally design hardware items to work together, but if a customer selects a blue porcelain knob, we will not be able to order a blue porcelain hinge.

The cabinetmaker should stock several lengths of machine screws to mount pulls and knobs because those that are provided with the hardware will sometimes not work. Generally, those that are packaged with the hardware are intended to be used with ¾-in. doors and drawers. If the cabinetmaker uses doors with overlaid backs or drawers that possess a subfront, he or she will need longer screws.

Besides hinges, drawer guides, shelf mounting systems, and knobs and pulls, there are many other hardware items which the cabinet builder will use from time to time. Most notable of these are lazy susan systems, panel tilt-out trays, pop-up shelf systems, and locks for cabinet doors and drawers. Literature on these items is available from the dealers who supply them.

SUPPLIES

Supplies include all those consumable items that are used to fasten together the cabinet, prepare it for finishing, and set it in place. Whenever possible, these items should be purchased in bulk to save on the expenses of fabricating cabinetry, even in the small shop. This naturally means committing to a particular system of assembly and then buying to fill the needs of that system.

Glue

Nothing is more important in making strong wood-to-wood joints than glue. In the 1960s, the woodworking trades depended mainly on polyvinyl glue (white glue), but in most general-purpose applications cabinetmakers now use a yellow glue called aliphatic resin glue. It is much stronger than white glue, and it dries faster. It is recommended for most cabinet building functions. Sometimes, the woodworker will encounter the need for a special-purpose glue. In water-resistant applications such as in laminating together the members of wooden cutting boards, most woodworkers choose a plastic resin glue. Many of these are

available. They generally must be mixed with water just before spreading, they have a rather slow setting and drying time, and they can be somewhat brittle. Epoxies can also be useful, especially on the occasional job requiring plastic components to be incorporated into the woodwork. Some adhesives can be purchased and spread in caulking-style tubes. These are useful for mounting paneling and in a few other circumstances. Contact cement is not usually employed as an adhesive for wood but is frequently used for fabricating plastic-laminate countertops. There are several varieties of contact cement available, and these are discussed more thoroughly in Chapter 10.

Wood Filler Pastes

Some cabinetmakers have resisted the use of fillers and putties, considering them in some way an inferior way of dealing with the tiny cracks and holes in wood which they were developed to deal with. This is probably another case of failing to understand the material, however. Fillers were never intended to be a substitute for either wood or quality workmanship. On the other hand, high-quality filler pastes have been developed that come close to matching the color of the various cabinet woods and which accept wood finishes in an acceptable way. When used to touch up a seam rather than to make a seam, fillers can be an enhancement. Fillers can also be used to fill nail holes anywhere on the interior of cabinets. Further, since a face frame is usually nailed onto its cabinet box, some cabinetmakers will fill these nail holes with filler paste before finishing. (See Figure 4-10.)

Nails

If the cabinetmaker does not have pneumatic nailing equipment, he or she will find that it is necessary to stock only a few types of nails for use in the assembly of cabinetry. (See Figure 4-11).

FIGURE 4-10 Filler can be used in fairly tight seams and in nail holes.

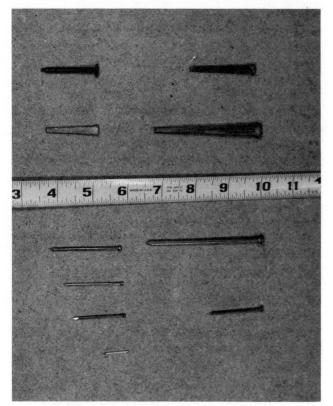

FIGURE 4-11 Useful nails in cabinet construction and installations. *Top (L-R):* 6d cut, 10d cut, 16d box, 4d box; *bottom (L-R):* 1 1/2-in. concrete, 4d cut, 6d finish, 5d finish, 4d finish, No. 18 × 3/4 in. brad.

For most fastening of the box, finishing nails will be required. These have a small head which can be ''set'' or buried slightly below the wood's surface. Since the holding power of nails is partially a factor of nail length and thickness, we should choose the largest possible nails that can be used without splitting cabinet members. If there is an ideal size of finishing nail to be used within the trade it is probably the six penny (6d), which is 2 in. long, or the five penny (5d), which is 1¾ in. long and slightly narrower. The five-penny size is a little harder to locate, but many woodworkers prefer it because it is less likely to cause splitting when driven edgewise into plywood and MDF. Either of these nails is suitable for joining cabinet members.

Where the nailed surface will not be visible, it is best to use box or common nails because of their somewhat superior fastening power. These nails have a large flat head, and many have a coating which gives them additional holding strength. The five-penny and six-penny sizes are suitable for most cabinet work, and so is the four-penny (4d) size, which is 1½ in. long. For attaching backs, the four-penny box nail may be used, or perhaps even a smaller nail.

For installing cabinets on walls where studs are pres-

ent, many people still use sixteen-penny (16d) nails. These are 3½ in. long—long enough to penetrate the nailer, the back, and drywall and to hold firmly in the stud. On the other hand, most modern installers, for a variety of reasons, affix their cabinets to such walls with drywall screws (see below). For mounting cabinets to masonry walls, ten-penny (10d) cut nails are sometimes employed, although it is probably a superior practice to insert lead or plastic shields into such a wall and to screw into these. Similarly, when it is necessary to install a cabinet over a brick or concrete surface, we have the option of using short (4d or 6d) cut nails or concrete nails or of using shields and screws. The principal problems with cut nails are that they often break loose too much masonry material and do not hold properly, and that driving them in can cause enough vibration to jar cabinetry and ''kick'' it out of its level position. This is the nature of cut nails; the flat, square tip actually breaks masonry material, and the nail's tapered shape is supposed to act as a wedge in the hole that is created.

Brads are actually small finish nails. Their size is indicated by a gauge number (like wire) and their actual length. These are most useful for attaching edging to shelves and for attaching molding or trim to cabinets on the job site. Since the edging or molding we use is usually a hard wood, the most useful gauge is eighteen (number 18), narrower gauges bend too easily. Because most trims and edgings are made from material that is only ¼ in. thick, brads need not be longer than ¾ in. long.

If pneumatic nailing equipment is available, several nail sizes can be eliminated. Compressed-air-driven fastening is a great deal faster than using a hammer and nails, and it is wise for even small shops to invest in this type of equipment. (When choosing a compressor, horsepower and tank pressure are less important than the supply of air at the tool. Make sure that the compressor you purchase has a high-enough cubic-foot-per-minute rate to feed your guns.)

Guns and fastener systems are available to perform almost every function of cabinet assembly. The nails available are long enough for joining all cabinet members and have a head that is suitable for finished surfaces. Brad or pin guns are suitable for applying edging or trim. Staple guns are often used for attaching backs and for drawer box assembly. (See Figure 4-12).

Screws

In certain applications, wood screws or drywall screws are the best fasteners to use. We pointed out earlier, for example, that countertops should be fabricated in the shop and then brought to the job site and installed with screws from beneath. This is superior to nailing the decking in place and then covering it with plastic laminate. Most hard-

FIGURE 4-12 Pneumatic guns. *Upper left:* Finish nail gun; *lower left:* brad gun; *upper and lower right:* staple guns. Note the clip of fasteners with each tool.

ware items require screws for incorporation into the cabinet unit, but specifically designed screws are almost always included in the packaging for these. Screws may also be employed effectively in several other ways.

Screw sizes are based on gauge and length. It is not necessary to understand how gauge sizes are determined as long as we remember that higher gauge numbers indicate thicker screws. The most commonly used gauge in the cabinet trade is probably number 8, with slightly smaller and larger gauges also utilized frequently.

It is probably a good idea to remind ourselves of the differences between wood screws and drywall screws. The chief advantage of wood screws is that they are tapered and therefore become more securely bound within the wood fibers as they are tightened. For this reason, many woodworkers insist on using them in all applications. There are several advantages to using drywall screws instead, however. (Keep in mind that in a few cabinetmaking applications the superior holding power of the tapered screws will be significant.) Drywall screws are harder than most wood screws. This makes them at least as strong as wood screws for horizontal, weight-bearing uses such as installing cabinets. Also, drywall screws often require no clearance hole and almost never require a tapping hole. Further, drywall screws are available with a "finish" head that may be easily hidden. It is acceptable on semiexposed surfaces and perhaps even on some finished surfaces. Finally, these screws are designed specifically to be driven with ease. They possess either a cross-point (Phillips) head or a square-hole head which will not slip when driven with a screw gun or a variable-speed drill. Makers of conventional wood screws often manufacture these with a slotted head, making for much slower installation.

The common screw usages are as follows:

1 in.	For securing subfronts to drawer faces
1¼ in.	For countertop fastening
1½, 1¾, 2 in.	Intermediate sizes useful for making cabinet-to-cabinet joints on the job site
2½, 3 in.	For mounting cabinetry to walls

Dowels

Cabinetmakers who assemble face frames with a dowel system should naturally stock an appropriate size of wood dowels for this purpose. These should have grooved ribs or a spiral groove machined into them to allow excess glue to escape during clamping. A very common size is ⅜ × 1½ in.

Sandpaper

Many cabinetmakers enter the trade by first learning a healthy respect for the value of proper sanding and for the virtues of sandpaper. Since sanding is so necessary to the production of good-quality wood products and since the process of sanding can be laborious and time consuming, it is important to choose the best abrasives for each job.

There are four types of material used to make sandpaper. The softest, flint, is not of much use to the woodworker since it wears away so quickly. Garnet paper wears longer and can be used with good results, especially for hand-sanding operations. When using an oscillating or vibrator sander, garnet paper will not last long, however. For use with power-driven sanders, aluminum oxide abrasives are superior. Virtually all sanding belts are made with this material. Aluminum oxide sandpaper is the most versatile abrasive used in the cabinet trade, and the longest wearing. Silicon carbide has similar hardness properties to aluminum oxide. It is available in the finest grits and is often backed with waterproof paper. It is best suited for the type of sanding which is performed between applications of finish such as lacquer.

There are also two types of "coat" available. Open-coat sandpaper has spaces between its grit particles for channeling away loose wood particles as they are cut away by the abrasive. It tends to fill up with wood particles less quickly than closed-coat sandpaper and is therefore used with the softer woods, such as spruce. For sanding the hardwoods, closed-coat abrasive sheets are preferred because they possess more cutting surfaces.

The grit of a sheet of sandpaper is a factor of the size of the particles used and their density on the sheet. The lower the grit number, the more coarse will be the sandpaper and its finish on the wood. In other words, if we have a large amount of material to sand, we will employ the coarser papers with lower grit numbers, such as 60. If we have less material to sand and we want a smoother surface, we select the smoother papers with the higher grit numbers, such as 120. For sanding coats of clear finish, we want even finer abrasives—perhaps a grit rating of 220. In stocking sandpapers, it is best to experiment and determine your own preferences and then to buy in useful quantities.

PLASTIC LAMINATES

Plastic laminates are available in a great variety of patterns, colors, and textures. They may be purchased in sheets as narrow as 36 in. or as wide as 60 in., and these sheets may be as long as 12 ft (144 in.) or longer. We discuss this material in more detail in Chapter 10.

CHAPTER SUMMARY OF CABINETMAKING SKILLS

In choosing the solid woods, sheet goods, and other materials for fabricating cabinetry, the modern cabinetmaker considers the tastes of the customer first. Other considerations include not only availability and cost but also the woodworker's own preferences and tools.

Most hardware items are purchased in bulk to save on costs, and this requires the shop operator to make a commitment to certain "standards": a hinging system, an adjustable shelf system, or another system that may be used over and over. Knobs and pulls are usually a customer option.

The woods selected for building cabinets are either primary or secondary. Primary woods are those employed in visible locations—most often the faces, finished ends and backs, doors, and drawer faces. Secondary woods make up the rest of the cabinet.

Primary woods are usually hardwoods or hardwood plywoods. The most suitable grade of solid material for cabinetry is FAS (firsts and seconds), or select when using certain woods. The grades of plywood that should be used are either A-2, where both sides of the cabinet member may be seen, or A-3, where only one side will be visible.

In secondary cabinet locations, pine is most often chosen where solid material is preferable. Where sheet goods are desirable, there is a choice among softwood plywood (A-D where one ply surface will be completely hid-

den and A-B elsewhere), medium-density fiberboard, hardboards, and other types of material. (With all plywoods, shop grade is often acceptable for cabinetwork, but it should be inspected before purchase.)

The productive cabinet shop will also be stocked with a supply of carefully chosen glue (aliphatic resin glue is best for most applications), nails, wood or drywall screws, and other fasteners.

Larger cabinet operations will already be committed to specific cabinet manufacturing techniques and fastening systems, asking only that their employees learn those techniques and systems. For the person who is beginning to build cabinets in his or her own shop, it is tremendously important to work within the limits of tools and space available. As we have observed in earlier sections, experience with cabinet operations is the best teacher, and material selection, purchasing, and handling is no exception. The primary skill to be learned with regard to choosing materials is a hands-on familiarity with the characteristics of as many woods, wood products, fastening systems, and hardwares as is reasonable. On the other hand, people need not be afraid to tackle major cabinet projects because they are unfamiliar with the tremendous variety of cabinet materials. There are no right and wrong choices—only choices that seem to suit the person's needs and cabinetmaking philosophy.

FIVE

CUTTING: SAFETY, SPEED, AND SAVING MATERIALS

SAFETY CONSIDERATIONS

As with all steps of cabinet production, cutting should be thought of as a goal-directed process. In using the sharp blades and the powerful motors that are applied, the cutter or miller should have safety as the foremost goal. In the days before government agencies began to enforce the codes that required effective guards on table saws, radial arm saws, and jointers (less than 20 years ago), many millers simply did not use them, complaining that they were bothersome, in the way, or even unsafe. The theory was that being careful was enough precaution in utilizing such tools. Unfortunately, the woodworkers who thought this way were wrong. No one is perfect in concentration, and it only takes a tiny distraction to bring about an accident that could cost the operator a deep cut, loss of a finger, or an even worse injury. Furthermore, such injuries can occur when there is no break in concentration at all, as when a piece of wood pinches the rear of a table saw blade and kicks back. There is no substitute for properly functioning guards. There is no substitute for safety.

BASIC PRINCIPLES OF CUTTING

With safety always in mind, it is still possible to develop speed in cutting out cabinet parts—a speed that comes from efficiency, *not* from being in a hurry. This type of effi-

ciency is based on some very basic, common-sense principles. We need to know which pieces to cut first, for example, and we must be familiar with the arrangement of the cutting list. The speed with which a job is cut is one more way of reducing the costs of cabinet production.

Another major cost-saver in cutting is saving material or reducing waste. A good miller can often find ways of getting one or more ''extra'' pieces out of a sheet of plywood or hardboard. The efficient, accurate cutter also develops a knowledge of which leftover pieces are useful and which belong in the trash bin.

The basic principles of cutting apply to all milling situations, whether in a large cabinet shop where one or two employees may do nothing but cutting, or in a very small home shop where the miller is also the designer, the assembler, and the installer.

Shop Layout

Proper location of equipment and stock bins is a principle that is often overlooked, not only in the literature of woodworking but also in the setup of some cabinet shops. It is so obvious that the jointer, the planer, and the ripping and cutoff saw(s) should be near the area where materials are stored that it should perhaps not need to be mentioned. Nonetheless, there are shops that are set up in absolute violation of this guideline. (See Figure 5-1.) The planners of

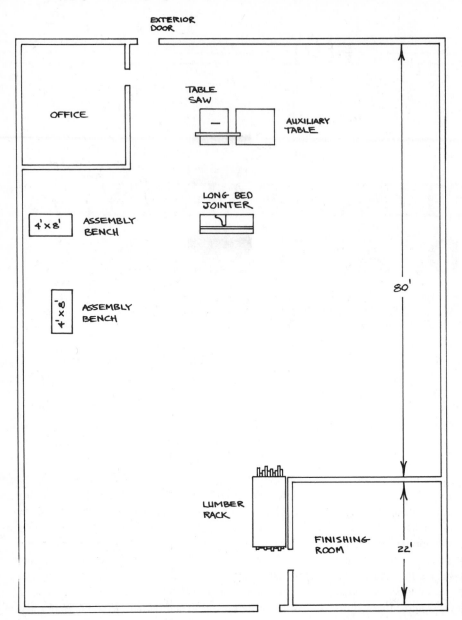

FIGURE 5-1 In a shop like this, the storage bin for solid material is ridiculously far from the table saw, jointer, and planer.

some shops apparently never consider the proper placement of material bins either, locating them far from the closest exterior doorways. (See Figure 5-2.) Even with dollies or carts for moving material around in such shops, the waste in effort and work hours is ridiculous.

The material bins for both solid and sheet materials should be located so that they can easily be restocked from a delivery truck. Ideally, it is possible to back a truck in, open a large door, and fill the bins at exactly the same time that the truck is unloaded. (See Figure 5-3.)

The table saw (and/or radial arm saw if one is used), the thickness planer, and the jointer should be directly in front of the material bins if at all possible. There should be enough distance between the stock bin and the stationary tools so that the longest pieces of stock may be pulled from

storage without interference, but the pieces to be cut should not have to be moved far for milling. (See Figure 5-4.) In addition, the stationary tools should be close enough together that they can be used in conjunction with one another. Most shops possess a table saw and a jointer as minimum cutting equipment. The jointer may be positioned either to the right or the left of the table saw so that solid stock may be edge straightened and then cut with only minimal movement. Many cabinetmakers think it most convenient to position the jointer on the right side of the table saw for two reasons. First, it is almost never necessary to have extra room on the right side of the table saw. When we cut a large board, it overhangs the left side of the saw table, not the right. Thus the jointer will never be in the way of table saw cutting operations. [For the same reason,

FIGURE 5-2 Here the sheet goods bin is placed appropriately close to the table saw but is too far from the closet doorway.

FIGURE 5-3 Stock bin located for ease of restocking.

if the jointer is placed at the left of the table saw, no part of it should be higher than the surface of the cutting table. (See Figure 5-5.)] A second reason to position the jointer on the right side of the table saw is so that material may be edge straightened and set directly on the cutting table to the right side of the table saw fence. This is convenient when we switch from the edge-straightening operation to the ripping operation. Finally, some boards (especially

FIGURE 5-4 Good setup for cutting. Note that materials may be pulled from the bins and cut with ease. There is adequate space between the storage bins and the stationary power tools.

alder) will need to be straightened again after one or two rips because they may produce a new bow or warp as they are ripped into narrow pieces. It is obvious that the jointer and the table saw are tools that were made for each other.

Cabinetmakers who require a thickness planer because they prefer to use unsurfaced solid materials should similarly position the planer so that it may be used in conjunction with the jointer. This way, solid stocks may first be smoothed or flattened on one side, then fed into the planer to obtain the desired thickness, and then brought right back to the jointer for edge straightening.

The fourth stationary tool that is often employed for cutting out cabinet parts is a radial arm saw. Although a

FIGURE 5-5 Convenient jointer and table saw arrangement. Since the jointer is on the left side where long pieces overhang the saw, the jointer fence is lower than the surface of the cutting table.

radial arm saw may be used for both ripping and cross-cutting (cutting to length), most cabinetmakers who use such a saw employ it only for cutting stock to length. There are several reasons for this.

In the first place, ripping is not as safe on the radial saw as it is on most table saws. More of the blade is exposed above the cutting table than with a table saw. Furthermore, the arrangement of the saw with the motor above rather than below the cutting table creates a tendency for the stock to "lift" from the cutting table—a tendency that can be especially troublesome with narrow, light stock. Also, the arm of the saw itself can contribute to blocking vision. When ripping material on a radial arm saw, we must extend an arm or the push stick under the arm of the saw in order to feed material through.

The radial arm saw is not nearly as versatile as a table saw for cutting the cabinet project. Changes in ripping width are slower, accuracy is more difficult, and the radial arm saw is not really designed to rip 48-in. sheets into narrower pieces. Since its blade rotation is away from the table, it generally will cause more vibration, chipping, and splintering. (If choosing a multipurpose saw, it should be obvious from the discussion that a table saw is far superior to a radial saw.)

Although a radial arm saw is not the most desirable of tools for ripping, it can give excellent service when used for length cutting. When properly set up and incorporated into production, it is in fact superior to the table saw for this type of cutting. In fact, many large shops employ one person to do virtually nothing but rip on the table saw and another to do nothing but cut the ripped materials to length on a radial arm saw.

When used as a cutoff saw, the radial arm saw should obviously be located close enough to the table saw to allow ripped materials to be passed on conveniently for length cutting, but not so close that the manipulation of materials around these tools will interfere with their operation. The ideal location for this tool is probably to the right of the ripping table, but situating it to the left is not terribly inconvenient. The saw itself should be located against a wall with a long, narrow table extending on each side. The length of the table depends on the length of stock usually being worked with and the space available. The longest pieces incorporated into a cabinet are seldom over 12 ft long, and the table extension on each side of the saw need not be this long. However, we frequently work with pieces up to 96 in. in length, and a cutoff table that is slightly longer than this on each side is not too long. Some owners of small shops recognize the value of a saw devoted entirely to cutoff and manage to build into their facilities a radial saw table that is only 10 ft from end to end. Regardless of table length, such a cutoff saw will be most effective if there are no obstructions along the wall where it is positioned, for a minimum of 10 ft in each direction. The radial

arm saw is suitable for use in cutting finished lengths of both solid stock and sheet goods.

Another type of cutoff saw is the panel saw. This is a nearly vertical framework into which sheet goods may be set, "locked" in place, and cut to length. The saw and motor assembly is similar to a portable circular saw which moves along metal guides. It is often counterweighted or fitted with a spring to make it easier to operate. A panel saw requires less floor space than a radial saw, but it is obviously not a suitable tool for cutting face frames and other narrow stock.

In some cabinet building environments, such as cabinet factories, the emphasis is on speed and standardization rather than on building a customized product. Here, some cutting tools may be remote controlled or fitted with automatic feed systems, or the motors may be larger and more powerful. Still, the principle of proper tool placement, as well as all the principles of safety, speed, and material savings, will apply.

Cutting System

A second principle of cutting has to do with developing and following a system. That is, types of materials should be grouped appropriately and all cut together. On an individual job with more than one cabinet unit, we cut all the doors at one time, all the pieces for the cabinet bodies at one time, and so on, with each different type of cabinet part. This allows for a minimum of setup changes and material handling.

This type of organization is partly established by a well-written cutting list. For example, it is advantageous to cut all the solid materials on a job at the same time. For this reason, it is easiest to read and follow a stock bill with all face frame pieces listed together (on one page or one section of a page if possible), all drawer parts listed together, and so on. Some layout men and women list all the parts for each case on a separate piece of paper together with the drawing for that cabinet, but this results in a lot of unnecessary paper shuffling as the miller progresses through the cutting of a job. Thus the proficient cutter must get used to the characteristics of cutting lists as developed by the cabinet designer, looking for types of materials that may be grouped together and scanning for miscellaneous items.

A very important principle in cutting might be called "prioritizing"—knowing which types of materials should be cut first to aid in the speed of production. In small shops, this is tremendously important because of space limitations. Even in larger shops, where space is less of a problem, it is still necessary to cut first those items that will require the most fabrication time. Furthermore, certain cabinet parts should be cut out of the straightest or the best-looking material in stock.

The cabinet components that generally require the most preparation time are doors and drawers. Frame doors and doors that are fabricated by laminating together planks of solid stock are the types of doors that require the most time to get ready for mounting on a cabinet. The pieces must usually be doweled or milled in another way to be fit together. After the pieces are glued, the door must often be recut to exact size or receive further machining or detailing before it may even by sanded and hinged. Even when using plywood doors, the preparation time can be substantial, especially if each door and drawer front must be edged to cover the plies. The drawer boxes for a job must also be made ready for installation into the cabinet box at the appropriate time. This point in cabinet assembly is generally prior to door mounting because it is easiest to mount drawers before the cabinet back is mounted, whereas doors are usually the very last step in cabinet assembly. If drawer parts are to be joined with glue and nails in common butt joints, drawer assembly can be very quick, but the employment of any type of interlocking joint naturally slows down the drawer assembly operation. In much less time, the cabinet bodies may be cut out, dadoed and rabbeted, and assembled with a face frame. Ideally, the doors and drawers are ready for mounting as soon as the cabinets are ready to have them mounted, and cutting out these components first helps to establish this type of timing.

In addition to establishing priorities that have to do with timing of production, the mill man or woman must cut certain specific pieces out of the best material in stock. When we purchase material for a job, our suppliers generally do not want us to pick through their entire supply of material and select the best pieces for our job. Suppliers not only want to sell materials right off the top of their supply stacks—they need to, or after a few "select" purchases they will be left with inferior materials in their own warehouse. Therefore, when we buy a quantity of hardwood and plywood for a job, we sometimes wind up with some pieces that are straighter or more attractive than others. Since the cutter must keep waste to a minimum, it is important for him or her to know how to use not only the straightest, most beautiful pieces but also the less perfect ones.

There are two rules to follow in selecting the appropriate quality of material for individual cabinet parts. One of these might be called the "rule of visibility." This is especially important for veneered materials because the pieces to be cut are fairly large. The more visible the part on the finished cabinet when it is complete and installed the more attractive the piece must be. On a job with ply doors (or ply panels on a frame door), it is best to cut the doors first, from the most attractive sheets available. Finished ends and finished backs are next in visibility ranking, then open shelves. Least important in terms of what will be seen on the finished cabinet are toekicks and drawer parts. The other rule to remember has to do with whether the individual piece is to be fastened into the cabinet box. If the piece is to be glued and nailed into the cabinet unit itself, it need not be as straight as pieces that are to become parts of doors. Some sheets of plywood possess a twist that will be impossible to correct. When the door is mounted, the hinges will hold one edge (and two corners) even in relation to the face frame. Another corner will contact the face when the door is closed, but the fourth corner will contact nothing when the door is closed. Almost nothing is more unattractive on a cabinet than this type of twisted door. When solid materials are employed to fabricate the doors on a job, the straightness of the stock selected may be even more important. When pieces are joined into a frame or a plank door, the gluing and clamping operation itself can contribute to development of a twist in the door, especially if clamping is done without a press to ensure door flatness. It is absolutely essential to use the straightest available pieces for cutting out doors. With particularly long doors, the cutter may search through an entire stock of hardwood to find the best boards for cutting out the required parts.

As a final word on the priorities of cutting, it should be pointed out that all the hardwood stocks need to be cut before the cabinet bodies. For all the reasons we have discussed, it is important to get production moving on doors and drawers before the cases are detailed and assembled. In addition, it is most convenient to cut out all the face frame pieces immediately after cutting the solid parts for drawers and doors. This helps to ensure that the assembled face frames will be ready for incorporation into the cabinet box at the appropriate time. If European-style cabinets are under construction, the cutter need only cut a sufficient amount of edging for the cabinetry before proceeding from solid material cutting to sheet good cutting. A satisfactory order for cutting follows. (See Figure 5-6.)

1. Estimate the total amount of solid stock required on the job. Select appropriate pieces by width, straightness, and appearance. Edge straighten (and surface straighten, if necessary).
2. Cut drawer faces and pieces for fabricating solid plank doors. (These will generally be the widest pieces on the cutting list, and they will often require cutting to exact size after gluing.)
3. Cut the parts for frame doors.
4. Cut face frame pieces.
5. Cut miscellaneous solid stock. (Scan the entire cutting list.)
6. Cut any edging, molding, or trim necessary for the job.
7. Cut plywood doors.

E. Jay Cee Cabinet Shop Tucson, Arizona 85714		DATE	PLAN#	JOB# 5	
PRODUCTION ORDER AND CUTTING LIST		CUSTOMER Charlie		Sheet 1 of 3	
Face# Case#	Solid Oak - Solid Oak - Solid Oak				
	3/4 Misc	3/4 x 2½	3/4 x 2	3/4 x 1¼	
Face 1	1-3x31½		2-19	1-19	
			1-31½		
1A	1-2⅛x35¼		1-35¼		
	1-5x19		2-19		
2	1-3¾x31½		1-31½		
			2-9	1-9	
3	1-3 1/16 x31½		1-31½		
			2-16½	1-16½	
3A			2-31½		
			2-20⅞	1-20⅞	
3B	1-3 1/16 x31½		1-31½		
			4-10	1-10	
4			2-16		
			1-31½	1-31½	
5	1-3 1/16 x30		1-30		
			1-26½	1-26½	
5A			2-30		
			1-13	1-13	
5B	1-2 1/16 x30 det				
6	1-1x30	1-26¾	1-78	1-34	
	1-3 1/16 x30	2-28 det		1-29	
				1-10	
6A	1-3x30		1-30		
			1-13	1-13	

FIGURE 5-6 Easy-to-follow cutting list.

8. Cut finished ends and finished backs.
9. Cut open plywood shelves.
10. Cut plywood drawer faces and drawer sides, backs, and subfronts.
11. Cut cabinet backs if the same material is to be used for drawer bottoms.
12. Cut drawer bottoms.
13. Cut all cabinet box parts: wall ends, bottoms, partitions, and so on.

Most of the basic principles of cutting that we have discussed so far have had to do with speeding up the cutting process in particular and cabinet production in general. The remaining principles are aimed at saving material.

Almost without exception, materials should be cut in the size order largest to smallest. In the cutting order just presented, this is the reason for cutting the wider drawer faces before cutting the stiles and rails of frame doors; it is the reason that cabinet backs are cut before cutting the smaller pieces needed for drawer bottoms when these components are made from the same type of material. (See items 2 and 3 before item 4, and item 11 before item 12.) When the miller begins to cut out a group of similar cabinet components such as face frames, he or she will encounter a list of pieces such as the one in Figure 5-6. This is a well-designed stock bill, with a miscellaneous column devoted to various widths and each other column devoted to only a single width. The list is also convenient because it reads from left to right as the stock width decreases. The proficient cutter would find the widest piece (in the example, this is the 5-in. piece on case number 1A), estimate the lineal footage needed to cut all the pieces of this width, make a rip, and then do all the length cutting necessary to get the pieces of that size. As the pieces are brought to finished size, they are marked with a case number and sorted so that all the parts to an individual face frame are together for detailing. If the cutter has ripped too much material to a certain width, the extra pieces may be used to rip narrower pieces. When pieces are cut to length, the cutter should again pay attention to getting the longer components first. In our example, this means arriving at the "¾- × 2-in." column and cutting the 78-in. piece first, followed by the 35¼-in. piece, then the seven pieces which are 31½ in. long, and so on, until at last the two 9-in. pieces are cut. As the longer pieces are cut, the shorter ones can be taken from waste, and if we have estimated well, most of the material left over will be suitable only for edging, molding, or perhaps the fireplace.

Another significant bit of knowledge to have is when to make length cuts before ripping. In cutting the cabinet job, it is usually best to rip materials to width first and then to make a series of length cuts, but there are a few exceptions when cutting certain pieces from plywood panels or other sheet goods. One group of pieces that usually should be cut to length first consists of the plywood doors. In custom cabinetry, there is no standard door width, but on a single job there will usually only be a few different lengths of door. Therefore, the cutter should most often cut plywood doors by crosscutting the plywood sheet to the desired door length and then ripping each plywood panel into the door widths needed.

The practice of end cutting sheet goods can also save material when cutting out any pieces that are substantially wider than half the width of a sheet of plywood. Most sheet goods with which we work will be 48 in. wide, and most cabinetry that we build will be 24 in. deep or less. It is obvious that plywood sheets are best if ripped first when we can achieve two rips out of each sheet. But when we require pieces that are as wide as 40 in. or more (as with many cabinet backs), ripping the sheet may leave us with pieces so narrow that they are useless. In such cases it is best to cut to length first and then to rip the material to the correct width.

A final consideration with regard to extending the use of wood products is knowing when to dispose of leftover pieces rather than to save them. This may seem too obvious for inclusion in a book of this nature, but the shop which is cluttered with waste pieces that can never be used is both inefficient and unsafe. Being a miller requires developing a sense for what can easily be used in production and what cannot. Narrow pieces that can be made into nailers, hold-downs, sleepers, and drawer guides should be saved if they are of standard length or longer. Molding and edging may also be made from narrower pieces of solid stock. However, any scrap that does not fit conveniently into the cabinet building system should be ruthlessly discarded.

SURFACING OF SOLID MATERIALS

Surfacing of solid materials is almost always performed with a jointer and a planer. Surfacing is not necessary if the cabinetmaker purchases solid boards that have already been surfaced, but there is one major advantage to performing our own surfacing of solid stock—it is possible to eliminate much cupping, twisting, and bowing in the boards to be used in the cabinet project. (See Figure 5-7.) Perfectly straight boards are not only a pleasure to work with but also contribute to square cabinetry and tight, even seams.

It is important to remember that a thickness planer will do nothing to make a board flat. Its rollers will follow the contour of each board that is fed into it. Consequently, if a bowed or twisted board is fed into a planer, it will come out smooth on the other end, but still bowed or twisted. A cupped board will be flattened out by the rollers temporarily, long enough for the cutters to do their work. A cupped

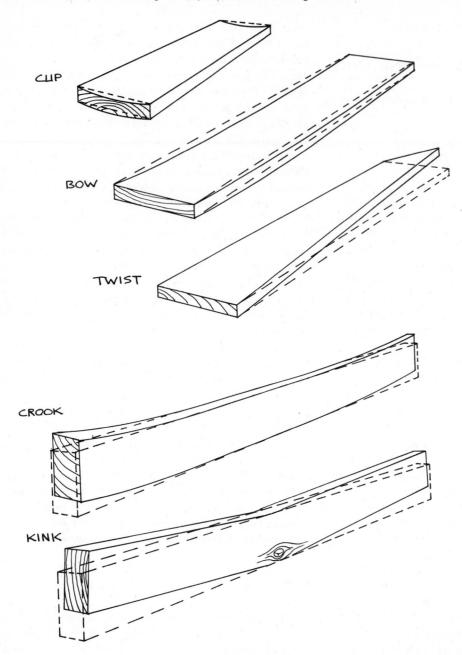

FIGURE 5-7 Types of warp.

board that is fed into a planer will still be cupped when it comes out at the other end. In addition, a cupped board may be cracked by the pressure of the rollers. To remove these types of warp in a board, it is necessary to flatten one of its sides on the jointer before feeding it into the planer.

The size of a jointer is an important factor in surfacing. The width of the bed naturally determines the width of boards that can be effectively surfaced on a jointer. In dealing with bowed or twisted boards, the length of the bed is very important. The longer the flat and stable surface on the infeed end of the jointer bed, the easier it will be to deal with twists and bows in solid stock. If a shop does a good deal of surfacing, as when it employs primarily un-surfaced stock in production, it should be equipped with a long bed jointer at least 8 in. in width. If a jointer is to be used in this way, it must be more powerful than if it is used only for edge straightening.

In using *all* power tools, it is imperative to read and understand the operator's manual and gain familiarity with the tool through visual inspection and respectful use. Anyone using such tools should be aware of their applications and limitations. Tools must be grounded; guards should be in place and functioning properly; the work area needs to be kept clean; loose-fitting clothing, long sleeves, and jewelry must not be worn; all the safety rules of the shop should be observed.

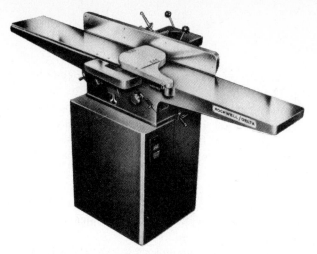

FIGURE 5-8 Long bed jointer. (Courtesy of Delta International Machinery Corp.)

Using the Jointer

Although there are many different jointer models, each with its own individual features, all jointers will have five basic parts that operate in the same way: the cutterhead assembly, which performs the actual removal of material; the cutter guard, which is designed to keep the dangerous spinning cutters covered; the infeed table, across which material is fed into the cutters; the outfeed table, which catches the surfaced wood; and the fence, which directs the angle and line of material feed. (See Figure 5-8.)

When surfacing is performed, the jointer should first be inspected and adjusted. The bed should naturally be clean, and a coat of wax should be applied to the tables and fence if necessary. Material should glide over all parts of the jointer easily, and paste waxes will reduce friction substantially when properly applied and buffed. The outfeed table should be exactly the same height as the highest point of the cutters in their rotation. Ideally, a wood surface is milled by the cutters and moves smoothly to the surface of the outfeed table. The miller should determine the depth of cut according to the width and hardness of the materials to be surfaced and make the necessary adjustment in the height of the infeed table. The fence should be locked after correct placement according to the width of the stock to be milled.

Each board to be surfaced should be inspected visually to see if it is flat or warped. Then milling can begin. Flat boards or boards with a cup are the easiest to surface. These are simply fed into the cutters evenly until they are smooth on one side and the cupping is removed. Bowed boards should be fed through the jointer "belly up." This way, the board can be surfaced a little at a time, removing material at the ends of the board first, progressing toward the middle until the board is flat enough to be fed into the planer. The most difficult type of warp to deal with is a twist. If a twisted board is laid on a perfectly flat surface, one of its four corners will fail to touch the surface. This type of piece must be fed across the jointer so that one of its edges remains in constant contact with the jointer tables. This is done again and again until the raised-up corner comes in contact with the surface of the jointer tables. It is very important to keep even and constant pressure on the same edge of a twisted piece with each pass through the jointer cutters. If the board is badly twisted, this type of surfacing procedure will result in a piece too thin for cabinet building purposes. Such a piece may still be used by first ripping it into widths slightly larger than finished widths. This allows the twist to be taken out of each piece with the removal of much less material on the jointer.

Some general rules apply for feeding all material through the jointer. If at all possible, wood should be fed into the cutters "with the grain" rather than against it. (See Figure 5-9.) This reduces chatter, reduces risk of kickback, and yields a smoother surface because wood fibers are cut

FIGURE 5-9 With the jointer, it is best to feed stock with the grain.

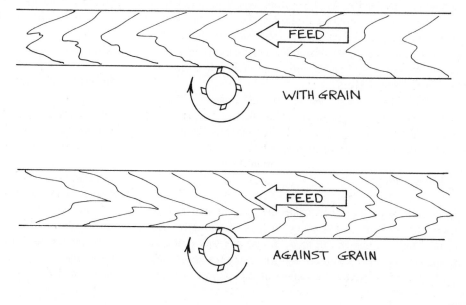

WITH GRAIN

FEED

AGAINST GRAIN

FEED

FIGURE 5-10   Rubber-surfaced and notched push blocks.

off rather than torn out. If it is necessary to mill the stock against the grain, or if the stock has a wavy grain figure, as in curly maple, this tearing out of the wood fibers can be reduced. It is obvious that reducing the depth of cut and feeding the stock more slowly can help. With some jointers, the fence may be set at an angle not quite perpendicular to the blades so that stock may be fed across the cutters ''indirectly.'' This also reduces the tear-out tendency. Another option, if stocks are fairly narrow, involves the table saw. Pieces are first ripped, then given one fairly flat face on the jointer as usual, and finally made smooth and brought to finished thickness by edge feeding on the table saw.

Each piece that must be fed across the jointer cutters should be fed at a steady pace and with continuous pressure against the bed and fence. The rear hand does most of the work in pushing the stock across the jointer; the front hand holds the stock firmly against the fence and jointer tables. The right and left hands alternate front and back positions in feeding most stock. After the front hand passes beyond the cutterhead, it should be lifted and placed on the stock as the rear hand. Stopping the feed is generally to be avoided. If it is necessary to stop for some reason, the stock should be drawn back a fraction of an inch before slowly beginning to feed again.

Push blocks are convenient and aid in safety. These may be flat and rubber-surfaced, or simple-to-make notched push blocks. (See Figure 5-10.) They should always be used when feeding thin or narrow stock.

Using the Planer

After solid stock has been made flat and smooth on one side with the jointer, it is ready for final surfacing by use of the thickness planer. In many ways, this tool is much simpler to use than a jointer. After adjustments are made, the tool itself controls the evenness of cut and rate of feed.

Almost all thickness planers have the cutterhead on top. They mill the top face of the material being fed. The bottom rollers keep the material even with the cutterhead so that we are left with parallel milled faces after machining. Therefore, the face of the stock that was made flat and smooth on the jointer must be on the bottom when feeding the planer.

All the material for a job should be planed at the same time. This way, the last cut will yield pieces that are of exactly the same thickness—a clear advantage for the rest of the cabinetmaking process.

In most cases, the finished thickness for the stock is not achieved in a single pass through the planer, but in several. The depth of each cut should not create a heavy load for the tool. Most cabinet shop planers are designed to remove about an ⅛ in. of hardwood at a time in wide pieces. The depth setting for the first pass through the planer should be about ⅛ in. less than the thickest piece of stock. We simply make enough passes of stock through the planer to reach the desired thickness. As with the jointer, it is advisable to feed so that cutting is with the grain rather than against it.

EDGE STRAIGHTENING

Edge straightening, or preparing one edge of a solid board so that it may be cut accurately on the table saw, is a much easier and less expensive process than surfacing. It requires no planer, and woodworkers who have not yet invested in a jointer can find alternatives that are feasible. Since it is a single-tool, single-setup operation, it is much less time consuming than is solid material surfacing. Since we are dealing here with the edges rather than the faces of boards, materials can be fed across the cutters quickly, and we do not need a wide bed on the surfacing tool. The power required to drive a jointer for this type of work is also much less than for surfacing.

Using the Jointer

The types of warpage that must be dealt with in edge straightening are crooks and kinks—edgewise bellies in boards caused by the uneven loss of moisture which occurs in most boards. (See Figure 5-7). As with surfacing of bowed boards, these pieces of solid stock should be fed through the jointer with the ''belly up.'' If the crook or kink is substantial, it may be advantageous to cut the board in half with a crosscut before performing the edge straightening. This will reduce waste, provided that the shorter pieces of solid stock will yield the finished size of some pieces on the cutting list. If it is necessary to get longer pieces out of such a board, the fastest technique to use on the jointer is to make a series of four or five jointing

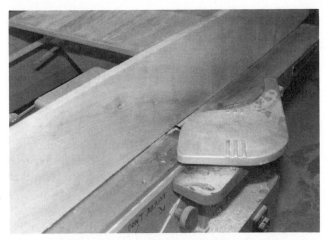

FIGURE 5-11 Taking a large crook or kink out of a warped board quickly. The leading end rests on the outfeed table, and the trailing end of the board is cut several times. In actually milling the piece, the guard will contact its surface.

FIGURE 5-12 Roller support that may be used in conjunction with the jointer and other tools. Note the use of the straight edge to adjust the height of the roller to be exactly even with the outfeed table on the jointer.

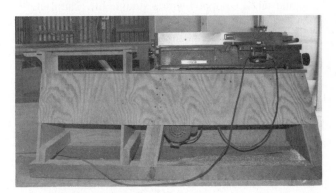

FIGURE 5-13 "Built-on" extension to the jointer outfeed table.

cuts on one end and then to turn the board end for end and repeat the process. When following such a procedure, it is easiest and safest to make the cuts on the trailing end of the board. The leading end of the board rests on the outfeed table, the kink or the crook is directly above the cutters, and the cutter guard is moved out of the way by the trailing end of the board as it is fed across the jointer. When the warp is reduced sufficiently, the entire board can be fed across the jointer cutters from end to end for final straightening. (See Figure 5-11.)

When using the jointer to do edge straightening, the outfeed table bears much of the weight of individual boards and provides nearly all the balance required as each jointing cut ends. It is obvious that stability, ease, and safety are all increased with the length of the outfeed table. Large, long-bed jointers (8 in. and more) have outfeed tables that are long enough to deal with most stock sizes that are employed in the cabinet trade, but such tools are often too expensive for small shops. Owners of such shops often invest in a smaller jointer and develop a way of effectively extending the weight-bearing capabilities of the outfeed table. A roller device such as the one shown in Figure 5-12 can be set wherever necessary to "catch" stock as it leaves the outfeed table and support its weight. The height of the roller can be adjusted to be exactly the same as the height of the jointer. Such a device is extremely versatile in a small shop because it can also be used in conjunction with other tools. Another option is to build a narrow table with exactly the same height as that of the outfeed table. Some cabinetmakers will even build an extension to the outfeed table which becomes part of the tool itself. Figure 5-13 shows a relatively small and inexpensive jointer with such a "built-on" table extension.

Alternatives to the Jointer

Like all cabinetmaking operations, use of the jointer is simply a goal-directed activity. But since the jointer is usually not the first major tool to be bought in the beginning shop, it is good to note that anything which safely provides straight edges on solid stock is an effective substitute.

One method of avoiding the necessity of using a jointer is to buy surfaced lumber which has already been straightened on the edge. Some lumberyards will perform

FIGURE 5-14 Router setup in a table for edge straightening. The fence is used to adjust depth of cut.

this type of milling for a charge. Still other suppliers sell certain types of hardwoods in common cabinet-use widths—1¼ in., 2 in., and so on. This material is sold by the lineal foot rather than by the board foot. It is ready for cutting to length. The drawback to this method of substituting for the jointer is its cost. Milling operations done at a lumberyard can be very expensive.

A heavy-duty router can be used as the substitute for a jointer when equipped with a straight bit. The router is mounted beneath a table with the cutter projecting to a height at least equal to the thickness of the stock. A straight edge is used as a fence, and we add a strip to the outfeed surface of the fence, exactly even with the cutting edges. This converts the table router into a "sideways jointer." (See Figure 5-14.) Boards are fed across the table against the fence until they are straight. This can be a very safe and effective method for edge straightening. The high speed of the router contributes to a very smooth edge.

The table saw can also be used for edge straightening. The fence is not used in this operation, but we do not "freehand" either. (No matter what anyone says, *never* freehand a cut on the table saw. Neither wood nor tools look attractive when spattered with blood.) To perform edge straightening on the table saw, a "jig" or shop aid

must be constructed. The jig consists of a long board fitted underneath with a wooden strip or runner to glide in the miter-gauge slots of the saw table. At the rear of the board is fastened a block to prevent kickback. The surface of the board should have sandpaper strips or other grips glued to it. Each board to be straightened is laid on the jig with its trailing end firmly against the antikickback block. The sandpaper grips help the miller keep the board in position. The jig is simply pushed through with the board in place. This is a ripping cut, and a straight edge is achieved in one pass. (See Figure 5-15.) The principal drawback to this method is that it is difficult to deal with long boards.

Another technique that can be used as replacement for the jointer is simply to strike a chalk line across the board to be straightened, clamp it in place, and plane to the line. This is a time-consuming process, but it can be speeded up somewhat by using a motor-driven plane.

There are a number of ways to achieve uniform edges for cutting, but there is really no substitute for a jointer. It is the fastest and most convenient method for attaining perfect edges, and it has other applications that are important to the cabinetmaker.

RIPPING MATERIALS TO WIDTH

Ripping materials to width is most often performed with a table saw, for reasons that have already been pointed out. No tool is of greater value in the wood shop than a well-maintained table saw of good quality, and choosing the right one should be very important to the serious cabinetmaker. If planning to use a table saw for anything more than light use, the woodworker will probably prefer a saw of at least 2 horsepower which will perform at a voltage of 200 and above. For even occasional heavy loads, such as ripping eight-quarter (8/4) hardwoods, the horsepower rating should be at least 3. Ripping materials can be rapid, safe, and precise with the right table saw.

Using the Table Saw

Along with power and precise machining, it is important to look for well-designed safety features. Some tools may be more dangerous to operate than a table saw, but we use this tool so much more frequently than most power tools that it is wise to give it the utmost respect. A machine that

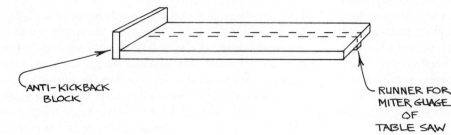

ANTI-KICKBACK BLOCK

RUNNER FOR MITER GUAGE OF TABLE SAW

FIGURE 5-15 "Jig" can be used with the table saw for edge straightening.

will cut hard maple would have no trouble in damaging human flesh. At the very least, the saw should be equipped with a blade guard, a splitter, and antikickback "fingers." The splitter is simply a piece of metal which is thinner than a saw cut. Mounted directly behind the saw blade, it prevents a piece of wood from pinching the rear of the saw blade and binding. The blade guard is a lightweight cover for the top and both sides of the saw blade. It reduces the chance of accidentally contacting the blade with a finger or hand. All the guard systems should be kept in place. All safety precautions should be understood and followed. A thorough discussion of safety practices is included in saw manuals for new saws, but when ripping, the following concerns are particularly important because they are *not* obvious.

1. Hold the material firmly. Tentatively held material can kick back or get away from the operator.

2. Develop an "automatic" reach for the off button. Know exactly where it is and what type of pressure will operate it quickly.

3. Make and use push blocks and sticks that are comfortable to use. Using a push stick is especially important when ripping narrow stock such as molding. (See Figure 5-16.)

4. Use clean, sharp blades. Many old-timers like to remark: "If I'm going to get cut, I want a clean cut." This may be ill humor, but dull, gummy blades or blades with burn marks can contribute as much as careless operation to binding and kickback.

5. Learn the "feel" of the saw. This may seem insignificant, but it can be of great importance. If

FIGURE 5-16 Push stick and a push block. The block, with its superior control features, should always be used unless its bulk interferes with the operation of the table saw guards. (Guard removed in this photo only for clarity.)

something does not sound right, or if there is a peculiar vibration, turn off the machine and inspect *immediately*.

6. Avoid mental "set." Performing the same operation again and again leads to "sleeping" at the saw. Take breaks when you feel bored or when cutting seems too easy.

7. It is all right to be quick, but do not hurry, especially in changing setups. For example, it may seem a bother to disconnect the power supply when making adjustments, and you may avoid trouble a million times without doing it, but it may be the next time that you accidentally hit the power switch and pay the price.

8. Keep the floor clean around the saw, especially the area where you stand to feed material through the saw. When sawdust builds up in this area, take a few minutes to sweep it out of the way.

All table saws have a similar design. The basic parts are used in the same way. When ripping, we are chiefly concerned with proper use of the fence, table, and blade as well as the splitter and blade guard. (See Figure 5-17.)

The blade is mounted on an arbor that can be raised or lowered, depending on the thickness of stock to be ripped. The height of the blade is usually adjusted by turning a wheel on the front of the tool. After choosing the right blade (see the later section "Saw Blades") and inspecting it for sharpness, it is important to set the blade height properly. The top of the blade should be approximately ¼ to ½ in. above the thickness of the stock to be cut.

After the miller has set the blade height, the cutting list should be consulted. Again, the widest rips are made first. The miller finds this largest ripping size and adjusts the fence for it. Some fences are mounted on a guard rail with reliable setting marks, and the miller has only to line up the cursor line on the fence with the correct setting and lock the fence in place. With this type of fence, new rip settings can be made safely without turning off the saw. (See Figure 5-18.) Many cabinetmakers consider the investment in such a fence well worth the price. If the saw is equipped with a standard fence and guide rail system, it is best to make the rip setting with a tape measure. With the saw *off*, and after the blade has *stopped completely*, the cutter may raise the blade guard and measure between the fence and the teeth of the blade. Then the fence is locked into position. When using this system, it is ideal to use a scrap of wood for a trial cut and verify the actual dimension. If the sample piece is too narrow or too wide, the fence position must be adjusted. It is obvious that we want to keep the number of setups to a minimum, to save time.

The miller now checks the cutting list and determines how many rips are needed to get all the pieces of a partic-

FIGURE 5-17 A 10-in. table saw. (Courtesy of Delta International Machinery Corp.)

FIGURE 5-18 This type of fence can be set rapidly and safely without turning off the saw. (Courtesy of Biesemeyer.)

ular width. This is a type of estimation and addition carried out simultaneously. The cutter should think in terms of feet rather than inches and add a certain length to the total to account for waste. The amount of waste is a factor of several things: length of pieces needed, length of boards in stock, and the quality of boards used. Cutting the 2-in. column in Figure 5-6, the miller would probably estimate the need for about 72 ft of 2-in.-wide stock. Arriving at this estimate is not very difficult. Starting at the top of the column, we should count the two 19-in. pieces as an approximate total of 3 ft. We add 2½ ft for the single 31½-in. piece, 3 ft for the 35¼-in. piece, and so on. The total for this estimated addition is about 64 ft. If we are working with oak firsts and seconds in 12-ft lengths, there will not be a great deal of waste, since most of the pieces are fairly short. Six rips of the 12-ft stock should conveniently yield the 64 ft we need plus an extra 8 ft for cutting around larger knots and other flaws. The cutter may believe that this is calling it too close and make another rip, yielding a total of 84 ft of 2-in. stock to work with. Anything extra can still be ripped down for the narrower stock on the list. Working in alder or some other woods might require allowing for even more waste. Once the ripping is accomplished for one width, the length cutting should be performed. If cutting to length is performed on a second saw, such as a radial arm saw, it may be wise to leave the same setup on the table saw until all the pieces of that width have been cut to length. This avoids ever having to make a second setup at the same width dimension. Then the miller is ready to consult the cutting list for the next smaller width.

The table saw is a nearly indispensible tool, but since cabinetmakers use it for dimensioning large pieces of wood and plywood, it should have tables or supports on the left side and in the rear. These will bear the weight of any material that is too long or wide for the steel table of the tool itself to support. (See Figure 5-19.) These weight-bearing tables should be sturdy so that they do not rock or wobble during the cutting operation. They should be built to the same height as the saw table itself or only slightly less. The surface of these supports may be constructed of wood, but they naturally function best when very smooth. Ideally, wood tabletops have a clear varnish or lacquer applied. Then, in beginning a substantially long cutting period, all the surfaces that will come into contact with the wood being cut can be prepared by cleaning, waxing, and buffing. This includes the steel saw table, the fence, and the support tables.

Finally, the user of a table saw should be reminded to check the tool frequently for adjustments that may be necessary, especially when more than one person is operating the saw. For safety's sake, the nut that holds the blade in place on the arbor of the saw should be checked for tightness. Accuracy calls for occasionally checking to be sure that the fence is perfectly parallel to the saw blade.

FIGURE 5-19 Notice the use of support tables in cutting long or wide pieces.

The manual for the saw will explain in detail how to do this. When beginning to cut a job, the user should always check to be sure that the blade is set to cut perpendicular to the saw table. This can be done as follows:

1. Cut off the power supply.
2. Raise the blade as high as possible.
3. Set a framing square on the saw table and against the side of the saw blade.
4. Use the blade-tilting mechanism to adjust the blade to exactly 90°.

The table saw is preferable to any other method of ripping material, but there are alternatives.

Using the Radial Arm Saw

The radial arm saw can be a very versatile tool. It can be used for cutting compound miters, for shaping, rabbeting, and dadoing as well as for cutting cabinet materials to size. As a tool for ripping, it is a feasible alternative to use the table saw if set up and used properly.

The radial arm saw consists of a vertical arm support in its rear, an arm, a wood guide fence and tabletop, and the motor and saw assembly, together with several controls that are found on no other tool: clamps, latches, and lock pins for various applications of the saw. To understand these control mechanisms fully, the woodworker should consult the manual that comes with the tool. (See Figure 5-20.)

For ripping material to correct width, it is important to make sure that all guards are in place. There is an upper blade guard which should be rotated downward to lightly contact each workpiece that is fed through the saw. This helps to reduce the up-and-down vibration caused by the

FIGURE 5-20 Radial arm saw. [Courtesy of Dewalt Division of Black & Decker (U.S.) Inc.]

upward rotation of the saw blade when ripping. There is a lower blade guard which reduces the chances of accidentally touching the blade on its side. The saw is also equipped with a splitter and antikickback device.

In a way, the radial saw is difficult to use for both ripping and cutoff. For cutting materials to finished length, we have seen that the radial saw is a useful tool and that its usefulness is increased by extending the table and fence to the right and left of the saw. When ripping, these extensions of the table are not only in the way but can be unsafe. The table extensions are exactly where the operator needs to stand when feeding material across the table. (See Figures 5-21 and 5-22.) A few shop operators circumvent this problem by making the table extensions movable. (See Figure 5-23.)

When crosscutting, the line of cut on the radial saw is perpendicular to its fence, but for ripping, the saw and motor assembly must be turned 90° to the right or left so that the line of cut will be parallel to the fence. To do this, the arm is first raised enough for the blade to clear the surface of the table. The motor and blade is then revolved for

ripping. For narrow pieces (up to approximately 8 in.), we use the "in-rip" position by rotating the motor assembly to the left. For wider rip settings, the "out-rip" position is used by rotating the assembly to the right. The arm of most radial arm saws is equipped with a measuring gauge, but most people who use this saw for ripping are inclined to measure the actual distance between the blade and the fence to get the desired ripping width. The saw is locked into position, turned on, and then the arm is lowered until the saw blade cuts a kerf in the saw table. The guards should be positioned before beginning to cut the cabinet materials. For each width-of-rip dimension, the saw must be raised and positioned, and then a new kerf must be made. Since cutting out cabinet parts requires many different rip settings, it is wise to cut a channel out of the saw table directly below the arm, perhaps ⅜ in. deep, and to fit this channel with a wooden insert that can be replaced easily when the number of saw kerfs makes the surface of the table undesirable.

Since most radial saws will not rip material to widths greater than 18 in. with their standard setups, the cabinet-

FIGURES 5-21 and 5-22 Ripping material to width on the radial arm saw. Notice that table extensions would be in the way for ripping. Also note the position of the out-rip fence close to the vertical arm support of the saw, allowing us to rip materials over 18 in. wide. [Courtesy of Dewalt Division of Black & Decker (U.S.) Inc.]

5-21   5-22

FIGURE 5-23 Movable extension table for the radial arm saw. Note the wheels for easy movement.

maker who uses this tool for ripping is presented with a problem. How are we to rip materials that are close to 24 in. in width, as we must for much cabinetry? The solution is to make the primary fence (the one built in by the factory, which is in the best location for crosscutting) removable, and to build in a second fence much closer to the vertical arm support in the rear of the tool. (See Figure 5-22.) This increases the maximum ripping width. It should be easy to remove and replace the primary fence so that time is not needlessly wasted in changing setups, but this fence must be secured properly when it is in use, for the sake of safety.

For ripping sheet goods into even wider segments, as sometimes must be done in building cabinets, the cutter who uses the radial saw must use a "subtraction technique." For example, if a 30-in.-wide piece is called for, and it must be ripped out of a standard piece of plywood (48 in. wide), the cutter should set the saw in the out-rip position and make the setup at 18 in. from the fence to the *outside* of the blade. When the rip is made, we are left with the desired piece on the outside of the blade. When using this technique, the saw operator should check for slight

variance in the particular sheet being used before cutting. Some pieces of plywood may not be exactly 48 in. wide.

As a final note on using the radial saw for ripping, it should be stressed that material must be fed against the direction of blade rotation only. This is especially important with the radial saw since it is possible to feed the stock from either end, depending on the in-rip or out-rip positioning of the motor and saw assembly.

All in all, the radial arm saw can be used for ripping material to proper width, and with some adaptation may be employed for both ripping and cutting off, but it should not be used for ripping if a table saw is available.

Naturally, there are systems and tools for ripping wood to width other than the table saw and the radial arm saw. A portable circular saw may be used in conjunction with a straight edge, for example. However, the serious cabinetmaker will prefer the speed and precision of stationary power tools.

CROSSCUTTING

Crosscutting, or cutting materials to length, is done most efficiently with a well-maintained radial arm saw, although many cabinetmakers prefer to use their table saw for this as well as for ripping. In addition, it is possible to cut sheet goods to length using a panel saw, and some woodworkers use a motorized miter saw ("chop saw") for cutting the pieces of a face frame to length.

Using the Radial Arm Saw

Using the radial arm saw for length cutting can be a very safe process, but the operator should not take the tool lightly. Again, it is necessary to be familiar with the recommendations of the manufacturer of the saw as presented in the manual, and to follow all safety rules. Specifically, when cross-cutting with the radial arm saw, the operator should pay close attention to the following not-so-obvious precautions.

1. Do not turn the saw off until it has reached full speed, and do not turn the saw on unless it is fully stopped. This can cause loosening of the nut that holds the blade secure.

2. Equip the saw with a counterweight or spring that will return the saw and motor assembly fully to the rear of the table after each cut.

3. Do not attempt any freehand cuts. The forces developed by the rotating saw can drive a piece of stock, or a hand, directly toward the blade.

4. Unplug the tool or otherwise disconnect the power source before attempting to change blades or make other adjustments.

5. Do not pull forward too quickly on a cut. This can result in the blade becoming jammed or pinched. It is also damaging to the motor.

6. Avoid making cuts which produce pieces of waste that are small enough to be grabbed and hurled by the blade. Also avoid waste pieces that can become wedged in the upper guard or between the blade and the fence.

7. Hold stock firmly against the fence.

8. Do not remove the antikickback device. Adjust it to be just clear of the workpieces.

When crosscutting, the workpiece is held securely against the primary fence of the saw table, and the blade is drawn across the material just enough to make the desired cut. This is a right-angle cut, and the cutter should be careful not to allow sawdust or wood chips to be trapped between the fence and the workpiece, as this can change the angle of the cut.

Most millers use the left side of the radial arm saw table as the measuring side and the right side as the waste side. The left hand holds the stock against the fence while the right hand brings the saw forward.

Much cabinet stock (especially solid materials) must be squared at the end before the first cut to finished length is made. The miller simply gets in the habit of cutting a few inches off the end of each piece, trimming checks as well as the irregular ends of all solid pieces. Cutting to length can then proceed by measuring in one of two ways.

One system of measurement is simply to measure from the square end of the stock, mark each individual piece that is needed, and position the stock so that the blade cuts right to the mark. This can be slow, but it may be necessary for long pieces, especially if there are no extensions on the saw table. If the radial saw is being used only for cutting to length and table extensions have been built, an accurate scale may be installed directly onto the table or fence. A hardware system is available for this specific purpose, or the cutter may install a steel measuring tape that will measure accurately from the blade. (The measurement should be checked for accuracy when blades are changed.) A sliding block-and-clamp device can be used with the measuring tape as a gauge. (See Figure 5-24.) The block is slid along the scale to the desired length measurement and clamped in place. The squared-off end of the stock may then be positioned against the block, and the piece cut to the exact length needed. This is a fast and safe measuring system for cutting custom cabinet parts. It is especially useful when making repetitive cuts at the same length.

The miller naturally develops his or her system to cut out a cabinet job, but certain practices are naturally superior. First, as pieces of stock are cut to length (from largest to smallest, of course) the cutter should check off each piece on the cutting list. This helps to avoid missing a piece or

FIGURE 5-24 Easy-to-install and accurate measuring gauge for length cutting on the radial arm saw.

cutting extra pieces. On a well-designed cutting list, each face or case has its own number, and the miller who performs the job of cutting pieces to length should mark each piece with its number so that cabinet components do not get mixed up or lost. Marks should be made on the back side of each part so that they will not necessarily be sanded off. As a group of materials is cut, the components should also be sorted and stacked according to face or case number. This saves a great deal of time in marking and detailing individual parts for dowels, rabbets, and dadoes.

When most ripped materials are cut to length, the sawing operation is across the wood fibers, sometimes causing a good deal of splintering or tearing away of these fibers on one side. This side or face of the cabinet component naturally becomes the back or rear side so that the splintered face will not show on the finished cabinet. The miller usually makes a decision as to which side is better on a piece of wood. For crosscutting on the radial arm saw, this means cutting "good side up." Some knots and other flaws in the stock appear only on one side. If these flaws will not affect the strength of the cabinet, they do not need to be cut out altogether; they are simply hidden on the rear side of the cabinet part. If there is a slight warp in a board, it is cut with its "belly up." Any splintering or tearing away of the wood fibers will thus be on the same face of each cabinet component as the other flaws in the piece.

The amount of splintering on the inferior side of a piece is generally greater when using a radial arm saw than when performing cutoffs with a table saw. In fact, this is why a few cabinetmakers insist on doing their length cutting on the table saw. However, this tendency can be minimized on the radial saw by using the appropriate blade and by keeping the kerf small in the tabletop. If the kerf becomes too large, it may be filled by fitting and gluing in a piece of wood or by mixing a fast-hardening epoxy resin and pouring it into the kerf. When the glue or resin is dry, a new kerf may be cut into the saw table.

Depending on the placement of the fence on a radial arm saw, the maximum width of a crosscut on the tool is approximately 15 in. Wider stock may be cut to length on this saw in one of two ways. If the presence of some splintering will not matter on the cabinet member, as with some partitions and wall ends, the cutter may use the saw's measuring gauge for two cuts, each about half the width of the material to be cut. The clamp gauge is set to the desired measurement, the material is positioned against it, and it is cut about halfway across. The saw and motor assembly is returned to its starting position behind the fence. Then the piece of stock is simply flipped over on the table, repositioned against the fence and clamp gauge, and again cut about halfway across its width. This completes the cut. When it is important to protect one face of the stock from splintering, the first "half-cut" may be made by using the clamp gauge as before, but the material is then turned end for end on the table instead of flipping it over. The cutter can make an exact "half-cut" from the opposite edge of the stock by using a framing square or a tape measure to make a reference mark on the wood.

The radial arm saw may not be the perfect tool for ripping, but it is excellent for crosscutting materials. When used as a partner to the table saw in a cutting operation, it makes for rapid and safe cutting.

Using the Table Saw

For cutting sheet goods to length, the table saw is used in much the same way that it is used for ripping. The guards are always kept in place, and the fence is used to feed material through the saw. Setting the saw up to cut the correct dimension is slower than on the radial arm saw unless the table saw is equipped with an accurate ripping fence. This is especially significant when cutting pieces to length because in this type of cutting there are a larger number of setups than in ripping. Also, pieces of stock can be cumbersome to cut to length on the table saw. When cutting to

length on the radial arm saw, we can simply position an 8-ft-long piece on the table and draw the blade through it, but when performing the same operation on the table saw, we must properly support the weight of such a piece and feed it through the blade. Some saws have a special sliding table that allows easy feeding of long pieces. Most cabinetmakers do not do most of their length-cutting on the table saw, but when cutting plywood doors or wide cabinet components such as backs, a table saw is the best tool to use.

In general, to cut pieces to length on the table saw, the operator simply sets the fence at the appropriate distance from the blade and makes all the cuts to the desired dimension. Again, the cutter begins with the largest piece and progresses to the smallest.

One problem with length cutting on the table saw has to do with achieving the longer length dimensions that will be required to construct some cabinetry. The ends for a pantry or an oven cabinet are often close to 7 ft long; countertops must often be made to be this long or longer. But most table saws are not designed with a table that is capable of taking pieces this long between the fence and the blade. The maximum setting for most saws is near 48 in. This is not a major problem, though. The miller simply employs another "subtraction technique." The fence will be used, but the desired piece is not delivered between the fence and the blade. Rather, the long piece will be delivered to the left of the blade, where the waste is usually delivered after a cut. The desired length is marked on the piece of stock from which it will be cut. The miller then measures back to this mark from the opposite end of the board and uses this measurement to set the position of the fence. It is important to allow for the width of the saw cut itself. The measurement should therefore be made from the fence to the *outside* of the blade instead of the inside. For example, if the cutting list calls for a plywood finished end that is 95 in. long, and it must be cut from a piece of stock that is 96 in. long, the cutter will wind up setting the fence exactly 1 in. from the outside of the blade. This will be approximately $7/8$ in. between the inside of the blade and the fence, depending on the blade in use. The splitter is a great advantage on this type of cut since it actually helps to keep the stock against the fence to achieve an even cut. Naturally, the piece needs to be supported adequately as it is fed through the saw since a long and heavy section of the piece hangs over the left side of the saw table. (See Fig. 5-25.)

The miller should not use the fence of the table saw for making length cuts of narrow stock on the table saw. The fence should never be used even as a gauge in cutting such pieces. It is too easy for such pieces to become twisted between the blade and the fence. The operator's hand can be drawn violently toward the saw. Even if the miter gauge is used to feed such material, the saw blade can transform

FIGURE 5-25 Using a table saw to cut a long cabinet member. The cutter has used a subtraction technique to arrive at the desired dimension. Note the use of the support table on the left of the saw.

a small piece of wood into a missile that can do damage to the operator or others.

To perform length cutting of narrow stock (under 12 in.) on the table saw, the fence is moved completely out of the way and stock is fed with the miter gauge. Even lengths of face frame material may be cut in this way. The cutter should make sure that the miter gauge is adjusted to make perfect 90° cuts in conjunction with the table saw blade. This is easily done by loosening a knob or lock on the miter gauge, positioning the face of the gauge correctly by use of a framing square, and then retightening the knob or lock.

Some cutters who use this method will extend the face of the miter gauge by attaching a straight piece of hardwood to it. There are usually screw clearance holes in the miter gauge for this purpose. The added piece stands higher on the table than the stock to be cut, and the blade height is adjusted to cut through the stock but not through the guide. This allows the guide to be used to push stock well past the saw blade. In a way, this is a safety feature, but the guard and splitter must be removed in order to use such a guiding system. (See Figure 5-26.)

When using the miter gauge and performing length cuts of narrow material on a table saw, it is advisable to put marks on the surface of the saw table at exactly the place where the tips of the blade will make their cut. These marks should be readily visible and located in front of the blade. It is thus easy to position stock in exactly the right place for each cut before the cut is actually begun.

Length cutting on the table saw can be an effective process. It will generally yield a more splinter-free cut than a radial arm saw. Its chief disadvantage is lack of speed. It is usually necessary to measure out and mark the dimension for each cut, even with repeated sizes. This is time-consuming. The operator should never move pieces (especially short pieces) away from the moving saw blade with

his or her hand. A stick may be used, or the saw may be turned off. Once again this takes time.

With some types of length cutting, the table saw is superior to the radial arm saw. Since the table saw will generally yield more splinter-free cuts than a radial saw, it is better for cutting plywood doors. In fact, for cutting these the miller consults the cutting list to find the longest door size rather than the widest. On a custom cabinet job, many doors will have the same length, but widths may be inconsistent. The miller should determine how many 48-in.-wide crosscuts will be needed to get all the doors of a particular dimension. The fence is set up at the correct dimension, and these cuts are made. The miller may then make the setups necessary to rip each door to its individual width. When grain must be matched, as with paired doors or flush overlay doors, the doors should be marked as they are cut to indicate how they are to be mounted on the cabinet. This may be especially important if the doors are to be lipped because we do not want to run the lip on a paired edge. What many cutters do is make the rip setup that will be used to achieve the paired door size and then, before turning on the saw motor, to set the board on the saw and draw one or two lines across its face where the blade will pass through. The marks become a reminder to us (or to whoever lips the doors) not to put a lip on that particular edge of the door. The marks should not be deep or heavy, so that they are easy to sand off in the normal preparation of the doors.

Cabinet backs are another cabinet component that can

FIGURE 5-26 The face of the miter gauge may be enlarged so that pieces are pushed well past the saw blade. Note, however, that it would be undesirable to use the splitter with such a system.

most easily be cut to length as well as width on the table saw, whether the cutter does most length cutting on the table saw or not. Such material may be anything from ¾-in. plywood to ⅛-in. hardboard. With grainless material such as hardboard, the cutter can frequently reduce waste by crosscutting sheets for pieces that are less than 48-in. in length. Because cabinet backs are usually about 30 in. wide, ripping a sheet will leave a waste piece about 18 in. wide. A few such pieces can occasionally be used for fabricating bottoms for small drawers, but other than this, such leftover pieces are almost useless. Waste reduction is an important goal. Plywood backs are usually mounted on a cabinet with the grain running vertically, and the miller must of course follow the width and length dimensions as prescribed on the cutting list. A seam can and often must be made in a plywood back which is at least ¼ in. thick. If the cutter keeps this in mind, he or she can often reduce waste by calling for a joint in some cabinet backs. This must be done somewhat judiciously, however, since unnecessary labor can frequently be more expensive than wasted materials.

As a final safety note related specifically to cutting thin cabinet members such as cabinet backs and drawer bottoms on the table saw, precaution should be taken not to allow the edge of any such material to be caught between the fence and the table. This can be a particular problem with ⅛-in. sheet goods. Many fences allow an adjustment to prevent this, but if not the cutter will find it advantageous to position a thin strip of wood next to the fence so that there is no possibility that the edge of thin stocks will "creep" under the fence. Many cutters will drive a box nail through this safety strip near one end. The nail extends below the surface of the saw table and prevents it from moving as stock is fed across the tool.

As we have seen, the table saw can be made to fulfill the duty of length cutting, and it is particularly well suited for cutting certain types of cabinet parts to length. In general, however, a cabinet shop will function more effectively when most ripping is done with the table saw while most length cutting is performed with a radial arm saw specifically set up for this purpose.

Alternatives

Dissimilar to material ripping, there are a few real alternatives to the stationary power tools when it comes to length cuts. For cutting face frame parts to length, a good setup may be constructed which utilizes a motorized miter box (a chop saw). This may be a wise choice for the cabinetmaker who is investing in a table saw but prefers to avoid the additional investment in a radial arm saw, which is used almost exclusively for cutoffs. The chop saw should be mounted at a convenient height. Table and fence extensions should be added on both sides of the saw. It is easy to construct an accurate gauge and clamping block system for this tool (similar to that described for use with the radial arm saw) so that continual measuring of stock is not necessary. This tool is also very versatile in the shop, especially for mitering. If a motorized miter box is used as a substitute for the radial arm saw, the cabinetmaker will probably do all cutting of sheet goods on a table saw.

A panel saw is not generally used as a substitute for any tool. It is designed to make crosscuts on wide sheets of material. Of course, it will do a quite adequate job of length cutting on most cabinet body components.

SAW BLADES

Saw blades are available in a variety of sizes and designs according to the number, arrangement, and type of teeth, but choosing the correct blades to equip our saws is not as difficult as it would seem. The decisions are based on the design of the saws to be outfitted and the jobs to be performed by them.

Tool design dictates some blade requirements. One of these is arbor diameter. Most stationary power tools employ a ⅝-in. diameter arbor, and it is best to buy blades that will fit all the saws in the shop. This way, for example, a particular blade can be used on both the table saw and the radial arm saw. Blade diameter is also a factor. Most radial arm saws are capable of taking a 12-in. blade, but the 10-in. size is more common for table saws and chop saws. The larger, 12-in. table saws are substantially more expensive. For the serious cabinetmaker, smaller diameters of blade (under 10 in.) are usually not used except on portable circular saws.

Saw blades may possess steel or carbide teeth. Most modern cabinetmakers opt for the more expensive carbide blades for most cutting situations because the tips hold their sharpness through much more cutting than do standard steel blades. The all-steel blades can give reliable service if they are kept sharp, especially in the 12 in. size.

Ripping blades are designed to cut with the grain, with fewer teeth (20 to 36) than other types of blades. These blades are used only for long periods of ripping, particularly with hardwood and softwood solid stocks.

Combination blades are sometimes referred to as general-purpose blades. They possess 40 to 50 teeth, and they may be employed for both ripping and crosscutting. Most combination blades can be used for cutting plywoods, hardboard, particle board, and plastic laminates as well as solid materials. A good blade will yield pieces with little splintering.

A cutoff blade or fine blade may have 60 to 100 teeth. It is never used for ripping solid material, but it makes very

FIGURE 5-27

smooth cuts in all materials that the cabinetmaker uses. It is particularly useful on the table saw for cutting plywood components to width and length, and on a radial arm saw for cutting any type of material across the grain.

Plywood blades are made entirely of steel. They have very many small, fine teeth for cutting narrow, splinter-free kerfs in plywood. This blade is often used for cutting plywood doors. (See Figure 5-27 for an illustration of the blade designs discussed.)

CHAPTER SUMMARY OF CABINETMAKING SKILLS

Cutting out the cabinet job requires great consciousness of safety and efficiency. To achieve these ends, the first concern of a shop owner should be in properly locating material storage bins and the stationary power tools that will be used.

In choosing stationary tools, the cabinetmaker should consider safety features and versatility. In the ideal shop, we use a jointer for straightening, a planer for surfacing, a table saw for ripping, and a radial arm saw for length cutting. But it is probably most important to possess a table saw before any of the other tools because of its great versatility. All cutting and even edge straightening can be performed with a table saw. The jointer is probably of more significance to the developing shop than the thickness planer since it is possible to purchase surfaced solid stocks, whereas it is not as easy or inexpensive to get straightened materials. No matter which saws are employed, the miller should understand the uses of the several types of saw blades and choose the right one for each cabinet cutting job.

Operators should learn great respect for the power of their cutting tools. Instruction manuals should be carefully read and understood, all guards should be kept functioning and in place, and the capabilities and limitations of each tool must be considered. If possible, and if space permits, weight-bearing tables should be constructed to assist in use of the table saw, the radial arm saw (or chop saw), and the jointer.

A good miller is able to understand a cutting list. He or she can perform the following:

- Estimate the amount of stock necessary to cut each type of cabinet component.
- Scan quickly and locate components largest to smallest for reduction of waste.
- Recognize those components which require the most preparation time so that they may be cut first.
- Understand the function of each cabinet component so that decisions can be made as to whether or not slight defects or warps are permissible in the piece.
- Mark and organize cabinet components by case number to speed cabinet production.

In general, solid materials are straightened and cut before sheet goods. With most types of cabinet components, pieces are ripped to their correct width first and then cut to length. With some components, such as plywood doors and cabinet backs, this order may be reversed. For cutting certain types of longer pieces, the miller must master subtraction techniques.

Following the principles of cutting will result in reaching the goal of safe, fast, and wasteless material dimensioning.

SIX

MACHINING AND DETAIL WORK

PLANNING FOR MACHINING AND DETAILING

After cabinet components are cut to their prescribed dimension and marked with the appropriate case number, they are ready to be machined for assembly. This is the work of a detailer who reads the layout sticks or drawings, marks each cabinet part for the necessary detail (dado, rabbet, dowel hole, etc.), and machines it appropriately. The detailer has frequently had a good deal of experience in several of the cabinetmaking processes, enabling him or her to isolate components quickly, determine exact locations of each detail, and to anticipate any problems that may develop in assembly, sanding, finishing, and installation. In larger shops, the detailer is called on to understand fully all the cabinet construction details called for by the cabinet designer. In the smaller shop, the detailer may often be the cabinet designer. In either case, it is important for this woodworker to have a clearly defined cabinetmaking philosophy to serve as a guide in developing and using systems of assembly that are effective.

Most of the systems and routines that are used in the machining process are simply a carrying out of the decisions made in cabinet designing which we discussed in earlier chapters. The types of joints to be used in assembling face frames, for example, are not decided on after the stiles and rails are cut, but before the production plan is even drawn. (For a discussion of the advantages and disadvantages of the several types of cabinet assembly details, see Chapters 2 and 3.)

In this chapter we look at the various techniques that can be used to machine the several types of details used in cabinet construction. As with most facets of cabinetmaking, there are several tools that can be used to carry out the same machining operation, and the reader should consider which of these would work best for him or her. As an example, dadoes may be cut into box components with a table saw, a radial arm saw, or a router. In smaller shops, with only one saw, the woodworker may cut all dadoes with a router so that there is no need to make several changes in the setup of the saw. In some shops, there may be the luxury of having one table saw for cutting and another for cutting dadoes and other details. Then the woodworker may opt for setting up a dado head on the table saw and running all the dadoes there, since the actual machining time is faster. With large cabinet jobs, with many dadoes to cut, even a small shop can save time by replacing a saw blade with a dado head and detailing with the saw. In following the discussion, therefore, the reader should consider the number of setups that are necessary to carry out a particular operation on a particular tool and the difficulty of making and using each setup, as well as the tools that are available.

BOX COMPONENTS

Box components will often require dadoes, rabbets, and miters to fulfill various functions in the cabinet. A dado is a rectangular groove cut into a piece of wood away from its edge or end, either with or across the grain. It is generally designed to receive the edge or end of another piece of wood. Rabbets are similar cuts or channels cut into the surface of a board right at its edge, and they are most often used for wood-to-wood joints, but they are sometimes cut only to reduce the thickness of a piece that must be scribed to the wall of a house. The most common reason to cut a miter in the shop is to conceal the core layers of plywood which would otherwise show on the finished cabinet, particularly where toekick meets finished end. In addition, the detailer will often cut notches into partitions and other cabinet members to receive nailers and hold-downs, and to prepare other special details.

Rabbeting

There are several situations that call for cutting a rabbet. First, the inside rear edge of a finished end must be rabbeted to receive and conceal the back if the cabinetry under construction is a free-standing piece (furniture).

If the cabinetmaker plans for trimless installation, all primary (visable or fully exposed) cabinet members should be rabbeted wherever they will contact walls or soffits. This includes the following:

- The top edge of upper face frames
- The top edge of upper finished ends
- The rear edge of finished ends
- The edge of any face frame stile that will be positioned against the wall

The top edge of base-unit finished ends may be rabbeted so that hold-downs and nailers may be fastened without driving nails through the face of the finished end. The top edges of wall ends on uppers should be rabbeted to receive the top of the cabinet. The top should also be secured to finished ends on upper units with a rabbet, even if there is no scribe needed for mounting to the ceiling or soffit. (Many cabinetmakers refer to these as dadoes since they are often the same width and depth, and since they are usually machined with the same setup as other dadoes on the job.)

In addition to the box components, some types of cabinet accessories may also require rabbeting: square-lipped doors, some types of drawer fronts, and occasionally certain parts of heavy-duty drawers and slide-out shelves.

The first step in rabbeting is determining where the details are necessary and what size they should be. This information is usually standardized within a particular shop, and should always be indicated somehow on the production drawing or layout stick for a particular cabinet. With the drawing system, the designer will usually call for rabbeting with a written notation, such as "rabbet—½ in. × ½ in.," and an arrow. (See Figure 2-10.) A similar notation will usually be found by the detailer who is interpreting a layout stick. For example, near the lines that represent a finished end on such a stick may be the notation "rabbet for back— ¼ in. × ⅜ in." The detailer will generally check for accuracy of the dimension of all pieces as he or she marks and machines them. If a finished end on a base cabinet is to be rabbeted to receive a ¼-in. back, for instance, the detailer checks to be sure that it is ¼ in. wider than bottom shelves, partitions, and so on.

At the same time, a check should be made to verify that the width and height of the back are correct. Using the drawing system, the actual dimensions of the back are quickly taken and compared to the measurements indicated on the production drawing, less the thickness of material that will be left after rabbets are cut. [On a 40-in. base with two rabbeted finished ends (again ¼- × ⅜-in. rabbets), the back should be 39¼ in. wide.] Following the stick system would be similar, in that the detailer takes the actual dimensions of the back, but this is compared to the actual measurement between the rabbets indicated on the layout stick. If the piece is small enough, it is even possible to skip measurement altogether and to set the layout stick against the actual back and verify its fit this way. Similar procedures can be used in checking the sizes of each cabinet component. The detailer simply asks again and again: "Will this piece fit the way that it should according to the layout plan?"

It is naturally best to make all rabbeting cuts at one time so that only setup changes are kept to a minimum. Therefore, marks are made to indicate those edges that will require machining. If it is desirable to stop the rabbet before reaching the end of the individual piece, as for rabbeting the inside edge of a face frame that contacts a finished end, a mark is made to indicate the exact place for the detail to be stopped. Otherwise, the marks for rabbeting need not be exact. They only serve as a reminder of which edges require machining. Exactness comes from a careful setup. Generally, when all marking is finished, the details are machined.

Rabbeting with the Table Saw. Rabbets are made on the table saw in one of two ways. In both methods, the splitter and guard must be removed.

One way requires no dado head, but it requires two different setups of the saw (unless the rabbet's width and depth are the same) and two separate passes of the same piece across the table. For the first cut, the height of the blade is set for cutting the rabbet's depth, and the fence is positioned from the outside of the blade to cut the rabbet's width. All the pieces that are to receive this detail are then machined at once, rabbeted face down. For the second cut, the blade's height is set for the desired rabbet width. When the second cut is completed, a thin strip of wood will fall away and lie on the table. This should *NOT* be delivered between the blade and the fence or it may turn into a harmful missile propelled by the saw. Therefore, the distance between fence and blade is the same as the thickness of board that will be left after the rabbet is made. For example, if a ½-in.-deep rabbet is to be made in a ¾-in. board, the fence is set ¼ in. from the inside of the blade for this second cut, which is made edge down. (See Figures 6-1 and 6-2.)

To rabbet with a dado head on the table saw, there is usually only one setup to make, but this may take some time to prepare. If there is a cutting blade on the saw, it must be removed from the arbor and replaced with the blades and chippers that make up the dado head. A board

FIGURE 6-1 First rabbet cut on a table saw.

FIGURE 6-2 Second table saw rabbet cut. Note that the waste will fall away harmlessly to the left of the blade as the cut is completed.

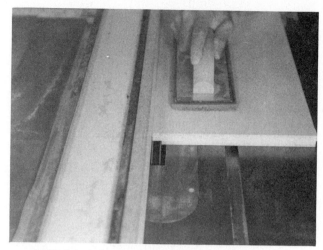

FIGURE 6-3 Rabbeting with a dado head. Note the wood protector strips on the fence.

must be screwed or clamped to the fence to prevent contact between the metal fence and the cutters. With the dado head just below the surface of the table, the fence position is set to control the width of the rabbet. Then the motor is turned on and the dado head is raised slowly to yield the desired depth. When this is done, the cutters will be removing material on the underside of the protection board that was added to the fence. Pieces are simply fed across the saw, rabbeted face down, to yield the detail. (See Figure 6-3.)

Rabbeting with the Radial Arm Saw. The radial arm saw is not often used for rabbeting when other options are available, but the operation may be performed on this tool. A dado head is mounted on the arbor to replace the blade. The elevating arm is then turned to raise the arm enough so that the motor may be rotated into a vertical position and locked. This places the cutters of the dado head in a horizontal position, parallel to the table of the saw. Instead of the upper and lower guards of the saw, the tool is fitted with a special shaper guard. The saw and motor assembly is rotated into ripping position. Material will be fed against the fence, and the width of the rabbet cut is therefore controlled by moving the saw motor back along the arm far enough to locate most of the dado head behind the fence. The projection of the blade beyond the surface of the fence is the actual rabbet width. The arm is raised or lowered to adjust to the desired rabbet depth. Stock is fed with its unrabbeted face down, against the table and fence. As you will recall, the direction of feed must always be against the rotation of the blades. (See Figure 6-4.)

Rabbeting with Routers. Many cabinetmakers run all rabbeting operations in their shops with a router. This is for two reasons. First, a router is a relatively inexpensive investment. For example, if the woodworker

FIGURE 6-4 Performing a rabbet operation with a radial arm saw. [Courtesy of Dewalt Division of Black & Decker (U.S.) Inc.]

FIGURE 6-5 The router may be fitted with an edge guide for rabbeting.

FIGURE 6-6 Table-mounted router used for rabbeting.

FIGURE 6-7 Rabbeting can be accomplished with a panel router. (Courtesy of Safranek Enterprises Inc.)

prefers to keep his or her table saw in specialized use as a cutting tool, one or more routers can be purchased and put into specialized use as detailing tools with much less expense than a second table saw. Router bits and accessories are also less expensive to buy and maintain than dado heads. A second major reason for using routers to machine details is that they can be very convenient to use. Setup changes are managed quickly, and when the tool is not in use, it may easily be stored out of the way.

Cabinetmakers who plan to make heavy use of a router for cutting dadoes and rabbets should caution themselves to buy "heavy-duty" tools that are designed for this type of work. With rabbeting or dadoing, we are removing a good deal of material in one pass or cut, and light-duty routers are not up to this type of regular use.

A router may be used for rabbeting in one of three ways: hand-held with an edge guide attached, mounted into a table that is equipped with a fence, and as part of a panel router tool. (See Figures 6-5 to 6-7.)

Many cabinetmakers reserve the use of one hand-held router for rabbeting and for dadoing shelf standard "grooves." The tool is kept fitted with a sharp ⅝-in. straight bit and an edge guide. Only two adjustments are ever necessary with this router. Rabbet depth is controlled by raising or lowering the router bit in relation to its base. Rabbet width is dictated by adjusting the position of the edge guide. To run the detail, each piece to be rabbeted is simply placed on a stable, flat surface and secured in some way so that it will not move (clamped or set against blocks that have been secured to the table). Then the router is passed along the board. The router base glides on the face of the wood while the edge guide is held against its edge. The operator should wear both ear and eye protective gear. (The router is a very safe tool when used properly, but too many users do not give enough attention to protecting their ears from the high pitches produced by it.) This rabbeting system is especially good in small shops because it costs little and requires only limited space to use. Larger custom shops also use it because it is as fast as most other systems.

A table-mounted router can also be used to make rabbets in the various cabinet components. With a straight bit in the router, adjustments are very simple. Depth is determined by cutter height, and width by fence position. On the other hand, since a table router is most often used to cut decorative edge details, it is nearly impossible to reserve the use of one such tool only for machining rabbets and similar details. Frequent bit changes are necessary. Also, most tables constructed for use with a router are relatively small, and feeding longer pieces (such as tall bookcase partitions) across the setup can be less than convenient. Nevertheless, the table router can be used to yield a precise, clean rabbet. Pieces are simply fed through the setup face down and edge against the fence. Again, ear and eye protection is important. The table-mounted router system is best applied in smaller shops, where it is impossible to specialize the use of one router to a single detailing operation. It may also be applicable in very large shops where there is the luxury of specializing a table router to one rabbeting setup.

A panel-routing tool is simply a metal framework, similar to the type used with a panel saw, with a router mounted in it. The framework is designed so that workpieces are machined while in a nearly vertical position. The router, with its base, may be moved up and down only, but it is designed to perform both dadoing and rabbeting. With the straight bit again in the tool, depth of cut is controlled by moving the router in or out in relation to its base. Rabbet width is controlled by positioning the router and base in the desired position along its metal guides and locking in place. Workpieces are fed through the setup edgewise and horizontally. The edge of the board rides upon a metal fence, and the face of the board slides along the metal framework. If the router is machining the bottom edge of the board, as is usual, feeding is from right to left. A panel router is a very fast detailing system. Its main drawback is a fairly high price tag. Often employed in the largest shops were the volume of production is high, it is especially useful for repeated cuts.

Rabbeting with a Shaper. The shaper will cut rabbets of excellent quality when fitted with cutters of the right kind. Setting up for width and depth is similar to using the table-mounted router. There is a fence to locate for control of rabbet width, and the spindle, with its cutters, can be raised or lowered to dictate depth. Material is fed across the tool with its edge against the fence and its face on the table. (*Note*: The direction of rotation is reversible on many shapers, and the operator should take care to feed workpieces against the rotation only.) Still, shapers are not generally used for rabbeting in most shops unless there are many pieces to run. The shaper is a major investment, and setting it up to run a few rabbets may not be the wisest use of the tool. Most cabinetmakers opt for another method of machining to do the limited number of rabbets called for in the usual cabinet job.

The best rabbeting system and tool is a matter of choice, to some degree, but some systems are used more frequently than others in the trade today. For rabbeting of plywood and particleboard members, most cabinetmakers use either a hand-held router with an edge guide or dado head mounted in the table saw. To rabbet certain types of cabinet members, especially hardwood face frames or frame doors, it is usually better to employ a combination blade on the table saw and to make two setups and two cuts. This reduces tearing when rabbeting across the grain on hardwood members.

Dadoing

Dadoes are most often cut to give strength to the cabinet box. As discussed specifically in Chapter 2, ends, partitions, tops, shelves, and bottoms may receive dadoes. Trade standards suggest that their depth be ¼ in. The width of a dado is determined by the thickness of the cabinet member that will be received into it.

When adjustable shelf standard is called for on a job, vertical dadoes should be run to receive each piece of standard. Recessed standard not only looks superior to surface-mounted standard, but is easier for the assembler to locate and install. Naturally, the dimensions of these dadoes are a factor of the type of shelf standard employed, but they are most often ⅝ in. wide and approximately ⅛ in. deep. The detail's location in relation to the edge of the cabinet member is a factor of the width of the board. For ends and partitions that are 11¼ in. in width, as is very common for upper cabinets and bookcases, most cabinetmakers place the dado 1¼ in. in from each edge. A general rule that may be followed is to locate the dadoes for shelf standard about 1 in. from the edge for each foot of width in the board. Thus, in standard base cabinets that are to receive shelf standard, the dadoes should be located about 2 in. from each edge.

If finished ends are to receive rabbets for backs or for a scribe, the location of the shelf standard dado is naturally affected. The distance from the edge of such a board to the dado for shelf standard must be increased by the width of the rabbet. For example, if the finished end of a standard base cabinet is to receive a 1-in.-wide rabbet for back and scribe, the detail for adjustable shelf standard would be cut not 2 in. but 3 in. in from the rear edge.

Finally, the detailer may need to consider whether shelf standard dadoes are to be run the entire length of ends and partitions from top to bottom, or if the standard is to be stopped a reasonable distance from the ends. Again, this is usually a shop standard. Since shelving will almost never be mounted within several inches of the top or bottom of a cabinet, some woodworkers prefer to end the shelf standards a certain distance from the ends of components, saving a bit on the cost of metal shelf standard. They develop a setup for "stop dadoes" as part of the detailing process.

Others believe that the few pennies' worth of standard saved is not worth the additional effort of stopping the dado mid-cut and squaring it out with a chisel. Their reasoning is sound.

Certain cabinet accessory components will also require dadoing. Drawer sides are sometimes dadoed to receive backs, a double dado may be run to secure the sides to the front or subfront on a drawer box, and all members of a drawer box are usually dadoed to receive the drawer bottom. The depth of all these details is a trade standard at ¼ in. Hampers, hinged pantries, and lazy susans are also constructed by using dadoes, and these, too, are usually ¼ in. deep.

The first step is again to mark all pieces for dado location. The description is a bit artificial at this point; in an effective operation, box parts are marked for all details at once—rabbets, dadoes, and miters—and then the actual machining is also carried out without interruption.

A detailer will naturally develop his or her own specific operation in marking cabinet body parts, but the system will follow either the shop drawing approach or the layout stick approach. In a shop drawing system, the detailer refers to the individual sketch or drawing for each case, determines where and how each piece will be fit into the finished cabinet, and marks with two lines the exact placement of each dado. (While doing this, the detailer marks the location for rabbets, miters, and all other details, to avoid handling the same piece more than once.)

The production sketch has written measurements that must be read and then measured out on the individual piece. Some addition or subtraction may be necessary to translate the written measurements on paper into the real measurements that are used to make detail marks. Figure 6-8 is a production drawing which gives all the necessary information for detailing and building a particular cabinet box. Focusing on the drawing, we would gather all the pieces

of the box. If these were properly marked and stacked by the cutter, this is quite simple. The next thing to do would be to identify each component and locate the details needed on it. The finished end would be the easiest to identify since it is wider (12½ in.) than the other material on the cabinet, and since it is very likely cut from some type of A-2 plywood, whereas the other cabinet components may be of MDF or fir plywood. This piece would be marked for a rear-edge rabbet (⅜ in. deep by 1½ in. wide). This does not have to be a careful mark since the accuracy of the rabbet will come in setting up the machinery to cut it. It does matter, though, which edge the detailer chooses for the front edges of all cabinet components so that there is less possibility of an assembler building the cabinet backwards. Using an accurate tape, we would next place lines for locating dadoes, especially if a router setup is to be used for dadoing. With table saw dadoing, the accuracy of these lines is less important, since the fence is used to place dadoes exactly where they are called for. Measuring from the bottom of the finished end near the front edge, we place small lines as follows:

- At ½ and 1¼ in. for the dado to receive the bottom.
- At 9¼ and 10 in. for the lower shelf.
- At 18 and 18¾ in. for a shelf.
- At 29¼ in. to receive the top. (This is a rabbet, but it is marked and machined just like the other dadoes on the piece.)

The other box components, other than adjustable shelves, are distinguishable only by length, since they all have the same thickness (¾ in.) and width (11 in.), and since they may all be made of the same type of secondary material. The adjustable shelves should be 10⅝ in. wide to

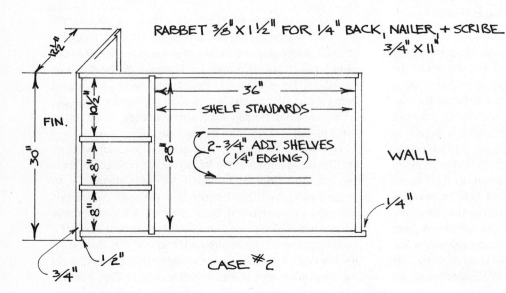

RABBET ⅜" × 1½" FOR ¼" BACK, NAILER, + SCRIBE
¾" × 11"

FIGURE 6-8 Production drawing showing construction details in a cabinet box.

12½"

FIN.

30"

10½"

8"

8"

36"

SHELF STANDARDS

2-¾" ADJ. SHELVES (¼" EDGING)

20"

WALL

¼"

¾"   ½"

CASE #2

allow for the addition of the edging noted in the drawing, and these shelves receive no details. In case 2 (Figure 6-8), if all dadoes are standard depth, the various pieces have these lengths:

- Wall end, 29 in.
- Partition, 28½ in.
- Top, 49¼ in.
- Bottom, 50 in.
- Fixed shelves, 12½ in.
- Adjustable shelves, 35¾ in.

Marking of the other components should proceed similarly to that for the finished end. The partition's left side would receive four dado lines—at 8¼, 9, 17, and 17¾ in. when measured from the bottom. Its right side, as well as the left side of the wall end, should be marked with reminders to run the dadoes or grooves for shelf standard. The placement of these dadoes (about 1¼ in. from the front and back edges) does not need accurate marking since, again, this type of accuracy comes from the actual machine setup. The dado, or rabbet, is marked on the wall end to receive the top, with a mark at 28¼ in. from its bottom. Measuring from the left, both the bottom and the top will receive a dado marked with lines at 12¼ and 13 in. The bottom will receive a second dado, located by measuring from the left and placing lines at 49 and 49¾ in.

With the case completely marked, the detailer proceeds to other individual cabinets and drawings on the same job since they are likely to have similar types of details. When the entire job is marked, setups are made and machining begins.

Dadoing with the Table Saw. The table saw, with a dado head in place, may be used to cut dadoes in much the same way as it is used for cutting rabbets. The desired width of the dado is set when mounting the dado head in place on the arbor of the saw. With the blade-and-chipper style of dado head, the detailer picks the appropriate size and number of chippers to be set in place between the two blades of the dado head. Such a dado head will usually have a ⅟₁₆-in. chipper and a number of ⅛-in. chippers. It may also have a ¼-in. chipper. By using different combinations, it is possible to set up for dado widths from the minimum ¼ in., using only the two blades, to a maximum of ¹³⁄₁₆ in. or more, in ⅟₁₆ in. increments. For selecting finer adjustments, a cabinetmaker will often make cardboard or paper spacers that can be positioned on the saw arbor between the blades and chippers of the dado head. We can thus arrive at dadoes of perfect width, even for accepting plywood that is not standard thickness. (*Note*: As an example, ¾-in. A-2 plywood often has a true thickness of less than ¾ in., but greater than ¹¹⁄₁₆ in. Cabinetmakers

FIGURE 6-9 Blade-and-chipper dado head and adjustable dado head.

who want perfect dado joints with such material often use spacers to achieve these cuts.)

A second type of dado head that may be used on the table saw for either rabbeting or dadoing is also available. Often called an adjustable dado, its width of cut is set by "dialing" the single blade within its eccentric mount. Many such dado heads may be set up to cut any width between ⅛ and ¹⁵⁄₁₆ in. The quality of adjustable dado heads has generally been improved in recent years, and they are used much more frequently in today's trade than they used to be. Setting up for dado cutting is much faster with this type of dado head, and changing from one width to another is also much easier to do than with the blade-and-chipper style of head. On the other hand, using an adjustable dado head can result in more chipping than is desirable on some types of material, particularly when cutting across the grain as we do so often in machining cabinet details. Since it results in cleaner cuts, the blade-and-chipper type of dado head is probably considered superior by most cabinetmakers. (See Figure 6-9.)

To set the depth of a dado cut on the table saw, the arbor is naturally raised or lowered to the desired height. The placement of dadoes may be controlled by proper positioning of the fence. If a dado is desired ½ in. from the end of a board, as for the bottom dado of the finished end in Figure 6-8, the fence is set and locked this distance from the inside of the blade. The end of the cabinet component is placed against the fence, and the piece is fed through the dadoing setup face down, perhaps using the miter gauge for control. It is important to keep good downward pressure on each piece that is fed through the dado setup to ensure even dadoes of the correct depth. Right-handed woodworkers should use the miter gauge and feed the material with the left hand while maintaining downward pressure with the right hand. Since this pressure should be applied close enough to the dado head to do some good, special care must be taken to avoid an accident. The use of a push block to apply this downward pressure is advisable. (See Figure 6-10.)

It is also possible to run dadoes on the table saw without the fence, using only the miter gauge as a guide in feeding the material. In fact, this procedure may be nec-

FIGURE 6-10 Cutting a dado in a finished end. Note the use of the fence and the hand position.

essary with longer pieces. Naturally, it may be wise to extend the face of the miter gauge with a straight piece of wood. This will improve control. When running dadoes in this way, the detailer should place marks on the saw table in front of the dado head to indicate the exact machining location of the cutters. The marks indicating dado location on each box component can then be lined up exactly and safely in front of the dado head without turning off the saw after each cut. Each dado is perfectly lined up, and the cut is made, again holding the material firmly against the face of the miter gauge and with even downward pressure. (See Figure 6-11.) The results will be as good as when the fence is used for a guide, but the great advantage in employing the fence is in time savings. On smaller jobs, this will not be significant, but on larger ones it will, since the number of setups will be reduced. When machining details, we keep

FIGURE 6-11 Dadoing without a fence on the table saw. The operator matches marks on the cabinet part with marks on the saw table itself.

setup changes to a minimum, and all components to get the same detail are machined at one time. For example, if we set up to run the shelf standard grooves with a dado head on the table saw, we machine every end and partition on the job which requires this detail before setting up differently.

Employing the table saw to cut dadoes is an effective method. Depending on the type of material being machined, the dado head may produce some tear-out of face veneers. However, the system is fast, and there is no restriction on the width of components that may be machined in this way. Dado cutting with the table saw is practiced widely, in large and small cabinet operations.

Dadoing with the Radial Arm Saw. Like the table saw, a radial arm saw may also be fitted with a dado head and applied for cutting dadoes. Since the saw is a stationary tool with a good deal of power, it can be a timesaver. Since the depth of the dado is controlled by raising or lowering the arm, the detailer who uses this method must make sure that each piece to be machined is held down firmly against the table. If this is not done, the depth of cut may vary from one dado to another—creating a major problem for the assembler. It is also important to make sure that the arm of the saw is perfectly parallel to the table and that the surface of the table will not flex from the pressure applied to it. Dadoes cut on improperly aligned or insufficiently supported tools may vary in depth from one end of the cut to the other.

Accurate dado cuts on the radial saw depend on accurately made marks to indicate dado location. The cuts are usually made in a way similar to the way that pieces of stock are cut to length on the radial arm saw, except that no block or clamp is generally used for positioning pieces. Each component is placed flat on the table, and the marks to indicate dado location are aligned with the dado head. The piece is then held firmly against the table and fence with one hand while the other hand draws the saw motor out to make the cut. (See Figure 6-12.)

For dadoing certain types of cabinet parts, the radial arm saw is excellent. There is no need to handle a piece more than once because all the dadoes on a single piece may be cut with the same setup. If the finished end of an upper is to be machined with dadoes of the same width to receive a bottom, two shelves, and a top (as in figure 6-8), it is simply positioned and cut four times in exactly the same way.

On the other hand, using the radial arm saw for dado cutting does have some drawbacks. First is the width limitation. If stock is wider than 15 in. or so (the distance from the fence of the saw to the position of the dado head when the saw is pulled all the way to its limit at the end of the arm), it cannot be dadoed with a single crosscut on the radial arm saw. To achieve dadoes in wider stock on the radial saw, the detailer must do one of two things: either

FIGURE 6-12 Dadoing with the radial arm saw. Notice that the width of cut is limited by the length of the arm. (Courtesy of DeWalt Division of Black & Decker (U.S.) Inc.)

turn each piece end for end so that dadoes may be achieved in two cuts or set up the tool as if ripping, and feed components through the setup with the fence as a guide. Both of these are more time-consuming options.

A second complication to dadoing with the radial arm saw is that a single depth setting may not be correct for all the dadoes on a single cabinet. This is because of the way we arrive at the depth setting on the tool. If set to yield a ¼-in.-deep dado in ¾-in. plywood, there will be ½ in. between the bottom of the dado head and the surface of the table. If the same depth setting is used for ⅝-in. material, it will yield a dado only ⅛ in. deep. Figure 6-13 is a production drawing indicating a box design that would present this problem. Instead of changing setups, many cabinetmakers circumvent this problem by putting a spacer board under the thinner stocks and then running the dadoes exactly as described earlier.

As with the table saw, employing the radial arm saw to cut dadoes can be a fast and efficient method. In fact, no system is much faster for dadoing of pieces up to 15 in.

Unlike the table saw, it is not really designed for quick and easy dadoing of wider stocks. Large cabinet shops may employ the tool in this way because they have the luxury of using other tools for machining wide pieces. The detailer in a small shop will generally do nearly all dadoing with a table saw or a router.

Both the table saw and the radial arm saw may be fitted with a dado head for cutting dadoes. This means that either method can be used to cut details that are straight, accurate, and square, but it also means that either method may result in some undesirable tear-away or chipping of face veneers, especially when cutting across the grain. For this reason, many cabinetmakers use a router to do their dadoing.

Dadoing with Routers. Routers, fitted with straight bits, are capable of machining precise dadoes with very little tearing of wood fibers. This is partly because of the high speeds developed by the tool. There are a number of ways to guide the router across material to be detailed, but regardless of the guiding system that is chosen, the woodworker should remember that dadoing involves the removal of a good deal of material in one cut. Therefore, it is important to utilize a heavy-duty router of good quality, to incorporate carbide-tipped bits (which will give long service and minimize burning), and to keep the dadoing bits as sharp as possible.

In all router–dadoing systems, the material to be detailed is clamped securely in position and the router is drawn across it. The base of the router rides directly on the surface of the material. The depth of cut is controlled by raising or lowering the router in its base. Obviously, the size of router bit determines dado width.

The proficient detailer will realize that the size of a new router bit will not necessarily conform to the exact width of cut desired. As we have already observed, the actual thickness of body components is not necessarily the

FIGURE 6-13 Production drawing for the box design of a base cabinet. The finished end is 3/4 in. thick material, while other components are 5/8 in. thick.

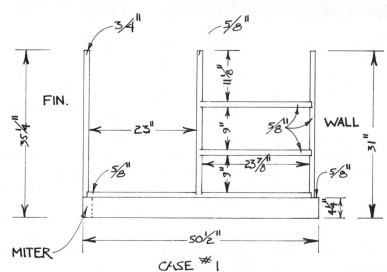

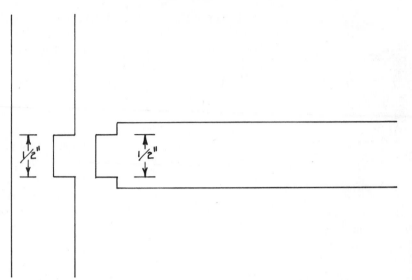

FIGURE 6-14 Blind dado joint. The shelf has been rabbeted, leaving a "tongue" that fits the dado channel exactly.

same as its nominal thickness. The cabinetmaker has several options available for dealing with this problem. One option is to accept joints that are not quite as tight as they could be, but many cabinetmakers would not even consider this. A second option is to grind the router bit to the exact size desired. The trouble with this approach is that we are wasting a lot of steel or carbide, and our bit will obviously not last as long. On the other hand, when router bits are sharpened, they lose some of their cutting width. Furthermore, a particular type of sheet good will generally be a consistent thickness. For example, sheets of ¾-in. A-2 birch plywood will consistently have an actual thickness close to $^{23}/_{32}$ in. Many types of plywood will have this actual thickness. Thus the first time a ¾-in. router bit becomes dull, it can be ground to cut dadoes for this type of plywood. A carbide cutting edge will give long service, so that this solution is not as wasteful as it would first seem. A third solution to the problem is simply to use a narrower-cutting router bit and cut each dado in two passes. This is time consuming, but many woodworkers use this solution anyway, at least in part. Actually, the modern cabinetmaker employs parts of all the above-described solutions to the problem. A hair's width of space is acceptable in the dado joints of most cabinetry, it is possible to build a collection of router bits to cut for the various common thicknesses of cabinet box members, and double cutting of dadoes is also employed from time to time. Naturally, there are other, more complex solutions (such as the blind dado illustrated in Figure 6-14), but the use of such joints is a designer's decision. Also, blind joints are usually reserved for furniture building.

Dadoing with a router requires the application of a reliable guiding system. A panel router cuts dadoes as well as rabbets, and there are other hardware systems available which employ a "built-in" router to create a stationary dadoing tool. (See Figure 6-15.) Large cabinet shops often

FIGURE 6-15 Stationary hardware that employs a router as a dado machine.

invest the money and space required for one of these tools, to speed up the dadoing process. Cutting dadoes with such a tool is very fast and simple. Since the router is guided to cut in exactly the same location time after time, it is a simple matter to position each piece of wood correctly against the fence, clamp it in place (such tools have their own clamps built in), and draw the router across it. The thickness of material is not a factor in controlling dado depth.

It is also very simple to construct an excellent router guiding system, a "dadoing jig," of wood. It consists of a fairly large, smooth board, parallel wooden strips fastened along the front and rear edges, and a hardwood strip to serve as a guide fence for the router. The fence must be mounted perpendicular to the two parallel strips. The edge of the router base glides along the fence for each cut. (See Figure 6-16.) With a base and legs, this dado aid can be set up as a stationary tool, or it can be kept as an easily moved and stored item in shops where space is at a premium.

FIGURE 6-16 Wooden guiding system used for dadoing with a router. Note the parallel front and rear strips and the perpendicular fence.

To use this jig, each piece to be detailed is slid into position beneath the guide fence. The dado marks on each board are lined up in the exact path of the router bit. The board is held in place with a C-clamp for machining. The router should be drawn across the surface of the board toward the operator, with the router to the left of the fence. This dadoing system can be used with speed to yield perfect cuts. When constructing the device, sufficient space must be allowed between the front and rear strips to allow for the widest frequently used stocks to be machined.

The choice of a dado-cutting system depends on several factors. Router systems will generally deliver cleaner dadoes more consistently than will dado head systems. The table saw, the radial arm saw, and the panel router are quite versatile because they can be used for both dadoing and rabbeting, but hand-held routers also have versatility. In addition, since routers are much less expensive than stationary tools, it is a very real option to purchase several routers and specialize their use. One might be outfitted for running shelf standard channels, another for cross-grain dadoing in conjunction with a wooden dadoing jig, and still another for rabbeting. The woodworker will naturally want to experiment with different approaches and choose the method best suited to his or her own shop and philosophy.

Mitering

Miter joints are used for several purposes. Moldings, edge trims, and frames (such as picture frames) are often joined with simple miters. The finished ends of base cabinets can easily be joined to toekicks in a miter joint. Figure 6-13 is a production drawing calling for this type of joint.

Marking pieces for mitering is very simple. Pieces such as the toekick require only a "reminder" mark such as an arrow pointing toward the end of the piece where the miter is to be cut. The miter will be cut all the way across the end of the board. Finished ends require a bit more care in marking, especially if mitering is to be done with a hand saw or portable tool. Of course, we mark for the miter at the same time that we mark for other details. After the front edge of the finished end is determined, perpendicular lines are drawn on the face of the piece to indicate the placement of the cut and its length. Note that the cut is a "stop cut." If cutting is to be done with a hand saw, a combination square should be used to indicate the angle of cut (45°).

Through cuts of narrow pieces can be done easily on the table saw or with a chop saw. The chop saw need only be set at its 45° setting. With the table saw, the saw blade should be tilted to achieve the miter angle. Feeding is done with the aid of the miter gauge. In using either tool, care must be taken to line up the cut correctly, or there is a good chance that the miter cut will shorten the toekick or other board. Other mitering setups are possible, of course. A "jig" can be made to allow miter cuts on the radial arm saw without moving its arm. A similar device can be constructed to use in conjunction with an edge sander. If there are only a few cuts, it may be just as fast to cut the miters by hand with a conventional miter box as it would be to change setups on a machine.

Clearly, the easiest and fastest way to make miter stop cuts is to use the table saw. The blade is tilted again, but this time the fence is positioned to achieve the cut in exactly the right place. For this operation the blade should be raised as high as possible, to prevent cutting too far on the bottom face of the end as the piece is fed into the saw. After all the stop cuts are made on a job, the blade can be returned to a safer height. (See Figure 6-17.)

FIGURE 6-17 Stop mitering a right-hand finished end to receive the toekick. Note that it would be impossible to feed from the front of this saw and achieve the same cut on the opposite (left) finished end.

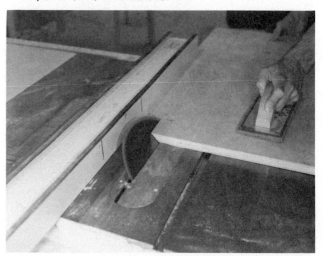

The blade of a table saw will usually tilt to the right, but some tilt the opposite way. However, few commonly available table saws are capable of tilting in both directions. This means that it is only possible to perform the mitering stop cuts for one type of finished end from the front of the saw. For example, a table saw that tilts to the right is readily adapted to stop cut miters on right-hand finished ends, but not for the same cut on left-hand finished ends. In this situation, some cabinetmakers will feed the left-hand finished ends from the rear of the saw, but this is not recommended, for reasons of safety. The ideal shop may have at least two table saws, with one capable of tilting each way, but this is clearly not reasonable for small shops. An alternative is necessary.

It is really not as difficult as it would seem to free hand a miter cut with a sharp crosscut saw. The keys are to find a way of holding the material securely, to make an accurate start on the 45° line marked on the bottom of the finished end, and to have confidence. Other realistic alternatives are to use a saber saw or a portable circular saw. Most such tools are adaptable to this use simply by tilting their bases to the correct angle. Then it is just a matter of cutting along the precisely marked line.

No matter how the miter cut is made, the detailer should not make the perpendicular cut from the front edge toward the stop miter cut. This should be left for the assembler to do so that the cut can be made to line up perfectly with the bottom of the face frame. (See Figure 6-18.)

There is another important mitering technique that should be mentioned here, since it is often used to make the joint between a finished end and a finished back on an island cabinet. The operation is performed on a table saw with the blade tilted toward the fence. Since the saw blade will actually be in contact with the fence, a protection board must be attached with screws or a clamp. We want as nearly perfect a cut as possible, so fence position is critical. The

FIGURE 6-18 An assembler should square out the notch started with a miter cut. It will match the face frame perfectly.

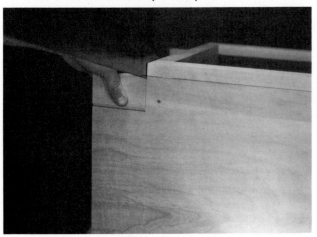

FIGURE 6-19 Mitering the rear edge of a finished end to be joined to a finished back. Note the protection board in place on the fence. The board should have a rabbet cut in it, as shown, to prevent the scrap piece from being pinched and hurled out by the blade.

blade should be lowered to make this adjustment and then turned on and raised to cut into the surface of the protection board. For a perfect joint, the blade should disappear into the surface of the protective board at a height from the surface of the table which is exactly equal to the thickness of the boards to be machined. Through some trial and error and with a few practice pieces, this adjustment is easy to accomplish. (See Figure 6-19.) In this operation, it is extremely important for the area behind the saw to be kept clear of onlookers. The thin triangular strip that is cut from the edge of the cabinet component can be transformed into a missile. To minimize this possibility, the protection board should have a rabbet cut into it below the point at which the saw blade enters it. This reduces the chance for the narrow triangular strip to become pinched between the saw blade and the fence.

Splining

A spline joint is a very effective way to join flat boards together edge to edge. (See Figure 6-20.) The most common use for this is in fabricating finished backs wider than 48 in. The cutter supplies two or more plywood boards with which to make the back. The detailer may choose to machine them for splining or to drill matching dowel holes for the joint.

The machining for a spline joint may be performed with either a table saw or a router. To cut the slots with a router, the detailer simply fits the tool with a specially designed splining bit, called a slotting cutter. Such bits vary in cutting depth and thickness, but for splining we probably choose a bit that will yield a slot at least ⅛ in. thick and ½-in. deep. For ¾ in. material, the cut should be thicker. The cut is made with the stock held securely in a horizontal position. The router base glides on the face of the stock while a bearing on the bit itself rolls along the edge of the board. The slots will match perfectly.

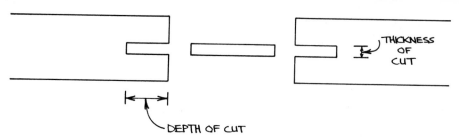

FIGURE 6-20 Construction detail for a spline joint. In 3/4-in. material, the spline should be at least 3/16 in. thick.

Cutting the slots with the table saw may be a bit more difficult. To yield slots that are thicker than ⅛ in., it is necessary either to make two cuts with each piece or to fit the arbor with a dado head. The height of the blade determines the depth of cut, and the fence is positioned to locate the slot. The boards must be fed edgewise through the setup. It is possible to cut perfect slots with this method, but it can also be difficult to hold the large pieces perfectly flat against the fence. Using the router is probably a superior method.

Regardless of which system is employed, the detailer should cut splines that will fit the slots properly, with enough room for a thin film of glue. It is also important to machine with the base of the router or the fence of the table saw in contact with the face of each board. This allows us the best chance of getting a perfectly flat joint, regardless of slight variations in the thickness of the boards to be joined.

Notching

It is sometimes necessary to cut notches into a partition to allow the installation of continuous nailers and countertop hold-downs. Since these cuts are very short stop cuts, set-

ting up the table saw to do them is probably a case of machining overkill. Such notches can be cut just as quickly and virtually as straight with a saber saw, even on a large job with many repetitive cuts. Using a band saw or a handsaw is a satisfactory alternative. Wherever a notch is necessary, the width and length of the cut are determined and marked on the board. If the partition to be notched is to be received into a dado, the detailer should remember to add the depth of the dado to the length of the notch cut. (See Figure 6-21.)

Mastery of the detailing process will require some experience, but the reader should not hesitate to plunge ahead with some of the systems we have discussed. It should be clear that there are almost always several ways to accomplish the same task, and determining the "best" way depends on the woodworker's own preferences as well as the types of tools available and the size of the shop.

FACINGS

Facings may be frames which lend strength to the cabinet, or they may be nothing more than edging used to cover the raw edges of sheet goods that make up the cabinet box. To machine frames, the detailer must interpret each produc-

FIGURE 6-21 *Left:* Base partition showing location of notches for nailer and hold-downs; *right:* upper partition showing location of notches. Note that the notches are 1/4 in. longer than the width of nailers. This is because the partition will be received into dadoes.

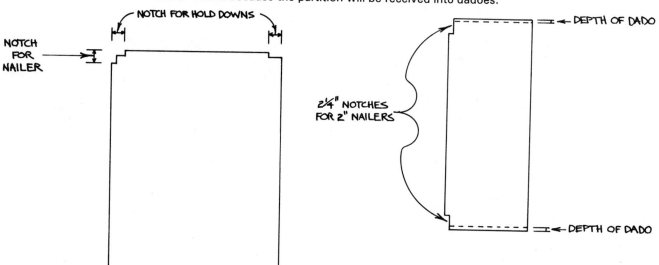

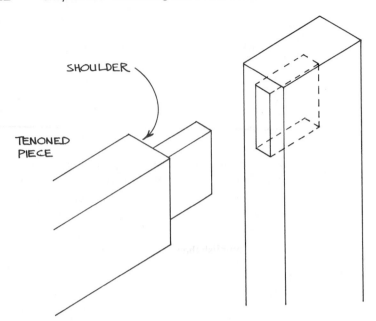

FIGURE 6-22 Basic design for a mortise-and-tenon joint.

tion drawing or stick in order to identify frame members and mark them to be precisely machined. There are three general methods for joining the members of the face frame.

Mortising and Tenoning

Face frames assembled with mortise-and-tenon joints are generally stronger than those assembled using other methods. This is one reason that a cabinetmaker chooses this system of assembly. Others employ the system because they consider it more old-fashioned and therefore superior. Constructing all face frames with the mortise-and-tenon system can be an expensive investment in time for most cabinetmakers.

There are many variations in the exact design of mortises and tenons, but basically each mortise-and-tenon joint consists of two parts which must be machined to fit together precisely. (See Figure 6-22.) On a standard face frame, the ends of all rails are shaped to make a tenon that will fit into mortises in the stiles and mullions. The ends of mullions are tenoned to fit mortises in the top and bottom rails.

Naturally, if the shop builds frames with mortise-and-tenon joints as a standard procedure, the detailer will be familiar with shop standards as to exact dimensions for all machining operations. When it is time to set up for detailing the individual parts, the length of the tongue-like tenon (and therefore the depth of the mortise) has already been determined by the designer. The thickness of the tenon should be approximately one-third of the total thickness of the stock. The detailer should first identify each piece of the frame by referring to the production drawing. Tenon location, since it will invariably be on the ends of pieces, need only be marked with some type of reminder as to

where the machining must be done. All marks should be on the rear face of each rail and mullion to serve as a reminder to perform all machining with the front of the stock as the reference. For example, if a fence is used as a guide in any part of the tenoning operation, the front face of each piece should be positioned against the fence whenever possible. This is also true when it comes to machining the mortise. (See Figure 6-23.)

Marking the mortise location is a matter of exact measurement. The detailer must figure exact machining location from measurements on the layout stick or drawing, accounting for the exact dimensions of the holes to be used

FIGURE 6-23 In machining mortises and tenons, the front faces of material are used as the depth reference. This face is therefore positioned against fences, and so on, as much as possible.

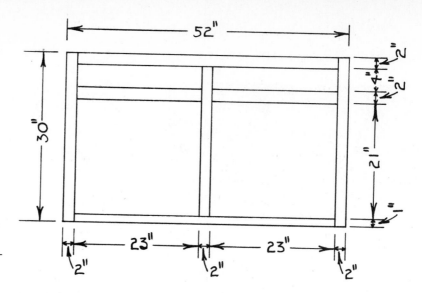

FIGURE 6-24 Production drawing for base cabinet face frame.

as mortises. Suppose that we are preparing to machine a face frame for a base cabinet. (See Figure 6-24.) The stock is ¾ in. thick. Our shop generally uses tenons that are ¼ in. × 1½ in. × 1½ in.). On pieces that are 2 in. wide, there will be a ¼-in. shoulder all the way around each tenon. Centering the mortise on each board will be taken care of by setting up properly (fence position on a drill press, mortiser, etc.). The depth of the holes will be determined with a proper setting for boring depth. Depth should be slightly more than the 1½-in. length of the tenons. The only exact marks needed are along the edges of the boards where we want to indicate the linear limits of the mortises. The top rail is 51 in. long, and the lines for the mortise will be exactly in the middle, at 24¾ and 26¼ in., measured from either end. The lines on the bottom rail should match, but since the width of this piece is less than the length of our standard tenon, an adaptation must be made. The depth of the mortise can be reduced to accept a shorter tenon, or the joint can be made as usual. The part of the tenon that projects all the way through the rail can then be trimmed off flush. The stiles should be marked as a pair. (Since these parts would be easy to machine or assemble in reverse position, it should be obvious how important it is to distinguish between the back and front of the pieces in the frame. If they are reversed, we may not get a flat joint.) Measuring from the top, the edges of the stiles should be marked at ¼ and 1¾ in. for the top rail. For receiving the tenon of the drawer rail, the stile should be marked at 6¼ and 7¾ in. To receive the bottom rail, an adaptation is again necessary. For the sake of strength, the mortise should probably be cut out to receive a full 1-in.-wide tenon. The mortises on either side of the mullion will match each other, and the mating tenons must be shortened to fit into the available depth. Measured from the top end of the mullion, our mortising lines will be located at 5¾ and 7¼ in. Other frames in the job would be marked similarly before machining begins. For the best possible fit, mortises should be machined first.

Mortising Systems. There are several methods for machining mortises. Most of these make use of drill bits to accomplish the task. Since drill bits are only capable of making round holes, it is necessary to utilize a system for squaring out a perfect rectangular mortise.

A mortising machine is an expensive piece of equipment, but it is capable of cutting mortises more speedily than other systems. It functions in much the same way that a drill press works except that the drill bit is surrounded by a very sharp square sheath or "hollow chisel" which trims away additional wood as the bit is punching its hole. What is left behind is a square hole. (See Figure 6-25.) The tool may easily be set to repeat the same boring depth on each cut. The table is equipped with a fence that may be set for proper centering of the mortise in different thicknesses of wood. The front or face of each piece should be set against the fence for machining to assure good, flat joints. For pre-

FIGURE 6-25 Hollow-chisel mortising attachment. Note the square sheath. (Courtesy of Delta International Machinery Corp.)

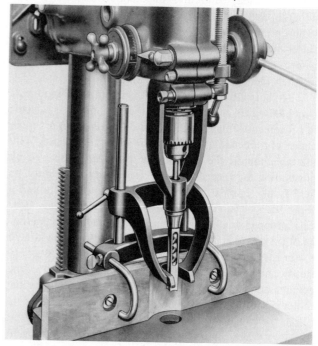

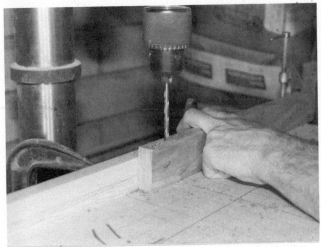

FIGURE 6-26 Drilling a series of holes for a mortise. Note the secure fence and the clamped stock.

FIGURE 6-27 Mortising with a table-mounted router. For better control a second fence is desirable.

cise mortising, each piece should be clamped securely against the fence.

A drill press can be set up to perform mortising. A fence should be clamped onto the table of the drill press as an aid in centering. The drilling depth should be determined and locked to be consistent for all holes. For each hole drilled, the face member should be clamped in place. The detailer begins by drilling the two end holes for each mortise, and then bores a series of overlapping holes in between. (See Figure 6-26.) Each mortise will have to be squared out by hand with a chisel and mallet. The time required is extensive. Other drilling tools may obviously be employed to do the boring for a mortise. A hand-held electric drill may be used in conjunction with a dowel-centering jig and a depth stop, or a horizontal boring machine is an option, but with these, the cabinetmaker must still chisel out the flat, square mortise. Owners of horizontal borers generally opt for drilling a lot fewer holes and joining their face frames with dowel joints.

A heavy-duty router, hand-held or table mounted, may be used for mortising. The thickness of cut is a factor of bit selection, of course. Depth of cut is again a simple matter of proper adjustment of the tool within its base. With the table router, the mortise cut is properly centered by positioning the fence. Each piece to be mortised must be held firmly against the fence (some cabinetmakers add a second fence, parallel to the first, as a pecision and safety aid), dropped down on the spinning bit, and fed to the limits of the desired cut. (See Figure 6-27.) Using a hand-held router requires addition of the edge guide as well as a very steady hand. The stock is clamped on edge securely. The detailer must get the cut started by carefully plunging the router bit into the stock with the tool on. This is done by tilting the router, with the edge guide against the face of the stock. (See Figure 6-28.) For achieving the precision

desirable in a mortise-and-tenon joint, the hand-held router method is probably not the most reliable. Of course, with any router mortising, it will be necessary to square out the ends of each cut.

The machines that can be used to cut mortises are all improvements to making the cuts with a chisel and mallet,

FIGURE 6-28 Using a hand-held router to cut a mortise. Note the less-than-reliable starting position.

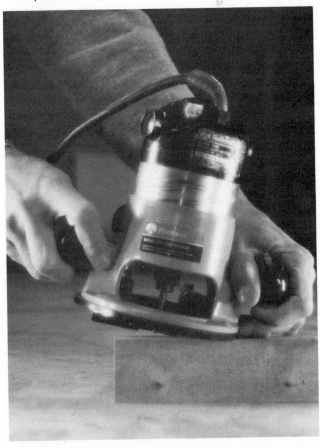

but most modern cabinetmakers have gone to entirely different face-joining systems, for obvious reasons. Cabinetmakers who invest in hollow-chisel mortisers are either "of
the old school" and believe that any other joining system
is the sign of inferior craftsmanship, or they are owners of
large custom shops where the volume of work justifies such
an investment. For even when the detailer has completed
all the mortises on his or her job, the tenons must still be
cut.

Tenoning Systems.   The tool that will most easily
cut away material to leave a tenon is a single-end tenoner.
Like the mortiser, however, it is not usually available in
the small shop.

It is fairly easy to machine rails and mullions on a
table saw, using either a dado head or a saw blade. In using
a dado head, the height setting for the blades and chippers
is critical in order that the tenons will fit perfectly into their
mortises. If the mortises were machined exactly on center,
one set up of the dado head may be used to mill away the
same amount of material from both faces of each piece,
leaving a tenon of correct thickness. (See Figure 6-29.) In
fact, with the tenons in our example above, the same setup
can also be used to make haunch cuts—the cuts that bring
the tenon to correct width after the thickness of the tenon
has been milled. This is because, in our example, the
shoulder that surrounded the tenon was exactly the same
(¼ in.) all the way around the tenon. Establishing the dimensions of the tenon is based on careful setups to remove
exactly the right amount of material on each shoulder cut.
The length of the tenon is controlled by using the fence.
The miter gauge is used for feeding each piece of material.
The tenoning cuts can be made on the table saw using a
combination or cutoff blade, too, by making a series of

FIGURE 6-30 Making the thickness cuts for
a tenon by feeding stock through the blade
vertically. This method can be unreliable.

cuts. On the first cut, the blade height is the same as the
length of the tenon, and the fence is positioned so that the
outside of the blade will make the shoulder cuts. Each rail
or mullion must be fed on end, with the front or back in
contact with the fence, and a perfectly vertical, steady position for each piece is important. A push block is an absolute necessity in this operation. To help keep the stock
firmly against the fence, a feather board may be clamped
to the saw table, or the push block can be designed to
"hook" around the stock. (See Figure 6-30.) If the materials for the frame are of a reliably consistent thickness,
this setup can be used to make the first two shoulder cuts
by feeding with one face against the fence and then the
other. After this first cut has been made on all pieces, the
setup must be changed to make a perpendicular cut to establish the shoulders of the tenon. Pieces are fed again with
the miter gauge, but it is important to line up each cut carefully because the fence should *not* be used to control tenon
length. The small scrap of wood that falls away as the
shoulder cut is completed can become pinched between
fence and blade. (See Figure 6-31.) If haunch cuts are necessary, the woodworker will probably want to do these with
some other tool. It is bothersome to set up the table saw
for these. The haunch cuts may be made using the radial
arm saw, a saber or band saw, or even a handsaw.

Some cabinetmakers find it convenient to machine
tenons with a dado head mounted in their radial arm saws.
This is effective if the tool is properly set up, with the blades
cutting perfectly perpendicular to the fence and the arm
exactly parallel to the table. The depth of shoulder cuts is
naturally controlled by adjustment of the height of the arm.
A block can be clamped or tacked in place to control tenon
length. The end of each piece is positioned against the block
and then cut. Of course, if the tenons are to be exactly in

FIGURE 6-29 Making the shoulder cuts with
a dado head on a table saw. On this operation,
it is all right to employ both the fence and the
miter gauge.

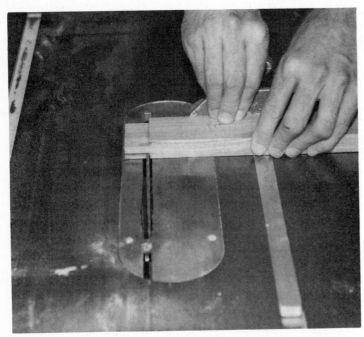

FIGURE 6-31 Completing the tenon shoulder cut on a table saw. Note that the fence is not used.

the middle of the pieces, all the widthwise shoulder cuts can be made with this one setup. After excess material is removed from one side, the piece is simply flipped over and machined on the other side. Haunch cuts are just as easy to make. We have only to raise the saw arm to the correct height.

Other than using a single-end tenoner, the fastest tenoning system is surely the radial arm saw equipped with dado head, but the table saw–dado head system is reasonably efficient as well. The table saw is perhaps a bit more dependable for accuracy, as well. A few other machines can also be set up or adapted to perform tenoning. The shaper can be fitted with a rabbeting-type knife to do the job, for example. On such a setup, fence position dictates tenon length, and the knife height controls the thickness of the shoulder cut. Pieces are fed with a miter gauge. The main drawback to this method is that the shaper knives can leave some splintered or chipped face members due to the way that they are designed to remove material. Of course, woodworkers with a lot of time on their hands may prefer to mark each tenon with a scratch line and cut it with a dovetail saw.

Making mortise-and-tenon joints is sometimes a necessity for the crafter of wood, and cabinetmakers should be prepared to make this type of joint. However, most practitioners of the modern trade do not assemble face frames with this method because today's customers are generally unwilling to pay for the additional time required. Face frames joined with mortises and tenons are unquestionably stronger than those assembled with dowels or

screws, but it can reasonably be argued that using mortise-and-tenon joints in the face frames of all our cabinetry is a case of overengineering. "Toe-screwed" face frames are a fairly recent development, but there is much evidence that dowel joints will last for hundreds of years.

Doweling

Dowel-strengthened butt joints are employed widely in the cabinet trade today and have been for a long time. Dowels can be purchased from many suppliers, the machinery for boring is not outrageously expensive, and the theory and operations to be used are simple. A cabinet shop of any size can easily employ this joining system for assembling face frames.

Identifying individual components and marking the frame for boring is quite simple. The marks that are made on each member will be reference marks for machining. The type of marking that a detailer must do depends on the tool to be used to bore the holes for the frame. If a doweling machine (see the horizontal boring machine in Figure 6-32) is to be used, it is not necessary to locate the center

FIGURE 6-32 Horizontal boring machine for doweling. (Courtesy Ritter Manufacturing, Inc. Antioch, Calif.

for each dowel hole. The pieces should be laid out on a bench in the way that they will be put together. All marks should be made on the back of the face members. Reminder marks are made at the end of each rail and mullion. Wherever end stock is to be joined to the edge of another piece (rail to stile, etc.), lines are drawn to indicate the exact place where end stock butts into the edge. Working from the drawing in Figure 6-24 and measuring from the top, we would mark the inner edge of the two stiles at 2 in. The top rail meets the edge of the stile between this mark and its top end. The same pieces would also receive marks at 6 in. and 8 in. to indicate the positioning of the drawer rail. Another line is drawn at 29 in., where the bottom rail will fit. If we are working from a layout stick for the same cabinet, we would mark it in exactly the same places, but the process would be even simpler. The layout stick would already have these full-scale locations marked on it. The stile would simply be set against its stick and the marks transferred. (See Figure 6-33.) Marking of the other frame members proceeds similarly. If the detailer is employing a doweling jig to position holes accurately, the center of each hole must be located and marked so that the centering line of the jig can be aligned. The easiest way to do this is to position the two pieces involved in each joint properly and then to draw a single line across the joint, marking both parts at once. A small square ought to be used as an aid in accuracy. (See Figure 6-34.) Incidentally, many dowel-centering jigs will require such marking to be done on the face sides of each piece.

With all pieces marked, boring of holes can proceed. The diameter of hole should be the same as the diameter of dowel to be used (usually $3/8$ in. in $3/4$-in. face frame stock). The depth of holes should be slightly more than half the length of dowel to be used. If a $1\frac{1}{2}$-in. dowel is used, as is very common, we should position the depth gauge on the drill or doweler to yield holes no more than $13/16$ in. in depth. The dowel holes should be approximately centered

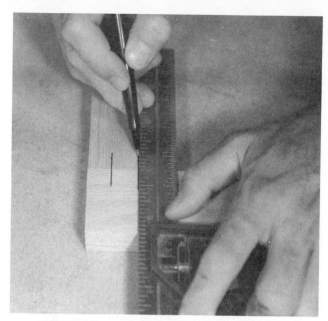

FIGURE 6-34 Marking for dowel jig centering on face members with aid of a square.

in the thickness of face stock. The table of a horizontal borer can be raised or lowered for this adjustment. It is also easy to set the dowel-centering jig appropriately and lock it in place.

With the horizontal boring doweler, each piece is properly positioned with its edge against the fence and its face down against the table. It must be held in this position securely while being machined. Many such machines are fitted with a pneumatic clamping device that performs this function. (See Figure 6-35.) Other machines have a built-on pressure device which is operated by hand. (See Figure 6-36.) The forward movement of the bit, through the fence and into the edge of the face frame, is controlled on most machines by a foot pedal. The principle of horizontally boring for dowel holes is so simple that it is easy to build one's own machine that does its work quite precisely. With such a "homemade" machine, stock is clamped into position against the table and fence as described earlier, but the motor remains stationary while the table is pressed back

FIGURE 6-33 Transferring marks from a layout stick to a face member.

FIGURE 6-35 Doweler employing a pneumatic stock-clamping system.

FIGURE 6-36   Doweler with a hand-operated stock-clamping device.

into the spinning bit to drill each hole. (See Figure 6-37 for the general design of such a machine.)

Proper alignment of face components depends on having reference lines marked on the surface of the doweling machine fence. These are located a convenient predetermined distance from the center of the drill bit. Again referring to Figure 6-24, the detailer would desire two dowels in each joint except where the stiles join with the bottom rail. Here there is not enough surface on the joint to fit more than one dowel. What is convenient in this situation is to use reference lines on the fence of the doweler which are ½ in. from the center of the bit. Centering of the end of the bottom rail is thus very easy—the outside edges of the piece are positioned at the reference lines on the fence. The matching hole in the stile is achieved in much the same way. We use the bottom end of the stile as a line. There is also a line marked on this piece exactly 1 in. from

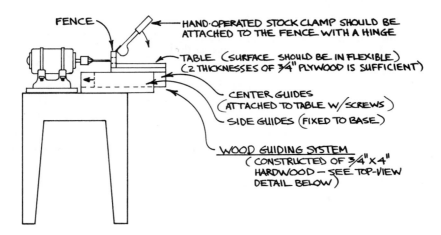

FIGURE 6-37   General design for a precise homemade doweling machine.

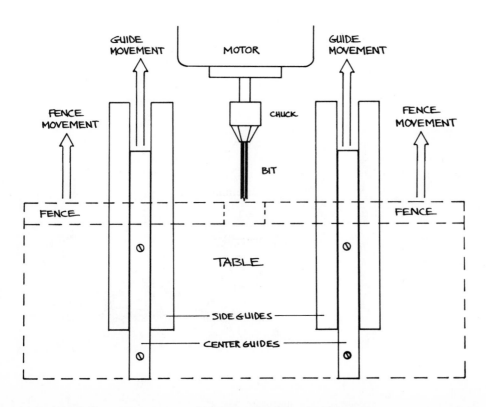

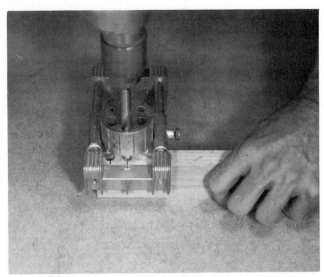

FIGURE 6-38 Drilling the end of a rail with a dowel-centering jig and hand-held drill.

the bottom. These are aligned with the reference lines on the fence. Machining of the wider spaces is similar, except that the pieces are not centered. The right-hand reference line is used for drilling one hole and the left-hand line for the other. With the end of a rail, for example, one edge is positioned even with one line, the hole is punched, and then the piece is moved slightly to position the other edge against the other line for boring. Marking for and drilling holes with a horizontal boring machine takes only minutes for each frame, and dowels function as round tenons.

Drilling with the centering jig obviously takes much longer, but it is still an easy operation to perform. The jig itself is equipped with a centering line or ''notch'' and a clamp. This notch must be matched with each dowel center line. Then the clamp is tightened and the hole may be drilled with a portable drill. (See Figure 6-38.) Joints made with this drilling system will be very flat. Proper use of the jig assures virtually perfect dowel alignment.

It should be clear from our discussion that there are great advantages in using the dowel joint as the basic face frame joint in a shop. There is only one machining operation to perform, and this is an operation that is easy to set up and use. With proper gluing, the resulting face frame joints will be flat and strong. Finally, the machinery necessary to do effective doweling does not have to be expensive.

Toe Screwing

The fastest method for putting together face frames is ''toe screwing.'' To use this method effectively, the cabinet-maker will usually have to invest in some equipment that is not inexpensive, but many large cabinet shops and cab-

inet factories have converted to this system. The principles involved are simple. All joints on the face frame are butt joints, strengthened with glue and with one or more screws which are driven at an angle from the rear side. (Refer to Figure 2-7.) Since screws hold better in side grain than they do in end grain, all end stocks are predrilled with a clearance hole and countersink hole at the correct angle so that the screws will thread into the edges of stiles, rails, and mullions. The screw acts both as a clamp for proper curing of the glue and as a permanent fastener with considerable strength.

Marking face frame parts for machining in this system is exactly the same as under the doweling system. All marking should be done on the rear because the face frame will be assembled face down. The ends of rails and mullions need only a reminder mark. Marks are made on the sides of all pieces to indicate the exact positioning of all end grains. Pieces are then ready for machining.

It is not usually effective to do toe screwing without the stationary tools designed for the operation. There are drill attachments designed for angle drilling of the type needed, but the tendency for the drill bit to ''walk'' when starting the hole is difficult to control. Furthermore, each joint must be clamped or held as flat as possible when the screws are driven or there will be a tendency for the face of each piece of end stock to be raised up. The stationary tools involved are usually in a pair, one specially designed to hold down each piece of end stock and drill the prescribed hole and the other to clamp down the joints of the face frame while screws are driven. (See Figure 6-39.)

Machining for this sort of frame assembly is very fast. Only end stocks must be drilled; no pilot hole is required in side stocks. This is half the drilling that is required for doweling. Also, there is really no need for extremely careful positioning of each piece in the drilling operation. With narrow pieces, one hole is bored approximately in the middle of the piece. Positioning for boring more than one hole is also approximate.

A careful setup is important, but obviously the setup will not need frequent changing. Drilling angle is a critical concern, and so is fence position. These should be adjusted so that the screw will be near the center of the stock thickness at the seam. The drilling angle, together with the factor of screw length (approximately 1 ¾ in. for ¾ in. face stock), also determines how close the screw will come to the surface of the frame when it is driven. If it is too close to the surface, there will be a tendency toward cracking the side grain material. The amount of material between the head of the screw and the seam is also important. The screw's effectiveness is limited by the strength of the wood fibers, and therefore, we desire as much thickness of material as possible for the screw head to ''bite.'' With proper fence and drill angle set, depths must be adjusted. The combination drill-and-countersinking bit will provide a

FIGURE 6-39 Stationary tools for face frame machinery and assembly. Faces are assembled face down on the large, angular-arranged table. Pneumatic clamps are used on both machines to hold materials flat against the tables.

clearance hole based on the gauge of the screw to be used (often number 6), and a larger-diameter, shallower hole to allow flush placement of the screw, all in one movement by the tool. Each plunge of the motor and bit comes after the end stock is positioned against the fence and "clamped" in place. With most machines of this type, a foot pedal controls both movements. The detailer simply positions a piece and depresses the pedal. A pneumatic plunger holds the stock in place, and then the bit moves at the prescribed angle through the wood. A face frame is ready for assembly in only a few minutes.

The reasons for employment of the toe screwing system are clear. It produces perfectly flat joints with minimal machining that can be performed by any employee. Each joint will also possess good strength. Those who use the system even claim that toe-screwed joints are stronger than conventional dowel joints. On the other hand, the system is not without drawbacks. In the first place, the holding power of screws does lessen somewhat with time, especially since we are here purposely avoiding tapered screws in order to reduce splitting. This may be an insignificant consideration in a conventional set of cabinets where most face joints are further supported by attachment to box members, and in a society given to discarding a set of residential cabinets every 10 years or so as a part of remodeling. But if we set out to build antiques of the future, toe-screwed face frames may not be the best choice. Small cab-

inet shops will not invest in the stationary tools needed for this operation because of the level of investment and because of the space required, and larger shops may also prefer not to devote the space to such highly specialized tools. Further, since no pilot holes are drilled, there is still some tendency toward cracking the side-grain members during assembly, particularly where the screw is driven close to the end of a board, such as when joining top and bottom rails to stiles. Finally, since the screw-joining method is fairly new, many modern cabinetmakers resist it because it simply seems less than craftsmanlike.

Each of the face assembly systems has positive and negative points to consider. The key in choosing among them is to ask ourselves for whom we are building. If a customer places a premium on old-fashioned crafting ethics and does not mind paying for the time required, a cabinetmaker will tend to use mortise and tenon, for example. But in committing to a system that can be used consistently for most modern customers, it is probably necessary to choose something faster—doweling, or in developing a large, high-production shop—toe screwing.

FRAMELESS METHODS (EUROPEAN DESIGN)

Frameless methods, or building cabinets in the European style, is perhaps the most recent major development in American cabinet construction. In terms of detailing or machining, it simplifies matters because the cabinetmaker deals with facings and box components at the same time. It is a cabinet design that is especially well suited to modularization and assembly line methods, but it is also easy to build custom cabinets in this mode.

Generally speaking, there are two systems of joining frameless cabinet components, and therefore two methods of machining to choose from. One method incorporates the conventional techniques and tools that we have already discussed, and the other employs specially designed assembly fittings for which details are machined somewhat differently.

Conventional Techniques

To build ''frameless,'' all box components must usually be edged with hardwood strips on the face. Otherwise, raw edges of sheet goods will be visible. The edging may be added either before or after dado and rabbet cutting, but it is usually better to cut the details first so that stop cuts are not necessary to avoid cutting through the edging. We do not want dado cuts to be visible on the face of the cabinet.

Machining for dadoes and other details is performed in the standard way, but location can be a bit different. The bottom shelf of an upper, for example, is received at the very bottom of a finished end. A rabbet, not a dado, is necessary. (See Figure 6-40.)

After all the details are cut, edging is added where necessary. Quarter-inch edging is convenient for this purpose, but slightly thinner or thicker edging may be used. Edging is usually applied with glue only, using no nails or brads, for the sake of appearance. It is usually best to sand the face of the edging before applying it so that there are no mill marks to deal with after the case is assembled. Some cabinetmakers prefer to use edging that just barely covers the edge of each box component—perhaps $^{13}/_{16}$ in. wide to cover components that are $^3/_4$ in. in thickness. The edging strips have to be positioned carefully in gluing, but a smooth seam can then be made by simply sanding. Others

FIGURE 6-41 Hardwood-edged cabinet components. *left:* Can be made perfectly flat by sanding; *right:* requires the use of a plane or flush cutter.

FIGURE 6-42 Flush cutting with a router. The operator must beware of trying to roll the bit over dadoes.

use wider edging which does not need to be positioned as carefully when it is glued in place, but they must use a plane or a router equipped with a flush-cutting bit to remove excess material and gain a flush joint. (See Figures 6-41 and 6-42.)

For ease in gluing on the edging, it is an inch or two longer than required to cover each component. (See Figure 6-41.) The excess length is cut off after glue is set. The edging on end stocks must then be notched to allow the pieces to be received into side sockets (partition to top, top to end, etc.). This may be done in any convenient way, but it is very common to use the jointer for this purpose. The depth of the jointer cut is set to be exactly the same as the depth of a dado. A stop cut is then made on the front of each piece to be received into a dado, feeding with its end

FIGURE 6-40 Box design for a frameless upper. All facing except for the top ''rail'' would be 1/4-in.-thick edging.

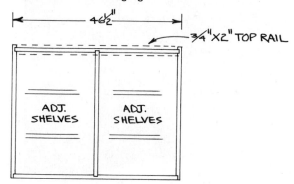

FIGURE 6-43 Using a jointer to notch an edged piece.

down against the table. (See Figure 6-43.) Notice that larger notches may sometimes be necessary. In Figure 6-40, the drawing calls for a top facing that is wider and thicker than the edging to be used on other pieces. This type of top rail is often built into a frameless cabinet for door clearance or to allow the placement of molding above doors. Naturally, the cutting list for this cabinet would have called for the top of the box to be narrower than the other components. The top rail should be flush with the other facings. The detailer would therefore cut a notch at the top of the partition to allow this rail to be fit into place.

Building European-style cabinetry with conventional methods is clearly quite simple. In reality, this is no new development at all. It is simply the application of a few furniture-making techniques to the building of installed cabinets. The only detail that is different from conventional cabinetry is the simple notch on the ends of some pieces.

Assembly Fittings

Cabinetry assembled with fittings requires no dadoes, no rabbets, and no glue except to add edging. In fact, shops that build exclusively using this system will often have incorporated methods to avoid the gluing of edge strips also. There are veneer tapes of various widths available in continuous rolls. The veneer is backed with a heat-sensitive glue and can be applied to the edges of components just as it comes off the roll. The necessary heat is supplied by a specially designed iron which may be hand held or table mounted. Pressure is applied at the same time as the heat, and the edging is in place. Any trimming necessary may be performed by sanding or by using a knife. The cabinet assembler puts the parts together with manufactured nylon and metal fittings. (See Figure 6-44.) The parts to each cabinet box are the same as with conventional cabinetry, but they are merely butted together and joined with the fittings. Machining seldom involves more than drilling holes in the surface of some pieces. The placement of these holes and their dimensions will naturally depend on the specifications of the particular fittings. This information is provided by the manufacturer.

Building in the frameless mode requires only a few techniques and tools which vary from the conventional, and it is possible for a shop to make products in both designs. In general, most shops are committed to one style or the other, however. Cabinetmakers who choose to build in the European style will probably want to rabbet the rear edges of cabinet components to receive backs. They will also depend heavily on a drill press, not only to prepare pieces to accept certain assembly fittings but also for hinge mounting. If a shop is totally committed to the European style, it will undoubtedly tool with special equipment such as multispindle borers.

FIGURE 6-44 Manufactured assembly fittings. (Courtesy of Julius Blum Inc., Cabinet and Furniture Hardware.)

MACHINING FOR DRAWERS

Machining for drawers employs many of the same tools and methods that are used in preparing details for cabinet boxes. With nearly all drawers, the bottom is held in position by slots cut into the other drawer members. (See Figure 2-16.) These slots are actually dadoes cut into the inside faces of sides and fronts or subfronts. Many cabinetmakers run the same detail in drawer backs as well. The slot is usually ¼ in. deep. The width of cut is naturally the same as the thickness of the bottom. The cut is made so that there will be approximately ⅜ in. of material below the drawer bottom to support it.

Detailers commonly use either a table saw or a table-mounted router for cutting drawer bottom slots. With the table saw, pieces will be fed across the tool, inside face down, with the bottom edge against the fence. Blade height contols depth of cut, fence position controls location, and kerf thickness determines the width of cut. For ⅛-in. bottoms, a conventional blade is used. If the drawer bottom material is slightly thicker, the detailer will often introduce a very slight wobble into the rotation of the blade. This is done by putting a thin piece of masking tape or cardboard between the blade and the stabilizing washer on its motor side. For thicker drawer bottoms, the fence may be positioned twice for two cuts on each piece, or a dado head may be used. With the table router, a slotting cutter is used, the same sort of bit as that used for splining. Pieces are fed across the setup with their bottom edges down and their inner faces against the fence. The fence position is set to control the slot depth, the height of cutters above the table determines the location of the cut, and width of cut depends on selecting a bit with correctly sized cutters. (See Figure 6-45.) Both systems are easy to set up and use. If a shop has the luxury of setting up one or more routers for this purpose, it may be the superior method. It would be absurd to specialize the use of a table saw to this task.

For drawers and slide-out shelves that must carry heavy loads, ½-in. bottoms may be desirable. These may be rabbeted to connecting drawer parts to maximize usable drawer height. This machining may be done in the same way that box parts are rabbeted.

For joining sides to drawer backs or subfronts, the cabinetmaker may choose simply to butt the pieces together, and no machining would be necessary. For greater strength, a dado may be cut into the sides to receive the back. Its position along the length of the side is a factor of the overall box design. To determine its exact location, the detailer will generally first find the point at which the bottom ends along the side and figure from there. If sides are rabbeted for a back or subfront, locating the detail is not a problem. Where no subfront is used, the front may be rabbeted to receive the sides. The length of this rabbet is a factor of several things: thickness of drawer side and drawer

FIGURE 6-45 Table routers for use in cutting drawer bottom slots.

guide, clearance, and the way in which the front is designed to fit into or over the facing. These details may all be run using setups similar to the ones used in machining box parts.

French Dovetailing (Dovetail Dadoing)

The French dovetail is an interlocking joint, sometimes used to attach the front and sides of a drawer. In machining the drawer front, a dado is cut in its rear face. This dado is substantially wider at the bottom than it is at the surface of the board. The ends of drawer sides are then shaped at the same angle to fit snugly into this dado. The necessary cuts are most easily cut with a table saw, table-mounted router, or overarm router. If a blind cut (not visible from the top of the drawer) is desired, a stop dado cut is needed. This type of stop cutting is performed more easily with a router.

The fronts should be first marked on the bottom edge as a reference in determining the exact location for each dado. It is simplest to mark the widest points of the angular dado. To do this, the detailer measures from the center of the front and places a mark at a point exactly half the width of the assembled box (See Figure 6-46.) This is the outer limit of the first cut. Then he or she measures back the thickness of the drawer sides and makes another mark. This is the inside limit of the dovetail cut.

Cutting dovetail-shaped dadoes on a table saw will require a series of cuts, and afterward, some chiseling by hand. The detailer should set the angle of the blade first, at about 10° in hard wood or 13° in softer woods such as pine. The blade is then raised so that its highest point is the depth of the desired dado. The fence is used to position

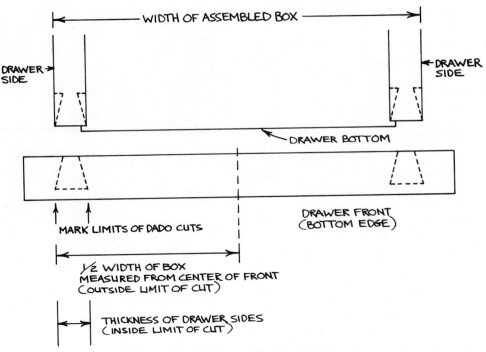

FIGURE 6-46 Marking for the dovetail dado cuts.

the cuts. It makes no difference whether the outside or the inside limiting cut is made first, but the detailer should align for it carefully, using practice pieces of stock, until the fence is positioned perfectly. Each front is then fed across the setup twice, once with each end of the stock against the fence. When all fronts have been machined with this setup, the opposite limiting cut must be made by setting up the fence on the opposite side of the saw blade. With both limiting cuts made, the detailer sets up the saw to remove material in between. It is usually necessary to flatten the bottom of the cut with a chisel.

With the dovetail dado cut, the detailer next must machine the mating ends for drawer sides to interlock. It is best to use sample stock of the exact thickness of the drawer sides for trial cuts until a perfect setup is achieved.

The saw is set up at exactly the same angle as that used for making the dadoes. Since the drawer sides will be fed through the setup front end down and face against the fence, the height of the blade is adjusted to determine the length of the detail and the fence position is used to control the thickness of cut. The blade should be tilted toward the fence. Full thickness is to be maintained at the very end of the sides, and blade height must be no more than total dado depth. (See Figure 6-47.) If this cut is made with a conventional saw blade, the kerf is square, and it is necessary to remove some additional material to make the side fit properly. It is better to use one of the blades from a dado head, with all its teeth beveled in one direction. The tail-shaped end of the drawer side should fit snugly into the previously cut dado.

FIGURE 6-47 Table saw set up for detailing drawer sides to fit into the dovetail-shaped dado on a drawer front. Notice that material C must be removed for the desired fit. Using the blade from a dado head, with all its top bevels in one direction would eliminate this need. B is the depth of the dado, and A is the thickness of drawer sides.

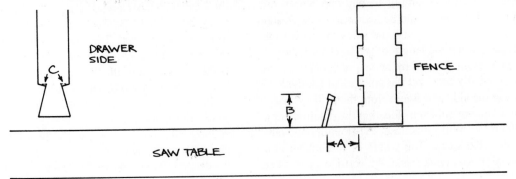

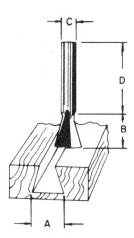

FIGURE 6-48 Dovetail bit. A is the widest cut width (side thickness), B is the depth of cut, and C and D are shank dimensions. (Courtesy of Porter-Cable Corporation.)

Using a router for the cuts involved in this joint is much easier since fewer setups are required. The table router and the overarm router are set up similarly for the dado cut, but feeding is slightly different—inside up on the overarm router but down on the table-mounted router. The cutting is accomplished by a bit designed specifically for this purpose. (See Figure 6-48.) The angle of cut is thus determined by the bit itself. Depth is controlled by raising or lowering the router bit. The fence is set to locate the dado. To make a stop cut, a mark should be placed on the table or fence so that the operator may stop the feed at exactly the right place. When stop cutting the dovetail dado, it is safer to turn off the tool at the end of each cut rather than trying to move the stock backward. Most overarm routers have a brake to aid in decelerating the rotation.

Sides may be easily detailed with a matching cut on a table router, but a router in the overarm position is not well suited to this task. It is possible with some overarm routers to put the motor in an under-the-table position and machine the drawer side details. This makes the overarm router, in effect, a table router.

In making the tail cuts on the table router, feeding is with the end down and the face in contact with the fence. The height of the cutter above the table should be the same as the depth of the dado cut or a bit less. The fence is positioned so that no material is removed at the very end of the drawer side. Again, sample pieces should be used until the perfect fit is attained.

If dovetail rabbeting (where matching bevels are cut onto the ends of drawer parts; see Figure 2-16) is desired, matching cuts are easily made with one setup. On the table saw, the subfront or front is given its bevel by correctly setting the blade angle and then feeding with the miter gauge. The fence is then put into position as described earlier to make the necessary cut on the front end of the drawer

side. The table router may be set up to make both bevels. The front or subfront is fed with its end against the fence, and the side is fed end down.

It should be noted that drawer sides are paired in making joints such as the French dovetail or the half dovetail. For example, if drawer boxes are to be joined with half dovetails in front and dadoes in the rear, the detailer must take care not to machine details on the wrong end of the drawer sides. This may seem a ridiculous error, but the mistake is easy to make. After the slots for drawer bottoms are run, sides should be paired up, inside to inside. The careful detailer may then put reminder marks on the front of each piece.

The French dovetail interlocks drawer parts very efficiently for carrying heavy loads. The easy-to-machine half dovetail is substantially stronger than a butt joint.

Double Dadoing

The double dado may be used to interlock the parts of drawers that may come into heavy usage. The strength of the joint depends on the inherent strength of wood fibers in the drawer parts. The details are generally cut to join front (or subfront) to sides. As explained in Chapter 1, the sides are dadoed to receive a portion of the thickness of the front or subfront. The front is dadoed to match. This detail is a rabbet on the subfront. We will discuss making the joint with a subfront. To make the necessary cut on a front, the detailer will naturally have to adapt setups for its design.

The drawer side is dadoed in any of the conventional ways that we have discussed. The dado's width should be half the thickness of the subfront or less—for strength, we want to preserve as much material as possible between the dado and the front end of the drawer. Its depth should be ¼ in. If the operation is performed on the table saw, pieces are fed with the front ends against the fence, using the miter gauge. Drawer sides must again be paired for machining.

Both ends of the subfront must be rabbeted on the exterior face to receive the detailed sides. Again, this may be performed in any convenient way. Routing with a straight bit may involve the quickest setup, using the table mount and fence. (For dadoing the drawer front rather than a subfront, the table saw may be easier—stock is fed on end, and adjustments for dado width, depth, and location are easier to control.)

Detailing drawers for assembly requires some precision. If employing butt joints to join sides to other drawer members, this is simply a matter of the one setup for drawer-bottom slots. If any sort of interlocking or semi-interlocking joint is used, precision is extremely important. There is no point in making such joints if they do not fit properly. But the reader should not hesitate to try his or her hand at this type of machining. The key is using sample pieces and making trial cuts until pieces fit satisfactorily.

(*Note:* Most built-in cabinetry does not include the making of dovetail joints. For a discussion of the possible procedures, see Chapter 13.)

Machining for doors is a complex process. It is a series of steps involving many of the techniques discussed in this chapter, but these steps are frequently interrupted by sanding operations, assembly operations, and other "subprocesses." To talk only about the machining involved is quite artificial, and we will therefore look at the machining involved as part of the overall door-making process. (See Chapter 8.)

OTHER MACHINING SITUATIONS

Other machining situations include cutting perfect circles, curves, and angles, shaping moldings, and the use of shaped details in jointery.

Circles

It is sometimes necessary to find a method for cutting a true circle. The cabinetmaker may accomplish this in one of two general ways: by drawing the circle and removing material to the line, or by setting up a cutting tool to do the job. If the drawing system is used, the marking is of course critical, but it is also easy to do. Working on the back side, a point is found that will serve conveniently for the center of the circle. Something rigid—a stick or a piece of shelf standard—will be rotated around this fixed point to draw the circle. It should be tacked to the center point with a nail. A notch or hole is put in the stick at any desired radius, and then a pencil is held in the notch, marking the stock as the stick is rotated. The cabinetmaker then cuts close to the line with a saber saw or band saw. The perfect circle is gained with careful sanding using an edge sander. (See Figures 6-49 to 6-51.) The sanding part of this process requires excellent skills, and many woodworkers prefer a different system.

A number of tools can be set up to cut the perfect circle without sanding: saber saw, band saw, router, and even a table router. The idea is to make the cut by rotating either the stock or the cutter from the fixed center point. Rather than marking the circle, we are cutting it. To use either the router or the saber saw, the base of the tool is attached to a rigid piece that can be nailed to the center of the desired circle. With the radius set correctly, we have only to turn the tool on and start cutting. (See Figure 6-52.) If a router is used in thick material, the cut should be made with a straight bit in several passes, to avoid burning and chipping. Care must be taken to keep the tool firmly fixed to its centering point with each successive rotation. With the saber saw, the blade may have a tendency not to cut in a perfectly vertical pattern. The tool should be equipped

FIGURE 6-49   Marking for a perfect circle.

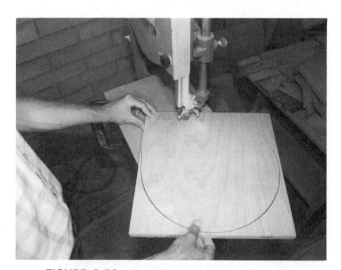

FIGURE 6-50   A circle may be cut "rough" on the band saw or rotated on a nail for a more exact cut. (See Figure 6-53.)

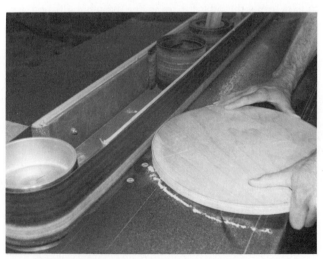

FIGURE 6-51   Finishing a true circle with an edge sander.

FIGURE 6-52 Cutting the circle with a router.

with a roller guide for the blade to ride in as it cuts, and a stiff blade should be used.

To use a band saw in circle cutting, the stock is naturally rotated rather than the tool. A centering point is found at the correct distance from the saw blade (the radius of the circle). Since a band saw table is generally not very large, it is often necessary to extend it. A large flat piece of plywood can generally be clamped directly to the band saw table for this operation. At the exact centering point, the detailer drives a nail so that it projects above the table surface less than the thickness of the stock to be cut. An awl or a small drill bit is used to make a hole in the rear face of the stock at its exact center. It is obvious that this hole should not go all the way through the stock. At this point, it may be necessary to make a starting cut so that the band saw can be properly positioned at the outside of the circle. If the outside of the circle is at the edge of the stock, the cut may be started here. (See Figure 6-53.) To employ a

FIGURE 6-53 A nearly perfect circle can be cut on a band saw by rotating the stock on a pivot point. Arrow points to a nail.

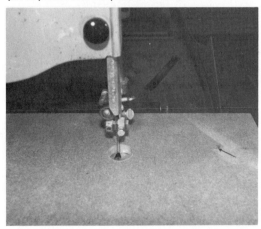

table router for this purpose, the setup is exactly the same. Since the router bit is called on to remove a good deal of material, the circle should first be marked out so that a "rough" cut can be made close to the line. Then the router is only trimming, and excellent results can be achieved.

Choosing among the several circle-cutting systems is largely a matter of preference, but the most reliable is probably the pivoting router method. Good results can be gained with any of the systems described, however.

Curves

It is obvious that curves must usually be cut with a saber saw, band saw, jigsaw, or coping saw. A jigsaw or coping saw is usually employed for the most intricate curves in the thinnest of woods. The band saw, if available, is probably most desirable for cutting most curves because it is never necessary to clamp pieces of stock in position for cutting. For pieces that are difficult to feed through the band saw, particularly large pieces, the saber saw is obviously superior.

What may not be obvious is how to mark pieces to be detailed. The detailer should remember the principle of "function first" for this operation. Arcs made to accept wine bottles should naturally be based on the design of wine bottles. If cabinet components need cutting to fit a curved wall, the detailer is following a pattern provided by the measurer. If a cabinet is to be mounted on a curved wall, it is important for the detailer to determine the exact positioning of each piece along the curve. This is easiest with a full-scale layout. Shops using the stick system of layout are more prone to provide this type of layout than are those in the production drawing system. Where repetitious cuts are necessary, as for making a wine rack, a pattern or template should be made from hardboard or another easily shaped material. The template can be used to mark every cut exactly the same. (See Figure 6-54.) Cuts should be made on the waste side of each line. A sanding drum is then used to sand to the line. (See Figure 6-55.) The position of the sanding drum is hard to control with a handheld drill. A drill press should be used for this purpose. The rotation speed of the drum should be kept low, and a coarse grit should be used on the drum to prevent burning. It is also best to feed stock with, rather than against, the rotation of the drum.

Angles

It is frequently necessary to adapt conventional setups to achieve unconventional cuts. It is very common, for example, to build cabinets that call for 45° joints. The designer frequently calls for this type of cabinet in order to incorporate a full-round susan in the kitchen base or upper. (See Figure 2-21.) There are other designs that also call for

FIGURE 6-54 Templates used by the detailer for marking various patterns.

FIGURE 6-55 Sanding a curve with a drum sander mounted in the drill press. In most cases, feeding of material is with the rotation of the drum.

this angle or some other angle to be featured in cabinet construction. In such cases it is usually necessary to cut box parts at a particular angle and then to machine a matching bevel into the stile of the face frame to be attached. Figure 6-56 gives plan views of two such cabinets.

If box parts will have a straight, continuous edge (as in Figure 6-56, left), they may be cut on a table saw. The fence is not used. Pieces should be fed with an extended-face miter gauge. A good alternative method is to mark the angle cut with a straightedge, make a rough cut outside the line with a saber saw, and then trim exactly to the line with a jointer. If the front edge of a piece is achievable only by making more than one cut (as in Figure 6-56, right), the procedure is slightly different. It may be possible to make portions of the cut on the table saw. This should be performed with the blade raised as high as possible, to reduce undercutting. The angled portion of the front edge is usually made with a saber saw. Irregularities in the edge must then be smoothed by sanding or another method.

Bevel cutting on the face frame or other cabinet com-

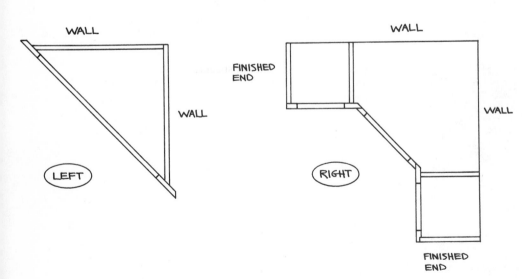

FIGURE 6-56 Cabinets that require angle cutting. *Left:* Arrangement frequently used as a built-in china cabinet. It utilizes small corner spaces as well. *Right:* An upper cabinet. The angled section will accommodate a full-round susan. If the top and bottom are to be cut from one piece, three cuts are necessary to yield the front edge. Cuts parallel to the rear edges of the top and bottom should be done on the table saw.

FIGURE 6-57 Feeding the shaper. Note the fence and guard. (Courtesy of Delta International Machinery Corp.)

ponent is almost always done on the table saw. This is performed exactly like a mitering cut made to prepare the joint of a finished end and back, with the blade tilted into a protection board mounted on the fence (see the earlier section, ''Mitering'').

Dadoes that must be cut at a nonstandard angle can be achieved by adapting one of the dadoing systems that we have already discussed. Marking pieces for such cuts is the same as in marking for conventional dadoes except that the marks are probably more important in positioning each cut. It is easy to get mixed up and make such cuts in the wrong direction, and the detailer should mark each piece to indicate the direction of the cutting angle. To adapt the table saw–dado head for this purpose, the fence is moved out of the way and the miter gauge is adjusted to the desired angle. Each cut is aligned with the dado head or with reference marks on the table, and feeding is done with the miter gauge. To adapt the router and ''dadoing jig,'' the angle of the router–guiding fence is simply changed from perpendicular to the desired angle.

Shaping

Wooden materials are frequently shaped on their edges. This may be done for decorative purposes, as in preparing moldings. There is a wide variety of contours that can be made, depending on the type of cutter chosen: coves, round-overs, beads, and ogees to name a few. In a few cases, edges are shaped to achieve greater strength in jointery, as when solid pieces are laminated edge to edge for tabletops and chair seats. Cutters for this type of shaping are available in pairs that will cut edges to match perfectly. These are generally tongue cutters and groove cutters, or a modification of these. Shaping of this type is almost invariably performed with a shaper or a table-mounted router, although it is possible to purchase such cutters that can be mounted in a table saw or radial arm saw. In using the router or shaper, the operator should keep the fence in place whenever possible and always feed against the direction of cutter rotation. (See Figure 6-57.)

CHAPTER SUMMARY OF CABINETMAKING SKILLS

The process of preparing cabinet components for assembly is referred to as detailing. It consists primarily of cutting dadoes, rabbets, miters, and notches into box parts; it also includes preparation of face frame members for assembly.

The detailer can choose from many different methods to accomplish each detail; the choice is generally a matter of tool availability.

It is important to consider tool versatility in choosing

tools for a cabinet shop and in managing the various steps in a cabinetmaking operation. For the preparation of box parts, it should be clear that a table saw is the most versatile of tools for machining. On the other hand, the productive cabinetmaker often seeks to specialize tool usage to avoid frequent setup changes. Heavy-duty routers can more easily be reserved to a particular detailing use than most tools, and they have great versatility. In large shops, a panel router can be employed with effectiveness for many specialized machining operations.

For face frame assembly, most cabinetmakers use a doweling system or, for large shops, a toe-screwing system. Although most craftsmen can and do make mortise-and-tenon joints, these are generally impractical for building large numbers of face frames.

In frameless, European cabinetry, conventional tools and systems can be adapted fairly easily for machining, but it is also possible to use specially designed assembly fittings instead of the conventional techniques.

The proficient designer not only understands the tools and methods that he or she chooses, but is also able to read and interpret production drawings or layout sticks and use this information to mark out individual cabinet parts.

SEVEN

FRAME ASSEMBLY AND GENERAL GLUING

BASIC PRINCIPLES OF GLUING

Since few wood products are made from a single piece of wood, the importance of glue and proper glue joints is hard to overestimate. Woodworkers should realize that adhesives or glues bond pieces together in two ways. One way involves the glue's penetration of pores in the wood's cell structure and holding pieces together with an intricate interweave between the wood and the hardened glue. Much more important, however, is that the glue forms a chemical bond with the wooden members of a joint. The significance of this knowledge to the woodworker is to destroy the myth that somewhat rough surfaces are best for bonding. In fact, smooth surfaces bond best, unless they have been burned or compacted by dull cutters.

In Chapter 4 the discussion of glues suggested that there is a wide variety of glues that may be used in the cabinetmaking trade. Every type of glue available has desirable properties when used for specific purposes. However, it is most common to employ one type of glue for most woodworking applications in a cabinet shop, and to use different adhesives only when our chosen "standard" glue will not be desirable. At the present time, yellow (aliphatic resin) is clearly the most popular general-purpose wood glue. In this chapter, then, primary attention will be on the use of this type of glue. The only tool necessary is

a full glue bottle. (Incidentally, most woodworkers do not buy glue bottles; they purchase only the nozzle tips. Many household items, such as shampoo and hand lotion, come in plastic bottles that may be rinsed out and used, as long as they will accept the twist-on glue bottle tips.)

Gluing theory is important for every serious woodworker to understand because it will affect the way that he or she performs gluing operations. Glues are applied to make long-lasting bonds between wooden cabinet members. The best glue joints can be achieved by following some general principles.

1. Prepare the surfaces adequately. Jointers, planers, and "knife" tools are better than saws for the preparation of edges and faces. Smoothness is important.

2. Use the right amount of glue. Too little glue yields a weak joint. Too much glue is wasteful, causes excessive swelling of wood fibers, and can leave a mess that will result in sanding and finishing problems. As their experience grows, cabinetmakers learn to "measure by eye." A small amount of glue may squeeze out of a joint as pressure is applied.

3. Spread the glue evenly. This ensures even ab-

sorption of glue and moisture. Some cabinet-makers use a brush or serrated scraper for this; others prefer their finger.

4. Spread glue on both surfaces. It is surprising how much this adds to the strength of the joint. (Obviously, this procedure need not always be followed. The cabinetmaker should consider the function of the joint. Face frames will generally be assembled with "single gluing," whereas pieces laminated for turning on the lathe should be "double glued.")

5. Apply sufficient pressure. For the narrowest possible seam line and for the best bonding, pressure should be applied. Soft woods require less pressure than harder woods. Many wood-workers tend to underestimate the amount of pressure necessary.

6. Align pieces carefully. Pieces glued out of square or in a twisted position will be forever out of square or twisted.

7. Apply pressure evenly. When joining longer surfaces, more than one clamp will be necessary. These should be spaced several inches apart, and a board (caul) should be placed between clamp and stock to help distribute the pressure evenly.

8. Allow sufficient time for the glue to set before removing pressure. This may require as little as 15 minutes for face frames in dry, warm conditions.

9. Remove excess glue after it has partially hardened into beads. Wet glue seeps into open pores and presents sanding and finishing problems. Fully hardened beads of glue will rip out wood fibers when removed.

10. Allow sufficient curing time before sanding and machining. The moisture in glue is absorbed into surrounding wood fibers. This causes swelling. If the joined pieces are sanded or detailed before this swelling has been removed by drying, the result is a dip.

In an assembly operation, cabinetmakers are relying on the glue itself for strength. Edge-to-edge and face-to-face joints may be made with glue only. If end stock is involved in a joint (as in most face frames), additional strength is necessary. In combination with "worked joints" such as mortises and tenons or dowels, glue will yield tremendous strength. A toe screw serves to stabilize the glue joint in a face frame. When nails are used in conjunction with glue, as in attaching the face frame to the body, they should be thought of as a gluing aid. Nails have fastening capability naturally, but they also function as permanent

clamps and as aids in alignment. The procedures recommended here are simple, yet they are of the greatest importance in joining wood.

FACE FRAME ASSEMBLY

Face frames can be assembled quickly and precisely by a craftsman who follows a few key principles. The face frame assembly table should be as flat as possible. This helps to ensure that the faces themselves will be flat. It should be large enough to accommodate most of the faces that will be produced, perhaps 3 ft wide and 7 ft long. It should be at a convenient working height, a height that does not require a lot of bending over the work surface. The framer should prevent glue buildup as much as possible.

Edges should be made as flat and smooth as possible before assembly of the frame. In some shops this is accomplished in the cutting or machining process. The cutter, for example, may use the table saw to rip stock ⅛ in. wider than necessary and then feed the stock on edge through a planer to reach the desired widths. Stock that has been milled in this way has uniform edges for assembly. The edges of face frame stock may also be prepared for jointery by sanding, but care must be taken to avoid uneven sanding. In shops where an edge sander is available, the framer may prepare edges simply by feeding each piece across the table of the machine, face up or down, with even pressure. Care must be exercised to make sure that the table is perfectly square with the sanding surface. Frame makers who are capable with a portable belt sander may use this tool for edge preparation. But since a 3- or 4-in.-wide belt sander has a tendency to rock side to side on stock that is only ¾ in., many woodworkers do not trust this system. If preparing edges with a belt sander, the frame maker should set up several pieces of the same width to be sanded all at once. This increases stability of the sander on the surface. If the belt sander is to be used, a block is affixed to the worktable to serve as a stop. This block may be tacked in place with nails, clamped in place, or set firmly by another method. Ends of pieces may then be positioned against this "stop block" to keep them from being thrown rearward by the belt sander. (See Figure 7-1.) Edges may also be sanded by hand with a flat sanding block. As a preparation to gluing, fine-grit sandpapers are superior to coarse grits. It should be noted that not all face members need edge preparation. Members that surround a drawer do not need sanding at all, and edges that will be on the exterior of the assembled frame should not be sanded until later in the cabinetmaking process.

We apply glue so that all surfaces to be in contact with other surfaces receive a coat of glue. With a doweling system this means that glue coats the entire surface of the dowel as well as the end of each rail and mullion. Since

FIGURE 7-1 Belt sanding interior edges of face members. Note the "stop block."

double coating is not necessary on a face frame, most cabinetmakers proceed through the steps that follow.

1. Apply glue to the end stocks first. A sufficient amount of glue is put into each dowel hole and onto the end surface of each rail and mullion at the same time.
2. Spread the glue to cover the end of each piece with a brush or fingertip. Avoid contact with the glue if it irritates the skin. (See Figure 7-2.)
3. Twist each dowel into its hole. This helps to spread the glue evenly and thoroughly. A small amount of glue should squeeze out.
4. With dowels inserted into all end stocks of a frame, treat the side stocks by putting glue into

FIGURE 7-2 Glue should cover the surface of each end stock.

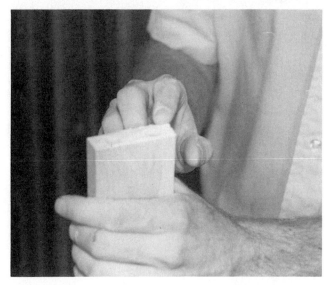

each dowel hole. Since it will not be possible to twist in each dowel, the glue should be distributed within the hole by swirling a tiny brush or stick around.

5. Assembly should be immediate, beginning in the middle of the frame and progressing outward. After swirling the glue in the edge-stock holes of an individual piece, the framer will generally assemble that piece with its mating end stocks.

In a mortise-and-tenon system, the procedure is similar. The framer applies glue to all contacting surfaces—cheeks and shoulders as well as the end of the tenon. Assembly must proceed from the middle of the frame. In either system, clamping begins after all joints have been assembled. If the face frame is to be assembled with toe-screwing equipment, gluing is simplest of all. For each joint, glue is spread on the end stock. Then the pieces are matched correctly, clamped down to the table surface, and screwed together. The most important gluing consideration here may be in avoiding excessive squeeze-out. Since the table itself should be maintained in a perfectly flat and smooth condition, we do not desire excess glue building up on its surface. Any excess should be cleaned up immediately, preferably with a damp cloth.

In toe screwing, no clamping is necessary. For clamping in one of the other face assembly systems, the procedure is simple. There are a variety of clamps available for use in the woodworking trades. (See Figure 7-3.) The best clamp to use in frame assembly is a manufactured bar clamp. It is capable of applying great pressure, and its parts are subject to very little bending or distortion. A good alternative is to use pipe clamps. These are fabricated parts mounted on lengths of steel pipe (not galvanized). They are much less expensive than manufactured bar clamps, they can be made to any convenient length, they are easily adjusted, and they are easily capable of applying sufficient pressure for face frame assembly. With either type of clamp, stock faces will contact the pipe or bar as the clamp is tightened. This is desirable as an aid in keeping the frame fairly flat while glue is setting, but the frame builder should be careful to avoid bent pipes that may result in "not-flat" joints. (See Figure 7-4). Certain other types of clamp, such as spring clamps, may also be helpful in building face frames.

A face frame is generally clamped in the following steps.

1. Position and tighten horizontal (across stiles) clamps first. There should be one horizontal clamp for each rail, and these should be underneath the frame. All clamps should be of the same type (with clamp fittings of the same size) so that the frame will be sitting fairly level. It is

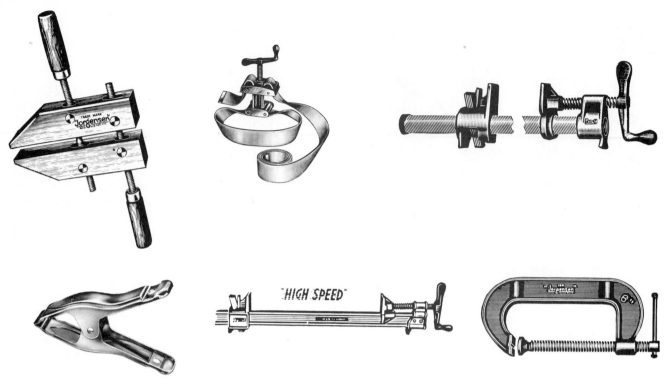

FIGURE 7-3 Some common and important clamps. *Top (L-R):* Hand screw, band clamp, steel bar clamp fixtures (pipe fixtures); *bottom (L-R):* spring clamp, steel I-bar clamp, carriage clamp. (Courtesy of Adjustable Clamp Company.)

FIGURE 7-5 Horizontal clamping of a face frame. Note that clamps have identical design and that a protective strip is in place to avoid marring the face frame. Also note the spring clamps used to prevent rails from bending away from the clamp.

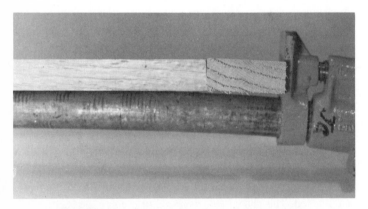

FIGURE 7-4 Using a bent pipe for clamping can lead to ''unflat'' joints. This type of pipe distortion will occur through overtightening.

advisable to put a protective wooden strip between the faces of the clamp fittings and the frame stock, especially with softer woods, to avoid marring the frame. (See Figure 7-5).

2. The horizontal clamps are tightened evenly. This contributes to a square face frame.

3. The framer should check to see that the rear face of the frame is in contact with the clamp bars or

FIGURE 7-6 Vertical clamping of a frame. Note the spacers employed to prevent contact of metal and wood.

FIGURE 7-7 Using a clamp to even an outside rail and a stile. Note that a pipe clamp is most suitable for this operation, since its clamp fittings are able to pivot on the pipe.

pipes. If not, stock should be tapped down with a hardwood block and hammer. With longer face frames, clamping pressure may cause the face to bow upward, away from the clamps. To correct this, a spring clamp may be used to hold the clamp and stock together.

4. Vertical clamps (across top and bottom rails) are placed next, on top of the frame. There should be a clamp running along each mullion. Since these clamps extend over the front of the frame, many cabinetmakers prefer to avoid contact between the bar or pipe and the face stock. (Metal and glue can react chemically to cause some discoloration of wood fibers.) Small blocks of wood are used as spacers between metal and wood. Each clamp rests on these rather than on the good side of the face frame. (See Figure 7-6.)

5. The vertical clamps are tightened.

The frame should be checked immediately for squareness and for evenness of joints. If every piece in a face frame has been machined and cut precisely, and if clamps are positioned correctly, no frame will ever need adjustment. Naturally, this type of perfection is unrealistic, and the cabinetmaker must have a standard procedure for checking the frame and for adjusting it.

Correct positioning should be checked first, beginning by looking for an even joint at the four corners of the frame where the top and bottom rails meet stiles. A visual inspection of these four corners is sufficient. If a minor adjustment is necessary, it should *not* be done by hammering pieces into alignment. The shock of a hammer blow across a mortise-and-tenon or dowel joint will often cause splitting. The edge of a rail may be aligned with the end of a stile by use of a pipe clamp. (For reasons that will be apparent, the pipe clamp is superior to the manufactured

bar clamp for this job.) One clamp face is placed against the end of the stile, and the other is positioned on the edge of the rail. (See Figure 7-7.) Just enough pressure is applied to align the stocks evenly. Then this clamp may be removed. The frame maker may then check for correct alignment of all other pieces by measuring with a tape measure and referring to the shop production drawing or layout stick if necessary. Adjustments are usually not needed but if they are, a bar clamp can be used as before to make slight movements in joint position.

Face frames assembled with dowels or tenons will usually be fairly flat, providing that pieces were milled and machined with some care on decent equipment. Belt sanding will remove any minor misalignment in faces. In fact, shops with a wide belt sander for preparing assembled face frames pay little attention to gaining flat-surfaced joints. On the other hand, a flat surface is desirable. Joints may be checked for flatness with any straight edge—the longer leg of a framing square is excellent for this because it is thin and allows us to see a clear definition of the joint. Correction of a ''bellied'' joint may be achieved by clamping the belly down to a straight edge. (See Figure 7-8.) Major misalignments should be corrected by cutting new pieces or by remachining.

The squareness of a frame may be checked with a framing square or with a tape. The proficient frame builder will use either method, depending on which is more convenient with a particular frame.

With many frames, the fastest and easiest way to check for squareness is with a framing square. Stiles and rails should naturally meet at a right angle, and the square may be easily positioned to check for this perpendicularity.

FIGURE 7-8 Clamping the belly out of a joint. Severe misalignment should be corrected by recutting or remachining.

FIGURE 7-9 Checking for squareness with a framing square.

(See Figure 7-9.) Continuous contact between the two legs of the tool and the face stock assures a square frame. If only the toes of the square are in contact, the angle is acute or less than 90°. If only the heel of the square is in contact with the stock, the angle is obtuse or greater than 90°. More than one corner of the frame should be checked, but it is not necessary to check every corner. A good rule is to "square from wide stock." For example, in an upper cabinet frame with 2-in. stiles and top rail and a 1¼-in. bottom rail, we would probably check only the joints that involve the top rail.

It is sometimes necessary or more convenient to check for right angles by measurement. If the angles of a frame or frame section are all right angles, the shape of the frame is a rectangle. This means that the two diagonal measurements of the frame must be equal. (See Figure 7-10.) If one diagonal is longer than the other, the frame or frame section is not square. The longer diagonal involves two angles which are acute, while the other two angles will be obtuse.

Adjusting a frame that is not square takes only a minute or two. The framer simply changes the position of one or more clamps so that longer diagonals are shortened. (See Figure 7-11 for reference in positioning clamps.)

With joints even and flat, and with the frame square, excess, squeeze-out glue should be wiped away to limit the absorption of moisture. The frame should be kept as flat as possible until the glue is set. Most cabinetmakers simply put each frame on the floor with its clamps in place so that assembly of the next frame may begin. The frame should not be leaned against anything while waiting for the glue to set, even though this practice conserves space. Twisted frames can be the result.

Proper drying time is important in the gluing of face frames. When a cabinetmaker refers to glue being "set," he or she means that the glue has dried sufficiently to allow removal of clamps. By saying that a joint has cured, we mean that enough drying has occurred to allow sanding and use of the frame in cabinet assembly. Even in hot, dry weather, several hours of drying time should be allowed for joints to cure before the frame is sanded. This is especially important in working with door frames because of the many sanding and detailing steps that may be required after gluing.

WIDE PANELS

Wide panels of solid material are often desirable or necessary in the cabinetmaking process. Some of the uses for wide panels are as follows: raised panels or plant-ons for

FIGURE 7-10 Checking for squareness by measurement.

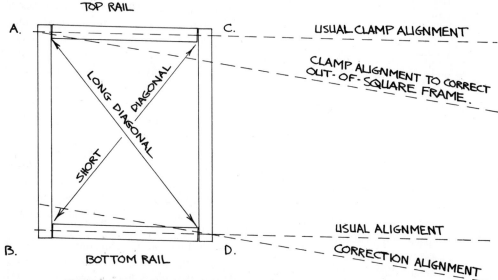

FIGURE 7-11 Clamp positioning can correct squareness of a frame. Acute angles *BAC* and *BDC* are at the ends of the long diagonal. Clamps are usually positioned parallel to frame members such as the rails in the drawing, but to shorten the long diagonal, clamp position is changed, bringing the frame square.

certain types of doors, plank doors, wide drawer fronts, desk tops, and some other furniture components. It is an obvious requirement for the cabinetmaker to have a useful system for laminating narrower boards together to achieve these wider pieces. The actual gluing procedures that should be used—surface preparation, glue spreading, and so on—are very much the same as those already described. In addition, the craftsman must remember several other key points.

Pieces should be oversized in length. This is a help in lamination beecause we do not have to concern ourselves with lining up the ends of pieces as we are gluing. Our focus can be more appropriately focused on gaining good seams and a flat panel. An inch or two of additional length is enough to be an aid without producing a great amount of waste.

Pieces should be a bit oversized in width. This allows the woodworker to do additional straightening of pieces on the jointer if necessary. It also eliminates the need for a protective strip between steel clamp parts and the stock. Some woodworkers will insist on using a caul anyway, to distribute pressure evenly, but this is probably not impor-

tant if the outside pieces of the panel are at least 3 in. wide. The width of the stock itself allows an even distribution of the clamping pressure along the seam. Each oversized panel must naturally be cut to its finished size. This should be done after the initial sanding of the panel.

Cauls are sometimes useful. If it is important to avoid marring an edge but still apply heavy pressure, or if the outside members of the wide panel are narrow ones, a caul should be used. A caul may be made of metal or a hard wood. The features of a caul are significant. Its edges should be perfectly square in relation to its faces; it must be at least as thick and as long as the material to be glued and wide enough so that it flexes very little. (See Figure 7-12.)

Pieces to be laminated should be fairly narrow. Flat-sawn lumber is cut so that growth rings (end grain) are somewhat parallel to the face of the board. Its opposite faces shrink and expand differently, and this causes warpage. Quarter-sawn lumber is cut from a tree so that its growth rings are more or less perpendicular to both faces. Expansion and contraction of the wood is fairly equal on either face of each board. (See Figure 7-13.) Keeping the

FIGURE 7-12 Clamping a wide panel. Note that cauls are thicker than stock to be glued and wide enough to distribute pressure. Also note that end grain direction of stock is alternated across the panel. This diminishes warpage by distributing expansion and contraction tendencies.

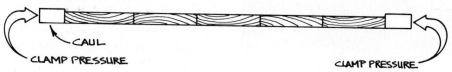

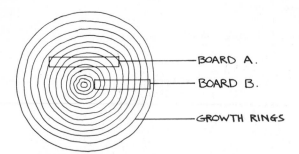

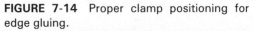

FIGURE 7-13 Differences in end grain as a result of differences in timber milling. Board A is flat sawn, and board B is quarter sawn.

individual pieces of a laminated panel rather narrow reduces the tendency for warpage. Pieces should be about 4 in. wide or less with flat-sawn four-quarter lumber, narrower for softwoods, and perhaps slightly wider for quarter-sawn lumber. Related to this, and extremely important, is that the woodcrafter should alternate the direction of end grain on each piece glued up to form the wide panel. (Again, see Figure 7-12.)

Clamp placement is significant in edge gluing of solid pieces. Bar clamps or pipe clamps are used most commonly. These should be spaced so that pressure is even. Thus the cabinetmaker will usually clamp within an inch or two of each end and then place clamps between, 6 to 12 in. apart. To promote flatness, "over and under" positioning of the clamps is desirable. This means that some bars or pipes will contact one face of the stock, while others contact the opposite face, ensuring that modest distortions in the clamp fixtures are equalized. (See Figure 7-14.)

When joining plywood pieces, we follow basically the same procedures as for joining solid stocks except that the joint is strengthened with dowels or a spline. If a spline

FIGURE 7-14 Proper clamp positioning for edge gluing.

is used, a bit of time should be expended in properly spreading the glue to ensure the best joint. Some workers will simply dump glue into the two kerfs that will be receiving the spline, run a bead of glue along the edge of the two pieces of plywood to be joined, and then clamp the pieces together. We may wish that this worked adequately for glue distribution, but it just does not. We can produce a far superior joint by using a brush or narrow stick of wood to spread the "dumped" glue to coat all the surfaces within each kerf. It is easier, and also ensures good results, to spread a coat of glue over all surfaces of the spline. If dowels are used, these may be twisted into place to effectively distribute glue. With all edge gluing, glue should be spread along the entirety of contacting edges for maximum strength.

Cabinetmakers who consistently use dowels in building face frames or in making other joints will usually buy dowels that are ready to use—with slightly tapered ends and a spiral groove to allow the escape of air and excess glue as the dowel is twisted into position. If a cabinetmaker is cutting up a dowel rod to make dowel joints, he or she should detail each dowel in a similar way. Tapers may be accomplished quickly by spinning dowel tips on a belt sander. A groove or kerf may be cut into the dowel with either the blade of a band saw or the abrasive edge of a belt on a belt sander. A length of dowel is spun around and drawn across the blade or belt at the same time. Naturally, this groove may also be cut with a small handsaw such as a dovetail saw. The grooving or kerfing should be done before dowels are cut to length.

When focusing on edge joining of plywood, it is pertinent to look at a few procedures that should be followed when it is necessary to join pieces of plywood end to end. This is occasionally required when building wood tops and other plywood components over 8 ft in length. Gluing practices are actually very much the same as those we have just pointed out, but the gluer must also be concerned with matching wood grain and color.

If two pieces of plywood must be joined end to end, the easiest way to achieve uniformity of color and grain is to join pieces that have been cut from the same sheet of plywood. With a premium grade of plywood, veneer on the "A" face will be consistent in color and figure as it comes from the supplier. This is true whether the veneer is plain or rotary sliced, but the plain-sliced veneer is easier to end join for good results. This is because the slices of veneer on a single sheet have been cut from adjacent portions of a tree. Pieces will have the same figure, and they will very nearly be the same width. With most sheets, these slices are either "book matched" or "slip matched." (See Figure 7-15.) As we shall see, the plywood factory has done part of the job for us.

To make the desired long piece, we must concern ourselves with keeping the grain direction running one way

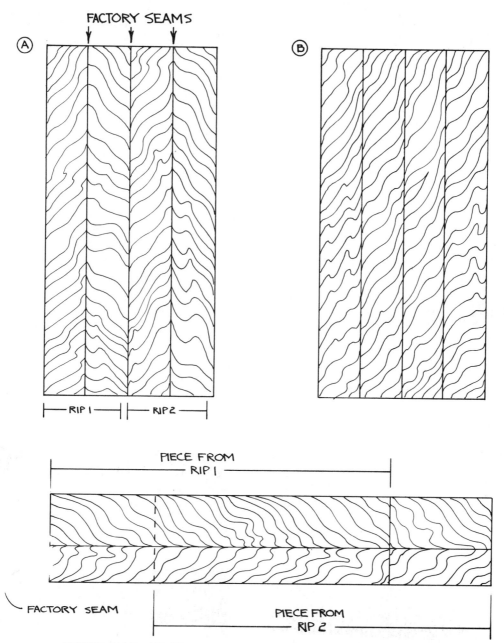

FIGURE 7-15 (A) ''Book-matched'' and (B) ''slip-matched'' grain figures. To perform end matching, rips 1 and 2 are made at the same width, taking care that veneer slices will be the same width. With grain running in the same direction, the piece from rip 1 is positioned on the piece from rip 2 and moved back and forth until the best end-to-end grain match is achieved.

and with aligning the factory seams. Two full-length rips are made to the required width, taking care that the factory seam(s) will be in exactly the same place on both pieces. To get the best possible match, one of these pieces is put on top of the other (with grain figure running in the same direction) and moved back and forth until the closest end-to-end match is found. We make a crosscut here and then spline and glue as usual. It may be necessary to perfect the

straightness of this cut on a jointer or by some other means before joining. When making such a crosscut or any connected milling, it is advisable to protect the veneer from chipping by putting a wide piece of masking tape along the line of cut. As soon as the end of our plywood piece is satisfactorily straight, the tape is removed. Obviously, this is a job that requires precise thinking, milling, and detailing in addition to gluing, but all the required operations are usually performed by one person in the shop. This avoids losing something in communication between workers.

Finally, the cabinetmaker should continually check for flatness while fabricating long or wide panels. In laminating solid stocks, many larger shops have the convenience of using slightly oversized thicknesses and reducing to finished thickness with a wide-belt sander, but edge gluing of plywood material always requires nearly-perfect alignment of stock surfaces. Veneers are simply not thick enough for excessive sanding.

BELT SANDING

Belt sanding is frequently performed on face frames and wide panels after glue curing in order to achieve perfectly flat components. This step allows easy machining of door parts and tight seams between the face frame and cabinet box. Larger shops will often invest in a wide, stationary belt sander for this purpose, but a hand-held, portable belt sander may be used to accomplish the same task.

Using a stationary sander is very simple, but it does require a thorough knowledge of the tool. In general, this machine removes material on the top surface of each piece that is fed into it. A conveyor belt keeps the rate of feed very consistent. It may be raised or lowered to accommodate varying thicknesses of material. Pressure controls on the tool must be monitored to stay within certain limits to avoid damage, and a suction system is necessary to draw off the large amounts of material that are removed. As with all tools that employ abrasives, grits may be changed by installing different belts.

If the woodworker has access to a wide-belt sander, he or she may become familiar with its operation and safety requirements by reading the manual and by observing and working with others who have a good understanding of its usage.

Setting up the sander usually begins with installing the desired belt. Tension on the belt is usually maintained with compressed air, and this pressure must be relieved before belts can be changed. The tool has a relief valve for this purpose. With the pressure released, the belts can be changed easily. (See Figure 7-16.) There is usually an arrow on the inside of the belt to indicate its correct direction of rotation.

After the woodworker has installed the right belt, he or she adjusts the height of the feed table to accept the material to be sanded. A wheel controls this setting, and a pointer and gauge on the machine gives the woodworker an approximate indication of the distance between the belt and the feed table. Many woodworkers get an accurate thickness setting on the tool by placing a piece of the stock to be sanded on the feed table and then raising the table until this piece just contacts the abrasive. This must naturally be performed with the tool off.

FIGURE 7-16 Installing a belt on the stationary wide-belt sander.

After setting the tool to correct thickness, the operator is ready to begin sanding. With most of these machines, it is necessary to engage three machine functions: the power feed, the belt drive, and suction to remove dust. Face frames, solid panels, and other stocks are simply positioned squarely on the feed table. (See Figure 7-17.) The power feed accomplishes even feeding, but the operator must observe sound safety procedures by avoiding loose

FIGURE 7-17 Feeding material through the wide-belt sander.

clothing, by keeping hands away from the power feed, and by remaining aware of how to operate the built-in panic break. Other procedures in effective, safe use of the wide-belt sander are as follows:

1. Monitor pressure gauges and keep pressure within the specified limits of the machine.

2. If pressure readings are too high, lower the feed table to lessen the amount of material being removed.

3. Sand components in ''sets''—all the face frames or door frames in a job—so that a consistent thickness can be achieved.

4. Feed the entire set of components before changing belts or thickness setting.

5. Sand in small ''bites'' without raising pressures beyond recommended limits.

6. Employ two people in the sanding process so that one may feed material into the machine and another can catch and stack pieces as they come out the rear.

7. Feed pieces to be sanded with the grain when possible.

8. Sand front and rear faces on alternate feeds for best results in flatness.

9. After frames and other components are fairly flat, install a finer grit belt for smoothness.

10. Service the machine frequently, and review safety procedures often.

When used properly, the wide-belt sander results in great savings in time and money. It is a large, very expensive piece of equipment, however, and owning one is wise only for high-volume shops with plenty of space. A few companies that own such a machine will perform sanding operations for smaller shops. This is a benefit to both parties, since the smaller shops can achieve savings in time, and since the owner of the sanding machine gets maximum tool usage.

Cabinetmakers without use of a wide-belt sander will usually achieve flatness in solid panels and face frames with a few hand tools and a portable belt sander.

The woodworker removes squeeze-out glue with a scraper or putty knife, ideally before the glue has fully hardened. Major surface misalignments (more than a hair's thickness) may be quickly removed with a sharp plane, but we use a belt sander for most coarse surface preparation.

Belt sanding should be performed on a table large enough to accommodate the entire frame or solid panel. Once again, the woodworker positions a stop block or two on the table to prevent movement of the workpiece. The table should be high enough to allow belt sander operation without a great deal of bending. In many shops, the face frame assembly table serves also as a face frame sanding table, since it is about the correct height. Cabinet assemblers will sometimes sand those face frames needed for each cabinet they work on. In fact, some assemblers prefer to do this sanding operation only after the face has been glued and nailed into place on the cabinet box.

Sanding a face frame with a portable belt sander requires development of good physical skill with the tool. The user learns a sense of balance and evenness of sanding by familiarity with it. This skill and sense are naturally easier to develop with a high-quality machine. Before investing in his or her own portable belt sander, a cabinetmaker should do some investigation. There are many portable tools produced today which are designed only for light-duty use. The serious woodworker will want to avoid these. Good-quality belt sanders are generally heavier in weight and higher in amperage rating than the cheaper kinds, and they will probably have an ''industrial'' rating. In a way, the craftsman uses the portable belt sander as an extension of the arm. We learn how to keep the sanding surface perfectly flat, and we learn to feel contours in the wood through the sander.

It should be obvious that the most careful sanding job on a face frame must be on the front, but some sanding is usually performed on the rear of the frame to ensure even joining with cabinet box members. Many cabinetmakers sand the rear of the face only where a flush contact is most important, such as along the bottom rail. Flatness is the only consideration, and we need pay little attention to grain direction.

It is easiest to sand the front of a face frame by beginning in the middle. This allows us to sand with the grain as much as possible. On a base cabinet face frame (Figure 7-18), we would sand the innermost rails first, allowing the belt sander to pass over and flatten the seam line where these rails butt into mullions. Next, we sand the mullions, allowing the head of the sander to pass beyond the seam line, where mullions butt into top and bottom rails, but not allowing the outside edge of the sander to ride over seam lines that have already been sanded flat. We continue in the same way, working toward the outer portions of the frame, until we sand the surface of the stiles. With this done, the frame is ready for mounting to the cabinet. Notice that each joint actually requires two belt sanding motions—the first with the grain of the end stock piece and all the way across the seam line, and the second with the grain of the side stock piece and not across the seam line. (See Figure 7-19.)

Some cabinetmakers resist certain usages of the belt sander, insisting that it leaves undesirable scratches in some soft wood surfaces. These workers usually prefer to spend a sustantially longer time in aligning their joints and then do surface preparation with a hand scraper. Considering the availability of reliable belt sanders and belts in fine (120) grits, their concern is probably unnecessary. It is possible to achieve excellent results with a belt sander by

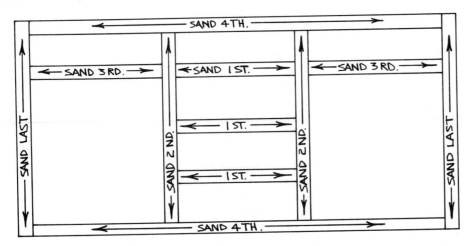

FIGURE 7-18 When sanding a face frame, we proceed piece-by-piece, working from the middle of the frame.

choosing appropriate belt grits and by following up with an oscillating sander. Craftsmen who insist on using a scraper should belt sand first and then finish up the surface with their scrapers. Properly sharpened hand scrapers have important applications, but preparing face frame surfaces is probably not one of them in today's trade.

In belt sanding wide panels, it is seldom necessary to have concern over cross-grain scratches because we are almost always sanding with the grain. Most cabinetmakers sand the rear face of each panel first. More material must generally be removed from solid panels than from face frames, and woodworkers generally use coarser belts for this type of work. On face frames, we frequently employ 80-grit and 100-grit belts, but we may choose 60-grit or coarser belts for the initial sanding of solid panels. If surfaces are quite uneven, we may even sand the panel cross-grain to speed up the flattening process and then remove scratches by additional sanding with the grain.

A belt sander can be used in surface preparation of laminated plywood panels. The procedures are similar to sanding solid panels except that we would neither use coarse belts nor perform cross-grain sanding. It is possible to sand through the veneer, and to avoid this, the woodworker will usually use a minimum of downward pressure and will lift the tool frequently for a visual inspection of the sanded surface.

Important points to remember in using a portable belt sander also include the following:

1. Turn the sander on and allow it to achieve full speed before setting it on the work surface.
2. Keep the sander moving to avoid pits and dips.
3. Take pains to keep the power cord out of the sander's path—it is easily damaged by a belt sander.
4. Allow the sander to work—do not force the tool downward against the workpiece.
5. Keep the dust collection bag in place or use a particle mask.
6. Learn the natural balances of the tool and keep the tool flat at all times.

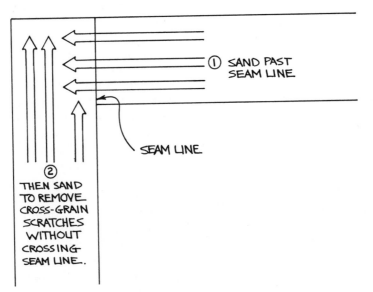

FIGURE 7-19 Each joint requires two sanding motions.

7. Use both hands, for good control.
8. Keep the belt sander properly lubricated and maintained.

A high-quality portable belt sander is an indispensable tool, even in shops with a stationary wide-belt sander. It is not only useful for fast surface preparation of frames and panels but in many other applications as well.

ALTERNATE GLUES

Alternate glues are sometimes the best choice for woodworkers. We generally use an adhesive other than "yellow glue" when the situation calls for it.

Using "White Glue"

If the cabinetmaker is gluing together a large or complex component or unit, yellow glue may begin to set before clamping and adjustments can be performed. Using white glue can be the answer. It is used in basically the same way as its yellow relative, but it allows increased working time because it dries more slowly.

Using Resorcinol Glue

If a water proof adhesive is needed, resorcinol glue is the best choice. It is frequently used in building outdoor furniture and in lamination of cutting boards and hardwood kitchen countertops. This is a two-part glue. We purchase it as separately packaged powder and liquid catalyst. These components are mixed in the prescribed proportions before application. It must be spread on both surfaces to be joined in order to work effectively, and it requires a curing time of at least 16 hours. Resorcinol glue is strong, with good gap-filling properties, but this is an impractical general-purpose woodworking glue because it can only be worked at temperatures of 70°F and above, it cannot be stored in its mixed form, it cures slowly, it leaves a dark seam line, and it can be brittle. Nothing is better in waterproofing applications, however. An adhesive that is quite similar in nearly all respects is powdered resin, which is mixed with water rather than a catalyst. Powdered resin glue is resistant to water, although not waterproof, and it does not have good gap-filling characteristics, but otherwise it is an adequate substitute for resorcinol glue.

Using Contact Cement

When an instant bond is desired, the best choice of adhesive is usually contact cement. It is most commonly used for laminating plastic to wood substrate in fabricating countertops, but it has other important usages for the cabinetmaker as well. Contact cement is quite useful in building furniture that requies bonding of wood to veneer or leather. A customer may desire a leather-covered desktop, for example. We frequently make curved cuts on plywood edges, and the most efficient way to cover the raw ply edge may be to apply a strip of veneer to it. These situations call for the use of contact cement.

Contact cement may be purchased in several different forms. Most have a base that can be thinned with solvent or lacquer thinner, but some are water based. The adhesive is applied somewhat differently from other woodworking glues. Since it has a gummy texture and adheres to almost anything, it is not easy to clean up. The woodworker usually applies it with a paintbrush or roller to avoid contact with skin and clothing. In specialized countertop manufacturing shops, workers often spray on the cement. Unless the craftsman uses contact cement with great regularity, it is usually best to purchase the least expensive brushes and rollers available. These may be used for a day or two of cement application and then discarded. A few people buy the water-based cement, which allows a soap and water cleanup of brushes, but they find that the time it takes to clean their application tools adequately is more expensive than their brushes and rollers. Naturally, it is possible to keep a brush or roller useful for several days by storing it in solvent between uses. It is important to apply thick, fully wet coats of the material, but we also want to avoid application to surfaces where it does not belong. Sloppy application results in unnecessary cleanup time.

Contact cement will not bond at all unless it is applied to both surfaces. The pieces are not joined until the adhesive has dried. This may take as little as 15 minutes and seldom longer than a half-hour under reasonably warm, dry conditions. When the cement is dry, the pieces may be placed together for an instant bond. Positioning of the two pieces is of the greatest importance because parts cannot be shifted after contact is made. (See Figure 7-20.) This is

FIGURE 7-20 Careful alignment of pieces is important when using contact cement to apply veneer. Note that the veneer is somewhat wider than the surface it covers.

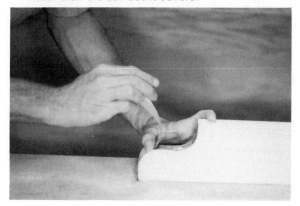

usually not a major problem, however. The cabinetmaker uses veneer, plastic, or leather that is somewhat oversized. If the backup material or substrate is the exact size needed, any excess of laminated material may easily be trimmed away. Plastic is usually trimmed with a router bit or a belt sander (see Chapter 10); leather and veneer are easily trimmed with a sharp knife. (See Figure 7-21.) A bigger potential problem in positioning is avoiding ripples and bubbles. We deal with this by allowing contact between the two pieces only in a small, controlled area. Clean pieces of wood, cardboard, or metal are kept between the two surfaces to be joined. This protective material prevents contact until we are ready to make the lamination over a confined area. For example, in positioning a large piece of plastic laminate upon its backup material, we would do the following:

1. After the cement has dried, we set the substrate piece on a firm surface, horizontally.
2. We lay thin, dust-free strips across the substrate, about 6 in. apart (this prevents contact between substrate and plastic).
3. We lay the oversized plastic sheet over the protective strips.
4. Working from one end to the other, we withdraw one or two protective wooden strips at a time and press together only that section of material without separating strips.
5. We continue removal of one or two strips at a time, following with pressure, until the lamination is finished.

In Chapter 10 we present a thorough explanation of this and other cementing techniques, in conjunction with illustrations.

With contact cement, no clamping is necessary, but before trimming, the laminator should make sure that good

FIGURE 7-21 Trimming excess veneer with a knife.

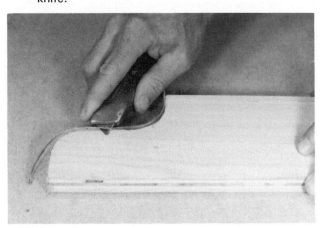

contact is achieved between parts over the entire surface. Heavy rollers are available for this specific purpose. The cabinetmaker who only does occasional cementing in this way may not want to invest in such a tool; the alternative is to use a hardwood block and a hammer and to tap the pieces together over the entire surface.

Using most types of contact cement requires adequate ventilation and reasonable fire precautions.

Using Epoxy Cements

There are basically two situations that call for the use of epoxies. One usage is in bonding together highly dissimilar materials, such as wood and metal. The other common cabinetmaking usage of epoxy has to do with its excellent hardness and filling properties. An occasional customer may request the craftsman to work in woods with large holes—a wood such as cedar or mesquite. With epoxy, it is possible to fill these large holes very effectively. Hardened epoxy can be drilled and machined with conventional woodworking tools and techniques. Thus it is possible to produce a "hole-less" panel out of wood that has fairly large holes. Since epoxies are clear, woodworkers will sometimes add color to the liquid epoxy so that it will come close to matching the color of their finished cabinetry.

Epoxy is another two-part adhesive. The resin and hardener must be mixed as specified by the manufacturer. The liquid may be applied with a stick or throwaway brush for laminating metal or ceramic to wood. For gap or hole filling, it is generally poured. Although waterproof, epoxy is not a suitable glue for large wood-to-wood joints. As with contact cement, working with epoxies requires good ventilation.

Using Hide Glue

Generally speaking, hide glue is not used with frequency in most cabinet shops. It may be good for constructing the "antiques of the future" because it is strong and does not become brittle. Application and clamping procedures are similar to those used for yellow or white glue, but it cures a bit more slowly.

Using a Glue Gun

An electrically operated glue gun can be useful in certain woodworking situations, especially when it is necessary to glue pieces in place rapidly in order to fit and cut other pieces. An example would be fabricating a door panel with "plant-on" moldings in some particular design such as the one called for in Figure 7-22. In the drawing, the designer has called for a solid stock frame to overlay a plywood back; in addition, he or she has called for a half-round molding to fill the space inside the frame. To avoid the use

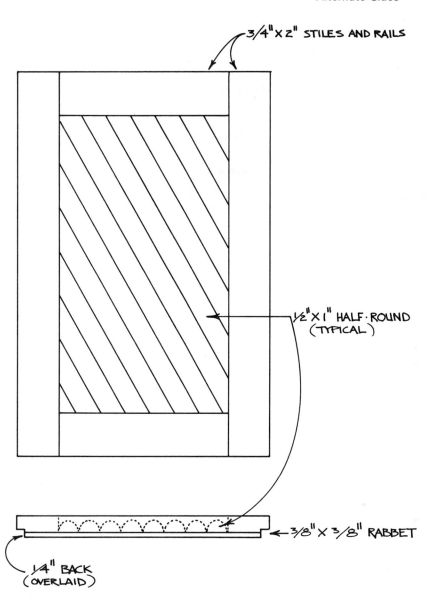

3/4" x 2" STILES AND RAILS

1/2" X 1" HALF-ROUND (TYPICAL)

3/8" X 3/8" RABBET

1/4" BACK (OVERLAID)

FIGURE 7-22 Door design that might call for use of a hot-glue gun and cartridges.

of staples and nails, the molding strips should be glued to the back panel. If the strips were in a horizontal or vertical arrangement, it would be possible to cut them to length (with one setup on the chop saw or radial arm saw) and glue them in place in one gluing operation. But this is not the case. The designer wants a diagonal arrangement of the strips. It is obvious that each strip must be individually marked and cut to size for proper fitting. The best way to do this is to cut a piece, glue it in place, and then to mark the next piece. We need a glue that can be applied rapidly to each molding strip just before it is set in place, and a glue that will set quickly, holding each strip in position so that the next can be properly measured and marked. The glue gun is a good solution.

With a glue gun, the adhesive itself comes in sticks or cartridges which are inserted into the tool. When the trigger of the gun is depressed, the glue cartridge is pressed

toward the gun tip. The tool also heats the glue so that it flows from the tip as a liquid. The gluer uses the tool tip to spread the glue. The glue begins to cool and harden immediately, but this is an advantage in situations like the one described.

A second type of heat-assisted gluing is often employed for bonding veneer tape to other materials. Within this system, the craftsman purchases rolls of veneer tape that has already been backed with heat-activated adhesive. An iron activates the glue by liquefying it. (See Figure 7-23.) Bonding is very rapid. The tape is extremely easy to apply because it may be positioned with ease, because there is no "gum" to clean up, and because the entire process is very fast. On the other hand, the bond created is not as secure as when contact cement is used, and it is also easy to apply the heat unevenly, with the consequence that there may be small unbonded gaps. The laminator who uses

FIGURE 7-23 Applying veneer tape with heat-sensitive glue and an iron. The process is faster than using contact cement, but the bond is not as strong.

this sytem must take care to apply good pressure to all sections of the tape after the adhesive has been heated and to inspect the bond carefully for flaws before declaring the job done.

Using Construction Adhesive

Construction adhesives are available in tubes that are designed to fit into a caulking gun. The woodworker may find this type of adhesive useful for mounting plywood paneling to flat wall surfaces. We can apply the ''glue'' in a way quite similar to using a conventional caulking cartridge—by cutting off the end of the tip, puncturing the seal within, and squeezing the handle of the caulking gun to make the adhesive flow. Construction adhesive is not suitable for joining pieces that require further machining.

CLAMPS

Clamps, in a great variety of designs, have been developed to fill particular needs within the wood industries. We have already observed the tremendous usefulness of bar or pipe clamps, but the applications of several others bear discussion. (See Figure 7-3.)

Using Hand Screws

Hand screws, or parallel-jaw clamps, have many uses in the cabinet shop. Face-to-face lamination is one application. In fabrication of legs for beds, tables, and other furniture, it is frequently necessary to join stock faces to get desired thicknesses. The joints must be strong because the laminated stock must usually be turned on a lathe or otherwise machined. The parallel jaws of a hand screw will apply pressure evenly and over a continuous area. This makes them extremely useful along ends and edges and across the midsections of stocks that must be laminated face to face. (See Figure 7-24.) This type of clamp is also used frequently for a firm hold on stock that is being milled, for holding stock on edge while it is being sanded, and for holding drawer boxes in position in mounting. (See Chapter 9.) Hand screws are virtually indispensable in a cabinet shop.

Using C-Clamps

C-clamps, sometimes called carriage clamps, are useful in many of the same ways as hand screws. They are capable of applying greater pressure than hand screws, but the face of the clamp does not distribute pressure over a large area. When laminating material for greater thickness, C-clamps and hand screws are usually used together—hand screws along ends and edges, and C-clamps in midsections. (See Figure 7-24.)

Using Band Clamps

The band clamp consists of a tough belt that can be wrapped around stocks to be glued and tightened in a ratchet fixture. Tightening is usually by means of a wrench. A band clamp is often used in the assembly of mitered frames such as picture frames, and it is also used in laminating to a curved surface.

Using Quick-Set Clamps

The quick-set clamp is actually a combination of the bar clamp and the C-clamp. Its design allows it to do the work of a C-clamp, only with much thicker material; its design also allows it to be used like a bar clamp, but with no con-

FIGURE 7-24 Hand screws and C-clamps used in face-to-face lamination.

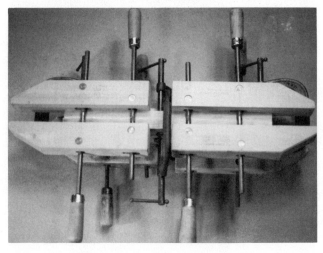

tact between the bar and stock. It is an excellent tool for furniture repair and for clamping a face frame to a finished end. (See Chapter 9.)

In addition to the clamps discussed here, there are a number of others that are much more highly specialized. As a minimum, even the small shop must equip itself with C-clamps, hand screws, and one or two band clamps in addition to its bar or pipe clamps.

CHAPTER SUMMARY OF CABINETMAKING SKILLS

Forming strong, durable joints is basic to cabinetmaking. It requires good machining and surface preparation with knife tools or abrasives, knowledge of glue characteristics, proper glue application, and the administration of sufficient, even pressure. Modern cabinetmakers employ yellow (aliphatic resin) glue for most wood-to-wood joints, but they also use a variety of other adhesives as the need arises.

In face frame assembly, the woodworker begins by assembling worked joints on the interior of the frame, progressing outward. Bar or pipe clamps are generally used for applying the required pressure to joints, and their position may be adjusted to achieve square frames. The framer first checks for correct positioning of stiles, rails, and mullions, and then determines squareness with a tape measure or framing square. While the glue is curing, the frame should be kept as flat as possible.

For assembly of wide solid panels, bar or pipe clamps are again most userful. Flatness is of the utmost importance, and pieces to be assembled are usually cut slightly wider and longer than necessary so that the gluer need not be concerned with perfect alignment of stock ends or with protection of stock edges from the clamp faces. Gluing is performed on the flattest surface available, and clamps are alternated over and under the stock as an aid in achieving flat panels. Pieces should be fairly narrow, and the end grain of plainsawn members should be alternated in gluing wide panels. It is also possible to edge-glue plywood into larger panels, using glue and pressure. The strength of these joints is enhanced with dowels or splines, and flatness is extremely important.

Frames and panels are usually belt sanded after assembly and sufficient curing. Large shops have a stationary wide-belt sander for this purpose, but a portable belt sander can also be used with great effectiveness, provided that the operator uses a good-quality tool and becomes familiar with it.

In addition to the cabinetmaker's standard glue and clamps, the trade also makes use of a variety of others. The proficient craftsman must become familiar with the usefulness of a number of adhesives and clamping devices.

EIGHT

FABRICATING DOORS AND DRAWERS

BASIC PRINCIPLES OF DOOR MAKING

Doors make the cabinet. In terms of appearance, this is nearly always true. Most cabinets are, after all, simply boxes used for storage. Drawer and door faces, with their individual designs in contour, shape, and texture, have a great deal to do with creating the unique character of a cabinet.

Building strong, attractive doors and drawer fronts requires nearly all the talents of the cabinetmaker. By learning the skills required for cabinet door fabrication, a novice craftsman is also learning to employ tools and techniques that are necessary in many other phases of cabinetmaking. This is why many shops assign newer and younger employees to "the door area." Learning door making will require some understanding of layout, the limitations and uses of raw materials, machine operation and safety, gluing, and frame building, as well as some experience with sandpaper. It is probably also true that working at the door table teaches the patience required of a fine craftsman. For most people, the "fun" jobs in a cabinet shop are layout, cabinet assembly, or milling—not door fabrication. Nevertheless, fine craftsmanship on doors and drawer facings is often an indication of cabinetry built with quality as a goal.

The door maker will find many tools either necessary or useful in his or her job. This range of tools includes stationary tools such as the shaper, portable power tools such as routers and sanders, and hand tools such as the scraper and chisel. Detailing for doors will require using many of the tools and systems discussed in Chapter 6, and it will require others as well. As the discussion unfolds, we will refer to procedures described previously and, in greater detail, to "new" procedures which are mainly pertinent to door construction. With most cabinet components, we can perform machining or detailing operations as a step; when box or face frame parts have been machined, they are ready for assembly and sanding. With doors, this is often not the case; parts are machined, partially assembled, partially sanded, machined in another operation, assembled further, and so on. We will therefore look at door preparation under three broad categories: plywood doors, solid plank doors, and frame doors. The cabinetmaker will, of course, desire some aspects of drawer front design to be similar to the doors on a job. When possible, he or she will use the same machining setups on both.

PLYWOOD DOORS

Plywood doors are the simplest of all types of doors to prepare. They may be nothing more than a piece of ¾-in. plywood cut to a finished size. This sort of door needs its

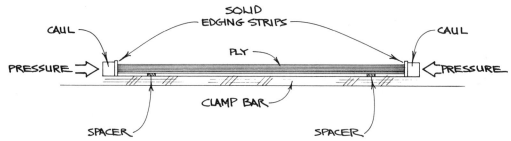

FIGURE 8-1 Gluing oversized edging to plywood. Note the use of spacers to prevent contact between the ply face and clamp bar. The spacers are also an aid in positioning the oversized edging on the plywood edge.

edges inspected for any voids that need filling, edge and surface sanding, and hinge mounting. There are some other options which are often called for, however.

Edging

Many plywood doors receive a hardwood or veneer edge on all edges. This step certainly improves the look of a plywood door, and it provides some protection to the veneer on the door, which can otherwise be susceptible to some chipping or splintering along exposed ends and edges.

If veneer is employed as door edging, veneer tape is almost always used. The tape is available in rolls with or without heat-sensitive adhesive backing. Veneer edging applied with contact cement yields fairly good results because the bond is quite secure, but it can take a good deal of time to prepare an entire set of doors and drawer fronts in this way. Using an iron and adhesive-backed veneer tape is much faster, but bonding is not as reliable. The edges of the veneer itself can splinter or chip if bonding is not perfect. In using veneer tape as door edging, many cabinetmakers prefer to spend the additional time in using contact cement. Others prefer the faster-applied heat-sensitive tape.

The use of hardwood veneer at least ⅛ in. thick is probably preferable to the use of veneer. It takes longer to apply than heat-sensitive veneer, but it probably takes no more time than cemented veneer. It is best to mount the edging with glue and clamp pressure only, because this yields an even seam line with no gaps. However, if no detailing is required on door edges, it is faster to mount the strips with glue and brads.

The thickness of the edging should be determined by the cabinet designer as part of the process of determining door size. The width of such edging may be a shop standard. Some woodworkers prefer to use strips that are only slightly wider than plywood thickness. It takes a bit more time and care to position the strips this way, but the excess solid material can be removed very rapidly with a belt sander. This is the best approach to take if the edging is to be applied with brads. We can also use this slightly larger edging in a glue-only system by using strips of masking tape for aids in holding the edging strips in position. Others of us use strips that are up to a ½ in. wider than ply thickness. This makes positioning of the edging very easy (see Figure 8-1), but excess material takes a little longer to remove. If a woodworker does a good deal of edging in this way, he or she can develop a router system for removing this material, using a straight bit and a custom-made base. (See Figure 8-2.)

The edge strips should be a bit longer than the edge of plywood to be covered. This way, we do not need to be concerned with aligning the ends perfectly. The edging should be applied to two opposing edges first. When the glue has set, we trim projecting ends of solid stock with a saw and apply edging to the other two raw edges. If the woodworker insists on mitering the corners of the edging where it comes together, he or she must carefully fit and cut each piece with a miter saw. Most door makers do not miter door edging unless it is thicker than ⅛ in.

Regardless of the type of edging and its method of application, the cabinetmaker next achieves a flush panel

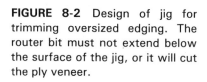

FIGURE 8-2 Design of jig for trimming oversized edging. The router bit must not extend below the surface of the jig, or it will cut the ply veneer.

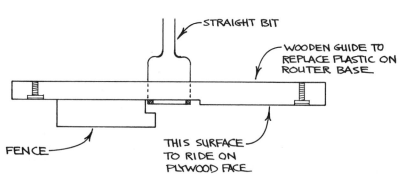

by trimming away edges of veneer or solid stock which projects above the surface of the plywood face. With veneer, it is easy to do this with a knife, but it is important to cut ''with the grain'' of the veneer to avoid damaging it. With the thicker solid edgings, excess may be trimmed with a router as suggested earlier, a plane, a fine-grit sanding belt, or a scraper (for small amounts). With flush joints between plywood and edging, the door panel is ready for final preparation with filler and fine sanding paper, unless edge or surface details must be added.

Edge Details

With a plywood door, or any other type of door, it is frequently necessary to do some machining along the edge of the door panel for purposes of decoration or function. If the detail is performed along the front edges of the door panel, its purpose is usually molding or decoration. Machining of this type is usually not done with plywood doors because it cuts away veneer and reveals interior layers of ply.

Machining performed on the rear edges of the door is almost always carried out for function. The most common of these operations are reverse beveling, lipping, and coving (for finger pulls).

Reverse beveling is easy to accomplish on the table saw. The setup is very similar to that used for mitering the edge of a piece of plywood. The woodworker attaches a protective board to the table saw fence, tilts the blade to the desired angle (usually 30°), and adjusts fence position and blade height to yield the cut. It is generally desirable to leave approximately ⅛ in. of straight door edge in machining this door. (See Figure 8-3.) This helps to protect the door face. Paired edges should not be machined. It is

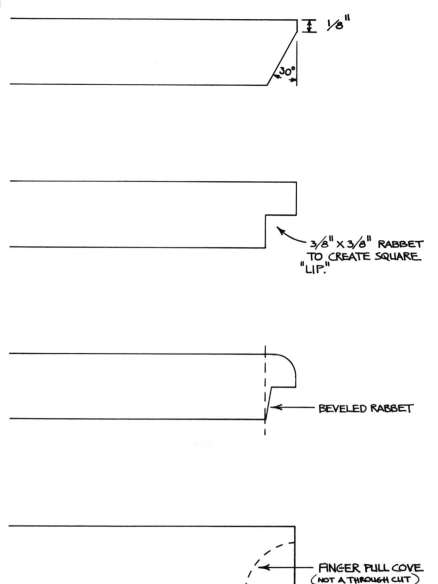

FIGURE 8-3 Drawer details often employed on the rear of cabinet doors and drawer fronts: (A) reverse bevel; (B) square lip; (C) round-over, beveled lip; (D) cove. The cove and reverse bevel may be used as a substitute for hardware.

⅛"

30°

3/8" X 3/8" RABBET TO CREATE SQUARE "LIP."

BEVELED RABBET

FINGER PULL COVE (NOT A THROUGH CUT)

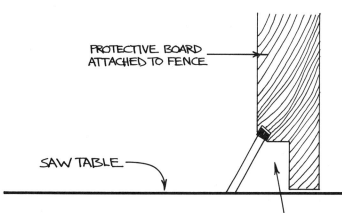

FIGURE 8-4 A protective board used for mitering or beveling should have a channel that allows waste to fall free.

important for the door detailer to use a protective board that has a groove in it to allow waste to fall away freely. Binding or pinching of the waste material is not only unsafe, but can cause the fence to be kicked out of position. (See Figure 8-4.) The 30° designation for cutting the bevel is a trade standard, based in part on the availability of specifically designed hinges.

Lipping is nothing more than rabbeting. The detail may be cut with any of the conventional rabbeting systems—dado head on the table saw (with a protective board on the fence), straight or rabbeting bit on the table-mounted router, and the others. All these systems will yield a square lip. (See Figure 8-3.) Shaper knives are capable of producing a square lip, but it is more common to purchase shaper knives that will yield a slightly beveled lip and round over the front edge of the plywood in one operation. (See Figure 8-3.) Lipping with the shaper can be very safe. The fence is in position to control the width of cut, and only a small portion of the cutter knives needs to project beyond the fence for lipping. Cutting height is controlled by raising or lowering the spindle and knives with a control wheel. Semiconcealed hinges are often used in conjunction with lipped doors, and rabbet dimensions usually conform to these hinges—⅜ × ⅜ in. It is possible with many shapers to reverse rotation direction, and the operator should make sure to use the correct rotation, depending on whether cutters are designed as clockwise or counterclockwise cutters. The shaper operator cannot be reminded too frequently to keep guards in place and to feed against cutter rotation. When lipping, and in feeding of most straight stocks, a shaper guard can be positioned which extends beyond the fence and covers most exposure to the blade. (See Figure 8-5.) Once again, paired edges should not be detailed.

Coving is performed on the rear edge of doors as a substitute for pulls and knobs. It is a purely functional detail and should therefore not appear on all edges of a door. In fact, we usually only machine a "finger-pull" cove along 5 or 6 in. of a door edge. It is therefore a start-and-stop operation, not a through cut. The cut should begin a couple

of inches away from the end of a piece and then stop after a predetermined length. It is very important that the cabinetmaker know where each door will be mounted on the cabinet, in which direction it opens, and whether the door is a pair or single. The general rule is to run the finger-pull detail as close as possible to where a knob or pull would be located. This means that the detail will be fairly close to the nonhinged edge of all doors, and that it will be near the top of base cabinet doors and near the bottom of upper cabinet doors. Long doors, such as for a broom closet, receive the detail at a convenient height to operate (about 4 ft from the floor). Paired doors must obviously be coved on the top or bottom end, but single doors may be detailed along the side edge. With lips and reverse bevels, drawer fronts are usually detailed in exactly the same way as doors on the job, but for machining the finger-pull cove, this is not always true. With low drawers, such as at the bottom of a stack, finger pulls are centered along the top edge. Drawers mounted higher, such as the ones found just below the countertop in most kitchens, receive their finger

FIGURE 8-5 Lipping with a shaper. An overhanging guard should be in position here, but it was removed for photo clarity.

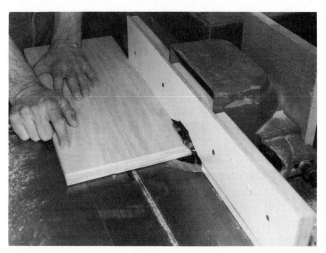

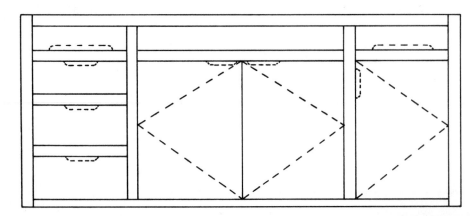

FIGURE 8-6 Appropriate finger pull locations on a base cabinet. Note that with the single door, the detail may be on the top edge.

pull in the center of the bottom edge. Also, coves cut into the bottom edges of drawer fronts are frequently longer than other finger pulls on a job. This makes them easier to find with the fingers. (See Figures 8-3 and 8-6.)

Cutting the cove is virtually always a router operation. If door personnel do the job, they will use the table-mounted router because this allows best control of the workpiece. The router is fitted with a coving bit and set at the desired height. The bit itself may be one with a bearing or roller guide, but this is not an absolute necessity since it is best to use the fence anyway. The door detailer should make reference marks on the fence so that each cut may be started and stopped correctly. In starting each cut, the right hand holds the door firmly against the table and fence to prevent kickback, on the feed end of the table (to the right of the cutter). With the tool on, the left hand brings the door edge against the fence. The entry cut is made. Feeding against cutter rotation for the desired length completes the finger-pull cove. The coving bit must be kept sharp to avoid burning, especially for the entry cut. (See Figure 8-7.)

In many cabinet shops, the door area is not responsible for detailing finger pulls. This job is left for the cabinet assembler to do as each door and drawer is mounted. This is a help in avoiding the mistake of running the detail in the wrong location. In this situation, assemblers may use a table router to accomplish the necessary details as just described, or they may elect to mount the doors first and cut the cove with a hand-held router. If this is the case, each door should be clamped motionless, the router should be fitted with both an edge guide and a coving bit that possesses a roller bearing guide, marks need to be made directly on the door for start and stop location, and the operator should wear protective glasses as an aid in vision. (See Figure 8-8.)

Surface Details

With plywood doors, decorative effects can be created on the face of the door by machining or by adding moldings. Machined details are usually created before the door re-

FIGURE 8-7 Preparing to make the entry cut with a table router.

FIGURE 8-8 A hand router may be used to cut a finger-pull cove.

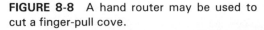

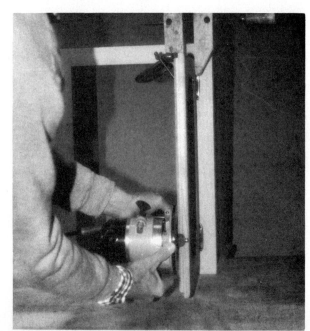

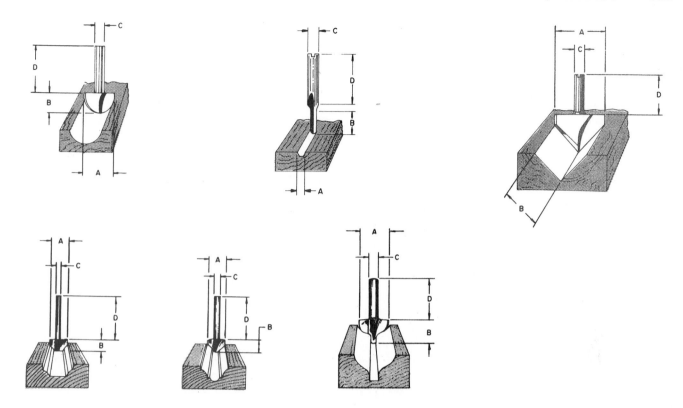

FIGURE 8-9 Bits used for surface ornamentation: (A) core box; (B) veining; (C) V-groove; (D) traditional; (E) classical; (F) ogee. (Courtesy of Porter-Cable Corporation.)

ceives any flaw repair or sanding, but if molding is to be added, the doormaker should sand the door face before applying the molding.

A router is used for machining surface details. An assortment of bits is available for this type of work, as follows: core box, veining, V-groove, traditional, classical, and ogee bits. (See Figure 8-9.) Surface routing may also require a template or pattern that can be adjusted according to the size of each door. The template usually consists of metal bars and fixtures which can be made to fit snugly around each door. To make the router capable of following the template, its base must be equipped with a projecting device called a template guide. (See Figure 8-10.) With the template securely in position on a door, the door detailer simply makes an entry with the tool on, making sure that the template guide is in contact with the template, and then follows the course of the template. For straight vertical or horizontal cuts on the surface of the door (as for imitating planks joined by tongue and groove), the cabinetmaker will often construct a wooden template.

Surface routing for decoration was fairly popular during the 1960s, but not currently. Knowledge of the tools and techniques used can still be important to the cabinetmaker, however. The shape created on the surface of doors by the routing process can help to create a style in the cabinetry, such as provincial or rustic.

Another method of "decorating" plain doors is to add moldings—strips of shaped wood that are laminated to the door faces. These may be physically arranged on the surface in a square design, a provincial design, or in other imaginative ways. The molding stock has a contour of its own which helps to create an appearance. The molding strips are mounted on each door a certain distance in from each end or edge, and they must therefore be cut (mitered) to size according to the size of each door panel.

Before applying anything to the surface of a door or drawer panel, it is necessary to do the final sanding on its face. Sanding up to and around molding strips is both inconvenient and ineffective.

FIGURE 8-10 A template guide may be installed in the base of a router and used for following the shape of a pattern.

If some type of edging was previously applied to the edges of the door, the seams between it and the plywood should be inspected for flaws. If the door maker finds small gaps, he or she should fill these with a good grade of filler paste.

If a belt sander is employed to trim edging, the entire surface of the door should be belt sanded to keep sanding texture even. Sometimes a scratch or mark is so deep that it calls for belt sanding. However, plywood doors generally require sanding only with an oscillating sander. Many cabinetmakers sand each door face twice, the first time with 100-grit paper on a sander that oscillates 10,000 times per minute, and the second with a finer paper such as 150 grit on a faster oscillating sander [12,000 oscillations per minute (opm)]. For specifics on using fillers and on finished sanding techniques, see the later section "Final Door Preparation."

Measuring the molding to be applied in a rectangular formation is very simple. The door maker simply subtracts the reveal distances from the overall dimensions of each door. For example, if door design calls for the molding to be placed 2 in. from each edge on a 12- × 20-in. door, horizontal strips will be 8 in. and vertical strips will be 16 in. in length, measured at the longest points of the miter cuts. If he or she is using curved segments, as with provincial molding, the door maker must determine how these will affect the sizes of straight segments.

The cabinetmaker may apply moldings with glue only or with glue and brads. Glue only is preferable because it yields no holes in the surface of the door, but this system is also much more time consuming. Pressure is desirable for proper application of the molding, and it can be difficult to clamp the strips into position without their slipping around on the surface of the door. Furthermore, the glue-only system requires a bit more glue to be used on each strip, and there is thus more chance of the adhesive squeezing out and marring the surface of the door, which has already been finished sanded. For these reasons, most cabinetmakers attach moldings to door faces with a small amount of glue and a few small brads. A brad gun for this purpose is extremely useful.

Careful placement of each strip is extremely important in avoiding misapplication of glue. Most door makers use tiny pencil marks (using a hard pencil) to mark the location of each corner joint of the molding on the face of the door. Such marks are easily removed with an eraser or fine sandpaper. It is also helpful to use a jig that will establish the reveal distance along each edge of the door, especially with longer strips. After the first piece has been firmly set in place, adjacent pieces should be mounted, rather than noncontacting strips, so that miter joints can be made as perfect as possible. Glue that squeezes out should be allowed to harden partially for easiest cleanup.

When we are creating a provincial shape on a set of cabinet doors, we can usually not carry out the same design on drawer fronts for the same job. Drawer facings are too narrow for this, whether the shape is rendered with router cuts or molding. The door maker often deletes the round shapes when adding detail to the drawer fronts on a provincial job. Other craftsmen consider the drawer front to be part of the door panel below it, set the two pieces edge to edge as they will be mounted on the cabinet, and apply moldings as if they were one piece. Still others make wood "plant-ons" with a modified provincial shape that can be mounted on the surface of narrow drawer fronts and tie in their design with adjacent doors.

A plant-on is simply a piece of wood that has been cut in a given shape, perhaps edge-detailed with a router (see the later section "Frame Doors"), finish sanded, and mounted on the door or drawer front. If the plant-on is very large, it should be mounted with only a modest amount of glue, allowing the door panel and the plant-on to flex and "breathe" independently.

A plywood door may receive almost any combination of the edge and surface details we have described. With this combination of details complete for the doors and drawers on a job, they are ready for final door preparation.

SOLID PLANK DOORS

Solid plank doors are similar to plywood doors in that they consist primarily of a continuous wood panel. The chief difference is that the panel cannot be cut from a sheet, but rather, must be laminated into door size by edge gluing several solid boards. The resulting door panel can receive a finger-pull cove on its rear edge, just as with plywood, but doors made of solid material seldom receive a lip, a reverse bevel, moldings, plant-ons, or solid edging.

Achieving Door Size

The first step in fabricating solid plank doors is to assemble boards into wide panels from which the doors may be cut. As mentioned earlier, the cutter selects straight boards with matching color for lamination. The pieces are oversized in length and width. Each piece is marked with a number or letter to make sure that lamination of each door includes all the necessary pieces and no pieces from another door. The laminator is responsible for making sure that end-grain direction is alternated to limit warpage. All the techniques for gluing, clamping, and wide-panel fabrication are employed.

It is especially important in preparing laminated solid doors to make seams as narrow and perfect as possible. With no glue, the pieces for each door should be laid out on a flat surface and pressed together to evaluate every seam on the door. If available, a saw table with the blade completely lowered is a good surface for this evaluation. The laminator or door maker remachines any imperfect edges on the jointer. This is why the boards were cut wider than necessary in the first place. With all its seams perfected, an individual door is ready for gluing and clamping. Since doors must be as flat as possible, the reader should be reminded of the importance of using a flat table and of equalizing over-and-under clamping pressure with each door.

Tongue-and-Groove Detailing

When used properly for joining side grains, aliphatic resin glue will create a bond stronger than the wood itself. There is no real need to strengthen seams between individual boards of a door panel by machining. Nevertheless, it may be desirable to shape the edges of solid stock for purposes of appearance. The best way to perform this detail is with a shaper, after all the individual pieces have had their edges perfected on the jointer. In employing this jointery system, it will be of the greatest importance to select perfectly flat stocks.

Two cutters are necessary for forming a worked edge joint, one to shape the tongue edge and the other to shape the grooved edge. (See Figure 8-11.) The door maker must make sure to mark each edge to be machined as either a tongue edge or a grooved edge. When doing a number of doors at once, it is otherwise easy to miss an edge or to mill it with the wrong detail. All pieces should be machined face down. Feeding must be firm and even, with no stops, to avoid irregularities in the detail. If irregularities do occur, the individual member may be restraightened on the jointer and fed again through the shaper setup. Gluing, clamping, and sanding the door panel may then proceed conventionally.

Sizing

After door panels have been sanded flush with a belt sander, they are ready for sizing. In cutting the panels to their finished size, we may use a table saw or radial arm saw as in most cutting situations, but we are dealing with panels that have irregular ends as well as edges that may be rough (from clamping) and not parallel. In many shops, the rough door panels are returned to the cutter after sanding for final dimensioning.

The cutter begins by establishing a straight edge on one edge of each panel. This is naturally easiest to perform on the jointer. The operation may require as few as one or two passes over the jointer knives.

Next, the cutter achieves a straight end on each panel, perpendicular to the edge just straightened. On a table saw, the way to accomplish this is to employ the extended face miter gauge. The cutter simply has to place the straightened edge of each panel against the miter gauge face and make a through cut near one end of each door panel. It is naturally vital to cut off only enough material so that a straight end results. The cutter may choose to make this first end cut on the radial saw by cutting each door panel with its straightened edge against the fence. If a door panel is too wide for doing the perpendicular cut in this way, it may be turned over for a second cut, provided that the straightened edge is kept against the fence and care is taken to make the two cuts meet perfectly. With a perpendicular corner, cutting may proceed conventionally on either the radial or table saw. The cutter should be sure always to use the straight end or edge as "reference" in each cut, positioned firmly against the fence.

The cutter who is sizing doors in this way should know what types of edge details are to be carried out on the doors. If a round-over or a cove is to be machined into the face of the doors, it may be a good idea to cut the doors face down rather than face up. The effects of any splintering by the saw blade will be eliminated by edge detailing. Cutters who use the radial arm saw for length cutting of doors will usually put a scrap piece of plywood or hardboard under the door for each cut as an aid in reducing splintering.

Edge Details

Cabinetmakers often add relief to solid plank doors (and frame doors) by machining along their face edges. Paired edges may or may not be detailed, depending on the preferences of the woodworker and the customer. Although it is possible to install shaping tools in either a radial arm saw or a table saw, most cabinetmakers carry out this operation with either a shaper or a table-mounted router. These tools will achieve similar edge-forming results, although the reader should keep in mind that shapers are more powerful and therefore capable of deeper, wider cuts. This is not too significant a difference in the types of edge forming discussed here, but it can be of tremendous importance in panel raising. (See the later section "Frame Doors" for information on panel raising.)

Cutter or bit selection is a concern, and there is a

FIGURE 8-11 A worked edge joint can be created with cutters that complement each other. (Courtesy of Delta International Machinery Corp.)

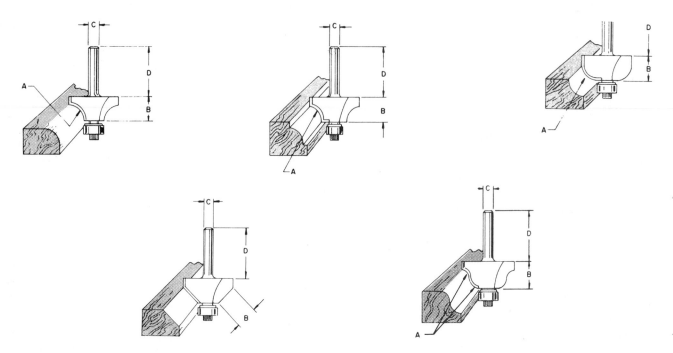

FIGURE 8-12 Edge-shaping bits: (A) corner round; (B) beading; (C) core; (D) chamfer; (E) Roman ogee. (Courtesy of Porter-Cable Corporation.)

variety of achievable contours. (See Figure 8-12.) Edge-forming router bits are usually equipped with a roller or bearing guide, but most door makers employ the fence of their table router in the edge-shaping process anyway. With the shaper it is vital to employ the fence whenever feeding stocks with straight edges.

Doors should be fed through the tool face down. The cutter is likely to cause some undesirable tearing of wood fibers at the end of each cross-grain feed, but two techniques may be used to limit the effects of this tear-out. First, cross-grain feeds should be made before with-grain feeds. The cutting done on with-grain feeds effectively cuts away much of the flaw created by cross-grain feeds. The other useful technique is to use a "follow block." This is nothing more than a scrap piece of wood that is held firmly behind the trail end of each workpiece as it is machined. It backs up the cross-grain wood fibers to limit tearing. (See Figure 8-13.)

Another technique may also be important to the door detailer. When cutters tend to burn slightly or when the cutting load is slowing tool speed (lugging down), it can be helpful to make two detailing cuts rather than one. The first cut should remove the bulk of material, and the second can then yield the sort of smoothness desired. More than slight burning indicates dull cutters or uneven feed. Double cutting will not solve these problems.

To keep door and drawer appearance consistent, drawer fronts should be given the same edge detail as the doors on a job. The detailer should edge form all the doors

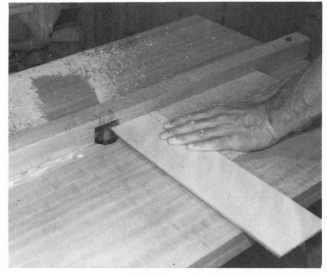

FIGURE 8-13 Edge detailing with a table router. Note the "follow block."

and drawer fronts on a single job with one setup of the tool. This ensures uniformity.

FRAME DOORS

Frame doors allow more variety of design than any other door. They can also involve a complexity of cabinetmaking processes, but the cabinetmaker thinks of frame door construction only as an involved but entirely solvable problem. Of greatest importance is completion of steps in order.

Arches and Curves

Many frame doors require cutting an arch or a curve in the top rail or in both top and bottom rails.

A door detailer must first mark rails for the curved cut. For many doors, especially arch top doors, this is a simple matter of positioning a pattern and marking with a pencil. Since doors have no standardized width, it is necessary to have arched patterns of several lengths in order to be able to mark rails as short as 6 in., as long as 18 in., and any length in between. (See Figure 8-14.) The height of each arch must be exactly the same, but since each arched rail has straight, horizontal segments where it joins door stiles, each arch pattern may be used to mark a range of rail lengths.

Another style of door calls for marking the interior of each rail with a segment of a true circle. (See Figure 8-15.) The door detailer must find the center of each rail and draw a line dividing the rail into two lengths. He or she then marks an intersecting line at a point equal to the width of the door stiles, measured from the outside of the

individual rail. The circle segment may then be drawn. It must intersect both inside corners of the rail as well as the point of the center line marked previously.

The chief difficulty in doing this is finding the correct centering point from which to draw the arc. The exact center location for each length of rail can be found mathematically, but most cabinetmakers use trial and error. To find and mark from a center, we need a perfectly square, fairly long reference board (60 in. is enough) that is ¾ in. thick and about 6 in. wide. We put a line down the length of the board and attach it to our work surface with a couple of nails. Each rail is centered on this line and held securely. We can tack a finishing nail into the reference board at a point along the center line to serve as the center. A length of shelf standard, with so many holes to slip around the nail and through which to project a pencil, is suitable to draw the arc. (See Figure 8-16.) If the curve is too small, we move the centering nail farther away from the rail; if it is too long an arc, we move the nail closer. Cabinetmakers who build this type of door with any frequency will label each nail hole to indicate the length of rail for which it may be used and save their reference board for future use. It is easiest to start with the shortest rails and proceed progressively to the longest. After rails have been marked, they are ready for cutting and interior edge sanding.

If door design calls for a raised panel on an arch-top or curved-rail door, the door maker should mark these by using a pattern. For arch-top doors, we may use the same pattern that was used for marking the rail on the same door. For marking raised panels of curved-rail doors, we first cut and edge sand the rail and then use it as a marking pattern. It is important not to cut off too much material on these curved cuts.

Cutting and Sanding Door Rails

We have already discussed the superiority of using a band saw for cutting curves and arcs like those which appear on door rails. The cut should be made slightly to the waste side of the line.

It is important to edge sand the curve of a door rail before any other machining is done on it so that irregularities and saw marks do not affect detailing. Edge forming

FIGURE 8-14 Marking arched rails from a pattern. The arch must be centered on the rail.

FIGURE 8-15 The rail of a door may have a curve that is a portion of a true circle.

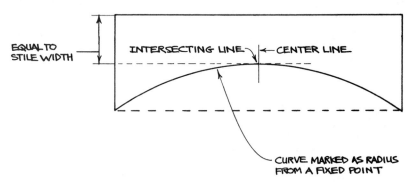

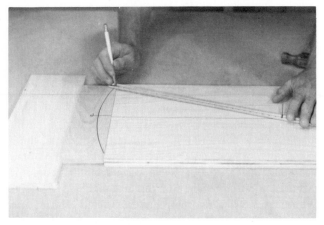

FIGURE 8-16 Marking a true circle segment on a door rail.

a curved piece requires removal of the fence on either the shaper or the router. Workpieces will be guided against a bearing attached to the cutter itself, and this will transfer dips and bumps in the edge to the shaped detail.

As pointed out in Chapter 6, we can sand curves most easily with a sanding drum mounted in the drill press. (See Figure 6-55.) Sanding to the curved line should be with drum rotation rather than against it.

Door Frame Assembly Systems

Shaper Assembly Systems. Probably the most widespread use of the shaper in the cabinet trade today is in machining door parts for assembly. In two setups with the appropriate cutter set, a door maker can achieve edge details that function in three ways. (See Figure 8-17.) The details are a male and female set, therefore creating an effective worked joint in all four corners where stiles and rails meet, like a mortise and tenon. The knives also cut a slot for insertion of an inset panel and give an attractive shape to the interior edges of the door frame.

FIGURE 8-17 Shaper knives—door set.

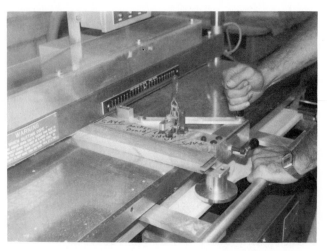

FIGURE 8-18 Feeding rail ends for a frame door. Note that the operator uses a built-in clamp to hold material and a follow board.

For milling of all straight stocks, the fence should be used, positioned parallel to the miter gauge slot in the table.

To limit the effects of tear-out, the miller should machine rail ends first, employing a follow board for each feed. The following procedures should also be followed:

1. Position the over-blade guard low enough to put downward pressure on each piece as it is fed through the cutter.
2. Use the miter gauge for feeding, and make sure that its face is perfectly perpendicular to the fence.
3. Hold each rail firmly with its end against the fence and its edge against the miter-gauge face.
4. Feed face down and evenly. (See Figure 8-18.)

After all rail ends have received their detail, it is time to run the interior edges of all door frame members. With a single-spindle shaper, this involves changing to the cutter that yields an inverted detail to the one run in rail ends. Blade height should be set carefully to achieve flush surfaces at all the frame joints. Fence position must also be determined carefully so that the two details will match correctly. The miller should also do the following:

1. Keep the over-blade guard low enough to press stock against the table.
2. Use a narrow feather board to keep narrow pieces pressed against the fence.
3. Hold each piece firmly, edge against the fence and face down.
4. Feed short pieces with a push block, a follow board, or both.

FIGURE 8-19 Safety ring guard. (Courtesy of Delta International Machinery Corp.)

In many shops, straight stock for this type of door is edge formed before it is cut to length, primarily to avoid having to feed short pieces through the shaper. This can be an excellent idea for milling door stiles, but if we do this with the door rails, it is impossible to follow our rule of milling rail ends first. If the door frame consists entirely of straight pieces, the milling operation is now complete.

To edge form the curved rails of a door frame, the miller has to remove the fence. Fenceless shaping may be

the most dangerous in the cabinet trade, and it should be performed only by personnel who are safety conscious and completely familiar with shaper operations. Some woodworkers even refer to the shaper as "the finger eater," but it can be used safely. There are guards that may be used. A safety ring will help to prevent accidental contact with the knives from above. (See Figure 8-19.) Probably even more protective is the clear spindle guard, which covers the knives more completely. (See Figure 8-20.) The shaper

FIGURE 8-20 A clear spindle guard may be used for edge forming of curves. (Courtesy of Delta International Machinery Corp.)

table must also be fitted with a pin against which stock pieces may be positioned as each cut is begun. Since we have to begin each feed at the very end of the rail, the shaper knives will have a tendency to grab the piece and draw it in. To prevent this, we position the workpiece against the support pin and bring the leading edge for the cut into the spinning knives until contact is established between the wood and the depth collar on the spindle of the shaper. The depth collar acts in exactly the same way as the bearing on a router bit. As the cut continues to completion, the curved door rail should remain in contact with the depth collar only, not the support pin. With short pieces, the door detailer will want to take an extra precaution by attaching a strip of wood to it with nails or screws. Short pieces may then be held firmly with hands far from the cutter. The curved rails should be milled right before or after edge forming of straight frame members so that the cutter height setting can remain identical throughout the milling of a particular job.

With curved rails now milled, frame members are ready for sanding and assembly. However, assembly of the frame cannot take place unless the back panels are also ready to be incorporated into the doors. If the back panels are to be flat, they are usually pieces of plywood that only need sanding to be ready for door assembly. If door design calls for raised panels, these laminated solid pieces must also receive their edge forming on the shaper.

A raised panel cutter produces some of the widest and deepest details that are achievable on the shaper. Driven by a motor with sufficient power, the cutter is capable of removing a great deal of material in one pass. With lighter-duty shaper motors, it is frequently necessary to make more than one pass to achieve the desired detail.

One of the first things that a door detailer should decide in preparing to do panel raising is whether to make the surface of the raised panel even with the surface of the door frame. This is a common practice in shops that possess a wide-belt sander because both frame and panel can then be sanded at one time with the stationary tool. The detailer simply shapes the rear edge of the panel with the panel-raising cutter just enough to allow this arrangement. Other shops generally prefer to allow the panel face to project beyond the surface of the door frame, performing all machining on the face side of the panel. (See Figure 8-21.)

In creating the "surfaces-even" panel, our first height setting would be exactly high enough to make the surfaces even. We would run this detail on the rear surface of all doors by feeding face up. Then we adjust cutter height so that milling the panel face down will leave an edge thickness lean enough to fit grooves in style and rail edges. This is the critical dimension in carrying out the detail. In this way, depth of cut takes care of itself. Similarly, for the true raised panel, cutter height is adjusted so that the panel will fit into edge slots. Since solid stocks will swell, this fit should not be too snug.

Other procedures that are important in panel raising are as follows:

1. If curves are present on the panel, machine these ends first, using no fence, but rather an efficient guard, depth collar, and support pin.
2. Attach short curved panels to larger boards for feeding.
3. Employ the fence in feeding all straight stocks.
4. Make cross-gain feeds first to limit tear-out.
5. Use the miter gauge to straight-feed short or narrow panels (similarly, if panel raising is performed on drawer front edges, feed these pieces with the miter gauge).
6. Use the over-cutter guard to provide downward pressure on workpieces.
7. Hold workpieces firmly and feed against cutter rotation.

It should be noted that it is possible to create raised panels with tools other than the shaper, but a shaper is clearly the best tool to use for this job if it is available.

FIGURE 8-21 Edge forming for a raised panel and a "surface-even" panel.

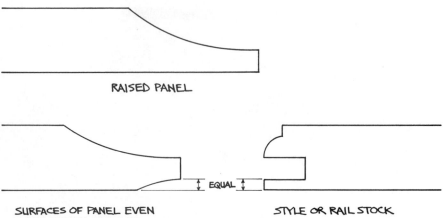

RAISED PANEL

SURFACES OF PANEL EVEN WITH FRAME SURFACE

EQUAL

STYLE OR RAIL STOCK

When all pieces have been machined, the door maker must sand certain portions of the door parts before they can be assembled. The large edge detail of a raised panel is much easier to reach with sandpaper at this stage than after the piece has been incorporated into an assembled door. It is similarly wise to finish sand the following sections: the rear face of the door panel (unless it will be even with the rear surface of the door frame), both faces of an inset plywood panel, and the inside edge detail on all frame members (except on the portion of the stile that is to receive rail ends).

Router Assembly Systems. The entire process of machining for doors with a shaper can be duplicated with a table-mounted, heavy-duty router. Tool manufacturers now provide carbide-tipped router bits that will accomplish edge forming and panel raising for door production.

Machining for doors with the table-mounted router follows the same procedures and safety guidelines as those we have pointed out for the shaper system. There are some important differences, however. Most tables used for routing are made from wood, and they possess no miter-gauge slots which can be used to feed rail ends or other narrow stocks. Some woodworkers adapt by either dadoing a slot into the surface of their router table or by setting up their router in the wood extension of their table saw. (See Figure 8-22.)

Generally speaking, the router can be an excellent tool for the type of edge forming required, but most cabinetmakers are not satisfied with panel raising with a router. Panel-raising router bits can vibrate a great deal, and they produce a narrower cut than shaper knives are capable of. The investment in a heavy-duty router and accessory bits is obviously going to be much less than purchasing a shaper and its cutters, but before deciding to "tool up" the router for door detailing as a shaper substitute, the reader is advised to consider its limitations. One possibility is to invest in the door-edge-forming bits and not the panel-raising bit. In this way, we are able to produce the decorative inner edge shape and interlock the stiles and rails. We can use this tool system with flat panels and with raised panels formed on the table saw.

The router can be used for a second sort of assembly system. The door maker actually uses dowels to join door faces and employs the router in machining a slot for insetting a panel or back. Any interior edge decorative detail must be machined separately.

To prepare stiles and rails in this system, the door detailer fits the router with a splining bit (slotting cutter). The bit should be equipped with a roller bearing for guiding curved rails. The fence should be used for feeding straight stocks. We position the slot so that the back of the inset panel will be about ⅛ in. from the rear face of the

FIGURE 8-22 Saw table extension fitted with a router. This allows use of the T-slots in conjunction with the router.

door frame. This is controlled by adjustment of cutter height above the table. It may be necessary to make two passes for each piece to make the thickness of the slot conform to panel thickness. Quarter-inch plywood is used most often for the inset panel, and it is usually a good deal thinner than its nominal thickness.

Material should be fed face down to contribute to an even door frame. Rails are detailed with through cuts, but stiles must be machined with stop cuts so that the slots do not appear on the top and bottom of assembled doors. (See Figure 8-23.) Since it would be nearly impossible to add a decorative detail to the interior edge of the door frame after the door is assembled, this machining must also be completed before assembly.

FIGURE 8-23 A back panel may be installed in slots machined with the router. Note the stop cuts necessary on the slot and round-over detail.

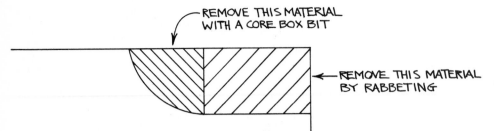

FIGURE 8-24 A wide cove for a raised panel may be created by combining rabbet and core box routing operations.

We may create a rectangular raised panel for inclusion in this type of door assembly system by first rabbeting each edge on a table saw and then using a core box bit in the table router to yield a wide cove detail. (See Figure 8-24.)

A router assembly system for doors can be effective as long as the door maker realizes and works within the tool's limitations. With detailing complete, the door maker will want to sand certain portions of the doors before they are assembled.

Table Saw Assembly Systems. Cutters are available for a table saw which will allow cutting the same types of matching edge details that are possible on a router or shaper, but few cabinetmakers do this. It does not contribute to tool specialization, and a router or shaper is simply more convenient.

A dado head or saw blade is sometimes used instead of a spline cutter to cut the slots in edges of door frame stock for installation of a back panel. A saw blade may not cause as much tear-out in wavy-grained stocks such as maple as will a knife tool such as a slotting cutter. Also, it is possible to set an adjustable dado to cut slots for plywood panels in one pass. One drawback to using a saw blade or dado head for slot cutting, however, is that they have a larger radius than a slotting cutter and therefore cannot cut as close to the ends of stiles on the stop cuts.

Probably a more important use of the table saw in door detailing is as a tool to form a bevel-edged raised panel which can be used in conjunction with any of the assembly systems we have described. A beveled panel naturally creates a much different appearance than a coved panel or a panel with an ogee. Shaper cutters are available that will cut the bevel, of course, but many cabinetmakers still do the operation on a table saw.

Unlike most angled cutting done on the table saw, the setup for beveling a raised panel requires tilting the blade away from the fence. On most saws, this means that the fence will have to be positioned to the left of the blade, and the required feeds will be a bit awkward at first for right-handed detailers. Since the panels have to be fed on edge and the blade projects through the table surface so close to the fence, it may be necessary to make a new insert to provide the maximum surface over which to feed edges. With the correct angle already set, the arbor is lowered and a solid wooden insert is positioned. It should be held firmly down with the fence as the spinning blade is raised through it.

Probably the biggest potential problem in making doors with a beveled panel is how to allow for the natural and substantial expansion of the panel's width due to variations in temperature and moisture. If the beveled edge of the solid material fits into the slots of the door stiles too snugly, expansion of the panel is enough to crack the door frame. Solutions are to machine a flat portion onto the outer section of the bevel or to increase the width of the panel mounting slots in the frame stiles. The contours created allow for a good deal of expansion and still yield an attractive beveled detail. (See Figure 8-25.)

Fence position should be such that thickness of the panel at its edges and ends will fit properly into the slots cut into stiles and rails. Blade height should be just high enough to allow the outside of the blade to project through the panel's surface. Each feed must be firm, with the rear face of the workpiece flat against the fence. Ends should be cut before edges. (See Figure 8-26.) Since it is impossible to use a guard, the door detailer should exercise care in performing this operation. Of course, the panel's edges and its rear surface should be sanded before assembly.

Other Door Assembly Systems. Many shops assemble door frames with dowel-supported butt joints. As we have observed, doweling may be employed in assembling doors with inset back panels. And as we shall see, dowels are often used to join door frames which will receive an overlaid back. (A shop may also use mortise-and-tenon or toe-screwed joints.) Dowel joining of door frames proceeds exactly as it does for face frames (see Chapters 6 and 7), except that the door maker must take a little care to position dowels far enough from stock edges to prevent an ensuing detail cut from revealing the dowel. This is naturally of most concern with coves and other wide and deep edge details. This may be an even more important concern when toe screwing is used to join door frames since we obviously do not want to hit a hardened steel screw with a router bit or saw blade.

Assembling Frame Doors

In assembling frame doors with inset backs, a good deal of machining and sanding is necessary before doors can even be put together. The actual gluing and clamping procedures

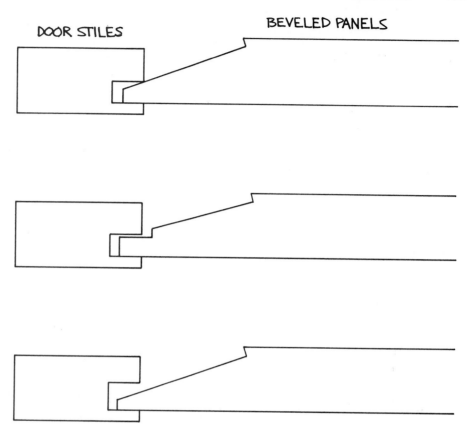

DOOR STILES   BEVELED PANELS

FIGURE 8-25   *Top:* The problem: Expansion of the beveled panel can ruin the door if the fit is too snug. *Middle:* One solution is to flatten a portion of the bevel. *Bottom*: A second solution is to widen stile slots (not rail slots).

FIGURE 8-26   Beveled panel raising with the table saw.

are quite similar to those used for building face frames, but there are a few differences.

Door frames must be as flat as possible so that they will fit cabinet openings without a raised corner—and achieving perfectly flat doors can be difficult. Some large shops use a specially designed press to ensure flatness, but effective equipment of this type can be expensive to develop. Woodworkers utilize a number of different techniques in an effort to get flat doors. Some have success with using C-clamps or hand screws to hold down each corner of an assembled door frame while it is curing. (See Figure 8-27.) Others will stack up a number of doors on a perfectly flat surface (such as a steel saw table), separating door surfaces from one another with plastic-laminate-covered boards, and then use bar clamps to press the entire stack flat against the table. These methods are time consuming and yield varied levels of success.

In reality, the key to building flat doors is probably precise cutting and machining as well as good material selection. A door maker cannot really do anything to achieve flat doors out of stock that was not cut square. It is equally important for frames to be assembled on a table which is perfectly level and flat. When beginning a set of doors, the door maker should take a few minutes to check the work surface with a level. Clamps are also a concern. The pipe or I-bar of the clamp should be straight and free of hardened glue.

The pair of clamps used on an individual door frame

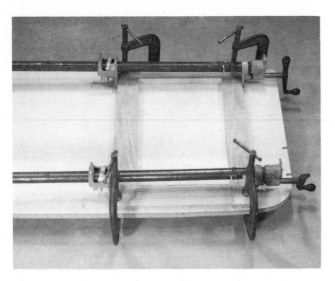

FIGURE 8-27 Clamping the corners of a door frame to a plastic-laminate-covered board to promote flatness.

should be as nearly identical as possible. They are positioned beneath each rail. The door maker should apply glue as to any frame, to coat all portions of the stile and rail that come into contact. The inset panel must naturally be in place when the frame goes together. It is all right to apply a small amount of glue to hold a plywood panel in place within the frame slots, but this procedure should *not* be followed with panels made of solid material. In fact, we should take care to avoid glue establishing a bond between the solid panel and stiles. Here again, the panel can expand in width to break the door. The panel should be attached only to the center of the top and bottom rails with a few drops of glue in the frame slots and a brad driven from the rear of the door. Since the panel will sit somewhat loosely in its frame, the door maker must take care to center it before the brads are driven into place. Also, some cabinetmakers put a packing material into the frame slots, adding stability to panel positioning. A few of the tiny adhesive-backed rubber door bumpers that come in a box of hinges are suitable for this.

The outside edges of the rails should line up perfectly with stile ends. The door must then be checked for squareness with a measuring tape or a framing square. Then the frame should be allowed to cure under pressure, resting on a flat surface. When glue is dry, we have a door with interior details and surfaces that are essentially complete. Before the door can receive any outer edge details, its frame must be sanded flat with a belt sander. Then the door will be ready for final sanding and hinging.

In assembling doors with overlaid backs, the sequence of operations is slightly different. If the door design calls for curved or arched rails, these details are marked, cut, and edge sanded as with any other door. We proceed by preparing the straight inner edges of the door frame, just as we would do for a face frame. The stock edges may be sanded or machined with the jointer or planer. If knife tools are used, the stock used should be oversized in width. Then it is possible to assemble the door frames, using dowels or another method. Even edge joints, squareness, and flatness are still very important concerns.

After sufficient curing time, the door frames are ready for sanding. The primary purpose for sanding at this stage in door making is to achieve perfectly flat faces on both the front and rear of the door. If we are using a wide-belt sander, feeds should alternate face up and face down until the doors are flat. The doors should be fed so that they are sanded with the grain of the rails. This makes later sanding processes easier. If we are using a portable belt sander, we should sand the rails first, allowing the head of the sander to go well beyond the seam lines. Then we may sand the stiles, being careful not to cross the seam lines. Of course, there is no need to avoid cross-grain sanding on the rear of the door frame because it will be entirely covered by the plywood back.

Interior Edge Machining

With the front surface of the door frame made flat, the door maker may use a table router or shaper to render its interior edge details. Since the operation cannot be carried out with a fence in place, the detailer should employ extra caution.

In setting up the shaper, we need a depth collar to control the width of our chosen detail. A spindle guard offers protection and a support pin can help to limit kickback. Cutter height naturally controls depth of cut. To feed, we set a frame on the table face down, surrounding the cutters and support pin, pivot one edge of the frame into the spinning cutters and against the depth collar, and feed firmly against cutter rotation. Hand and finger position should be near the outer edges of the frame, but close enough to the cutters to exert control. If feasible, grip-surfaced push blocks can be very helpful. To change grips, as for feeding the corner of the frame, the operator should draw the workpiece slightly away from the depth collar, change hand position, and then reinitiate feeding at a point of the frame that has already been cut. If possible, the door detailer should not allow feeding to pause in the corners when the depth collar is in contact with a stile and rail at the same time, since this can contribute to some burning. Feeding continues in a circuit until all four members of the frame are detailed. (See Figure 8-20.) Before committing to this system, a cabinetmaker should realize that it will be impossible to render the inner edge detail all the way into the corner of a frame with a shaper. The large diameters of shaper cutters and depth collars will simply not permit this. This is one reason that many cabinetmakers prefer a table router for detailing assembled frames. Nonetheless, the detail or sticking, stopped exactly the same distance from each corner on all frame members, can be attractive. If cutting

FIGURE 8-28 Detailing the inside edge of an assembled door frame.

results in tear-out, or if the cutting load is too heavy for a single feed on each door frame, it will be necessary to reduce the amount of material being removed by lowering the cutter or by changing to a larger depth collar. *Do not feed with cutter rotation* on a shaper as a solution to tear-out.

Many cabinetmakers consider the table-mounted router to be superior to the shaper for detailing of assembled frames, not only because it can edge form all the way into each corner, but also because it is safer for this operation. There is much less of a cutter to be wary of, and the tool is far less likely to kick back. It is even possible to feed stocks backward as a solution to tear-out, provided that the operator is not using a very large cutter and has good control of each workpiece. However, it is still advisable to feed against cutter rotation as much as possible.

In setting up the router, we need only to fit it properly with the desired bit (with depth collar or roller guide) and adjust it to the desired height. Feeding is quite similar to shaper feeding—face down, hands clear of danger but close enough to the cutters for control, in a circuit around the inside edge of each door frame, and with an effort to avoid hesitations that can cause burning. (See Figure 8-28.) The detail is round in each corner.

Mitering

Cabinetmakers occasionally employ mitering operations in making doors. The entire width of stiles and rails may receive miter cuts for joining. If so, all inner-edge machining should be complete before the frame is assembled. This will yield square-cornered rather than round-cornered details. (See Figure 8-29.) It is possible to use dowels in a mitered face joint simply by drilling the dowel holes perpendicular to the mitered ends. The actual miter cuts are most easily cut with a motorized miter box. Still another option is to create a miter only for the edge-formed width of stiles and rails. (See Figure 8-30.) This will also produce a square-cornered detail, and stiles may be joined to rails

FIGURE 8-29 Mitered door frame. Notice the square-cornered edge detail.

FIGURE 8-30 A square-cornered edge detail is also achievable when only the shaped portions of stiles and rails are mitered.

175

in one of the conventional ways. The stop miter necessary on the stile is easiest to cut feeding with a miter gauge on the table saw. With either miter system, backs may be inset or overlaid.

Attaching Overlaid Backs

Cabinetmakers generally rely on glue for attaching overlaid plywood backs to the rear of door frames. Larger shops employ a door press to clamp the backs in position until glue cures (Figure 8-31), but many cabinetmakers use a staple gun or brad gun in addition to the glue (Figure 8-32).

Positioning of the back can be important. If the doors are to be lipped or reverse beveled, as such doors often are, the cabinet designer will usually call for plywood backs with overall dimensions that are slightly less (perhaps ⅛ in.) in both width and length than the dimensions of the assembled door frames. This is an aid in outer-edge sanding and detailing. The door maker should keep the edge of the back away from the edge of the door frame except at paired edges. On paired edges, these edges must be flush. (*Note:* Some doors, such as arch-top doors, cannot be reversed by turning them upside down, and therefore the door maker must know how such doors will be mounted on the cabinet in order to determine which edges are paired.)

The front surface of the plywood backs must be finish sanded before they are mounted. In mounting overlaid backs, the craftsman will usually use a piece of thin carpet or another sort of clean padding as a covering for the work surface. This offers some protection for the door face that must be laid on the worktable face down in order to attach the back. With a frame laid out, the door maker applies glue to its rear surface. The glue should be applied near the edges of the frame for good bonding, but the wood-

worker should avoid using so much glue near the inner edges that it will squeeze out onto the already sanded surface of the back. Then the plywood back is laid into position carefully. It must not slip around or glue may be smeared onto the visible surface of the back.

If the doors are to go under a press, two short brads should be driven through the rear of the back to prevent movement as pressure is applied. The door maker positions backs to several doors of the same or nearly the same size in this way, stacks them in the press, and then applies pressure to the whole stack.

If staples or brads are to be used, positioning is quite similar, but the cabinetmaker drives a series of staples or brads to support the glue. In driving the fasteners, we need to be careful not to miss the door frame or we will have a damaged door face. It is also necessary to position fasteners far enough from the edges to be missed by blades and cutters in ensuing lipping, beveling, or coving operations.

Staples give more secure fastening, but the smaller brad holes are easier to fill. Using a door press not only yields better-looking door backs, but it brings savings in preparation time. In the small shop, it may be a quite realistic alternative to stack doors between two flat, rigid surfaces and to press the backs on using bar clamps.

Regardless of how the frame door is machined and assembled, with its back installed, it is ready for outer edge detailing. Rear edge forms—lips, bevels, and coves—can now be achieved just as they would for plywood doors. Front-edge forms—coves, round-overs, beads, and so on—may be rendered with the same techniques as those employed for solid plank doors. Before performing any machine operation on the outside edges of a frame door, the door maker should do two important things. First, he or

FIGURE 8-31 Press used to clamp door frames and backs.

FIGURE 8-32 Attaching the door back with a staple gun.

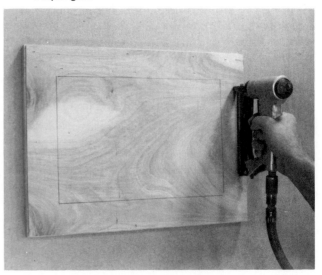

she should sand all the ends and edges of each door so that irregularities do not affect machining. A stationary edge sander is excellent for this, but a craftsman may also hand sand each door edge with a block. Workers who are steady-handed with a portable belt sander may clamp each door on end and sand. No matter which sanding technique is used, the woodworker must take care not to oversand. Second, a proficient door maker will want to avoid mistakes by going through all the doors on a job and marking paired edges. These will often not receive a detail.

It is obvious that door production may proceed in a variety of ways. Cabinetmakers choose their door-making systems based on the look they are striving to create in an individual cabinet job as well as their own available tooling. Door designs are products of imagination, and as long as there are doors on cabinets, cabinetmakers will create unique looks and search for new assembly systems.

FINAL DOOR PREPARATION

Final door preparation can be thought of as three processes: filling, sanding, and hinging. Filling and sanding create smooth, uniform surfaces that are pleasing to the eye and to the touch. These phases of door making require patience and some hard work, but they are also sources of pride. Hinging is a purely functional activity.

Using Fillers and Patches

In general, filler pastes are used to repair any flaws that are too large to be sanded out but too small to be patched with wood. (In building new cabinets, it is seldom necessary to patch because we cut around major flaws in our raw materials, but it is often necessary to patch in furniture repair.)

Some craftsmen resist the use of fillers, and, of course, perfect joints require no filler. On the other hand, the pastes now available truly come close to matching wood materials in color and stain acceptance, if not in texture and grain figure. Using filler is far better than leaving a small gap in a seam or a nail hole.

Filler paste should have a smooth texture when applied, but it should not be too thin or it will shrink so much that it does not fill the void. Thinning is possible with solvent or lacquer thinner. It is easiest to apply with a flexible putty knife. Good pressure should be applied so that the hole is actually filled rather than just covered. Excess should be removed immediately. (See Figure 8-33.) Woodworkers commonly use filler in the voids of raw ply edges, nail or staple holes (if these were handdriven, they may first need to be set with a hammer and nail set), and in slight imperfections along seam lines.

Patches are thin pieces of wood that are used to repair larger defects in a surface. Patching is a type of inlay work.

FIGURE 8-33 Applying filler paste with a putty knife.

The woodworker first cuts away a section of the wood surface to eliminate the flaw. The shape of this cutaway is usually triangular. Most important, it must have straight edges and a flat bottom so that it will be fairly easy to make a new piece of wood conform to its contours. We should mark the three points of the cutaway with the tiny point of an awl and then make cuts with a sharp utility knife, guiding its point along a metal straightedge. An effort should be made to keep the blade straight and pressure even so that each straight-line cut may be achieved in one pass of the knife. Then we carefully remove all the material between the cuts with a sharp chisel.

The patch itself may be cut in a similar way, but we first have to get the patching material to its correct thickness. If we are working with a finished surface, as when repairing the veneer on an antique, it is vital to make the patch material exactly as thick as the cutaway's depth before it is glued in place. With unfinished surfaces, it is of course possible to glue the patch in place and then sand it flush with the surrounding surface. Probably the best way to achieve exact thickness is to edge cut an oversized piece on the table saw. If the slice is imperfect, we are losing very little material by throwing it away, resetting the saw, and cutting a new slice. With a piece of perfect thickness, we cut it with a straightedge and knife to fit into the cutaway and then glue and clamp it in place. (See Figure 8-34.)

FIGURE 8-34 Triangular patching job.

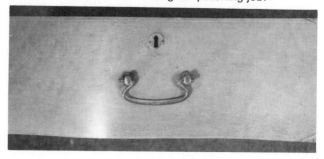

Sanding by Hand

Some portions of a door require hand sanding. Broad, long surfaces can usually be effectively sanded with power sanders, but edge forms or details most often can only be made smooth with hand sanding.

In sanding any detail, the door maker often encounters mill marks and small burns which require heavy sanding. The coarse grits of sandpaper (60 to 80) are used to remove these irregularities. If the detail will appear on the front of the door, it should also be sanded with a finer-grit paper (120 to 180) so that heavy abrasive scratches may be removed. Papers used for sanding of face details should be at least as fine as the paper we plan to use for broad surface sanding.

Edge-form sanding is with the grain when convenient, but certain portions cannot easily be sanded without cross-grain sanding. The door maker therefore sands along each detail, regardless of grain direction. In narrow edge forms, we can reduce the effects of cross-grain sanding by following with finer paper. On broad edge forms such as those shaped by a raised-panel cutter, we can do our final sanding in short strokes with the grain, or it may be possible to use an oscillating sander. (See Figure 8-35.)

If it is feasible, the door maker uses a block as backing for sandpaper, and if possible, this block should be shaped to fit the contour of the edge form. The block for sanding a lip may be just a square-edged piece of wood with the abrasive creased and folded around it. This type of block allows the door maker to sand both surfaces of the rabbet at once. (See Figure 8-36.) Backing for sanding a cove shape may simply be a dowel wrapped with sandpaper. (See Figure 8-37.) Rounded-over or flat edges at the outside of the door (or unassembled door component) may be sanded with a flat block or even a power finishing sander. With many other edge forms, it is often easiest and fastest to back the paper with a finger.

FIGURE 8-35 Sanding a broad edge form with a small oscillating sander.

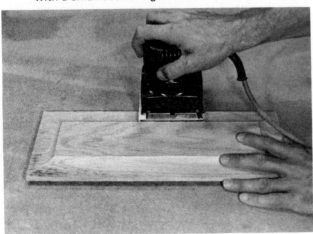

FIGURE 8-36 Hand sanding a door lip.

The sharp corners or edges of a detail should also be eased or broken. Sharp, perfectly square edges are not very functional because they are more likely to splinter, and splintering is bad for the door's appearance as well as the skin. It takes only a moment to draw sandpaper along each edge.

FIGURE 8-37 Hand sanding a cove.

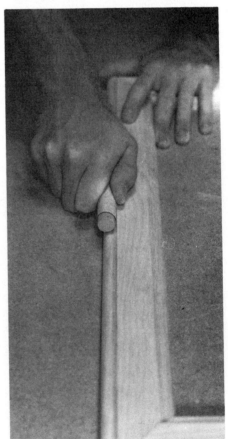

Belt Sanding

It is appropriate to belt sand certain portions of a door in its preparation. We have already observed that coarse sanding is necessary in preparing solid laminated doors and panels. This should be followed by belt sanding with a fine grit (100 to 120) as a transition to using a finish sander. Door frames should be surface sanded similarly with a belt sander.

In addition, it is sometimes wise to belt sand certain plywood door surfaces (veneers). The rear faces of overlaid door backs often require belt sanding, especially if they are attached with brads or staples. Occasionally, the front face of a plywood door or door component will possess a scratch or flaw that may be removed easily with light belt sanding. The key is to use a fine-grit belt and to lift the sander frequently for inspection of the veneer. Another useful technique is to apply a small amount of water to a shallow scratch and allow it to dry before sanding. This swells and raises the wood fibers a bit, allowing them to be sanded. As in all belt-sanding operations, we should obey the following:

1. Make sure that the workpiece is firmly held.
2. Allow the tool to reach full speed before sanding.
3. Make long, with-grain strokes, end to end if possible.

4. Allow the flat part of the sander to travel all the way to the end of the workpiece.
5. Keep the sander flat and keep it moving.
6. Overlap each stroke widthwise with the previous stroke, working gradually to sand the entire width of the board.
7. As much as possible, avoid changes of direction (back and forth) in the midsection of the workpiece.

Using Finishing Sanders

Most finishing sanders function by oscillation of their base or pad. Most of those in use are powered electrically, but some pneumatically operated finish sanders have recently become available. Cabinetmakers frequently refer to finishing sanders as vibrators. (See Figure 8-38.)

The pad of a finishing sander may be rectangular, accepting half-sheets of sandpaper, or it may be square, taking quarter-sheets. Some pads are even round.

Most half-sheet sanders are designed for general sanding, with no-load pad speeds of 10,000 oscillations per minute (opm). They remove stock more quickly than quarter-sheet sanders, and they are a favorite among cabinetmakers. Large production shops frequently use these as their only finishing sanders. They are operable with one hand, but they are far more effective when operated with

FIGURE 8-38 Oscillating sanders. The larger half-sheet sander is a favorite general-purpose sander. The quarter-sheet sander is used for superior smoothness. (Courtesy of Porter-Cable Corporation.)

two. In softer woods, their oscillations can leave swirls—tiny circular sanding scratches—especially at places where the direction of tool movement is changed. The swirls are fairly easy to sand out with a higher-speed sander or by a bit of hand sanding.

Quarter-sheet sanders are designed to yield greater smoothness than their bigger brothers, with speeds of 12,000 opm. Many cabinetmakers develop the habit of using one of these sanders on door and drawer fronts and on all other primary surfaces. They follow a belt-sanding procedure with a half-sheet model, using a medium-grit (100) sandpaper. Then they sand the same surface with the smaller, faster sander, employing a finer-grit (120 to 150) paper. Their product is smooth and more swirl-free. The tool is designed for one-handed operation.

It is appropriate to use an oscillating sander on many portions of a door. On plywood or solid plank doors, both the front and rear surfaces of each door should be "vibrated." On frame doors, the doormaker will usually use a finishing sander to prepare the front and rear faces of each frame as well as both faces of a raised panel or plywood back. In addition, the quarter-sheet sander may easily be used for sanding some edge forms, notably round-overs and some wider coves.

In using any oscillating sander, the operator should obey the following guidelines:

1. Turn the tool on and allow it to reach full speed before setting it to the surface to be sanded.
2. Move the sander with the grain.
3. Keep the pad of the sander flat on the surface (do not tilt and sand with an edge or corner of the pad).
4. Make long strokes, allowing the front or rear end of the pad to pass beyond the end of the stock.
5. Make successive strokes overlap in width.
6. Use fairly slow strokes under controlled pressure, allowing the pad and abrasive to work.

The last sanding operation on a door is to ease the sharp edges with a bit of sandpaper. Doors are then ready for hinging.

Using a Scraper

Used judiciously, a sharp scraper can be a valuable tool in door production. Most modern cabinetmakers do not use a scraper for the preparation of large flat surfaces, but it does have applications in various cabinetmaking processes. In door making, it can be shaped with a grinder (Figure 8-39) to conform to particular shapes and used instead of or in addition to sandpapers to achieve smooth edge forms. (See Figure 8-40.) Scrapers also have a few modern usages in cabinet assembly that we will look at in Chapter 9.

FIGURE 8-39   Grinding a form into a scraper.

FIGURE 8-40   Using the scraper on a formed edge.

Hinging

Hinging is an operation that may be performed by door personnel or by an assembler. The rationale for the assembler performing this operation is to avoid mistakes. As we have observed, some doors are not reversible. A single arched-top door must be hinged on the correct side for correct mounting. An assembler usually has the best knowledge of how doors are to be hinged on a cabinet under construction.

Different door designs call for different hinging systems. The most common cabinet hinging systems in use today are butt, strap, semiconcealed, demountable, pin, and European (fully concealed). It is quite easy to position hinges and attach them by screwing into the wood or another method, but additional machining is necessary to mount certain kinds of hinges.

Butt hinges are often used on flush inlaid doors and shutters. They are easiest to mount when they are simply screwed into place on the edge of a door. Most cabinetmakers fit the hinge carefully into a shallow notch or mortise on the edge of the door for a smaller gap between facing and door, however. (See Figure 8-41.) The mortise may be easily cut with a straight bit in a portable router. We must use a template guide and jig in this operation. (See Figure 8-42.) The mortising may also be done on a table saw with a dado head, feeding each door on edge with the miter gauge and using the fence as a guide in positioning the mortise properly on the door edge. The drawback here is a danger of torn-out wood fibers on the door faces. Hinges (nearly all hinges) should be positioned within a few inches of the end of the door. The pin of a butt hinge should protrude above the door's front face. These hinges may also be mounted as strap or surface hinges.

Strap hinges may be used on flush, inset (lipped), or overlaid doors, depending on hinge contour and door thickness. These are merely set into position on the front surface of the door and screwed in place.

Semiconcealed hinges have varying contours that allow them to be mounted to the rear face of a door and wrap around its edge form so that it may be attached to a cabinet's face frame. Styles are available to fit the edge contours of inset, slab overlay, and reverse bevel doors. Many

FIGURE 8-42 Cutting the shallow mortise with a router and jig. Note the template guide.

such hinges will attach to the front surface of a cabinet's face frame; others, called knuckle hinges, attach to the edge of a face frame.

Most semiconcealed hinges are inexpensive and easy to mount. No special machining is necessary. The cabinetmaker places each door face down on a protected work surface, measures for hinge position near the edge of the door, punches small pilots with an awl, and screws the hinge in place. Appropriate hinge position is about the width of a hinge from each end of the door, and many craftsmen actually use the hinge to measure for placement. Hinge manufacturers will also sell a template jig that speeds up the hinging process. (See Figure 8-43.) It has spring-loaded stop pins that allow the jig to be used at either end of each door. The tool is simply set in correct position and struck with a mallet to position the hinge correctly and punch all three screw-starting holes at once. A screw gun or a variable-speed drill will drive the screws most quickly. Phillips head screws are vastly preferable to slotted screws. (See Figure 8-44.)

Demountable hinges are used as a system in many large shops because they are easily mounted and adjusted. They are designed to function similarly to semiconcealed hinges in that they may wrap around a particular door edge form: inset, slab overlay, or reverse bevel. The pin assembly or knuckle is exposed on the front of the cabinet. A single demountable hinge will be mounted to the cabinet face just like a semiconcealed hinge, with screws.

Demountable hinges are attached to a door by a clamping effect that is operated with the tightening of a single screw, but doors must receive additional machining

FIGURE 8-41 Flush door with mortised butt hinges.

FIGURE 8-43 Hinge template jig for fast location of hinge screws. (Courtesy of Amerock Corporation.)

FIGURE 8-44 Mounting a semiconcealed hinge with a variable-speed drill. Note the Phillips driving tip and padding for door-face protection.

FIGURE 8-46 Preparing a door for demountable hinges on a stationary routing machine.

with a router. The cabinetmaker employs a bit called a T-slot cutter to cut the necessary detail into the edge of each door. A special hinge routing machine makes it easy to locate the position for the T-slot and cut it. Smaller shops often invest in such a portable routing machine. (See Figure 8-45.) Shops with more space might purchase a stationary model. (See Figure 8-46.) It is possible, but not as reliable or fast, to buy only the T-slot bit for this machining operation. The woodworker could guide each feed with an edge guide, for example, but the reason for using demountables is to increase speed. The cabinetmaker who uses them should probably be committed to the whole system. When T-slots have been cut, the hinge is attached by inserting its wing clamps and tightening the single screw. In this system it is frequently just as fast to use a conventional screwdriver to fasten the hinge in place. Since they are so easy to attach, it may be wise to leave the hinges off until the cabinet assembler is ready for doors. The completed doors are more easily stored this way.

FIGURE 8-45 Portable demountable-hinge routing machine. (Courtesy of Amerock Corporation.)

Pin hinges are mounted to the rear surface of each door with screws. The pin or knife of the hinge projects through an angled slot which must be cut through the edge of the door. The necessary machining is generally performed with a jig designed to fit into the slots of a table saw. (See Figure 8-47.) The jig should have a protruding edge against which to position each door edge. The rear face of the door lies against the surface of the jig. The angle of the jig's surface in relation to the saw table allows us to make a through cut and achieve the type of slot we need to achieve—just large enough for the angled pin assembly to fit through. (See Figure 8-48.) The door maker usually marks the jig as an aid in positioning for each cut.

Most pin hinges possess oval-shaped and circular screw holes for hinge mounting. In screwing the hinges into position, we should drive screws only into the oval-shaped holes because they allow the assembler some adjustment in door mounting. The assembler will drive screws through the circular "locking holes" after doors are perfectly positioned on the cabinet.

European hinges also require machining to be

FIGURE 8-47 Cutting a beveled slot for the pin hinge. Note the angle of the jig surface and the protruding lip used to position each door.

FIGURE 8-49 Drilling the back surface of a door to receive the "cup" of a European hinge.

VARIABLE OVERLAY

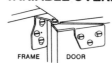

FRAME   DOOR

FIGURE 8-48 Pin-hinge mounting arrangement. Note the beveled slot. (Courtesy of Amerock Corporation.)

mounted. This involves drilling carefully located holes in the rear face of each door. Drilling must be a stop operation with a special bit available from the hinge manufacturer. It can be quite difficult to create the required hole without a drill press.

In creating a setup that can be used to drill a set of cabinet doors, the drill operator must refer to specifications provided for the particular hinge. The drill bit itself will determine the correct hole diameter, but the craftsman needs to set the table and depth gauge of the press to control depth. Depth must be enough to accommodate the hinge cup without getting too close to the front face of the door. Individual hinges, with predetermined specifications for size of overlay, call for particular placement of the hinge holes in relation to the vertical edge of the door. Once this location has been determined (some throwaway sample pieces are suggested), the woodworker should attach a fence to the drill press table so that the edge of each door may be positioned against it, accurately controlling the lateral position of hinge holes for repeat boring. (See Figure 8-49.) Naturally, if the cabinetmaker does not have access to a drill press, he or she will not often want to use this style of hinge. If a job calls only for a few such hinges to be installed, it is possible to create a jig or pattern that allows routing of the hinge cup hole. A portable drill will not work well for this operation.

The hinges are secured in position either by screwing

FIGURE 8-50 Machine for drilling and insertion of European hinges. (Courtesy of Julius Blum Inc., Cabinet and Furniture Hardware.)

or by pressing in specially designed friction fittings that are already attached to the hinge cup. Cabinetmakers who are committed to the European design will invest in special drilling and press-in tools. (See Figure 8-50.)

After doors are hinged, they should be stored somewhat carefully. They should be kept off of the floor where they can pick up moisture, and hinges should not contact faces if they are stacked.

ASSEMBLING DRAWER BOXES

Assembling drawer boxes is a very simple process. We have already taken a look at tools and methods that can be used for machining drawer parts. In general, we simply fill and sand drawer parts as necessary, spread glue properly, and drive fasteners.

Preparing Drawer Components

Just as in certain phases of door assembly, it is best to repair flaws and to sand drawer parts before they are assembled into a unit. The same tools and procedures are also applicable.

If sides, subfronts, and backs are composed of solid material, little filling is generally necessary. Hardwood plywood members should have top edges inspected for voids that require filling. With softwood plywoods, faces as well as edges may need filling. Drawer bottoms may require a bit of filler paste (on the better face) only if they are made of softwood plywood.

Drawer members need sanding as follows:

- *Sides:* on both faces and the top edge.
- *Subfronts and backs:* on the inner face and the top edge.
- *Bottoms:* on the face (not at all with hardboard).
- *Edges:* all vertical members should be eased substantially to prevent splintering unless they were previously rounded over with a shaper or router.

Some softwood faces may need belt sanding if they are very rough, but otherwise all the faces may be sanded with an oscillating sander. Since drawer components are secondary surfaces, fine finish sanding is generally not considered necessary. The drawer builder can use a half-sheet sander with medium-grit (100) paper. Edges are most quickly sanded with a stationary edge sander, which can also be used to ease the sharp edges very rapidly. (See Figure 8-51.)

FIGURE 8-51 Sanding the edges of a drawer box part.

FIGURE 8-52 Fastening drawer members with a brad gun.

Fastening Drawer Components

Whether or not we are using a subfront, assembly of the drawer should begin at the front. This helps to assure flush, even joints at the front of the drawer box, where it matters most. We spread glue along the surfaces of the front or subfront that are to contact the sides and then drive our fasteners. If the joints are straight butt joints, it is advisable to use staples rather than nails for their superior holding power. For drawers that are to be under heavy loads, wood screws or drywall screws may be a good choice as fasteners, but the drawer assembler should predrill a countersink and clearance hole in the drawer side for these, and more important, should also drill a pilot hole for the screws into the end of the front or subfront. Otherwise, the screw may do more to weaken the drawer than to strengthen it. The fastest systems employ a pneumatically driven staple gun or nail gun for fastening. (See Figure 8-52.) The guns save a great deal of time, and they are a wise investment even for one-woodworker shops with any sort of consistent work flow. Naturally, use of pneumatic guns requires having a compressor and buying specially designed nail or staple clips. With both sides joined to the front by spreading glue and fastening, we can attach the back to the sides in the same way.

If the drawer bottom is to be supported in a slot cut into the back, the bottom must obviously be positioned before gluing and nailing the back in place. Cabinetmakers who use this system usually install backs that are slightly loose, side to side, in the drawer slots. They put a small amount of glue into the slots to bond the bottom to the rest of the box. This is an aid in keeping the box square.

Some cabinetmakers still prefer to use a narrower back that allows the drawer bottom to be installed last. They slide the bottom into the slots cut in the sides and front, turn the drawer over, and drive nails through the bottom into the back. The bottom fits snugly into the rest of the

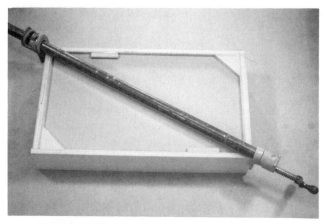

FIGURE 8-53 Clamping the long diagonal of a drawer box for squareness. Note the glue blocks.

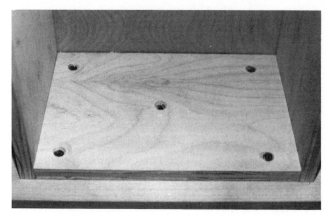

FIGURE 8-54 Drawer front may be attached to the drawer box with screws.

FIGURE 8-55 Drawer front adjustment fitting. (Courtesy of Julius Blum Inc., Cabinet and Furniture Hardware.)

drawer box to hold it square, and no glue is used in the drawer bottom slots.

Regardless of which system is used, the drawer builder should check each drawer box with a tape or square to ensure its squareness. The box should be checked near the drawer bottom. If an adjustment is necessary, the longer diagonal of the box may be shortened with a bar clamp. Then a small glue block or two can be positioned under the drawer bottom to keep it square. (See Figure 8-53.)

The completed drawer box may require attachment of a front if it is of subfront design. The drawer builder may do this, or the task may be left for the cabinet assembler to complete. Obviously, the front should be sanded before attachment. The attachment system should be one that allows adjustments. In a conventional cabinetmaking situation, screws are used for this fastening. (See Figure 8-54.) Suppliers of hardware for European cabinetry can often make special fittings available for this purpose. The fittings call for predrilling to be installed, but they allow fast and easy adjustments. (See Figure 8-55.)

CHAPTER SUMMARY OF CABINETMAKING SKILLS

Creating strong, beautiful doors is vital to quality cabinetmaking, and to do so, a woodworker must not only develop tool-handling knowledge and abilities, but also develop a good sense of procedural order to follow. It is especially helpful to be aware of those final preparation processes that must be accomplished in the midst of assembly. Many door and drawer segments are much more difficult to sand after doors are wholly assembled.

Plywood doors may receive edging, which may be clamped in position or ironed on. Their rear edges may be detailed on a table saw, a table router, or a shaper to achieve a lip, a cove, or a reverse bevel. Surface details may be routed into the surface of such a door or be added on as molding or plant-ons.

Solid plank doors must be laminated from oversized pieces and sanded smooth before they are cut to finished size. They may then receive rear edge details just like a plywood door. In addition, solid doors often receive a front edge detail, which may be run on a shaper or router. The contour of such a formed edge may vary greatly.

To construct frame doors, the cabinetmaker may have to follow a series of machining steps that is frequently interrupted by sanding procedures. Arched or curved rails must be marked out and cut if they are called for in design. Raised panels must be cut to match these curves and arches. The edges of these pieces, and all door frame members, must be sanded for smooth machining.

The shaper, with the correct knives, can be used to shape frame members in such a way that they can be put together in a strong joint, receive an inset panel, and yield decorative sticking or molding. It is also the best tool for panel raising. Safe shaper operation requires care, especially in operations with the fence removed. Edge forms on all pieces, and both faces of a raised or flat panel, should be sanded prior to assembly. With the door assembled, it may further receive outer edge details, front and rear, just as a solid plank door.

The table-mounted router can achieve results similar to a shaper, but it is not an effective instrument for panel raising. It is frequently used for edge forming of the interior edges of assembled frames that have been joined with dowels. Such frames require interior edge sanding before assembly, and they require surface sanding before routing or back application. The router is especially helpful in shaper-less shops which routinely use overlaid backs.

Overlaid backs must be finish sanded on their faces before they are attached. Then they are glued and pressed on, or they may be glued and stapled on with a pneumatic stapler. With backs on, these doors, too, may receive outer-edge detailing.

Final door preparation consists of appropriate use of fillers as well as applications of belt and oscillating sanders with abrasives ranging from coarse (60) to fine (180).

The cabinetmaker has a variety of hinging systems to choose from. Some require investment in special tooling systems. Semiconcealed hinges are inexpensive and easy to use, making them a favorite in small shops.

The fastest drawer assembly system is with pneumatic stapling equipment. Used in conjunction with glue, staples yield good strength even in butt joints. Before assembly, drawer components should be prepared with some medium-grit sanding.

Before any assembly step, the question should be: Is any sanding necessary before this assembly is completed? Makers of doors and drawers will achieve excellent results, without unnecessary work, by continually reminding themselves of their ultimate product.

NINE

ASSEMBLING THE CABINET

THE WORK SPACE

For many cabinetmakers, assembly is the most enjoyable part of their work. This phase, after all, is a fulfillment of all the other cabinetmaking processes. Box components are cut to size and machined for assembly. The face frame is assembled and sanded flat. Doors, drawers, and other accessories are ready and waiting to be installed.

A particular cabinet may take as little as an hour or two to assemble, but many take substantially longer. To build good-quality products without sacrificing a great deal of time, cabinet assemblers should set themselves up efficiently and develop their own comfortable assembly system.

Cabinet assembly can require a number of tools. Therefore, the setting up calls for good organization of the necessary tools in a convenient work space. The ideal work space consists of a firm, level, fairly large (3 ft × 7 ft minimum) table on which to assemble the cabinet. Surrounding the table should be a good deal of free floor space. This allows the cabinetmaker to reach any part of a cabinet under construction easily. The work surface should be at a convenient height, probably between 2 and 3 ft. from the floor. Nearby should be a smaller auxiliary table for storing tools and supplies. In addition to a box of hand tools, the cabinetmaker should have a belt sander, finishing sander(s),

and a reversible variable-speed drill within easy reach. These are essential. If available, other valuable timesaving equipment—nail and staple guns, saber saw, portable router, and so on—should not be far away. The area needs good lighting.

Developing one's own assembly procedure is largely a matter of choosing a sequence to follow. This naturally has a lot to do with the type of cabinet design generally used in a shop, but the cabinetmaker also makes some sequence choices, such as whether to attach sleepers to the bottom before or after a cabinet is assembled. It is surprising how much these relatively minor decisions have to do with developing assembly efficiency. Such things are learned from experience. Of primary importance is to follow the same sequence again and again.

ASSEMBLING THE BOX

Assembling the box means preparing for face frame attachment. As the assembler begins an individual cabinet, he or she should first gather all the necessary parts: box components, face frame, sleepers, and material for hold-downs and nailers. Some sanding may be necessary before gluing and nailing anything together. If the face frame was not previously sanded, it should be belt sanded now, before a partially assembled case is sitting in the way on the assembly table. Secondary surfaces—box insides—should also be sanded. A half-sheet oscillating sander with medium-grit paper will do the job. Scratches and other visible marks should be removed. Fir plywood interiors may need some filling.

The assembler should also make sure that notches have been properly cut where necessary. Most partitions require notching to allow the placement of continuous nailers. This is especially important in upper cabinets, where notches are more difficult to cut after assembly.

True assembly, the joining of components, can now begin. In general, each part-to-part attachment is made by spreading glue and then nailing. A nail gun is of tremendous value, and it should be kept lubricated and maintained according to manufacturer specifications. The operator must learn to position the gun accurately and hold it firmly while firing. The gun selected for a purchase should be relatively light and easy to handle. It should possess a safety that will allow it to be fired only when in contact with a surface. When firing the gun, the operator's free hand should be far enough away from the gun to prevent injury from a misdirected nail. (Misdirection can be caused by poor alignment of the gun or by a wood fiber irregularity that the operator cannot detect.)

If a base cabinet is to have front-to-back hold-downs, these may be attached to the top of each partition and end, flush with the front and the top edge. In a sink cabinet, the hold-downs should not be attached in the sink area. (See Figure 9-1.)

The bottom of a base cabinet needs sleepers attached to it. These should be no farther than 18 in. apart, and the assembler should make sure that a sleeper is positioned fairly close to every partition. Of course, a sleeper is not necessary near an end that contacts the floor. Since most base cabinets have a toe space, the front of each sleeper should be held back a certain distance. The toekick will later be attached to them. (See Figure 9-2.) With some cabinets, and furniture pieces too, the sleepers and toekick may

FIGURE 9-1   Attaching hold-downs for a base cabinet.

FIGURE 9-2   Attaching a sleeper to the bottom of a base cabinet.

be built as a separate unit and later attached to the bottom of the case with screws.

In upper cabinets, strips of shelf standard may be installed before assembling the box. The assembler usually needs to cut four strips of standard for any section of cabinetry that is to receive adjustable shelves. The strips must be exactly the same length, and their rectangular holes (where support clips are inserted) must match vertically. The assembler may cut pieces to length with a hacksaw, a saber saw (with metal cutting blade), or a special cutting tool made for just this purpose. (See Figure 9-3.) Aluminum strips are easy to cut with some types of snips. The assembler then affixes the strips of standard to partitions and ends with the special nails provided for the standard or with a staple gun. The standard has holes that allow the use of either. Naturally, it is important to avoid staples so long that they can be driven all the way through the cabinet

FIGURE 9-3   Tool for cutting shelf standard to length. (Courtesy of Knape & Vogt Mfg. Co.)

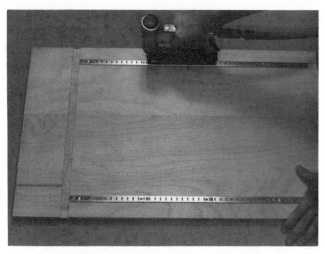

FIGURE 9-4 Attaching shelf standard with a pneumatic staple gun.

FIGURE 9-6 Attaching a finished end to the bottom of a base.

member. (See Figure 9-4.) It should be noted that some cabinetmakers prefer to install the shelf standard only after the cabinet has received its stain and lacquer or other finish.

With hold-downs, sleepers, and shelf standard in place, the main body of the cabinet box may be glued and nailed together. This is simply a matter of dealing with one joint at a time. We apply glue in a dado or rabbet, insert the end of the piece which is designed to fit, nail, and proceed to the next joint. In a few minutes, the box is together and ready for its face frame. (See Figures 9-5 to 9-7.) In this work, the assembler should remember the following:

1. Begin by assembling interior joints (these usually involve the ends of fixed shelves).
2. Assemble components with their front edges up.

FIGURE 9-5 Attaching a wall end to the bottom of a base unit.

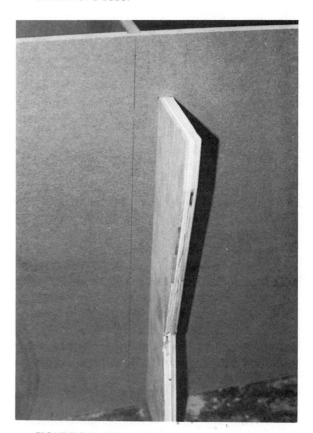

FIGURE 9-7 The cabinetmaker used a line on the reverse side of a dado to attach the partition to this bottom.

3. At each joint, make sure that these front edges are even so that the face frame can be attached flat.
4. Use a nail near each end of a joint, but be careful not to split fibers of the end stock that receives the nail.

189

5. In general, space nails 5 to 6 in. apart.

6. If hand nailing, use finishing nails on all primary and secondary surfaces and box nails on concealed surfaces.

7. Refer to the production drawing or layout stick to make sure that the arrangement of components is correct (it is possible, and even easy, to confuse an arrangement and build a particular cabinet in reverse).

8. Leave the back off until the face frame has been attached and drawers have been mounted.

Some cabinetmakers draw faint pencil lines on the opposite side of a dado as an aid in locating nail positions, but with a nail gun it is fairly easy to sight along a dado to position the gun.

ATTACHING THE FACE FRAME

Attaching the face frame takes only minutes if the box is flat. With the box assembled, the cabinetmaker can immediately glue and nail the face frame into place. Of course, if the craftsman is building without a frame, edging was added to the front edge of the cabinet components as part of the detailing process. When this type of box has been assembled, its face is already in place.

The assembler uses quite conventional techniques to attach a face frame. First, it is a good idea to lay the frame on the assembled box and make sure that it fits properly before glue is applied. A mistake (heaven forbid) is easier to correct before the face frame is attached. This also allows us to mark any portions of edge stock that will not be covered with a face frame. (See Figure 9-8.) The marks tell us where not to spread glue on the edge stock. Next, we set the frame aside and spread the necessary glue. The cabinetmaker should take care to cover the entire edge of the box wherever it contacts the frame, particularly on the edges of finished ends and cabinet bottoms where face and box are to meet in a perfect flush joint. The frame should be set and nailed in place immediately. (See Figure 9-9.) Again, there are a few guidelines to obey, as follows:

1. Begin nailing on the outside of the cabinet and work toward the middle.

2. Nail first along seams that must be made flush, such as finished ends and bottoms.

3. Allow a small amount of the stile's width to overhang finished ends.

4. Keep the top edge of the bottom rail exactly even with top surface of the cabinet bottom. (See Figure 9-10.)

5. Align partitions to be parallel with mullions as you nail. (See Figure 9-11.)

FIGURE 9-8 Marking a portion of edge stock that will not be covered by the face frame.

FIGURE 9-9 Attaching the face frame with a nail gun.

6. Use a measuring tape to make sure that longer fixed shelves are nailed to the frame parallel to the bottom.

7. In general, space nails 6 to 8 in. apart.

8. Nail through the face into each hold-down.

9. Where possible, nail through the frame into fixed shelves.

Driving nails through very hard woods with a hammer can be difficult. It can also split a frame member. The cabinetmaker should drill a pilot hole for each nail, using a bit that is just slightly smaller than the nails to be used. It also helps to rub each nail with paraffin or beeswax before driving. With a nail gun, we can usually solve the problem by raising air pressure, as long as we stay within the recommended limits of the gun.

For a base cabinet, the toekick is usually mounted right after the face frame. With a handsaw, the assembler makes a cut in finished ends to complete the mitered notch begun by the detailer. (See Figure 9-12.) The assembler must also cut a small notch in the mitered end of the toekick. Glue is then applied to the top of the kick, the mitered cut, and the front of all sleepers before nailing. (See Figure 9-13.)

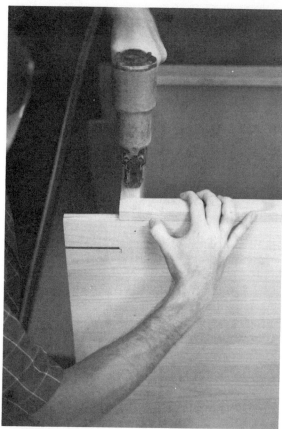

FIGURE 9-10 Aligning the bottom rail with the bottom of the box.

FIGURE 9-11 A partition must be aligned parallel with a mullion.

FIGURE 9-12 Cutting to the mitered stop cut in a finished end. Note that the cut is even with the bottom of the mounted face frame.

FIGURE 9-13 Attaching a toekick. Notice the notch cut into its surface to fit around the finished end.

As soon as possible after the frame and the kick have been nailed into position, seams should be examined for tightness. The cabinetmaker may desire to apply clamping pressure across certain seams, especially where flush joints are desired. In applying these clamps, cauls should be used to protect the face and to yield even pressure. (See Figure 9-14.) Cabinetmakers will frequently stand the cabinet up on its bottom while under clamp pressure. This way, they have access to the rear of the cabinet, where nailers can be measured and installed. (In building "premium-grade" cabinets, nailers are installed after backs are in place.)

Several things can be achieved while waiting for glue to dry. It is a better practice to measure for nailer length directly from the assembled cabinet rather than to take dimensions from a production drawing or layout stick. This is why many shops do not list nailer lengths on the cutting list. The assembler can position a length of nailer material where it is to be installed in the case and mark for a cut of perfect length. (See Figure 9-15.) An upper cabinet should receive top and bottom nailers. A base cabinet requires a top nailer as well as nailers positioned appropriately so that they may be used to affix rear ends of drawer guides. (See Figure 9-16.) Nailers are fastened by nailing through cabinet members which they contact. (In premium-grade cabinetry, the finished end is rabbeted to receive both the back and the nailer. They are fastened by driving staples or box nails through their rear face and into the edge of the finished end.)

Another task that can be performed before clamps are removed is to apply edging to the front edge of any fixed shelves in the cabinet. These are raw edges of plywood or other material not covered by the face frame. The edging may be ¼-in. strips of the same type of hardwood used for

FIGURE 9-15 Marking a nailer's length directly from the case.

FIGURE 9-16 Nailer positioning in a base cabinet. The short horizontal nailer is for mounting a single drawer. The vertical nailers will be used to mount a stack of drawers. Side-mount glides will be used.

FIGURE 9-14 Clamping the seam of a finished end.

the face frame, or it may be the iron-on variety. (On cabinets with flush inlaid doors, fixed shelves must be edged before the cabinet is assembled so that the thickness of the edging will not interfere with operation of a door.)

SANDING THE ASSEMBLED CABINET

Sanding the assembled cabinet is like other sanding operations. When clamped joints have cured sufficiently, the assembler can remove the pressure and begin the cabinet's final surface preparation. This begins with removal of any glue that squeezed out during the clamping procedures. This glue will interfere with filler application and router and sander operation.

The portable router, fitted with a flush-cutting bit, can be very helpful in gaining a perfectly flush joint between the stile of a face frame and plywood on a finished end. The ball-bearing guide contacts the plywood surface while we feed with the base of the router flat on the surface of the face frame. (See Figure 9-17.) Some shops use a slightly different bit which trims excess material and cuts a V-groove exactly at the seam line, but most custom cabinetmakers prefer a flat seam. The operator may employ reverse feeding to keep chipping to a minimum.

Filler should be applied wherever necessary. There may be tiny seam gaps where the face frame joins a finished end or cabinet bottom. There may also be such gaps where hardwood edging was applied to fixed shelves. The use of filler paste to fill nail holes on the primary surfaces of a cabinet may be an issue. Some cabinetmakers do this as a matter of routine, while others prefer to leave this filling to be done as part of the finishing process. The cabinet finisher can mix stains with putties to match the final color of surrounding wood surfaces. Still, nail holes can never be made to disappear, and it ultimately saves time for the assembler to fill them with paste before sanding.

Seams involving the cabinet bottom or fixed shelves may be sanded or scraped smooth. For long seams, some

FIGURE 9-17 Trimming face frame overhang on a finished end with a router and flush cutter.

FIGURE 9-18 Smoothing the seam between the bottom rail and cabinet bottom with an oscillating sander.

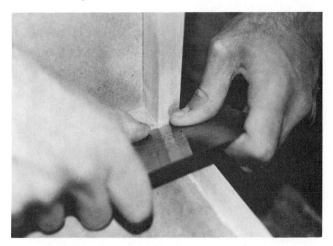

FIGURE 9-19 Smoothing a seam near a mullion with a flat scraper.

cabinetmakers employ a belt sander for part of this sanding. A half-sheet oscillator is used most frequently. (See Figure 9-18.) Paper grits should be medium (80 to 100). The position of paritions and vertical frame members limits the use of these sanders, and scrapers are frequently used to complete the smoothing-out process. (See Figure 9-19.)

A scraper must be kept sharp for it to be effective. To sharpen it, we simply mount it firmly, edge up, in a vise or hand screw and draw a file flat across it a number of times. For faster cutting, the scraper's cutting edges may also be knurled over slightly.

A finished end should be sanded to a fine surface. The belt sander may be used with a fine-grit belt, but quite good results can be achieved using only a finishing sander. Procedures are similar to sanding flat door surfaces except that we often have to do the sanding with a finished end in vertical position. If so, it is imperative to maintain good control of the tool. (See Figure 9-20.)

The last sanding operation on an assembled cabinet is on the face or face frame. If the front of the face frame was not previously belt sanded, it may be sanded at this point. Some cabinetmakers will belt sand the face again, to make removal of extra filler paste a bit faster. It is again a good idea to finish sand twice: first, with a half-sheet oscillator and medium-grit paper, then with a quarter-sheet

FIGURE 9-20   Sanding a finished end in the vertical position.

sander and fine-grit paper. At butt joints, we again sand first with the grain of an end stock piece across the seam lines, and then we sand with the grain of the side stock piece up to the seam line. (Refer to Figure 7-19.) Some touch-up sanding by hand may be necessary. Finally, the cabinetmaker should ease all sharp corners on the cabinet with sandpaper.

Differences for Frameless Cabinetry

It should be noted that European cabinetry may be constructed and sanded in much the same way as framed cabinet work unless assembly fittings are employed to make the joints. Pieces are glued and nailed together in dado and rabbet joints. However, the facing or edging is already in place, and there are no major new seam lines to fill or sand. If seam gaps were filled and components sanded prior to assembly as they should have been, the only filling that might be required is in nail holes. Finished sanding is probably necessary on finished ends. The front facing of the components may require a bit of belt sanding before the finished sanding to achieve perfectly flush joints.

When assembly fittings are used, all finished sanding can be complete prior to assembly. The assembly fittings

are attached by press-in or screwing methods. Then components are merely pressed together, still beginning in the middle of the case. If alignment of the fittings has been careful, there is generally no need to fill or sand anything. In using this system, components can even be assembled after they have been lacquered or otherwise finished.

The builder of European cabinetry may want to attach the cabinet back as soon as possible.

MOUNTING CABINET ACCESSORIES

Mounting cabinet accessories follows a certain system in a shop. A few cabinetmakers choose to mount cabinet doors and drawers only after the finish has been applied. Most, however, do this task as soon as the cabinet has been put together and sanded.

Drawers and Slide-out Shelves

Drawer mounting is easiest when the cabinetmaker has access to the rear of the cabinet box. Most cabinetmakers attach the back as soon as the drawers are properly mounted.

Regardless of the drawer guiding system to be used on a cabinet, the assembler should first situate the cabinet level on the workbench. In this way, when the same cabinet is leveled on the job site for installation, drawers will operate just as they did when they were first mounted in the shop. This is usually just a matter of setting the case upright, resting a level on it, and putting a wedge or two beneath the cabinet as needed to make it level.

Side-mounted guides are probably the most popular today. Many different types are available, varying in weight-bearing capacity and other features, but they are all mounted in basically the same way.

The assembler must attach a guide assembly to each side of the drawer. The manufacturer supplies exact information to locate the assembly, but the front end of the guide generally extends all the way to the front of the drawer box. Screws should be driven through the slotted holes to allow minor adjustments. (See Figure 9-21.)

It is also necessary to attach a guide assembly inside the body of the cabinet. In face frame construction, it is often possible to screw the metal guide to a straight piece of wood, which in turn can be fastened properly into the cabinet. This is much easier than reaching inside the cabinet box to attach the guide. The system also allows very easy and perfect positioning of the drawer within the case. There are four steps in using this technique.

First, the cabinetmaker attaches each metal guide member to a piece of wood (½ in. thick, minimum by 2½ in. wide, minimum) that is exactly long enough to reach from the rear of the face frame to the front of the nailer.

FIGURE 9-21 Attachment of a drawer guide to the box. The worker should attach through slotted holes until the drawer has been adjusted.

FIGURE 9-22 Attaching a guide member to a board. The metal guide extends beyond the wood for an overlaid drawer front.

(See Figure 9-22.) If the drawer front is to be overlaid, the metal member will extend beyond the front end of the wooden strip about the thickness of the face frame. Flush drawer fronts obviously call for the wood and metal to be approximately even at the front.

Second, both assembled wood-and-metal drawer guides are attached to the cabinet, but only near the front. If possible, the cabinetmaker should avoid nailing through the front of the face frame. (See Figure 9-23.)

Third, the drawer box, with its metal guide members in place, is inserted. The assembler may use hand screws, or a helper, to hold it closed. (See Figure 9-24.)

Fourth, with the drawer box held secure, we position the rear end of the wood-and-metal assembly to hold the drawer exactly where it is and nail through the nailer to

FIGURE 9-23 Attaching a side guide to the face frame.

FIGURE 9-24 The drawer box is held in position with hand screws.

hold it in place. (See Figure 9-25.) Glue blocks and locking screws may be added for strength. When the hand screws are removed, the drawer functions properly. We may want to adjust the vertical position of the drawer front, but drawers mounted this way usually require no other adjustments.

FIGURE 9-25 The rear end of the wood-and-metal guide can be moved into exact position and nailed.

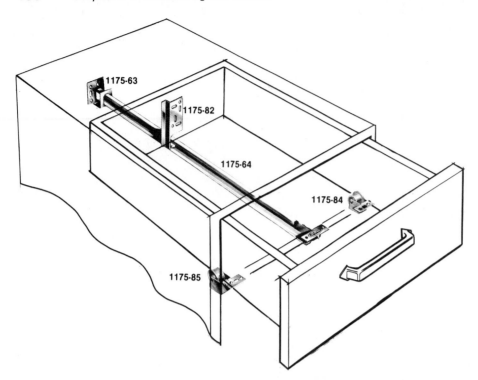

1175-63

1175-82

1175-64

1175-84

1175-85

FIGURE 9-26 Roller and bracket position in a three-roller guide. (Courtesy of Knape & Vogt Mfg. Co.)

"Three-roller guides" are also easy to mount, and they remain fairly popular. The assembler first finds the center of the bottom rail in a drawer opening and marks it. The under drawer rail is centered here and secured with staples or screws. The assembler then installs right- and left-hand nylon rollers, at the very ends of the bottom rail. A bracket is then attached to the rear of the drawer back. On it is the single roller that will guide in the centered drawer rail. This rear roller must be centered and must extend below the drawer box. With hand screws holding the drawer in its closed position, the assembler screws or staples the rear mounting bracket in position against the nailer. (See Figure 9-26.)

There are several possibilities for guiding drawers with wooden members. Perhaps the simplest is often found in the finest furniture. The assembler merely affixes a piece of wood to the cabinet for each drawer side to slide on. Shims, thin strips of wood, are used for adjustment. A very inexpensive technique that may be used for guiding light-weight drawers is for the assembler to attach a strip of wood to the center of an under-drawer rail. It projects up into the drawer space approximately ¼ in. The assembler may cut a notch in the bottom of a drawer back to fit around this projection, slide the drawer into its hole, and attach the rear end of the guide rail to a nailer in the back. (See Figure 9-27.) With either of these systems, a strip of wood should also be attached front to back above the drawer. This "tip rail" keeps the drawer horizontal as it is pulled out.

In attaching wood guides, every effort should be made to avoid driving additional nails through the face and sides of the cabinet. In a furniture type of design, it is a simple matter to screw or nail the guides into position from the

inside. Screws are preferable because they are easy to extract. Initial misplacement of the wood guide is easy to correct. When guides are positioned perfectly, glue blocks may be added for additional strength. In using a notched back design, the woodworker can give the front of the under-drawer rail a T-shape by adding a nailing strip to its rear end. Attachment is from the rear again, through the nailing strip and into the back of the frame.

Adjustments to wood-guided drawers are often made by the addition of shims. These may be small pieces of wood that are glued in place, or manufactured nylon tabs with an adhesive backing. To raise a drawer, we position such a shim on top of the under-drawer rail so that the sides will glide upon it. To keep a drawer from wobbling side to side, we insert shims that will contact the outsides of the drawer box as it slides. With flush inlaid drawers, wooden pieces are often glued in place which will stop the drawer exactly where desired. (See Figure 9-28 and Chapter 13.)

As cabinetmakers gain experience, they will encounter other drawer-guiding options, but nearly all are variations of the systems we have just discussed. Guiding may be by virtue of specially made metal and nylon hardware, and the woodworker chooses sets of drawer slides that are appropriate to the needs of a particular job. For file cabinets, we can purchase heavy-duty slides; for quiet operation, we can buy guides with an epoxy coating; where extra width is important, we get a model that mounts under the drawer. Wooden guides are all based on weight and friction distribution. Regardless of the type of guiding system employed, however, the reader should note that the critical adjustments of fitting a drawer are made at the back of the cabinet. With the box sitting exactly as it should be when

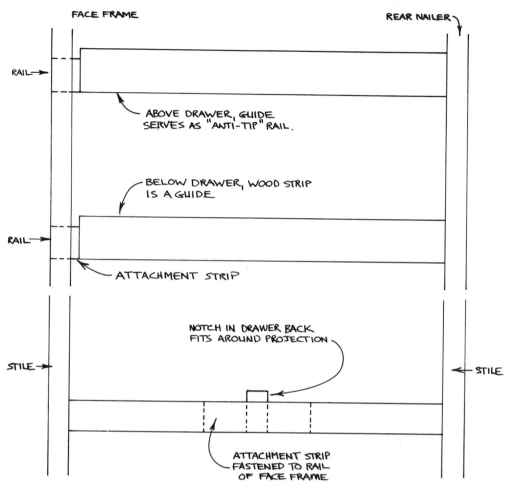

RAIL

ABOVE DRAWER, GUIDE
SERVES AS "ANTI-TIP" RAIL.

BELOW DRAWER, WOOD STRIP
IS A GUIDE

RAIL

ATTACHMENT STRIP

REAR NAILER

NOTCH IN DRAWER BACK
FITS AROUND PROJECTION

STILE

STILE

ATTACHMENT STRIP
FASTENED TO RAIL
OF FACE FRAME

FIGURE 9-27 Inexpensive wooden drawer guides.

FIGURE 9-28 "Stops" positioned to contact the rear of a flush drawer front.

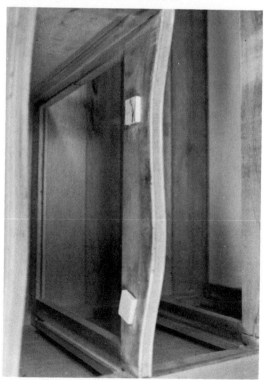

closed, it is easy to position the rear of the guide(s) perfectly.

Slide-out shelves should also be mounted before the cabinet back is attached. The cabinetmaker can mount these exactly like drawers. Side-mounted guides are almost always used. Some cabinetmakers do not like to use individual strips of wood for attachment of guides to the cabinet box as is often the practice in mounting drawers. They object to the appearance when cabinet doors are open. (See Figure 9-29.) The strips can be avoided by positioning a partition on which to mount the guides. (See Figure 9-30.)

Attaching the Back

As soon as drawers and slide-out shelves have been mounted, it is best to attach the back. This is generally the last step of assembly, which really establishes strength and rigidity in a cabinet. In building dressers and other furniture pieces, attaching the top also lends strength.

If it is feasible, the assembler should keep the cabinet in its leveled position while attaching its back. Otherwise, drawer alignments can be altered. Some cabinetmakers prefer to lay the cabinet over on its face (with padding between it and the workbench) for back attachment.

Most cabinet backs consist of a single piece of plywood or hardboard. It may be wise to draw lines on its rear face to indicate locations of partitions, fixed shelves, and some nailers. This makes it easy to drive fasteners without missing. To save material, a back may consist of two or more pieces. They meet at the rear edge of cabinet members to which they can both be attached, such as the edge of a partition.

With a cabinet that is to be mounted against a wall, the back is usually mounted with glue, supported with either box nails or pneumatic-driven staples. After spreading glue to cover the rear of the cabinet, the assembler simply positions the back and drives the fasteners. With installed cabinetry, there is no way to repair a back that becomes loose from the rear of the cabinet, and attachment must be secure. Therefore, fasteners should be at least ¾-in. long and spaced within a few inches of each other. No portion of the back should be allowed to project above the top of the cabinet or beyond a finished end. (See Figure 9-31.)

The backs of some cabinets are finished. They are usually made of hardwood plywood. Finished backs are mounted quite similarly to other backs except that the woodworker uses finishing nails for fasteners. Furthermore, the finished back must be made to meet a finished end in a miter or other finished joint. If the two cabinet

FIGURE 9-29 Slide-outs mounted on individual strips.

FIGURE 9-30 Slide-outs mounted on the partition.

FIGURE 9-31 Using a staple gun to attach a hardboard back.

members were mitered, the angle-cut edges are simply glued, positioned, and nailed together. Another option is to cover the raw edge of the finished back with a strip of hardwood edging and then to mount the back. The hardwood strip, sanded flush to both pieces of plywood, makes the finished joint.

Occasionally, pieces of plywood must be edge joined which are too thin for splining or doweling. Bookcases must sometimes have a ¼-in. back which is wider than 48 in., the standard width of a plywood sheet. These may be joined in two steps. First, they are glued on edge and clamped together. After the glue has cured, the clamps are removed and a thin strip is attached across the seam on its rear surface. Because of its minimal thickness and its toughness, plastic laminate is often used for this "scab." After sanding the finished surface, the wide back may be attached conventionally.

Door Mounting

As in hinging doors, the system used for mounting a cabinet door depends on general door design and the type of hinge chosen. In mounting any door, the step of determining exact mounting location is first. Doors are usually mounted with the cabinet lying level on its back. A finished back should naturally be protected with padding.

In positioning doors with butt hinges, the goal is to divide clearance space equally. Some designers list the length of such doors to be exactly the same as the height of the opening to be covered. In this case, the assembler slides the hinged edge of the door against the stile or mullion to which it is to be attached. This will be a snug fit, and the assembler uses a pencil mark or a tiny scratch to mark hinge location on the frame. Then the door can be trimmed as needed on the top and bottom and mounted in place with screws. More often than not, the flush inlaid door has already been cut very close to its trimmed size. If the cabinetmaker can trust a frame's squareness, it is a waste to spend a lot of time trimming a door that is also square. To mount the door in this case, the assembler proceeds as before, but there is not a snug fit. The amount of clearance between door and rail must be the same at the top and the bottom of the door. When this is achieved, the hinges are in the correct position to be marked. As an aid in holding the door while it is positioned, some cabinetmakers will temporarily attach strips of wood against the rear of the face frame. The strips may be clamped or tacked in place. They project into the door opening just enough to support the door in its horizontal position. Another option is to mount this type of door with the cabinet and door in their vertical position. A narrow strip of wood is used to establish the correct spacing beneath the door. (See Figure 9-32.) When using butt hinges, the pin of the hinge must project above the surface of the face frame exactly the same

FIGURE 9-32   Positioning a flush door to mark the location of butt hinges.

amount that it projects above the surface of the door. Otherwise, we do not have a truly flush arrangement.

Strap hinges are used for door mounting in the same way as butt hinges except that the assembler screws one wing of the hinge to the face of the stile or mullion rather than to its edge. He or she must also be sure to allow a tiny spacing between door and face member on the hinged side. The pin of the hinge should be centered on this tiny gap.

Doors with semiconcealed hinges are among the easiest to mount. With lipped doors, the cabinetmaker simply lays the door in its opening, presses the door into full contact with the edge of the frame, and centers the door vertically in the opening. To center the door, we determine how far the door will move up between rails and split this distance. Screw location can then be marked in the center of the hinges' screw holes with the point of an awl. With self-closing or spring-loaded hinges, the mounting base of the hinge must be flattened out slightly before these starting holes are punched.

Overlay doors with semiconcealed hinges are also easily mounted. The most important thing to control when mounting these doors is the amount of overlay. A straightedge is positioned along one of the cabinet rails to control vertical overlay. With a base, the straightedge is

FIGURE 9-33 Clamp-on strip for attaching doors.

positioned above the doors; with an upper, it is positioned below. The top or bottom edge of all the doors may then be set against this straightedge, and they will line up perfectly. (See Figure 9-33.) The amount of horizontal overlay is measured and marked on a stile or mullion. When the door's edge is held even with the mark, the door is in correct position. Holes are punched in the face frame. Again, self-closing hinges must have their mounting base flattened on the surface of the frame before holes are punched. (See Figure 9-34.)

FIGURE 9-34 Punching screw-starting holes. Note the straightedge used for vertical position. These are self-closing hinges that must be held flat for locating holes.

FIGURE 9-35 Machine for routing T-slots into the surface of a face frame. (Courtesy of Amerock Corporation.)

To mount doors with demountable hinges, the cabinetmaker must machine a T-slot into the frame of the assembled cabinet. This operation is easiest to perform with a portable routing machine made especially for this purpose. (See Figure 9-35.) The base of the machine has stops that may be set to contact a rail when set in place for machining, thus controlling vertical location of the T-slot. Naturally, the exact positioning of the machined detail depends on where along the edge of the door the matching slot was run for installation of the hinges. With the detail run, the asssembler simply slips the hinge into the frame slot and tightens the single screw to hold it in position. (See Figure 9-36.) This type of hinge allows easy minor adjustments of each door. The door may be moved horizontally, vertically, or in and out on a hinge. The assembler simply loosens one of the screws, makes the desired adjustment, and retightens.

Single demountable hinges are screwed to the frame like semiconcealed hinges. These can also be located in an opening, marked, and screwed in place just as in the semiconcealed system.

FIGURE 9-36 T-slots in a face frame.

FIGURE 9-37 A European hinged door attached to the face frame with an edge mounting plate. Screws C are through slotted holes within the mounting plate to allow vertical adjustments. Screw B attaches the hinge cup to the mounting plate, allowing horizontal adjustments. (Courtesy of Julius Blum Inc., Cabinet and Furniture Hardware.)

Pin hinges were created to be nearly invisible. Therefore, they mount to the face frame on the inside edge or on its surface behind the door. (Semiconcealed and single demountable hinges are available in models that must be attached to the cabinet in a very similar way.) Doors with this type of hinge are positioned to cover openings just like doors with semiconcealed hinges. When the exact position is attained, marking for screw placement is in one of two ways. Most surface-mounted hinges possess a small projection that will easily dent the surface of a facing. If such a projection is present, the cabinetmaker can mark exact hinge location with a single solid rap of the fist on the surface of the door over each hinge. The projection makes a mark that can be used for hinge positioning. The cabinetmaker only has to match the hinge projection up with the mark it just made and drive screws. When no projection can be used, as on many wraparound hinges that mount to the inner edge of the face frame, the cabinetmaker can usually mark the face frame with a pencil where the knife part of the hinge is situated. The first screws should be placed in the slotted holes to allow minor adjustments. Then the locking screws can be driven.

Doors with European (fully concealed) hinges are secured to the cabinet with mounting plates. These mounting plates are available in several different designs. Many are applicable for frameless design, attached to a vertical case member well behind the cabinet facing. (Refer again to Figure 4-5.) Other mounting plates may be attached directly to the front or edge of a face frame. (See Figure 9-37.) To determine mounting plate location, the assembler attaches mounting plates to the hinge cups on one door, opens the hinge arm, and holds the door to the facing in its open position. The screw staring holes can be marked easily this way. With one door properly hung, the assembler can make a template or take measurements that can be used

in positioning mounting plates for other doors on the same job. Adjustments can be made by loosening screws, moving the door, and retightening screws. (Again, see Figure 9-37.)

Virtually every modern hinge is available in a self-closing model, and most cabinetmakers use these as much as possible. The use of free-swinging hinges requires the assembler to attach a catch to hold each door closed. This is done with the doors mounted. The catch consists of two parts. The part to be attached to the case should be mounted first, beneath a shelf or on the edge of a stile or mullion if possible. The other part, a strike clip or plate, is then set upon it, screw projecting. Then the door is closed, and the projecting screw marks its own location.

Mounting Other Accessories

Many residential cabinets and furniture pieces require the assembler to attach components and accessories in addition to drawers, slide-out shelves, and doors. Most such accessories call for the use of quite conventional techniques, however.

Panels or false fronts must often be affixed to base cabinets in front of sinks or cooktops. These are simply drawer fronts without a box. They may be fixed and functionless, attached for the sake of appearance, or they may have small tilt-out trays mounted to their rear and hinged to the cabinet facing, allowing them to open. The assembler may attach fixed panels in any convenient way. To avoid nailing through their faces, most cabinetmakers attach them from the rear with screws. One efficient way is to glue and nail strips of wood to the edge of the opening in the frame that the panel is supposed to cover. The assembler then drills clearance holes through the strips and screws the panel into correct position. (See Figure 9-38.) For a tilt-out panel, the cabinetmaker first hinges the false

FIGURE 9-38 A fixed false front may be attached from the rear with screws.

front to the cabinet. It may be hinged with the same hinges that were used for doors on the same job, except, of course, that the hinges are on the bottom edge of the component rather than the side. For better concealment of the hinge itself, butt hinges (or a section of continuous hinge) may be used. These may even be mortised into the bottom edge of the panel, making for a virtually flush fit. Tilting trays are available from many hardware suppliers. They are simply folded sheet metal with holes drilled for attachment and a projecting metal arm that contacts the rear of the face frame to stop outward motion. The assembler positions each tray on the rear of the panel, parallel with its top edge and making sure that the projecting arm will function properly. Two screws are enough to secure the tray. The trays should be removed for finishing.

Narrow shelving units are sometimes attached to the rear of a door. This arrangement is frequently used in an upper cabinet spice rack or in a pantry cabinet. The rack of shelves is built by the assembler as a separate unit and then attached to the already mounted door with screws. The rack may have its own nailers, or the sides of the rack themselves may be drilled with clearance and countersink holes for attachment. (See Figure 9-39.) The assembler should be careful of two things in mounting such shelving

FIGURE 9-39 Attachment of a shelving unit to the rear of a pantry door with a nailer. Note the detail cut in the side of the shelving unit. Note that the side of the shelving unit is well away from the unhinged edge of the door.

FIGURE 9-40 A swinging pantry unit should be affixed with a continuous hinge.

units. First, he or she needs to consider screw location as it relates to door design. With some doors, the screws can only be driven into the door frame. Second, the shelving unit has the effect of deepening the door. The shelving unit requires additional clearance to open properly, and its side must be kept well away from the unhinged door edge. Large rear-door shelving may require additional hinges.

Swing-out pantry units must be rigid and well built to carry a good deal of weight. An assembler will also build this type of unit using conventional methods, but extra care must be taken in mounting the back (½ in. minimum thickness). The back establishes squareness and has a good deal to do with the rigidity of the accessory. The swing-out pantry should be hung in place with a continuous (piano) hinge to provide as much strength as possible. The continuous hinge is positioned and screwed in place like a butt hinge, with its pin projecting beyond the front surface of the unit. (See Figure 9-40.)

Lazy susans are of several types, as we observed in Chapter 2. Each type calls for its own detailing, assembly, and mounting techniques.

One type of lazy susan is the blind-corner susan. It consists of two shelving sections, each in the shape of one-fourth of a circle. The critical factor in fabricating and installing this type of susan is ensuring that the shelves will open properly. Some shops, particularly shops in the production drawing system, make it a practice to design and cut the pieces for these susans only after the cabinet is assembled. Full-scale layout can be used.

To come up with exact dimensioning for the susans, the cabinetmaker draws the features (plan view) of the space in which the susan is to be fit on a piece of sheet wood. It takes only a few minutes to measure and mark out the location of stiles, partition, end, and back. The cabinetmaker will draw the necessary arcs from the point where hinge pins are located. Remember that one shelf unit is mounted to the back of the door affixed to the face frame, and that this door is hinged backwards—opposite the return corner. The other shelf assembly is mounted on a narrow strip just inside this corner in such a way that the hinge pin will extend beyond the stile's inner edge. A nail is tacked into the hinge pin location to draw an arc for each shelf unit. By drawing the arc clear of any vertical members on the cabinet, the curved edge of the shelves is established. Then the cabinetmaker can draw in the location of the front and side support of the shelving unit at right angles. From the full-scale layout, dimensions of all pieces can be determined. (Refer again to Figure 3-27.) The shelves must be cut according to the arc swing drawn, and they should be dadoed into the front and side support. After assembly, the units can be hinged in place with conventional techniques.

Some susans, particularly in upper cabinets, are mounted by attaching the bottom to a turntable—metal plates that are rotated in relation to each other on ball bearings. The other face of the turntable is then mounted to the cabinet bottom. Attachment is done with screws, and a hole large enough for a screwdriver tip to fit through must be drilled in one of the attached wooden pieces.

Manufactured susans may be full round or pie-shaped, and both are fairly easy to install by following the manufacturer's instructions. (See Figure 9-41.) The bottom mounting bracket may be screwed directly to the bottom of the base unit, but a wooden strip needs to be installed in the cabinet for attaching the top mounting bracket. With the brackets in correct position, shelves are attached to the rotating center pole by friction. Screws are present in the base of each shelf for this purpose. The door to cover a full-round susan section is mounted like any other door, but in covering the L-shaped opening of a pie susan section, the cabinetmaker has to make a choice. The doors may be independent of the susan if they are mitered and hinged together, or they may be trimmed in size enough to rotate through the door openings. If they are to rotate with the susan, they are secured to the susan shelves with screws. To attach pie-shaped susans, the cabinetmaker will often have to assemble two base cabinets as they will be joined when installed. After brackets and doors are correctly positioned, the two cabinets may be taken apart again. In general, susans should be removed from any cabinet for finishing.

Slide-out cutting boards are frequently a kitchen cab-

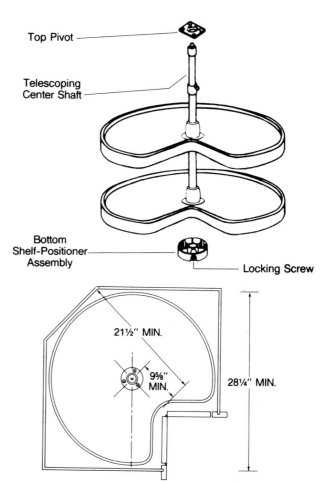

FIGURE 9-41 Installing a manufactured susan is simply a matter of affixing top and bottom mounting brackets and then securing the shelf to the pole with screws.

inet accessory. The laminated board that makes up the cutting surface should already be cut to size and sanded when the assembler gets it. It is fabricated just like any wide, solid panel except that it is usually made up of very narrow strips. If its front is not detailed and attached, the assembler should first run a finger-pull cove on the bottom of the front and attach it to the cutting board body with dowels. The cutting board slides in and out, kept on line with wooden guides. The guides themselves are made of solid stock, and they have a dado cut into them lengthwise. As with mounting drawers, the front ends of the guides are attached to the rear of the face frame first; then, with the cutting board inserted all the way into its opening, the rear ends of the dadoed guides may be correctly positioned and attached to a nailer with nails and glue blocks. To avoid nailing through the face frame, the front ends of the guides may be fastened to a strip of wood that is screwed to the face from behind. Sometimes, it is possible to attach these guides to the hold-downs directly above. The same system can be applied in building a slide-out writing surface into a desk.

A section of cabinetry may be devoted to tray storage. The width of such a section should be divided into narrow sections by thin ¼ in. pieces of plywood or hardboard. These should be easy to remove for the sake of finishing. Probably the best way to secure tray dividers at their top is to mount a piece like a shelf. Its bottom surface projects approximately ¼ in. below the edge of the top rail, but it has dadoes cut into it, appropriately spaced, to receive the top edges of the dividers. The shelf may be attached conventionally or with cleats that allow the assembler to avoid additional face frame nailing. Slots may be provided to receive and guide the bottom edges of the dividers by installing a similar piece right to the surface of the cabinet bottom. Some cabinetmakers prefer a single strip of solid wood with a lengthwise dado in it to hold the top of each divider in place. Some cabinetmakers let the bottom end of the tray dividers slide directly on the cabinet bottom and space them by attaching pieces of ¼-in. material in between.

There are many other accessories that can be installed in a given cabinet box, and the variety of possibilities will undoubtedly grow. A proficient, confident cabinetmaker does not hesitate to incorporate new hardware items into a cabinet job to meet a need. By generalizing skills and knowledges, the cabinetmaker will frequently develop his or her own accessory to meet the needs of a job.

FABRICATING FINISHED WOODEN TOPS

Fabricating finished wooden tops is necessary in several types of cabinetmaking situations. Furniture items such as desks often require wooden tops, and so do some built-in wall systems. Such tops may be created by edge-laminating solid materials or by applying edging to a piece of plywood.

Edged Plywood Tops

A plywood top is nearly always attached to the cabinet body after finishing, by driving screws from below, through holddowns. The plywood should have a thickness of at least ¾ in. The edging is applied flush to the top surface of the plywood, but it often extends below the bottom plywood face, covering a small amount of the frame and finished ends of the cabinet to which it is attached. The edging is often ¾ × 1½ in.

To be suitable for making a top, the piece of plywood should possess a thick, high-quality veneer face and perfectly straight square edges. Some cabinetmakers like to apply edging to factory edges as much as possible; others specifically cut away the factory edge, trusting their own jointer and their own abilities to render the straight edges

desired. The edging should be straight and even grained. Since the edging may receive an edge form, the cabinetmaker should decide whether to run the detail before or after the edging is applied. When nails are to be used to attach the edging, it is obviously better to machine the detail before application. It is also easier to feed the thin strips of edging through a shaper or table router than to feed an assembled top across the same setup. Edge forming after assembly, however, can be a benefit in glue-only applications of the edging. With either kind of application, the cabinetmaker should focus on making miter joints perfectly. If a miter is not necessary at a corner of the plywood, as when we are edging only along the front edge of a wall-to-wall top, the edging strip should be allowed to extend beyond the corner a small amount. This will make it easier for the top to be fit and installed properly by the installer.

To apply edging without nails, woodworkers should use edging that is oversized in width. This allows them to pay little heed to getting a flush top surface, and they can focus their attention on aligning mitered corners perfectly. The edging is simply glued and clamped to the edge of the plywood top. One strip is glued in position at a time unless it is possible to clamp opposing edges at once. Edging should project a small amount above the surface of the plywood, but the inside limit of a miter cut must be held perfectly even with the corner of the plywood. After all pieces have been attached, the edging is cut to its desired width. The top surface is made flush first, using a flush-cutting router bit and belt sander. With the top edge even and straight, the final width of the edging can be established by edge and end feeding the assembled top across the table saw. The easiest and most reliable way to do any edge forming is with a portable router, roller-bearing bit fitted. The top may then be finish sanded like a door.

Nailing the edging on is much faster and easier. Careful cutting and placement of mitered corners is still vital, and the cabinetmaker must take care of aligning the top of the edging flush with the top surface of the plywood. Clamps may be used, as in the attachment of a face frame to a finished end, to tighten small seam gaps. After glue has cured, the top requires only minimal filling and then finish sanding.

Cauls should be used to protect the face of any edging applied.

Solid Tops

Fabricating a wood top from solid materials is more expensive and time consuming than making edged-ply tops. The process, however, is easily described. It is simply the preparation of a wide solid panel. Pieces begin oversized. They are simply edge straightened and laminated together with end grain direction alternated on individual members.

FIGURE 9-42 The top of this TV stand was made to appear twice as thick by laminating end-stock cutoffs onto the bottom surface of the furniture top. Legs were made in the same way.

When its glue joints have dried enough, the top is sanded flat, cut to size, edge formed, and finish sanded.

Solid wood tops are not edged like plywood tops, but cabinetmakers do use an edging technique in order to give an appearance of additional thickness. When the top is cut to size, we save the ''scrap'' pieces. It is important to cut approximately the same amount off of each end, because we usually want matching end grain for both ends. The scrap pieces from the front edge and both ends are then cut to the same width, mitered where they will meet, and glued onto the bottom surface of the top. We should take care to glue the strips directly beneath the edge or end from which they were cut. The end grain will match, and the natural shrinking and swelling of wood fibers will affect the main body of the top and the ''edging'' in the same way. Hand screws and C-clamps may be used for pressure. After the joint has cured, we can sand ends and edges of the joint flat. Then the top can be completed as any other solid top, with edge forming and finish sanding. (See Figure 9-42.)

ALTERNATIVES TO PRIMARY SURFACE NAILING

Alternatives to primary surface nailing are sometimes desirable, especially in constructing furniture. This type of fastening can usually be accomplished by employing systems that we have already looked at. When designing and

assembling such cabinetry, the primary goal is to look for ways of concealing fasteners. If concealed fasteners are not feasible, the cabinetmaker can resort to worked joints of various kinds.

An obvious way to conceal the heads of fasteners is to drive them only through secondary and hidden surfaces. Machining a rabbet on the rear edges of finished ends to receive a back and nailers is a common practice. We can drive nails through the back surface of a piece and into the edges of the finished ends. The surface of the finished end need not be marred.

Angled nailing or ''toenailing'' can also be employed in certain circumstances. The bottom or fixed shelf of a furniture piece may fit into a conventional dado, but the assembler can usually drive a nail through the rear edge of the finished end and into the shelf or bottom at an angle to help support the joint. It is also easy to angle a nail through the surface of the furniture bottom and into the edge grain of the finished end inside the cabinet. Glue blocks—short, square-edged pieces—are very often glued in place to support this type of joint. (See Figure 9-43.)

Drawer chests often do not have a single-piece bottom. The bottom (and wood drawer guides between each drawer) are often frames that are assembled with dowels or mortise-and-tenon joints. (Again, see Figure 9-43.) The assembler can install fasteners through these into the finished end from the inside for good strength. Screws are superior fasteners in this application.

There are many possibilities for concealed screw usage in assembling a cabinet or furniture piece, but screws should generally be employed as a support for glued joints. A face frame may even be butt joined to a furniture piece with screws. The edges of the case are covered with glue and the face is clamped in place. While the glue is under

FIGURE 9-43 Glue blocks used to support a cabinet bottom. Note that the bottom is a frame rather than a single piece.

pressure, the cabinetmaker attaches a square wooden strip, like a long glue block, to the inside of the joint. The strip is glued and screwed into contact with both the rear of the face frame and the inside surface of the finished end. (See Figure 9-44.) Almost any perpendicular meeting of cabinet components can be glued together and supported with screws in this way.

Much European cabinetry is designed for concealed fastening. There is no face frame to attach, and cabinet components can be joined with assembly fittings which are not visible on any primary surface. (Refer again to Figure 6-44.)

Worked joints are frequently created to make nailing unnecessary. Most furniture with legs is partially assembled with conventional doweling or mortises and tenons.

FIGURE 9-44   In this furniture piece, the face frame is attached to finished ends with glue and an interior strip that is screwed to both face and end.

CHAPTER SUMMARY OF CABINETMAKING SKILLS

Craftsmanlike and rapid assembly of cabinetry requires good organization of space and tools. Most important are a firm work surface and surrounding space, good lighting, and a close-by array of fastening and sanding tools.

Assembling a cabinet calls for following joining systems required by the cabinet designer. In general, the assembler begins by sanding secondary surfaces. He or she can then put components of the box together with glue and nails, concealed fasteners, or another system. Innermost portions of the cabinet should be joined first, and the process continues outward until the box is complete. Pneumatic nailing equipment speeds up all attachment procedures, but these tools should be purchased and used with some care.

In most modern cabinet work, a face frame is attached to the box with glue and nails, but there are concealment options. Seams between the frame and a finished end are made as tight as possible by clamping. Nailers may

then be attached, and the piece sanded. Backs should not be affixed until drawers are mounted, however.

The cabinetmaker must gain familiarity with the many systems that he or she may be called on to use in mounting doors, drawers, and other accessories to the assembled cabinet. For drawer guiding, side-mounted and three-roller guides are used often in conventional cabinetry. Wooden guides remain in wide use for furniture. Procedures for hanging doors will depend on door design and the type of hinge employed: butt, strap, semiconcealed, demountable, pin, or fully concealed. There are a number of other accessories, which call for their own attachment methods.

The chief goals of assembly are to create a piece of cabinetry that is ready to have its finish applied and which will require a minimum of on-site adjustment by the installer.

TEN

FABRICATING COUNTERTOPS

BASIC PRINCIPLES OF FABRICATION

Plastic laminates are probably the most popular type of material in use today for the surface of countertops. Customers like it because it is less expensive than tile or marble, and because it is tough, durable, and easy to clean. It is also remarkably easy to work with. These tops are simply a wood bed or substrate that is covered with plastic.

Many cabinet shops do not work with plastic laminates, and conversely, some shops specialize in the fabrication of plastic-laminate tops and other products. Large, specialized countertop businesses possess saws and other equipment that make it very easy to build and cut tops, even those with beveled or formed edges. Cabinetmakers who prefer to stay out of the countertop fabrication trade will usually "subcontract" plastic-laminate work with such a business. Nevertheless, the cabinetmaker can easily create one style of plastic-laminate countertop—the self-edged top.

When a top is "self-edged," its front edge consists of a piece of flat plastic that meets the surface of the top at a right angle. A "formed edge" is gained by rolling the plastic top over rounded substrate materials to cover the front edge. A formed edge generally includes a small surface hump near the front edge, which helps to keep small

amounts of water on the countertop rather than on the floor. A "beveled-edged" top is like a self-edged top, but instead of two pieces of plastic meeting at a right angle, three pieces of plastic come together at 45° angles to form each edge. Similar arrangements are also possible in adding backsplashes.

Since the bed of a countertop is made of wood, the cabinetmaker may cut its components with conventional shop tools. We can cut the plastic sheets themselves with a table saw. Throwaway brushes and rollers are used to spread the contact cement that will hold it in place. After they are in place, the pieces of plastic may be trimmed and shaped with a router, a belt sander (in some situations), and a file.

The large pieces of a countertop bed, the surface itself and the backsplash, can be fabricated from ¾-in. particleboard or plywood. The most common application for plywood is where moisture repulsion is critical. Exterior plywoods are then used. Industrial-grade particle board is used for most tops, however. Industrial board is less expensive than medium-density fiberboard, and it is lighter in weight. Backing for edges may be of the same material, or pine may be used. The countertop builder uses very conventional fastening systems (glue, drywall screws, and staples or nails) to join the components.

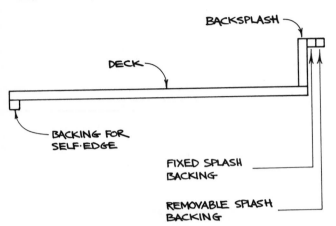

FIGURE 10-1 Top-structure cross section. Note how backing pieces are attached. In general, all pieces are 3/4 in. thick.

DESIGNING PLASTIC-LAMINATE TOPS

Designing plastic-laminate tops requires an understanding of how such tops are to fit over installed cabinetry and familiarity with a few trade standards. With this knowledge, the cabinetmaker can determine overall dimensions of a top and build it.

General Top Structure

Backing for the self-edge should not overlay the front edge of the top surface as it does with a wood top. Rather, the strip is added beneath the top, flush with its front edge. We can build a backsplash in much the same way. Two strips are attached flush to the rear surface of the splash, even with the top edge. The second strip should be removable. When the top is installed, this strip is removed so that the installer has only to shape the thin plastic itself to the contour of a wall. This projection of plastic is frequently referred to as ''scribe.'' (See Figure 10-1.)

Finished ends of a top are created exactly like the front edge. At a wall end, the top may have a backsplash or simply a scribe protection strip attached to the end of the deck. If a miter is necessary at the wall end, the top is constructed as usual. It is mitered after fabrication. (See Figure 10-2.)

FIGURE 10-2 Top-structure front view. This top meets a wall on the left but is finished on the right.

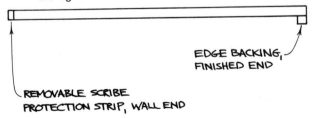

In general, then, permanent backing strips are added to the deck and splash wherever plastic edging is to be added. This material is usually 3/4 in. square (3/4 in. × 3/4 in. Removable scribe protector strips should be added wherever the plastic must contact a wall. These strips are 3/4 in. thick, but they vary in width, depending on how much plastic is desired for scribing. One-half-inch is usually enough width.

Dimensioning the Top

The first step in constructing a plastic-laminate top is to derive its overall size. This is naturally dependent on the design of the cabinet structure to which it will be fastened. The thickness of the plastic material is usually less than 1/16 in. and it is considered insignificant in dimensioning the top.

The overall depth of the top is 1 in. greater than the cabinet below, plus any necessary scribe. This includes the thickness of the splash with its fixed backing strip. Thus tops in a standard kitchen will be 25½ in. in depth. This takes into account a 1-in. overhang at the front edge, the 24-in. cabinet depth, and ½ in. of scribe.

The length of the top is equal to the length of the cabinet structure below, plus 1-in. overhang for each finished end, plus a small amount (perhaps ¼ in.) of scribe for each wall end. If a base unit is 50 in. long, with one wall end and one finished end, its top should measure 51¼ in. in length. This is true whether or not the wall end of the top is to have a splash.

It is a trade standard for the front edge of a top and the top edge of the splash to be approximately 1½ in. wide; splashes are usually close to 4 in. in height.

The dimensions of individual components of the bed can be determined from the overall dimensions. The width of the piece that is to make the main body of the top (deck) should be equal to the overall depth less the combined width of the scribe and fixed backing strip at the rear of the splash. In a standard kitchen top, the deck will be 24¼ in. wide. This allows for a 3/4-in. backing strip and ½ in. of scribe.

The length of the deck is the overall top length minus the scribe for any wall ends. (If a splash is to be affixed to the wall end, we must also subtract the depth of the backing strip.) In the 51¼-in. top mentioned above, the deck would be 51 in. long, unless its wall end must have a splash.

Once the cabinetmaker has established deck size, he or she can easily develop dimensions for cutting the other materials needed. The splash will be as long as the deck. If it meets a return splash at the wall end, its length will be the width of the deck, less the thickness of splash material (usually 3/4 in.). The top fabricator usually estimates the total length of support and scribe strips needed and cuts them to exact length as they are put in place.

ASSEMBLING THE COUNTERTOP BED

Countertop backsplashes are not attached to the deck until lamination is complete. The countertop builder attaches backing and scribe strips where needed to both the deck and the splash.

If the deck or splash requires scribe strips to be attached to the ends, these should be mounted first, flush with the surface and edges to be clad with plastic. The strips are set in place with staples or nails only. (See Figure 10-3.)

Backing strips should be attached with glue and fasteners. Fasteners should be driven from below so that there is no chance of their working up into the cemented plastic. The front strip on a deck and the top strip of a splash should be attached first, with side strips butting into them. (See Figure 10-4.) After backing strips are in place, scribe strips should be nailed or stapled in place on the rear of the splash. (See Figure 10-5.)

Before cementing the plastic into position, some surfaces need to be perfectly flattened, in particular those surfaces to be clad that were thickened by the addition of backing strips—finished ends and the front edge of the deck,

FIGURE 10-3 Attaching a scribe strip to a splash and deck with a staple gun. The strip is flush to surfaces to be clad with plastic.

FIGURE 10-4 Attaching backing strips to support self-edging.

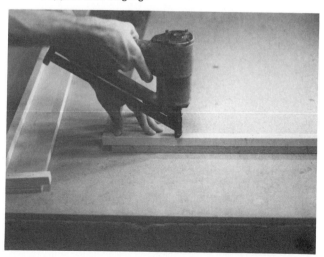

FIGURE 10-5 Scribe strips are added to the rear of the backsplash.

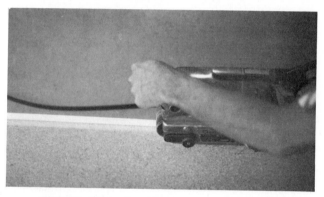

FIGURE 10-6 Excellent control of the belt sander is required for flattening the edge of a deck in this way.

and the finished ends and top edge of the backsplash. This flattening procedure is usually performed by sanding. It is possible to use a belt or edge sander for the operation, but many fabricators prefer the control of hand sanding with a rigid block. In this type of sanding, the power sanders can yield a dip or an edge that is not square, and using a block takes only a few minutes. (See Figure 10-6.)

On the surface of some countertops, we may be required to cut a curve or radius. This is frequently done on tops for island or peninsula cabinets, or next to walking areas. The round corners are less likely to cause injury. It is really rather simple to curve a self-edge. We simply mark the desired curve directly on the surface of the deck with a pencil and cut and sand to the line. The size of arc radius is a consideration. Plastic laminate will crack if forced to flex around extremely tight curves. Since an island or peninsula countertop frequently overhangs the finished back of the base below it by as much as 12 in., this is often not a problem. We simply cut a curve with a radius of 3 in. or more. Most plastic laminates will easily conform to this curve. (*Note:* To cut such a wide radius, we will be cutting all the way through ¾-in. backing strips; wider backing strips are necessary.) At the corner of some curved-edge countertops, a tighter radius is necessary. An example is where a face frame and a finished end come together on the cabinet and there is only a 1-in. countertop overhang for each. The solution is to go ahead and cut the tighter curve (as little as a 2-in. radius). The strip of plastic self-edging can achieve the turn if it is heated with an iron during application.

Another situation that may arise (rarely) is the need to fit the rear of a countertop to a curved or angular wall shape. This is no difficulty without a backsplash. We simply add enough depth or length to the overall size of the top to reach the deepest portions of the curve or angle in the wall. The installer then scribes it into place. Angled splashes are similarly bothersome but achievable. Straight segments of the splash are simply constructed and joined together at the desired angles.

Constructing a curved splash, however, requires another technique—building a curved backing. A similar procedure may be used in building furniture with curved surfaces. The first requirement is a pattern. As we have observed, the measurer generally provides a wall-contoured pattern for such cabinetry. We may be able to trust a blueprint with radial measurements, but on-site pattern making is most reliable. The shape of the pattern is used to mark and cut two identical pieces. Spacers are installed between the two pieces to create a form that is approximately as wide as the height of the splash. The cabinetmaker presses long strips of plywood into the form, laminating enough layers together with glue to achieve the desired thickness. Five layers of 1/8-in. material is sufficient. When the glue has dried, the curved splash can be cut to exact width and length. A curved backing strip may be cut to fit. The assembled unit may then be treated as any other backsplash.

APPLYING PLASTIC LAMINATES

With a properly prepared deck and splash, the plastic cladding goes on rapidly. In general, pieces are cut oversized, cemented in place, trimmed, and slightly beveled at joints.

The order of attachment is important. Vertical surfaces should be clad before horizontal surfaces, and the plastic should be applied to finished end surfaces before it is applied to front surfaces. This order yields the lowest seam visibility.

Sheets of plastic may be cut on the table saw in a conventional way, with a combination or cutoff blade. Carbide is highly recommended. When cutting plastic, it is of great importance to wear safety glasses or a face shield. Bits of plastic in the eye may not forgive us for lapses in safety.

The tiny edge of a plastic sheet can easily slip under the fence of the saw. With some fences, we can loosen a few screws, lower the face of the fence into complete contact with the saw table, and retighten the screw. (See Figure 10-7.) Another option is to place a thin strip of hardboard next to the fence while feeding plastic sheet goods. A box nail driven all the way through the strip will contact the front of the saw table and keep it from slipping. (See Figure 10-8.) Every piece should be about 1 in. wider and longer than necessary, and even more "extra" material may be desired for large surfaces.

If the top overhangs a finished end, the sides of the splash and deck should be covered first. With a curved radius deck, of course, we edge the finished end and the front with the same piece. As the reader will recall, cement is applied to the matching surfaces, allowed to dry, and then put together. Most important, perhaps, is getting adequate coating near the edges and ends of the substrate surfaces. Position adjustments are not possible after contact. The

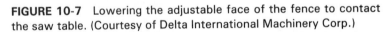

FIGURE 10-7 Lowering the adjustable face of the fence to contact the saw table. (Courtesy of Delta International Machinery Corp.)

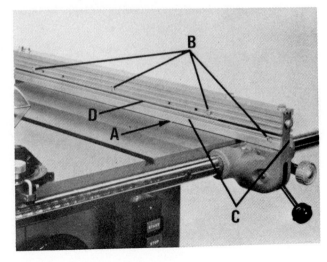

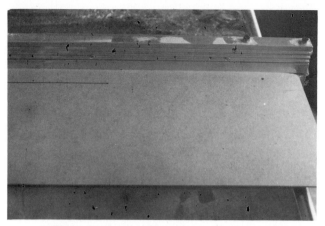

FIGURE 10-8 A strip next to the fence will keep plastic from creeping under the fence. Note the nail to prevent slipping.

piece should be pressed on with a roller or by tamping with a smooth block and hammer. Trimming may be immediate, with either a belt sander or flush cutter and router. (See Figures 10-9 and 10-10.) If the sander is used, some care should be taken to sand evenly. The top edge of the plastic must be perfectly even with right-angle surfaces of the deck and splash.

FIGURE 10-9 Trimming plastic with a router.

FIGURE 10-10 Trimming plastic with a belt sander.

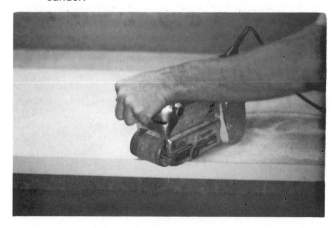

FIGURE 10-11 Preparing to attach cladding to the face of the deck.

Next, the fabricator cements plastic to the front of the splash and the face edge of the deck. (See Figure 10-11.) When spreading cement on the deck and splash, we make an effort to coat the edges of plastic that are to be overlapped.

If applying a strip to a curved surface, the laminator should proceed slowly around the curve, making sure that no ripples are developed. In a tight curve, the plastic should be heated with an iron before and during its application. An iron for applying heat-sensitive veneer is suitable, and so is a household iron.

Horizontal surfaces, the top of the deck and splash, are the last to be clad, following the same application principles. Here, with the largest pieces, is where we are most likely to need protective strips as an aid in positioning the plastic. (See Figures 10-12 and 10-13.) With the counter-

FIGURES 10-12 and 10-13 Positioning a large piece of plastic. Note the protective strips.

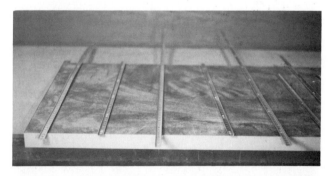

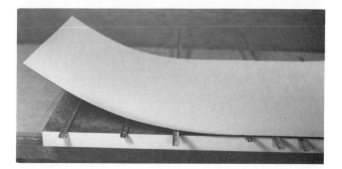

FIGURE 10-14 Four-flute laminate trimmer for easing edges. [Courtesy of Wisconsin Knife Works, 2710 Prairie Ave., Beloit, WI 53511, A Division of Black and Decker (U.S.) Inc.]

top now fully covered in plastic laminate, all sharp edges need to be eased. The portable router may be fitted with a trimming bit with angled flutes for this purpose. (See Figure 10-14.) The beveled router cut should be followed up by drawing a file over each plastic-to-plastic seam. Some cabinetmakers use only the file to ease edges. (See Figure 10-15.)

At this point, we may assemble deck and splash portions of the top. Clearance holes are drilled through the surface of the deck, about ⅜ in. from its rear and 4 to 6 in. apart. We then apply a thick bead of water-repellant caulking to the bottom of the splash and secure it to the deck screws. Scribe edges on the rear of the two pieces should be approximately even. The screws should be countersunk. (See Figure 10-16.)

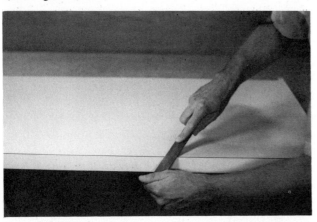

FIGURE 10-15 Easing plastic edges with a file.

FIGURE 10-16 Fastening the splash to a top. Notice the caulking squeezed out.

Ordinarily, the top fabricator's last step is to clean up, not only his or her tools and work area, but also the completed top. Small amounts of dried cement may have adhered to finished plastic surfaces. This can usually be rubbed off with fingers or a soft cloth. Larger or more stubborn messes may require solvent or lacquer thinner rubbing. Squeezed-out caulking material must also be wiped off the finished seam between deck and splash with a damp cloth.

COUNTERTOP SEAMS

Countertop seams are often necessary where base cabinets meet in a return. If one of the legs of the L-shaped countertop is fairly short, and if the countertop pattern and texture are not directional (not wood-grain patterns, etc.), it may be possible to avoid a seam. Plastic-laminate sheets are commonly available in widths of (36 and 48 in.). Some patterns may be ordered in widths of 60 in. Thus we can sometimes build a one-piece top in an L-shape. The bed of the top is designed and assembled as described earlier, but in the desired return configuration. A seam in the deck can be made with dowels or a spline. The sheet to cover the deck is applied in one piece over the entire deck surface and then trimmed as usual.

Seams in plastic-laminate materials may be necessary in some instances. If a straight section of top is quite long, the fabricator may have to join pieces of plastic end to end. Nondirectional patterns may be butt-joined in the same way for a return. Plastics with a directed pattern should be joined by mitering at a return. In fact, most L-shaped tops are mitered to meet in the corner unless a seamless top is achievable, regardless of pattern.

In making any plastic-to-plastic seam, the top fabricator should first decide whether to make a seam involving only the plastic or involving the entire thickness of the countertop. In specialized countertop shops, a large cutoff saw allows the workers to assemble straight sections of top and cut them, either straight or mitered, with the splash in place. (See Figure 10-17.) Straight sections of top are transported and joined at the job site. On the other hand, most cabinet shops generally do not possess this type of saw unless they build countertops in some volume.

High-quality mitered and butt-joined plastic seams are achievable in the smallest of shops. Assembed tops, or just the pieces of plastic, are scribed together.

Plastic-Only Seams

If it is possible to transport and install a countertop in one piece, a plastic-only seam may be the best choice. Making a perfect edge joint is probably easier in material that is less than ¹⁄₁₆ in. thick than it is in the combined thickness

FIGURE 10-17 Mitering an assembled countertop.

of plastic and substrate. Again, splash and deck are built and clad with plastic separately, then fastened together.

The fabricator first determines overall substrate dimensions for deck and splash, and then decides where to make any joints necessary in the substrate. These should not be in the vicinity of the seams that are to be made in the plastic. For strength, it is also better if a joint in the backsplash does not align with a joint in the deck. Another area to avoid in joining decking segments is anywhere that will be cut out to accommodate a sink or cooktop. Considering these restrictions, we assemble segments of the substrate, using dowels or a spline. It may be advisable to use a waterproof glue here if the joint is near a source of moisture. Flatness is extremely important, and we should machine carefully. Sanding over the surface of the joint should be light, with a block or belt sander.

The most critical aspect in creating this type of seam is cutting a perfectly straight line along the plastic pieces where they meet. The pieces should be a few inches longer than needed. One effective method of making the cuts is with a router, fitted with a straight bit. The top fabricator guides the base of the router along a straightedge clamped in place as needed. Obviously, the straightness and inflexibility of the straightedge are vital. (See Figure 10-18.) Of course, it is also possible to scratch a straight line with the tip of an awl, cut outside the line with a fine-point saw, and then remove material to the line with a sharp plane. The edges are set in place dry to evaluate the seam. High spots along the edge can be trimmed with a plane, although some cabinetmakers are capable enough with a belt sander to do the trimming. (See Figure 10-19.)

When the plastic edges meet satisfactorily, the pieces may be cemented in place. Placement is also critical. The fabricator should mark the location at which the seam is to be made and then spread the cement. Positioning the first piece should be no problem. The larger piece should be set first. We use protective strips to keep surfaces apart, use

the marks on the substrate for alignment, and press into place, removing the protector strips as we go. But we do not use a roller until both sheets of plastic are in place. Positioning the second sheet of plastic takes some care. With protective strips in place, we concentrate on the seam end. We overlap the first piece of plastic evenly with the second, by approximately ⅛ in. Several long strips of masking tape are strapped across the seam. The masking tape will stretch enough to allow the overlapping piece to be set in place, but it also provides a bit of clamping pres-

FIGURE 10-18 Cutting plastic with a router and straightedge.

FIGURE 10-19 Trimming a plastic edge with a belt sander. A plane probably gives better control.

sure across the seam. Holding the plastic as parallel as possible with the deck surface, we now push against the tape until the plastic edge drops into position. We press it firmly into place and then secure the rest of the surface. Rolling or tamping can then be performed, but it should be toward, rather than away from the seam. The top may be completed as usual.

Seams Involving Total Countertop Thickness

When sections of countertop must be joined on the site, it is necessary to give them perfectly straight ends that will not be difficult to join. Most often, this means a miter for a corner, but straight pieces are sometimes so long that they must be joined end to end on the job. The important task is once again the perfectly straight cut across the entire width of the top, usually at a 45° angle. Now, however, we are contending with greater thickness in the cut. Again, deck and splash should be dealt with separately.

The countertop deck should be constructed and clad with plastic as usual. The joinery cuts are made just before the edges are eased. A line of cut should be scratched into the surface of the plastic with an awl. Staying just outside the line, we can cut the deck with a 12-point crosscut saw or a saber saw fitted with a reverse-tooth blade. If a saber saw is used, it should be one with a bearing guide to keep the blade as perpendicular as possible with the deck surface. Also, if there is any chance of the saber saw base scratching the finished plastic surface, protection of some type (such as strips of masking tape) should be used. Trimming to the line proceeds most easily with a router. We employ a straight, carbide-tipped bit with enough length to cut the entire depth of the deck in one pass. The base of the router guides along a straightedge. A portion of the self-edging and its backing will undoubtedly have to be trimmed with a handsaw, a block plane, or a sanding block. Of course, the belt sander can be used instead of the router to perfect the line, but it will not yield as perpendicular a trimming cut as the router.

When the seam is satisfactory, the sections of countertop need to be temporarily fastened together with tight joint fasteners. These fasteners are bolt-tightened clamps that are actually embedded in the bottom surface of the deck. A router, still with its straight bit, is used to cut the required T-shaped detail in both sections of the deck. (See Figure 10-20.) With the sections upside down and properly aligned with each other, the top fabricator marks lines across the seam so that the T-shapes can be matched. A pattern may be clamped in position on the edge of the deck for the pattern guide of the router to follow. Some cabinetmakers simply draw the shape of their desired T-cut and freehand the cut.

After making the T-cuts, the fabricator inserts the fasteners and clamps the sections of top together so that

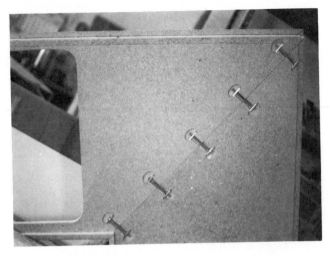

FIGURE 10-20 Tight joint fasteners used to clamp together two sections of countertop. Note the matching T-shapes routed into each piece of decking.

surfaces are flat. Self-edging strips should also meet satisfactorily. The top is then ready for affixing the sections of backsplash.

The top fabricator can make straight or miter cuts on sections of splash with a radial arm saw or even a chop saw. The keys are to use a fine (60 or more teeth on a 10-in.) blade and to position the unclad surfaces against the fence and table. End-joined splashes may be put together with a tight-joint fastener; mitered pieces may be screwed together. Finally, the splash is mounted to the decking with screws and caulking. After easing edges and cleaning away excess cement and caulking material, the sections of assembled top are separated for ease of transport.

PLASTIC-CLAD CABINETRY

Plastic-clad cabinetry is a frequent request in today's cabinet trade. Some people insist on plastic-laminate cabinetry because it is tough and easy to clean up. Others simply enjoy its appearance. To laminate plastic on the exterior of a cabinet, the cabinetmaker generally follows procedures quite similar to those used in countertop fabrication. He or she builds a cabinet and then simply covers its primary surfaces with plastic. There are, however, a few additional matters for the cabinetmaker to consider before launching into such a job.

A primary concern is tooling. There are a number of routers available which are designed specifically for trimming of plastic laminates. (See Figure 10-21.) These routers may have several features that are quite valuable in laminating plastics. They are lightweight and easy to control, even with one hand. Some have an offset drive spindle which allows the router bit to be very close to the edge of

FIGURE 10-21 Offset-base laminate trimmer. (Courtesy of Porter-Cable Corporation.)

the router base. Others have a tilting base to allow easy beveled trimming.

Certain types of router bits are designed for the sort of cutting that is done in plastic lamination of cabinets. In laminating over a face frame, we may cover the entire surface with a single sheet and then cut out the openings for doors and drawers. The face frame itself serves as a template. We can drill through the plastic and insert a conventional flush-cutting bit with a roller bearing guide, or we can employ a panel pilot bit with a plunge point. (See Figure 10-22.) The bit drills its own starting hole and then guides along the edges of the face frame. Where face members meet in a right angle, either bit will leave a rounded plastic corner that can be easily trimmed square with a file.

FIGURE 10-22 A panel pilot bit will self-drill through plastic and follow the ''template'' created by a face frame's edges. (Courtesy of Porter-Cable Corporation.)

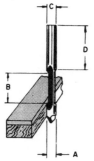

Material selection is another concern. A controlling factor here is whether the cabinet interior must be clad in plastic. Sometimes, plans call for plastic cladding on primary surfaces only. In this case, pine or alder may be used for face frames, and finished ends and backs may consist of medium-density fiberboard. Construction techniques are quite conventional. Ends should be clad before faces and finished backs.

If secondary surfaces of the cabinet must be clad in plastic, the cabinetmaker may want to use factory-coated sheet goods (such as Kortron, produced by Willamette Industries) for some cabinet box components. Another possibility is to apply plastic to sheet goods prior to cutting. Applying plastic prior to assembly works especially well when building cabinets of European design because there are no interior face frame edges to coat with plastic laminate. When planning to use such materials, the cabinetmaker should remember to cut material slightly oversized so that ends and edges can be trimmed on the jointer. Sheets coated on one side are suitable for wall ends, finished ends, and other pieces that have a concealed surface. (The outside of the finished end will be covered with plastic after assembly.) Sheets coated on both sides may be cut into shelves, partitions, and other pieces that will be secondarily visible on both sides. Exposed edges in the assembled cabinet (such as the front edges of shelves) are covered with plastic. Cabinet backs and nailers are often painted to match the color of the cabinet interior. Such cabinets can be put together using conventional means and then receive exterior plastic cladding. If the cabinetry is of face frame design, the interior edges of the frame should be clad first. Also, the cabinetmaker must decide how he or she plans to deal with cladding of the cabinet bottom. The bottom may be a piece of preclad material, but then there will have to be a seam between its surface and the edging of the edge of the bottom rail. Getting the seam flush can be tricky. There are at least two options. One is to make the cabinet bottom from unclad material, assemble the cabinet as usual, and then fit a single piece of plastic in to cover both the bottom and upper edge of the bottom rail. This process can be time consuming, because the plastic must be scribed to fit perfectly up to vertical components. Another possibility is to design the cabinet without a bottom rail. The preclad bottom can then be edged like a shelf.

Doors and drawer fronts are usually covered with plastic on such cabinetry. Since these are generally flat pieces, we do not usually encounter major problems in dealing with them, but there are several guidelines to remember.

First, doors must be clad on their rear surfaces as well as their faces, even if other secondary surfaces on the cabinet are not to be covered in plastic. This equalizes absorption of moisture through the two surfaces of the door. Failure to clad the rear of the door will almost certainly result in warpage. Even though a plastic-clad drawer front will usually be attached to a subfront, it is a good idea to coat its rear surface in plastic as well.

Whenever feasible, door and drawer edges should be clad before faces. This is not absolutely necessary, but it tends to conceal the seams in the plastic better. Unfortunately, it precludes our cutting the doors and drawer fronts from preclad sheets. Another difficulty with cladding ends and edges first is associated with flush inlaid doors. These frequently need to have edge material trimmed away in order to achieve a desirable fit. Obviously, this is undesirable on ends and edges that are already clad in plastic. To avoid this difficulty, most cabinetmakers apply the plastic edge-covering strips last, after the faces are covered. Another

possibility is to fit the doors and drawer fronts before any plastic is cemented on, and to allow enough clearance for the thicknesses of plastic laminate.

Finally, we need to consider interior drawer component surfaces. If it is necessary to prepare these with a hard plastic coating, it is clearly advisable to cut the parts from precoated sheets, assemble the box, and then cement plastic laminate onto the top edges. Since conventional yellow glue will not bond to Kortron or other factory-applied coatings, it is best to rabbet the front and rear of the drawer sides to receive the back and subfront. Drawer bottoms are sometimes painted to match the color of other drawer box components. If so, the painting should be done prior to assembly.

CHAPTER SUMMARY OF CABINETMAKING SKILLS

Plastic laminates are in wide use in fabricating modern cabinetry, as a countertop material and as cladding for the cabinets themselves. It is common practice to build tops in the shop, transport them to the job site, and then attach them to the cabinetry with screws driven from below. Cabinet shops frequently subcontract countertop fabrication to specialized shops, especially for creation of formed or edge-beveled tops.

Self-edged tops are relatively easy for an experienced cabinetmaker to build. A bed, backing for the plastic, is assembled and covered with plastic. The deck and backsplash of a countertop are usually not put together until they have been clad in plastic.

In determining bed dimensions, the top fabricator considers overall cabinet depth and length, overhang, splash attachments, and scribes. Thickness of the plastics is generally ignored.

In cementing the plastic in place, the only skills necessary are spreading cement and tamping or rolling surfaces together. Routers are used to trim rough-cut pieces of plastic to their exact fit size after cementing. Surfaces to receive plastic cladding are flattened by sanding. Curves may be cut with a saber saw or created by laminating thin strips of plywood.

Joining countertops in a miter or in an end-to-end joint is often by means of tight joint fasteners. The most critical operation in this process is making cuts in the plastic which will match perfectly, but this can be done reliably by using a router and straightedge. The fabricator can also sometimes avoid having to make seams to nondirectional patterns of plastic.

The cabinetmaker may also be called on to cover primary or secondary cabinet surfaces with plastic laminate. A special trimming router can be helpful in this, but each cabinet unit is usually assembled and then clad with plastic on primary surfaces. Where feasible, the cabinetmaker clads secondary surfaces prior to assembly, perhaps employing factory-finished materials.

ELEVEN

APPLYING FINISHES

PURPOSES OF A FINISH

The finish for an individual piece of cabinetry or furniture may be any of hundreds of possibilities. It may be that the cabinetmaker's chief finishing problem is in choosing a finish. There is no single finishing material that is best for every wood product, for every woodworker, and for every customer. In making a choice of finish, we need to consider first the particular purposes for finishing a single piece or a set of residential cabinetry.

The purpose of some finishes is to alter the color of wood surfaces. This is usually done by staining. Suppliers of stain make a variety of colors available, most of them adding hues of red, brown, and black to wood. Stains may also be custom mixed to yield virtually any color. A few cabinetmakers disapprove of the use of stains, insisting that staining detracts from the natural beauty of wood. The use of stains is largely a matter of taste, however. Color is, after all, a factor in creating an overall atmosphere within a house or office, and not everyone can afford walnut or other expensive species. Stains also serve to correlate or tie together woodwork, such as paneling and doors, with installed cabinetry. A particular stain may have the effect of either muting or accentuating the grain figure in wood, depending on wood species and the color of stain chosen.

Stains may have a base or solvent consisting of oil or water. Water-based stains are easy to clean up, but they are not frequently used as penetrating stains because the water tends to raise wood fibers undesirably. Water-based stains are often used over other paints and stains, as when the hobbyist is "antiquing" a furniture piece. Oil-based stains are undoubtedly more popular, but the finisher must allow them sufficient drying time before coating over with varnish, lacquer, or oil. In general, stains are easy to apply and wipe off with no special equipment.

The purpose of some finishes is to protect wood. Most of these function by creating a layer of essentially clear material on the surface of the wood. The coatings form a barrier between the wood and its surrounding environment. Most varnishes and lacquers will effectively repel alcohol and water, making them suitable finishes on kitchen, bar, and bathroom cabinetry. Lacquer dries much more quickly than varnish, but its coating is generally thinner. Shellac dries faster than other varnishes and yields thicker coats than lacquer, but it is not nearly as resistant to alcohol and moisture as its two cousins. Any of the three is available in varying degrees of gloss, from flat satin to high gloss. Tools for application may make a difference in choosing a clear coating. Brushing may cause some bubbles, but most of these bubbles will burst without producing a blemish if the material is properly thinned. Lacquer is most often sprayed on, making it desirable to invest in a compressor and other spraying tools. Varnish and shellac may be brushed on easily. Some modern urethane varnishes may be applied by hand rubbing to yield a smooth, tough finish. Lacquer is probably most popular because of its exceptionally fast drying speed. This is important to large shops because it speeds production; it is also significant in small shops because such shops usually do not have a dust-free environment for finishing, and a rapid-drying finish has less of a chance to collect and hold dust.

Rather than coating finishes, wood may receive penetrating finishes. Watco and Minwax are brand names for two such finishes. Linseed oil and tung oil are types of finishing material that also belong in this category. Oils and waxes are very easy to apply with only a few rags. Most are fairly clear and colorless, but they are also available in a variety of wood tones. Most of the finish applied is absorbed into the cell structure of the wood, leaving only a very thin film on its surface. When using oils and waxes, the finisher can usually heighten gloss and resistance to alcohol and water by treating the wood in several applications. Such finishes are often applied to the finest furniture and cabinetry. Since the oil is rubbed in, adherence of dust is not a major problem in a reasonably dust-controlled environment. This factor alone makes rubbed oil finishes an excellent choice for the woodworker who must do his or her cabinetmaking and finishing in the same area.

In choosing a finish, cabinetmakers probably rely on their customers to select stain color and gloss level, but it is usually up to us to choose materials and methods that will arrive at the desired finish. What this means is that we develop our own ''standard'' system for finishing just as with any other cabinetmaking process. In focusing on one system, the finisher must consider tooling, finishing environment, and required application/drying time in addition to features desired in the completed finish, such as color, gloss, and wood protection.

SURFACE PREPARATION

Surface preparation is probably as important to the achievement of a high-quality finish as any other factor. Nearly every operation in the cabinetmaking process has an influence of some type on surface preparation. Improperly stored wood will absorb moisture that can affect finishing adversely. The use of dull saw blades and cutters can cause compacting of wood fibers that inhibits the penetration of both stains and clear finishes, and this wood damage may not even be visible until the wood is finished. Regardless of finishing material and application technique, the best finishes are achieved on wood that is dry and smooth. Of course, most cabinetry consists of surfaces that are in-

tended to be true and flat as well. If wood materials have been selected, cut, and machined properly, such surfaces are generally created by sanding.

Sanding

In theory, a piece of cabinetry is ready for dust removal and finishing as soon as it leaves the assembler's bench. In practice, the proficient finisher inspects visible surfaces fairly carefully before going near a rag or paintbrush. He or she learns to look for particular flaws that can destroy an otherwise good finishing job.

One thing to look for is hardened glue, especially in spots most likely to be missed in sanding, such as inside edges of frames and frame doors. Spots caused by perspiration, water, or oil will also alter finish absorption. Glue can usually be removed fairly easily with a knife, and moisture spots can generally be sanded out, but oily foreign substances can be a real problem to eradicate. The only good solution is to keep oily materials well away from the wood. If a substantially flat and smooth surface is desired on porous woods such as oak, the finisher may want to apply filler paste and resand.

We should also inspect the sanding job, looking for irregularities caused by poor use of the scraper, deep scratches left by coarse sandpaper, swirls left by an oscillating sander, cross-grain sanding scratches (most likely where stile and rail join), and any other surface flaw.

We have already looked rather closely at sanding procedures in Chapters 8 and 9, but it is important here to reemphasize a few principles in the usage of abrasives since they are so important in finishing.

First, sanding with the grain is of tremendous importance. Cross-gain sanding not only leaves highly visible scratches, but also damages the wood's cellular structure. The flaw will be more, not less, visible after finishing, especially when adding color.

Second, but still related to the issue of sanding with the grain, is the judicious use of oscillating sanders. We have already observed that such sanders will leave swirled sanding marks. This is inevitable since the tool operates by rapid circular movement of the abrasive. There is no way that this sanding motion can be parallel to the grain. This does not mean that an oscillating sander cannot be used, however. Swirled scratches can be minimized by proper usage—moving the tool itself with the grain, use of a 12,000-opm sander and fine paper for final sanding, and perhaps a bit of touch-up by hand.

Third, we should initiate sanding with an abrasive only as coarse as necessary, and finish with an abrasive fine enough to achieve the desirable level of smoothness, but intermediate grits should not be skipped. Each sandpaper grit used must be coarse enough to sand out the deepest scratches left by preceding paper. Otherwise, we will have a finely sanded surface with any number of deep scratches through it. Some shops consider 120-grit papers to be fine enough for finished sanding, but others conventionally employ finer papers.

Dust Removal

The label on any container of wood finish will state quite specifically that surfaces to be finished should be free of dust and other contaminants. If a finishing booth is available, pieces should be cleaned before they are moved into the booth.

If compressed air is used to remove large quantities of dust, the line must be free of oil and moisture. Neither a brush nor compressed air alone will remove dust well enough for surfacing. All surfaces should be wiped well with a tacky cloth. These are commercially available and well worth the small investment.

STAINING

Staining wood products to achieve a particular color is a two-step process. The finisher first distributes the material and then wipes off the excess after a short time. The wood fibers act like a sponge, absorbing the oil base and the color it carries. Porous woods will obviously allow deeper penetration of the stain than will nonporous woods. A single board or veneer slice of certain woods (ash is an example) has wide variations in porosity. This is because each growth ring really has two sections: earlywood, which is formed at the beginning of a tree's seasonal growth, and latewood, which is formed later. Densities in earlywood and latewood can be substantially different. These woods will absorb more stain in their more porous sections, darkening the wood fibers more than in other sections, leading to great accentuation of the grain figure. (See Figure 11-1.) End grains also absorb stain more deeply and rapidly than do face or side grains.

An obvious help in staining that is frequently ignored is the information on the container label. After we have used the same type of stain several times, we can probably skip this step, but with any material that we have not used before, nothing may be more important. For example, instructions for some stains tell us exactly how to thin the material, while other cans specify that no thinning must be done under any circumstances. Optimum application temperature and drying time are also revealed here. Good staining results are possible only if the finisher understands how to control the resulting color and darkness on the product.

The final coloring on a piece of cabinetry is the result of several factors. Natural coloring in the wood should not be overlooked. Red oak and white oak treated with the same

FIGURE 11-1 Stained piece of oak. The earlywood and latewood absorb stain at different rates, accentuating grain figure.

stain will differ in color. Stain pigments are obviously a factor. Clear finishes to be applied after the stain is dry can also have an effect on coloration. Some lacquers and varnishes may possess a slight hue of their own, and even if they do not, clear coatings may tend to heighten the effect of certain pigments while softening the effect of others.

Darkness of finished pieces is a result of the degree to which wood fibers absorb the stain. The factors to consider here are porosity of wood fibers, appropriate thinning, and the suggested time for allowing the stain to stand before wiping. With most stains, darkness cannot be increased by allowing the material to stand on the wood surface longer than recommended, by applying more stain, or with second and third coats. Surface wood fibers become saturated, and deeper penetration of the stain ceases as the stain begins to thicken and dry. The desired darkness and color are arrived at most reliably through proper selection and mixing.

Application Procedures

The finisher should begin by making sure that he or she will be able to control color and darkness. This is done by experimenting on sample pieces that are as similar as possible to the cabinetry. Samples should not only be the same type of wood, but also should be sanded in the same way. If the job calls for even darkness, it will be necessary to find a means to inhibit the absorption of stain into end grains, and therefore some samples may also have to be machined similarly to end grains present on the cabinetry. We may want a few samples with a raised panel detail, for example.

End grains can be prohibited from absorbing more stain than side and face grains by applying a thin coat of sealer. Sealer is the same material as that used for clear overcoating, cut with thinner. The finisher treats end grains with this material and allows it to dry, at least partially, before applying stain.

Stain should be well mixed before application (unless instructions order us not to). Since bubble formation in a stain is usually of no consequence, cans of material may be shaken or stirred. The goal is to ensure that all pigments present in the stain are thoroughly distributed.

The finisher then treats the prepared sample pieces. It is a good idea to apply the material to the samples, allow it to stand, and wipe it off in the same way that we intend to do with the cabinet product. In evaluating color and darkness, the finisher usually applies a coating of the intended varnish or lacquer to some part of the stained surface. This allows us to see the effects of the clear coat. If adjustments are called for, this is the time to make them. The best way to alter color and stain depth (darkness versus lightness) is probably by changing to another stain or adding more pigment. We have already observed that it is usually fruitless to allow stains more soak-in time. To achieve additional darkness, we can usually go to a darker stain. For example, if "medium walnut" is too light, we can try "dark walnut." If stained samples are too dark, we can use a lighter stain or thin the material. It is frequently possible to mix light and dark stains to achieve the desired stain depth. (In thinning or mixing stains, it is again necessary to check the container label.) It is very important for the finisher to keep track of the stain "recipe" because it may be necessary to mix more stain later.

If we are attempting to limit the amount of material absorbed by end grains, end-grain samples need to be checked for the effectiveness of sealer. If too much stain was absorbed, we need to thicken the sealer; if too little was absorbed, the sealer needs more thinning. Again, the finisher should keep a recipe. (It should probably be pointed out that this type of absorption control is usually unnecessary. Some cabinet shops follow the procedure routinely, but most do not. Deep end-grain penetration by any penetrating finish material is simply a characteristic of wood. The decision of whether or not to "even out" color and darkness is entirely a matter of taste.

With the infinite color variety available from stain suppliers, the finisher does not usually have to do any mixing to achieve a desired color. If we have the wrong color, we can simply switch stains. Nevertheless, we can achieve subtle changes in color by adding pigments or mixing compatible stains. There is no reason for hesitation in this type of experimentation, even for people without an "eye for color." Custom stain mixing is, in fact, an excellent way to develop such an ability.

With adjustments made, the finisher can proceed with work on the cabinetry. It is an excellent idea, in any size of shop, to make sure that all pieces to be stained are finish sanded and ready for staining. This may include molding or trim, filler strips, individual shelves, or other small parts that are easy to overlook. If the finisher is controlling end-grain absorption, the thinned sealer should be applied wherever necessary with a small brush or rag.

It may also be necessary to mask off certain portions of a cabinet product. The working parts in some hinges and drawer guides may be adversely affected by finishing materials, but the finisher should use some discretion here. Stain will wipe right off of most metal surfaces. Most finishers do not mask off shelf standard strips, the steel sections of drawer guides, or most hinges, especially if lacquer is planned for the clear coating. (The thicker clear coats will usually not seep into a hinge, but they will put a thick coat over the hinge that has to be broken for the hinge to operate. With lacquer, this break in the coating is barely perceptible.) Furthermore, it is probably faster and easier to demount the doors, especially when using hinges that are easily remounted, such as the demountable type. Roller portions of drawer guides should definitely be masked. We cannot allow foreign material to penetrate the roller mechanism, but demounting and remounting are unnecessarily time consuming because we may wind up having to readjust the drawer guides completely. It is very easy to wrap a piece of masking tape around a roller. (See Figure 11-2.) Finishers should also decide whether or not they

FIGURE 11-2 Side-guide roller masked for protection.

intend to apply stain to secondary wood surfaces. Cabinet interiors should probably receive a sealer or clear coat if the cabinet's primary surfaces are to receive one, but application of stain to a cabinet's interior is a matter of choice. Most cabinetmakers will find, however, that it is usually less expensive to go ahead and stain secondary surfaces than to spend a good deal of time masking them off.

Pieces should be distributed in the finishing area in such a way that it will be possible to reach as many finished surfaces as possible without repositioning. Generally, upper cabinets are set upside down, and base cabinets rest on their toekicks. It is helpful to put a few scrap strips between a cabinet and the surface on which it rests. This will make it easier to wipe. Since drawers should be removed from their cases for finishing, the finisher should mark the rear of each drawer and its opening with a matching number unless the assembler already did so. Several drawers may be the same size, but they may each have been adjusted to fit uniquely into a particular opening. Cabinets with finished backs should be arranged so that we can move all the way around them.

If the woodworking area is to be transformed into the finishing area, thorough cleaning is necessary. Some cabinetmakers use inexpensive plastic drop sheets as temporary walls in an isolated portion of their shop. The plastic not only limits dust problems but prevents overspray from getting onto woodworking tools.

Most stains may be applied with a rag, a brush, or spraying equipment. The method is up to us unless the label tells us otherwise. The object is simply to apply the stain liberally, without missing any spots. The only real problem that can develop is overextending ourselves. Stain can be applied much more quickly than surfaces can be wiped, especially when spraying. Thus it is quite possible to put stain on more surface than one person can wipe adequately before the material begins to harden. Wiping semihardened stain off a surface is like trying to wipe away semihardened paint. In using spray equipment, some care should also be taken to prevent hardening of a finishing material inside the nozzle or tip. Most finishers remove the tip of their sprayers and immerse it in thinner while wiping.

With some experience, a finisher learns to allow just the right amount of soak-in time for stain. Here again is an occasion for checking the label. The instructions will tell us approximately how much time to allow. When we read this time limit, we should consider the temperature as well. Several degrees of temperature will substantially shorten the amount of time available to do the wiping. Ideally, we should be wiping off the last sprayed surfaces just before the stain begins to solidify. The wiping should not necessitate heavy rubbing, and the material we are removing should still be essentially a liquid.

The rags of cloths used for wiping should be soft, clean, and absorbent. This is obvious, and label instruc-

tions remind us of this anyway. A bit less obvious is that the rags should not be prone to leaving lint or threads behind. Woven material, the type in T-shirts, is appropriate. Torn sheets do not make very good wiping cloths. A box of new wiping rags, available from most paint stores, is probably well worth the money.

Goals in the actual wiping process are to apply fairly even pressure and to remove all excess. Generally, we wipe surfaces with a hand motion parallel to the grain, although this is not an absolute necessity. Often, as with frame doors, we follow the surface contours. The finisher should take extra care to remove all excess on such surfaces. It is easy to leave behind some unabsorbed stain in some places, especially where frame members meet an inset panel or back, and also along any machined edge form. Metal hardware should be wiped carefully, too. With the excess wiped off, pieces need curing time before further finishing work. Some stain may be ready to be covered with a clear finish in a few hours, but most cabinetmakers allow overnight drying.

Matching Colors

From time to time, the cabinetmaker is asked to build pieces to match existing cabinetry. It is necessary to follow someone else's design plans in fabricating the cabinetry, rather than following our own standards. Most of the necessary information for fabricating such pieces can be gained by measuring the components of the existing woodwork: stile and rail dimensions, exact cabinet depth, almost every feature. But one thing the cabinetmaker generally does not measure for is door design. We usually take one of the doors back to the shop. This allows us to re-create particular features, such as edge forms. It also gives us an example of finished wood. The color and the gloss level of the finish must often be matched.

The first matter for the finisher to consider is the effects of age on the sample piece. Clear finishes that are several years old may have yellowed a bit. To create the same effect on the new cabinetry, the finisher will frequently add color to the clear coating material. To varnish or shellac we add oil-based stain. Lacquer-based paints mix best with lacquer finishes. The colors used are generally light tan or yellow, and we need only very small amounts. Naturally, some experimenting may be necessary.

Establishing a matching stain color can also call for experimentation. It is important to build the piece from woods as similar as possible to those in the original piece. The finisher begins to arrive at the correct hue by choosing a stain that is already close to the sample door in color. Suppliers of stain will also provide a sample card illustrating colors of all their available stains. The sample card will give us a good idea of which stain to begin with. Then pigments are added as necessary to create the matching color. (See Figure 11-3.) Pigments or tints are available

FIGURE 11-3   Adding oil pigment to a stain.

from the stain supplier in virtually every color that we might need. The finisher first prepares several pieces of wood for experimenting. One of these is stained with the base stain and compared to the sample door. The idea is to look for colors present in the sample door but missing from our practice piece. Then we add some tint of that particular color. The tints needed most often are as follows: ocher (earthy yellow), raw sienna (brownish yellow), burnt sienna (reddish or rust brown), raw umber (medium gray-brown), burnt umber (dark gray-brown), toluidine red, vermillion (reddish orange), and lamp black. We can also purchase white and shades of blue and green. Mixing must be very thorough. When the finisher believes that the right color has been achieved, he or she should apply the clear coat finish over a section of stained wood, to be sure.

CLEAR COATING

Clear coating is the application of materials such as varnish, shellac, and lacquer. They protect wood essentially by adhering to its surface rather than by substantial penetration of the wood fibers. We have already looked at and compared some of the important characteristics of these materials. Now it is time for us to look at specific application procedures.

Further Surface Preparation

Before any wood surfaces are clear coated, they may need treatment in addition to the sanding and dusting discussed earlier. Some stained surfaces will require further sanding after the stain has fully dried. It is frequently possible to clear coat over penetrating oil stains without the additional sanding, but water-based stains raise the grain substantially and need to be sanded. The sanding should be light, with a very fine grit paper or steel wool. Since we are actually

removing wood fibers as well as some dried stain material, sanding motion should be parallel to the grain. The operation may lighten the color. Some woodworkers go over wood stained with oil in a similar way. After the sanding, the finisher must once again remove all dust with a tacky cloth.

Wood bleaching bears some mention here. This operation makes use of chemicals to lighten the coloring in wood. The bleaching of entire furniture and cabinet pieces allows the finisher to lighten and even-out color tones in wood surfaces. Dark walnut can first be bleached and then stained to an even fruitwood or maple color, for example. This is not a widely used practice in the trade today, but, of course, it may become more prevalent again in the future. The main purpose for using bleaches in today's trade is for treatment of dark spots and streaks on some surfaces. Even in these situations, the finisher bleaches only when a customer insists on perfect uniformity in color. Occasionally, we may find a door panel or a wood top with dark spots caused by a belt sander or dull cutters, and the bleach can help to soften the color in these spots.

The bleaching material is available from some suppliers of paint and stain. It is actually two different materials (sodium hydroxide and hydrogen peroxide) in two different bottles. They are applied with a rubber sponge to the wood, separately but one right after the other. When the solution is dry, some sanding is necessary to remove a salt material that forms. If more lightening of color is desired, we can repeat the procedure, but then it is often necessary to apply water to the surface and actually wash it before sanding. Wood bleach is caustic and should be used only after carefully reading the instructions (good ventilation and rubber gloves are vital). Many modern woodworkers simply do not use it.

Filling of open-grained woods is another practice that is used less frequently today than it once was, but unlike bleaching, it is sometimes an absolute necessity. Anyone who has ever applied a clear coat to the surface of oak, ash, or walnut can attest that the layers of finish do very little to fill the large pores. We can still see and feel tiny indentations in the wood over every pore. In general, this is acceptable. For many customers, the natural textures are even desirable. In deciding whether or not to do this sort of filling, the cabinetmaker should remember the principle of "function first." Perfectly flat, true, and smooth wood surfaces may have a substantial function in a desktop or table, but probably not in residential kitchen cabinetry.

Whether or not a cabinet project has been stained, the color of filler paste used to fill wood pores should be mixed with stain to match the color of finish. Then the finisher simply takes the time to give wood a coat of the filler paste. (Naturally, this filling step may be performed before staining if we are confident that the filler paste will absorb stain in the same way as the surrounding wood. In fact, since some sanding in necessary after the filler dries, many cabinetmakers prefer to fill pores with paste before staining.) When the filler has dried, we should sand the surface by hand, with very fine grit (300 grit or finer) sandpaper on a block. Since the goal here is flatness, block sanding is the most reliable method. With the pores satisfactorily flushed to the surface, the finisher must wipe away dust and inspect for desired color.

Seal Coating

The first actual clear coat applied to a wood surface is referred to as sealer or sanding sealer. Suppliers market sealers for specific coatings, but sealer is almost always the clear coat material cut with an equal portion of thinner. The sealer bonds more easily with a wooden surface than full-strength clear coats, allowing subsequent coats to attach more easily.

When the sealer is dry, it, too, must be sanded. The purpose of this sanding is to flatten irregularities in the first layer of finish caused by settling dust and tiny bubbles. Here, for the first time in the cabinetmaking process, the sanding is not on the wood at all, but rather, on the finishing material. This is both an advantage and a disadvantage. We do not need to pay attention to sanding in the direction of the grain, for the clear coating material has no grain. Yet we must be careful not to sand too heavily or we will cut through the thin sealer to the surface of the wood. Sandpaper grit should be very fine, between 220 and 300 grit. Sanding may be by hand, with or without a block, or with a quarter-sheet sander. Then tacky cloths are used to remove dust, and the cabinetry may receive one or more coats of uncut varnish, shellac, or lacquer.

Shading

Some finishers may apply additional coloring over the seal coat in certain areas of the wood, to achieve even color and darkness. This is called shading. The shading material is generally a stain which is slightly darker than previously applied stain. It is most often sprayed on lightly and evenly, and allowed to dry without wiping. Shading by spraying requires good operator control in order to get the coloring in exactly the right place. It is helpful to use an airbrush or a touch-up gun in this operation. (See Figure 11-4.) Some finishers mix coloring with their clear coating material for shading. Colored clear coat may be applied to the lighter sections of wood with a brush. Shading is entirely optional. Some admirers of wood consider the practice unnatural, but some customers may be seeking a finish that is completely even over the entire surface, and shading is a fairly fast and easy way to achieve this without bleaching. In general, shaded areas are not sanded until they are covered in the first uncut clear coat.

FIGURE 11-4 Shading lighter areas with a spray gun. (Courtesy of Binks Manufacturing Company.)

Brushing and Spraying

In production shops, one fairly thick clear coat is considered enough for residential cabinetry. The thickness of lacquer may be built up in several coatings. Some "high-solids" lacquers (Deft is a brand name for such a product) allow, and even recommend, very thick coats to be applied.

Temperature is a concern in any application of varnish-type material. Naturally, the container instructions call for a particular temperature range during application and drying, but there is another concern here as well. If an unfinished wood article is built or stored in a rather cool environment and then moved to a substantially warmer area for clear coating, a bubbling problem may develop, particularly when using slower-drying materials such as varnish. This is because wood fibers expand in the warmer environment, forcing out air. If the finisher's paint booth is substantially warmer than the assembly/storage area, pieces to be finished should be given some warm-up time before clear coating. Lacquer is not usually affected, since it may be dry to the touch in less than a minute. This is obviously another advantage of lacquer over shellac and varnish.

Another important factor is viscosity. The thicker a finishing material is—the more resistant it is to flowing—the more viscous it is said to be. Varnish usually has more viscosity than lacquer, for example. Finishes with high viscosity are more difficult to spray on.

One method for choosing between brush and spray applications of the clear coat is simply to follow label recommendations. The container will often recommend one system over the other. This is probably somewhat artificial, however. In reality, most cabinetmakers choose the material based on the tools they have available, ability to control dust and temperature in the application environment, and job requirements.

In general, most lacquers are meant for spraying, while most varnishes are better suited for brush applications, at least in small and medium-sized shops. Varnishes tend to be too thick for efficient spraying and can also form bubbles when aerated. Lacquers dry so fast that brushing them on will leave brush marks. However, a few varnishes may be sprayed and some lacquers (such as Deft) may be brushed with good results. Polyurethane and polyester finishes may also be sprayed. Quite recently, coatings have appeared in the industry which are called "plural-component" finishes. These consist of two parts—catalyst and resin—which are mixed together just prior to spraying.

In commiting to a finishing system, the cabinetmaker has to consider a number of factors, including the quality of finish desired, preferred finishing materials, and production volume.

To be sprayed on, finishing material must be "atomized." This means that it must be broken into tiny particles just prior to application. While still a liquid, these particles blend together on the wood's surface and create a coating of consistent thickness. When we choose a spray system, we are choosing, in part, among methods of atomization. Different atomizing systems will call for particular types of equipment. (See Figure 11-5.)

One method is air atomization. This works by aerating the lacquer, either just inside or just outside the nozzle of our gun. This type of atomization results in a good deal of overspray and waste but can produce an excellent finish.

For the small shop, a siphon-feed air system may be most appropriate. The lacquer is drawn out of a cup attached directly to the bottom of the gun. (See Figure 11-6.) It is easy to change from one type of material to another, and cleanup is fast. The viscosity of the finishing material must be fairly low, but atomization is very fine, and we can achieve fine results.

A pressure-feed system may be used in larger cabinet shops, where there is continual finishing to be done. For the fine atomization required in most woodworking, an external mix nozzle is desirable. In a pressure-feed setup, fluid and air are both delivered to the gun under pressure, and these pressures must be in balance.

Airless spraying is also a possibility. This system works by pumping the finishing material out of a small hole in the nozzle. It is a useful system when high production and great speed are important. The finishing material may be heated as an aid in atomizing, but this type of spraying will generally not produce finishes of the same quality as that produced by an air atomizing system. Airless systems can also be more hazardous, since fairly high pressure is required to apply the finish.

Air-assisted airless systems are a fairly recent development. This type of system atomizes partially by fluid pressure (as in airless spraying), and partially with compressed air. It yields fine atomization and a fine finish without the high waste factor involved in conventional compressed-air spraying.

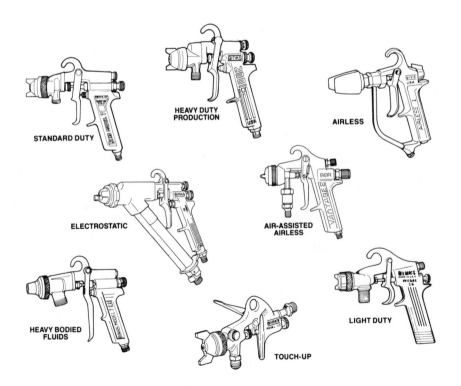

FIGURE 11-5 The method of atomization may dictate the choice of gun and nozzles. (Courtesy of Binks Manufacturing Company.)

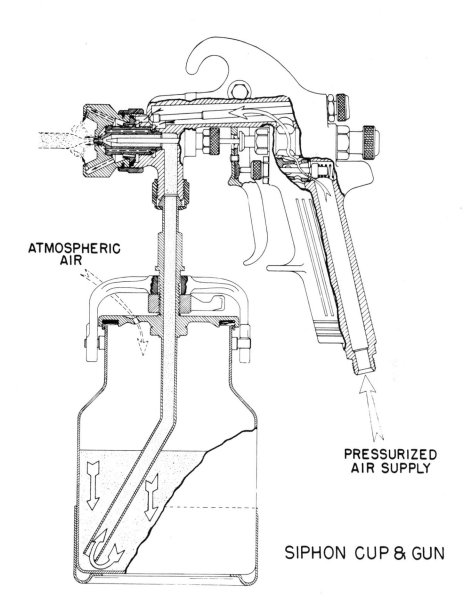

ATMOSPHERIC
AIR

PRESSURIZED
AIR SUPPLY

SIPHON CUP & GUN

FIGURE 11-6 Siphon cup and gun. (Courtesy of Binks Manufacturing Company.)

In high-production furniture-finishing operations, overspray and waste are reduced by spraying electrically charged particles. Electric charging creates an attraction between the finishing fluid and the product being sprayed. Plural-component finishes are applied by special pumps that control the flow rate of minerals, mix them, and send the finish through a spray gun.

Even in a small shop, investment in a good-quality spraying system and a respirator is often superior to brushing, particularly if the shop operator already possesses a compressor for driving other pneumatic equipment. Money invested is regained very quickly in time savings. Therefore, most shops use a spray system unless a particular job demands something else.

Sprayed lacquer is suitable on almost any interior cabinet surface: kitchen and bathroom cabinets, shelving units, and wall systems. Even desks and finished wooden tops may be clear coated in this way if we build thick enough coatings. Most lacquers are highly resistant to water and alcohol after three full coats.

Varnish, because is has more viscosity than lacquer, is often used on interior surfaces that are more likely to get hard use. With only two coats of varnish, we can build a thick finish on interior doors and the tops of some furniture items.

Brushes and Brushing Techniques

When applying varnish, selection of the right brush may be the most important consideration. A 75-cent throwaway brush is the right choice for applying contact cement, but it is among the worst choices for finishing. A good varnish brush should be made of nylon or natural bristle. It should have a chisel shape on its application end, but it must be full-bodied. The individual bristles of a varnish brush are generally tapered slightly and split at the end.

Before dipping into the varnish with the brush, the finisher should prepare the brush adequately. This means flexing by hand to remove loose bristles. The brush should also be dipped into the appropriate thinner (turpentine, mineral spirits, or another thinner will be specified on the can) and gently swabbed on a soft throwaway cloth.

Brushing on a clear coat should obey the following guidelines:

1. Begin in the middle of large surfaces, brushing toward ends.
2. Brush from wet areas into dry areas.
3. Generally, brush with the grain—better penetration is achieved by brushing cross-grain first, then brushing again parallel to the grain.
4. For ends and edges, brush to follow the edge forms or other contours of the wood.
5. To remove excess varnish from the brush after dipping into the can, tap or lightly scrape the brush against the side of a separate can—this helps to prevent bubbles.
6. Achieve wet, even coats.
7. Check for and brush out drips, runs, and other buildup, especially where surfaces come together (top–edge, etc.).

Sprayers and Spraying Techniques

To use an air spraying gun, it must be connected to an air line that is free of moisture and oil. When air is first compressed and then allowed to enter a feed hose, a good deal of the moisture present is liquefied. This water, if allowed through the spray gun, will do a lacquer finish a good deal of harm. Oil, too, may be present since the compressor head requires lubrication. Therefore, the air line used for finishing should be fitted with its own regulator and an extractor to remove water and oil from the air.

In most cabinet shops at the present time, the preferred spraying system is an air atomizing system, either siphon feed or pressure feed, employing an external mix nozzle.

Pressure and feed are important considerations in any spray-finishing setup. Pressure is measured in pounds per square inch (psi), and it should be kept low, just enough to atomize the lacquer. Feed refers to the measurable airflow, measured in cubic feet per minute (cfm). In general, external mix nozzles require a higher cfm rate than do internal mix nozzles. Also, a fluid nozzle is chosen partly on the basis of its orifice diameter in relation to the viscosity and the amount of material to be sprayed (higher viscosity and thicker coats require a larger-diameter hole). It should be obvious that pressure must be higher for nozzles with larger fluid-delivery orifices, and this means a heavier demand on the feed (cfm) capabilities of the compressor. A 1-horsepower compressor can only deliver about 4 cfm at 100 psi. Such a tool may not be capable of keeping up with the cfm demands of an external-mix air nozzle.

When buying a compressor, the cabinetmaker should consider the following: cfm rating, pressure rating, holding-tank volume, horsepower rating, the type of nozzle to be used in finishing, and the type of feed (siphon or pressure), as well as the air demands of other pneumatic equipment in the shop.

The lacquer may be supplied to the gun from a 1-quart cup attached directly to its bottom (often siphon feed) or from a separate container that is connected to the bottom of the gun through flexible feed lines (pressure feed). The separate container system is best for large jobs because the operator does not have to manage any weight in addition to the gun, and because it may hold up to 5 gallons of lacquer or more, making frequent cup refills unnecessary.

A good-quality spray gun has built-in controls for the regulation of spray pattern and lacquer feed rate. These are usually small knobs at the rear of the gun. Generally, we desire the maximum amount of lacquer that can be delivered to the wood surface without creating runs. The spray pattern is an ellipse or oval shape.

When clear coating with a compressed air sprayer, we should adhere to the following guidelines:

1. Use a large practice piece to check proper operation and adjustment of the gun.
2. Arrange the wide part of the oval spray pattern and use it vertically for most spraying. (See Figure 11-7.)

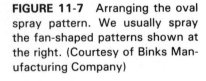

FIGURE 11-7 Arranging the oval spray pattern. We usually spray the fan-shaped patterns shown at the right. (Courtesy of Binks Manufacturing Company)

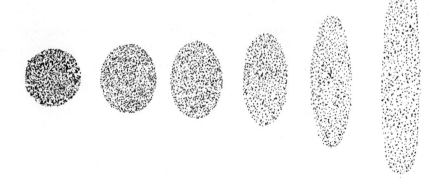

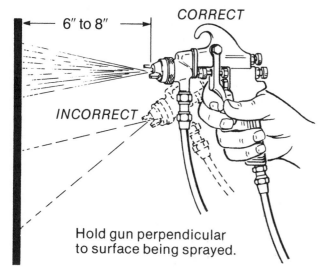

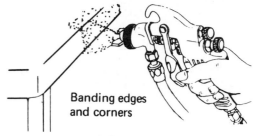

FIGURE 11-9

FIGURE 11-8 Hold the gun perpendicular to the surface. (Courtesy of Binks Manufacturing Company.)

3. Determine the proper distance away from finished surfaces at which to hold the spray gun (6 to 8 in.) and maintain this distance (too close, and we get thick, narrow bands of lacquer; too far, and a white powder develops).

4. As much as possible, hold the gun at a right angle to the surface being sprayed. (See Figure 11-8.)

5. Spray first in hard-to-reach places (cabinet interiors, inside face frame edges, door ends and edges, etc.), this "banding" allows overspray to accumulate on the outer portions of larger surfaces, taking the place of a stroke or two and preventing runs. (See Figure 11-9.)

6. Make spraying strokes from side to side as much as possible, and overlap the spray pattern of each stroke with the previous stroke. (See Figure 11-10.)

7. For interior corners, spray a section along the edge, and then work away from the corner.

8. Before each spraying stroke, pull the trigger and initiate the flow of air and lacquer with the gun aimed away from the wood surface, then proceed with the stroke.

9. At the end of each stroke, release the trigger.

FIGURE 11-10

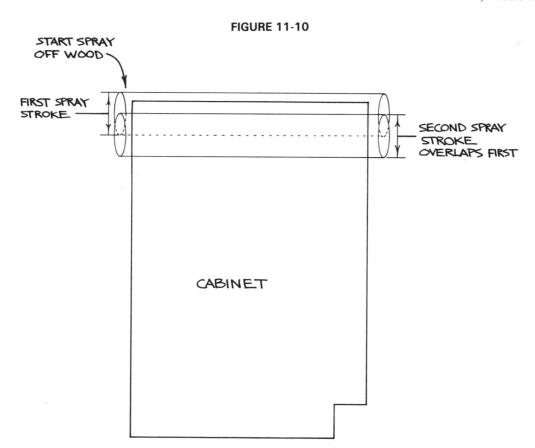

FIGURE 11-11 Immersing the air and fluid nozzles in solvent.

10. Achieve full, wet coats.

11. Arrange pieces such as finished tops, shelves, and doors vertically so that they can be sprayed with the gun upright.

12. During any pause of more than a few minutes, unscrew the gun tips to immerse them in lacquer thinner and hang the gun up. (See Figure 11-11.)

Spraying a finish is much faster than brushing, and it can produce some beautiful results. Air-driven sprayers are very common in both small and large shops, and the modern finisher generally operates on the assumption that "if it can be sprayed, use a sprayer." When spraying any finish, it is imperative to use a respirator. Conventional particle masks cannot take the place of a respirator.

Factory usage of finishing sprayers goes even farther. Furniture factories discovered some time ago that color and clear coating can be mixed and applied to wood articles in one spraying step. It is like shading on a massive scale. When we mix a color (stain) and a clear coating (lacquer), we are not staining the wood at all; we are more-or-less "painting" on a colored clear coat. If the coat is not colored too darkly, we can still see the wood grain. This system allows the finisher to avoid bleaching, stain wiping, and shading while attaining wood products with a very even coloring and a smooth finish. Factories are now using airless, electrostatic, and air-assisted airless sprayers to reduce waste and allow for the application of thicker coatings of lacquer.

Whether the finisher uses a brush or a spray gun, some procedures are the same. Whenever more than one coat is desired (and this is essential with lacquer), some fine sanding must be performed between coats. Indeed, some finishers sand after the final coat as well, with extremely fine (600-grit or so) paper. Some prefer to use steel wool (000 between coats and 0000 after the final coat). Naturally, after every sanding operation, dusting with a tacky cloth must follow. For a fine furniture finish, the last coat can be treated with a rub of pumice and oil, followed by another rub with rottenstone and oil. Whether the crushed stone is used or not, primary surfaces on most cabinetry should receive a rub with lemon oil or paste wax. Production-style shops do not usually perform this last rubbing out, but many custom shops do.

Cleanup should be immediate and thorough. The substantial investments necessary for decent brushing and spraying equipment is worth protecting. Professional painters and finishers realize the great importance of caring for their equipment, and they probably do a better job of it than some cabinetmakers. Lacquer thinner should be fed through the feed lines and the spray gun, and its tips should be immersed in thinner as well. A good storage place for the tips is inside the spray gun cup with a small amount of thinner. A varnish brush should be stored so that it does not stand on its bristles, suspended in solvent if possible.

WIPING WITH OILS AND WAXES

Wiping with oils and waxes should be thought of not as clear coating, but rather, as the application of a treatment that protects by penetration, solidification, and hardening of the wood's fibers. For staining effects, finishers may purchase colored oils in several shades, or they can add tints to the oil as they would for stains. Oil finishes are not only beautiful, protective, and long lasting; they are also extremely easy to apply. Cabinetmakers who have trouble in the application of other types of finishes usually fall in love with oils for this reason. If we can follow the container label directions, we can succeed with oil finishes.

After proper surface preparation, the finisher should make sure that the oil is properly mixed. Most oils need no thinning, and in fact should not be thinned, but they should be shaken or stirred well prior to application. Notice that it is perfectly all right to shake cans of oil vigorously, a procedure that is not advisable with many varnishes. Since oil penetrates instead of building a surface film, bubbles are unimportant.

In general, each application of oil involves flooding wood surfaces with the oil, allowing it time to penetrate the wood fibers (and perhaps adding more oil), and then wiping off the excess.

The finisher usually has a good deal of choice in application tools. Most oils can be flooded into wood with a brush, a roller, or a cloth. Some finishers even have success in spraying or pouring, although the oil manufacturers seldom recommend this. After the oil has been allowed time to penetrate (labels recommend certain times and temperatures), a cloth should be used for wiping. These should be soft and absorbent, like stain-wiping cloths.

Application and wiping motions may be parallel to wood grain or may follow surface forms. (See Figure 11-12.) Almost the only way to make any type of mistake is to allow the oil to harden too much before wiping. This will usually not harm the finish, but it can make the excess oil more difficult to wipe off.

FIGURE 11-12 Applying an oil finish to a door with a soft cloth.

After excess oil has been wiped away, the cabinetry is allowed to dry. Most oils require substantial drying time, from 12 to 24 hours, before further finishing treatment proceeds. The cloths used for application and wiping must be disposed of immediately and properly or they can ignite spontaneously, particularly when using linseed oil. The cloths may be burned, or discarded in a sealed, water-filled can.

It is possible to sand a wood surface while it is still covered with wet oil. Very fine (400 to 600 grit) wet–dry paper is used, sanding parallel to the grain. This procedure can be used instead of filling with paste to create a very smooth surface on porous woods. Tiny wood particles are worked into the pores with the oil. Naturally, this step is entirely optional.

After the oil has dried, we sand lightly over the finished surfaces with very fine paper or steel wool. Since the coating effects of the oil are minimal, sanding should be with the grain. Then dust is removed with a tacky cloth, and the piece is ready for additional treatment.

At this point, oil finishing may proceed in a few different ways. The container labels on different products may recommend different procedures. With most oils, we can increase gloss and depth of finish simply by applying more material, just as we did on the first coat. Tung oil finishes are built in this way. Other products, such as Watco, may be wet sanded, using 600-grit wet–dry paper and a lubricant (the oil itself or a wax).

After the finisher has built an oil finish with satisfactory depth and luster, primary surfaces should be polished, using a cloth—dry, with lemon oil, or with a very small amount of the finishing oil.

Many custom cabinetmakers use oil finishes on their best furniture products, even if they conventionally apply lacquer finishes to kitchen cabinetry. Furniture articles that have been scratched or nicked can often be repaired with additional oiling treatments. The mar can often be polished or wet sanded away, using oil as the lubricant.

Cabinetmakers used to do much of their oiling with linseed oil, but it is not the best choice for new wood products. Linseed oil can bleed out of a surface because it never actually hardens (polymerizes) like the other oils, it yellows, and it can alter wood color. Nowadays, most cabinet finishers use linseed oil only for restoring antiques. The goal in this type of work is to "maintain the integrity" of the old finish. (Actually, many of us believe that a modern oil should be used anyway. A hardening oil is better for aging wood, and it becomes part of its history as well. Most furniture restorers do not hesitate to use other modern materials, such as resin glues, and there is probably no good reason to avoid the superior oils.)

CHAPTER SUMMARY OF CABINETMAKING SKILLS

The best finish for an individual cabinetry piece is largely a matter of choice, and a cabinetmaker should not hesitate to try different finishing techniques. In general, however, lacquers are used for conventional cabinetry, and penetrating oils are employed for most furniture. Varnishes are usually applied only to surfaces that must endure heavy use such as desktops. Color is achievable by staining, applying color with the polymerizing oil, or mixing color in with a clear coat.

Surface preparation is vital to creating a high-quality finish. An unfinished cabinet should be protected from oil and moisture absorption. We inspect all surfaces carefully and sand as necessary, using successively finer grits and sanding with the grain. Dust must be removed with tacky cloths, and sections that must not be finished should be masked off.

Stain may be sprayed, brushed, or swabbed on, but the excess should be wiped away with soft cloths, following the grain direction or surface contours. Exact shades of color and darkness can be controlled by mixing stains or adding tints to a stain. Wood surfaces can be bleached, partially sealed, or shaded to achieve even tone and depth of color.

Clear coatings are lacquer, varnish, and shellac. To apply these, the cabinetmaker must learn proper methods of manipulating varnish brushes and spray equipment. Wet, even coats are the main goal. Stained materials may need light sanding before the seal coat is put on. The sealer is usually thinned lacquer or varnish, and successive coats are applied full strength, with light sanding between coats.

Oil finishes may be the easiest to apply in some respects, but they are high-quality finishes. They are very suitable in the small shop, where finishes have to be applied amid some dust. Surfaces receive oil, which is allowed to penetrate for 10 to 30 minutes and then wiped with a soft cloth. Greater luster, hardness, and coating features are attainable with successive coats.

TWELVE

INSTALLATION

TOOLS AND SUPPLIES

With cabinetry that must be affixed to the walls or floor of a house or building, the work of the installer is, in a way, the most visible. When the installer's work is done, the cabinet project is finished. The installer is therefore associated with the total cabinet product.

Installation requires many different tools. Most installers hold the opinion that they should have with them any tool which there is even a chance of using. Like the cabinet assembler, an installer should possess a full range of hand tools.

Power tools are a tremendous benefit to an installer, as we shall see, and most job sites do have a power supply, even sites of new construction. Electric power speeds up installation so much, in fact, that many shops invest in their own generators. The most important power tool for an installer is probably a variable-speed reversible drill or a screw gun. In the trade today, most cabinetmakers prefer to affix cabinets with drywall screws whenever possible, rather than with nails, and a screw gun is probably the best way to drive these and other fasteners. An installer also has use for other portable power tools, as follows: sanders (especially a belt sander), saber saw, circular saw, motorized miter box, hammer drill, and conventional drill. A router and power plane can also be helpful. Some installers take along a compressor and a brad or nail gun.

Certain tools are a necessity to an installer. A stool or short step ladder, padded props for mounting upper cabinets, furniture blankets, and dollies may all be a great help.

A cabinet installer needs a variety of fasteners, which are usually carried in a custom-made box with dividers. (See Figure 12-1.) Shims are necessary for leveling cabinet units. For touching up finishes, it is also wise to carry stain and colored putty that matches the finish color of a job,

FIGURE 12-1 Well-used screw box. The user obviously prefers drywall screws for fasteners.

lacquer, and any molding sizes or supplies that may be needed on an individual job.

TRANSPORTING CABINETS

Transporting cabinets is an operation often overlooked, yet it is rather important. The ignorance of a few principles can lead to substantial damage of wood products.

If possible, cabinets should be moved under cover. In very dry regions, a cabinet shop may be able to get by with an open truck, but even in such regions, pieces may need protection from the sun and heat, particularly if the articles must be transported for some distance. This is most important with unfinished wood. If a covered truck is not an option, cabinets should be arranged on the truck bed so that there is minimum exposure to the elements, or pieces should be covered with an opaque tarp for trips that may take more than a half hour.

Furniture blankets or other padding should be used to protect finished surfaces from rubbing together. The number of pads can be kept to a minimum by arranging pieces finished surface-to-finished surface, allowing one piece of padding to protect two surfaces at once. Unfinished surfaces, such as most backs, can be positioned against the outsides of the track or against one another.

If only a small truck bed is available, such as the bed of a pickup truck, cabinets may be stacked up and tied in place. Tying is important, since we want to prohibit movement as much as possible. Stretchy, soft furniture ropes are best, but we can also use conventional nylon rope. Wherever rope contacts a finished surface, we need to position more padding to inhibit rope friction. When substantial tightness is necessary, as when we are tying a stacked load down to the bed, loops in the rope can be used with great effectiveness. Any loose members—shelves, loose doors, and drawers—should be put inside cabinetry to inhibit movement.

The installer should take the time to double check to be sure that every piece of cabinetry and every necessary tool has been loaded. This is especially important when the installer divides time between installing and other duties. The craftsman who does nothing but install cabinetry is less likely to forget a tool or supply than the woodworker who divides time between installation and other duties. Nothing is a bigger waste of time than extra trips for missing items.

MOUNTING SYSTEMS

Mounting systems are only partly a matter of choice. The type of building material present in a particular home or office may call for a particular type of fastener.

FIGURE 12-2 Cabinets are frequently hung on studs.

Many walls and ceilings or soffits consist of plasterboard mounted over wooden "studs." The studs are usually fir 2 × 4's or 2 × 6's. (See Figure 12-2.) We can affix cabinetry to this sort of wall by driving nails or screws through cabinet box members and into the studs. Screws are superior. They can be driven with a drill or screw gun, avoiding the risk of damaging wood members with a hammer. This is especially important since we frequently have to drive fasteners at awkward angles when installing. Furthermore, driving a screw creates a minimum of vibration to alter cabinet adjustment and alignment, has greater holding power, and is easy to remove if we make a mistake. The screws most commonly used are 2½- or 3-in. drywall screws. It may occasionally be necessary to use screws up to 5 in. long in order to reach a stud by driving at an angle. It is possible to use wood screws, but using them often necessitates predrilling of countersink and clearance holes. Drywall screws may be driven without predrilling unless there is a possibility of splitting the nailer. An efficient installer will also avoid slotted screws as much as possible. If nails are chosen as the fastener, the most common size is 16d. (See Figure 12-3.)

Sometimes we require a fastener on the hollow section of a stud wall. The most common choices for this situation are toggle bolts and hollow wall fasteners, which actually tie the cabinet to the plasterboard. Toggle bolts consist of a machine screw and spring-operated wing. (See Figure 12-4.) To use it, the cabinet must be positioned exactly as it is to be mounted against the wall. The installer then drills a hole through the cabinet and wallboard, moves the cabinet away from the wall, and enlarges the hole in the wallboard only. The hole must be large enough to allow the collapsed spring wing to fit through. We then

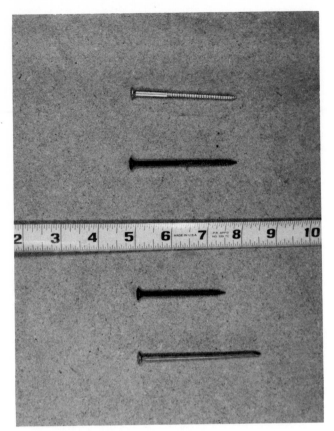

FIGURE 12-3 The superiority of drywall screws is based on their taperless, self-threading design. They are easily driven with a drill.

SPRING-WING TYPE

| Round Head | Flat Head | Mushroom Head | Button Head | Slotted Hex Head |

FIGURE 12-4 A toggle bolt will usually have a slotted head. (Courtesy of The Rawlplug Company, Inc.)

push the machine screw through the nailer, attach the spring wing to it, collapse the wings and push it through the drywall, and tighten. The spring wings spreads out behind the wallboard. A hollow wall anchor is made up of a machine screw and a metal expansion anchor. (See Figure 12-5.) It is used similarly to the toggle bolt. The cabinet is positioned as necessary, a hole is drilled through the nailer and

FIGURE 12-5 Hollow wall anchor. As the nut is tightened, the anchor compresses and spreads out on the rear side of the wall board. (Courtesy of The Rawlplug Company, Inc.)

wallboard, and the cabinet is moved out of the way. We push the fastener through the hole in the drywall and tighten the screw to expand the anchor against the rear side of the wallboard. Then we remove the screw, put the cabinet back where it belongs, and reinsert and tighten the machine screw.

Drywall may also be hung on rolled sheet metal studs in a wall. Upon this type of wall, cabinets may be mounted either by driving self-threading (sheet metal or drywall type) screws into the studs or by attachment to hollow sections of wallboard with toggle bolts or hollow wall fasteners.

Stud walls may also be covered with lath and plaster, but cabinets may be secured to this type of wall just as they would be to stud walls that are hung with drywall. We can also drive screws into wood lath strips if they are present.

Masonry walls, made of bricks or some type of block and held together by mortar, often make up the exterior of a building, and the cabinet installer often has to affix cabinetry directly to such walls. We can nail or drive screws to accomplish this. Nailing may be faster and easier here because nails allow one-step fastening. No drilling is generally required. After the cabinet is properly positioned, the installer simply drives as many cut nails or concrete nails as are needed, directly through the back and nailer and into the masonry. With softer block, such as burnt adobe, the nails are fairly easy to drive right into the middle of blocks; with denser material, such as brick, it is better to aim for seams and mortar joints.

With a lot of cabinetry, especially units that rest on the floor, driving cut or concrete nails is a perfectly adequate fastening system. The main reason for using other fasteners is probably to achieve greater strength.

Some fastener companies do manufacture special screws that are designed to be driven directly into masonry (Rawlplug markets one called a Tapcon). With these, the installer drills a clearance hole in the cabinet nailer and then drills a slightly smaller pilot or tapping hole in the masonry wall. The screw may be tightened with a screwdriver or socket. (See Figure 12-6.)

FIGURE 12-6 Screws for mounting directly into masonry. (Courtesy of The Rawlplug Company, Inc.)

**RAWL
LAG-SHIELD**

FIGURE 12-7 Lead, zinc, and plastic screw anchors. (Courtesy of The Rawlplug Company, Inc.)

Another system for fastening into masonry is to install a zinc, lead, or plastic screw anchor into the wall and then to screw into the anchor. The anchors are often called plugs or shields. (See Figure 12-7.) To use them effectively, the installer drills through the nailer, positions the cabinet as it is to be mounted, and marks the location for plugs with a punch. With the cabinet moved out of the way, we use a masonry bit to drill holes at each marked position (deep enough to accept the chosen plug), tap the plugs in, reposition the cabinet, and drive screws into the plugs. This is a friction system. As the screw is driven, the surrounding plug expands to "grab" the masonry material. Tapered screws, such as wood screws, and lag bolts are probably most effective in this type of mounting.

For tremendous strength, especially in dense masonry such as concrete floors, anchor bolts may be used. The fastener looks like a conventional bolt, except that it has a taper or "knob" on one end instead of a driving head. There is a washer and nut on the other end. Between the tapered knob and the washer is a metal sleeve. (See Figure 12-8.) This type of fastener is usually not called for, but it is used occasionally. The springs of fold-down-bed mechanisms may be secured reliably with anchor bolts. The tapered end of the bolt fits into a predrilled hole in the concrete, with the washer flush against the surface of the wood to be fastened in place. As the nut is tightened, the sleeve is forced against the tapered knob and compacted against the sides of the hole.

In certain regions we may encounter walls made of asphalt-stabilized adobe or other sun-dried adobe. These are actually among the easiest walls to mount to, because we can simply drive drywall screws into the material virtually anywhere. Holding strength is surprisingly good, especially in the asphalt material. With ordinary adobe,

FIGURE 12-8 Anchor bolt. When tightened, the sleeve and tapered end are forced together. Great fastening strength is achievable. (Courtesy of The Rawlplug Company, Inc.)

longer screws are sometimes needed, or the installer can use the expansion-style fasteners.

Island cabinetry must usually be attached to a ceiling, soffit, or floor. Most ceilings and soffits are simply horizontal stud walls, and we can attach to them with screws or nails. Incidentally, the mounting of an island upper is one of those situations in which it is awkward to nail. Arm swing on hammer strokes is limited by the distance between the top of the cabinet and fixed shelves. We attach to floors by first mounting cleats (wood strips) firmly to the floor, and then driving screws or nails through the toekick, finished end, or finished back and into the cleats. A cleat may be attached to the floor in one of the ways that we have just looked at for attachment to walls. When mounting into concrete, many installers prefer to use plywood as cleats because they do not split, allowing them to drive cut or cement nails very easily. Many others prefer to drill into concrete for placement of plastic screw anchors. Floors with ceramic, concrete, or clay tile in place must be drilled for anchors or there is substantial danger of cracking the tiles. (Most such flooring is actually laid after cabinetry is installed, however.) For brick floors, the installer often drives cut nails through the cleat and into the seams between bricks. It should be obvious that the installer has some choice of fasteners, but only within limits defined by the materials that were used in constructing the building.

CABINET PLACEMENT AND ALIGNMENT

Cabinet placement and alignment is easiest to do if the installer has a floor plan that shows where each numbered case goes, but we do not always have this luxury. The proficient installer must recognize characteristics of individual units which can indicate placement. This is a good deal like the recognition skills of the measurer. The installer knows, for example, that a cabinet section with no shelf and no drawers is probably the sink section, and it will usually be set on the wall directly over water supply and drain pipes. (See Figure 12-9.) Like the measurer, the installer must recognize wall, ceiling, and floor features which indicate the placement of appliances (discussed in Chapter 1). He or she should also be aware of the appliance dimensions on a particular job. We need to allow minimum spacings for free-standing appliances such as refrigerators and many ranges.

Upper cabinets will naturally have continuous tops, but their bottoms are often not continuous. Many uppers have short sections over a range, refrigerator, or sink. This knowledge helps the installer to determine location of appliances.

The presence of wall ends, return design for corners, and finished ends and backs are also significant. We need a finished end next to a refrigerator but not next to a free-

FIGURE 12-9 Water supply and drain pipes indicate placement of a sink section.

standing range or a dishwasher. Measurement can also be helpful. If cabinetry extends wall to wall, we know that its length will be only slightly less (½ in. for clearance) than the wall-to-wall measurement.

It should be easy to see that general cabinet positioning is simply a matter of common sense as well as a bit of familiarity with cabinet design and configuration. For the more exact positioning we need, the cabinet installer must first do some cutting.

Cutting for Fixtures

Before the installer can do any fitting, leveling, scribing, or mounting, holes may have to be cut in some cabinet components to allow various hookups. The back of a sink section is almost always cut for the pipes. If these pipes are fairly close together, many installers simply cut one triangular hole for all of them (Figure 12-10), but others cut a single circular hole for each pipe. The circular holes are easiest to cut with hole saws of a correct size, mounted on a mandrel. (See Figure 12-11.) Regardless of the sort of holes to be used, their location must usually be measured up from the floor and from some right- or left-hand reference. This can be tricky because it is often necessary to adjust the cabinet up, down, or sideways when it is leveled and mounted to the wall. To deal with this potential problem, we can follow one of two procedures. The fastest solution is simply to cut the holes oversized, allowing the adjustments of cabinet position without the pipes ever contacting the back. The other solution is to determine the exact location of the cabinet before cutting the holes. To do this, we have to determine a right- or left-hand reference

point based on adjacent cabinetry or appliances. (See Figure 12-12.) We also have to evaluate the floor's levelness to come up with an estimate of how high the cabinet must be raised in the vicinity of the pipes to achieve a level cabinet.

If the kitchen is to have a hood vented through the roof, it is necessary to cut a hole in the top of an upper cabinet for this vent. The necessity for this is indicated by a circular or rectangular duct projecting from the soffit. The hole should be slightly larger than this duct. It is fairly simple to position and cut the hole accurately, provided that the back of the cabinet is to be mounted against a fairly flat wall, and we can determine a right- or left-hand measuring point. Unless the cabinetmaker is installing the hood, he or she does not usually cut the venting hole in the bottom of an upper cabinet for it, especially in sites of new construction. This and other appliances are not usually present to be measured by the cabinet installer. If the hood is present, it is usually obvious how to position it properly, making measuring for and cutting the hole quite easy.

Some kitchens will not have a hood. This usually means that the range has its own built-in venting fan and ducting. If this is the case, the standard cabinet design may have been substantially altered to accommodate the ductwork. In any case, ducts for this sort of cooktop will gen-

FIGURE 12-10 Triangular hole for all the sink pipes.

FIGURE 12-11 Mandrel and hole saw for drilling circular pipe holes. (Photograph courtesy of Stanley Tools, Division of The Stanley Works, New Britain, CT 06050.)

FIGURE 12-12 Marking for holes on the rear of a sink section. Here the line on the wall indicates finished end location, based on the amount of room necessary for an appliance. The installer can measure from this line to determine pipe location, transfer measurements to the back of the cabinet, and cut.

erally require rectangular holes to be cut in the cabinetry. Usually, only one hole is required, in the cabinet back or bottom, but we may also have to cut fixed shelves to make room for the duct.

Electrical lines or other wires will often need to be fed into installed cabinetry by the installer. Different cities or regions may have different standards or codes which regulate these procedures, and the cabinetmaker needs to be aware of these codes in his or her own area. Generally speaking, however, the installer has to deal with two sorts of wiring feeds. One type is a ''pigtail'' or bare cable which projects from the wall or soffit. Used for bringing power to an electric range, hood, or oven, these cables are left bare because they are tied directly into a junction box in the appliance. For these, all that is usually necessary is a hole through which to bring the cable. Obviously, it is important to make sure that the line is not live. The hole we drill should not be in a highly visible location. We can usually bring it into the cabinet so that the appliance itself will hide it. In fact, if we do not like the exact place from which it protrudes from the wall, we can often move it by enlarging the hole in the wall board or by making a new hole. Of course, we have to make sure that damage to the drywall will be covered by cabinet backs. Speaker and antenna wires are usually brought into a built-in stereo unit in this way.

The other type of wiring that must often be brought into a cabinet is through a conventional plug or switch.

Again, it is important to check local codes. If access to a switch or plug is required in the back of a cabinet, it is usually only necessary to cut through a thin back. In secondary locations, it is usually all right simply to cut a rectangular hole in the back for the entire plate of the electric fixture. This allows access, but we do not even have to touch the fixture. The power supply for a garbage disposal is often cut into a sink section in this way.

On primary surfaces, we usually have to cut a hole small enough to be hidden by the cover plate. We will actually be bringing the fixture forward the thickness of the cabinet back. Most general hardware stores sell box extensions, in several thicknesses, for this purpose.

To use an electrical box extension, we first turn off the power supply to the particular box on which we are working. Then it is possible to remove the cover plate, remove the screws that hold the switch or outlet in its box, and mount the extension. The fixture may then be screwed back in place, now extended forward the desired amount by the extension. With careful measuring, we can cut the cabinet back to allow projection of the fixture through the cabinet back. After the cabinet is mounted, we simply screw the cover plate back on. This is the procedure to follow when we need to bring electrical and telephone fixtures through the finished back of a wall unit.

The installation of custom cabinetry may call for cutting in fixtures of many types. The space under a base cabinet (beneath its bottom) is even used to cover electrical conduits and cold air returns. (See Figure 12-13.) Position-

FIGURE 12-13 Section of base. Note the cold-air return cut into its bottom.

ing such fixtures and cutting for them properly takes an understanding of how pieces are to be positioned, careful measurement, and common sense. Sharp saws are a help, too. With all the access cuts made in a set of cabinets, the installer begins to position pieces for leveling and mounting.

Key Alignments

As an installer begins to bring cabinets into exact position for mounting, there are several features which are keys to proper installation of the entire job, especially in a kitchen. These must be considered before or at the same time as leveling procedures.

First, there are places in a kitchen where ends of base and upper cabinets must be in perfect vertical alignment. One such place is next to a floor-to-soffit cabinet such as an oven cabinet. If the ends do not align, there will be a gap between the oven cabinet and the stile of one of the connecting cabinets, or the oven cabinet will not be plumb and level. It is quite important that the oven sit level, and we want a tight gap wherever cabinets meet. Certain appliances, particularly eye-level range–oven combination units, cannot be mounted properly without perfect alignment of the base and upper. (See Figure 12-14.) The side of the appliance is perfectly flat and straight on both sides, and it contacts the sides of both base and upper units. It is obvious that the contacting stiles of base units have to be aligned with the stiles of the upper unit(s) above. It is also desirable, although not critical, to align the finished ends of base and upper units next to a refrigerator so that spacing between the cabinetry and appliance is consistent all the way up. Alignment in these situations is not difficult to accomplish using a 4-ft level. Whether the base or upper

unit is mounted first, it should be held in place with only two or three screws. This makes it easy to withdraw the fasteners in case an adjustment is necessary. If the upper is mounted first, we hold the level vertically with its face against the wall and its edge against the end of the upper. After centering the bubble, we simply mark the wall with a pencil to indicate the desired position for the stile of the base cabinet. (See Figure 12-15.) If the base has a finished end here, we can simply position it at the line. If it has a wall end, we will have to measure back the distance of the face frame overhang and mark a positioning line. All we are doing here is extending a plumb line. If the installer prefers to mount base units first, the procedure is reversible, of course. After gaining the desired alignment, we should remind ourselves to align as many fasteners as are finally necessary for all the cabinets.

Symmetry around windows and other wall openings is significant in many cabinet installations. In a kitchen, for example, the sink is usually centered under a window, and upper cabinetry should stop a certain distance from the edge of the window. This distance, called a reveal, should be the same on both sides of a window. If the cabinet layout was performed correctly, the installer only has to be

FIGURE 12-15 Extending a plumb line from the end of an upper.

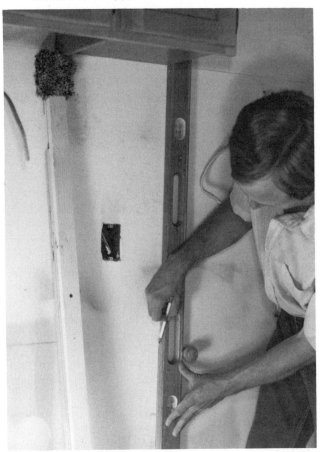

FIGURE 12-14 Spacing for an eye-level range and oven. (Courtesy of Whirlpool Home Appliances.)

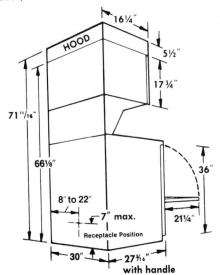

FIGURE 12-16 Cutting the overhang (scribe) of a face frame at a wall end.

concerned with minor adjustments of ½ in. or less. Still, next to a window, differences in reveal up to a ½ in. are noticeable. An installer may have to move an upper horizontally to equalize such reveal spaces. To do so, it is sometimes necessary to cut off the scribe—the face frame and cabinet material that overhangs a wall end. (See Figure 12-16.) If a cabinet has to be moved toward or away from a window, and it is attached to a return, the problem is more difficult to solve. To adjust toward a window, one solution is to build out the return cabinet from its mounting wall with shims. It may also be possible to add filler strips to the stile and bottom of one of the cabinets where they meet. To adjust away from a window a small amount, it is sometimes possible to cut a small amount from the stile and bottom of one of the units. (Refer once again to Figure 3-4.) If cabinet B must be moved to the right to equalize reveals, it may be possible to shorten the length of the cabinet by cutting its stile and bottom. If cabinet A must be moved toward the wall, we can cut its left-hand stile and scribe material.) If such cutting seems called for, we must first make sure that it will not inhibit door operation.

Wall-to-wall cabinetry is usually about ½ in. less than the finished space into which it fits. The installer should make it a goal to split this clearance approximately in half on the right and left ends of the cabinet. This allows us to use same-width molding strips to cover the gap at both ends without interfering with hinge position.

The space for a dishwasher or a trash compactor needs some attention. Most important is making sure of the correct width of the opening (24 in. for most dishwashers). Most kitchen bases are high enough to install a narrow rail across the space above the appliance. In fact, if this is possible, the cabinet designer will usually call for the rail on his or her cutting list. Since it is the exact length required, it can be joined with dowels to the cabinet stiles on either side of the opening and serve as a spacer. Most installers glue and clamp the rail in place to establish spacing. The rail should be backed up with a wood strip. The two stiles should also be checked with a level to make sure that they

are plumb. If the cabinet is square and mounted level, it should be plumb. Nevertheless, if necessary we can trim away a small amount of the scribe material on the stile if it will be a help in positioning the appliance.

Height measurements may be a key, too. In many kitchens, the tops of upper cabinets are positioned against a soffit or furred-down ceiling for mounting. Here the height has been determined for us. In a number of kitchens, however, there are no soffits or furred-down ceilings. In rooms like this, we can usually follow trade standards. Relevant standards are as follows:

1. The distance from a finished floor to the top of a standard (30 in.) upper is 84 in.
2. Finished countertop height in a kitchen is 36 in.
3. The distance from a countertop to the bottom of an upper is from 15 to 18 in., and 18 in. is most common.

A few appliances also require minimum distances in either width or height. Many free-standing ranges, for example, are 30 in. wide. Adjoining base units must be this far apart. Eye-level ranges such as the one shown in Figure 12-14 require a minimum distance between finished flooring and the upper's bottom rail.

On individual cabinet installations, there may be key alignments in addition to those we have looked at. A proficient installer determines exact cabinet positions by remembering the principle of "function first." The cabinets are only one component of a kitchen or any other room, and their primary purpose is to serve the user. Thus we have to consider appliances, clearances, finished floor and countertop height, and reveals in addition to the simple goal or matter of cabinet placement. We want to create the easiest possible job for other installers (tilers, appliance installers, etc.), and ultimately, we want to achieve the most functional and beautiful area for the user of our cabinets.

Locating Fasteners

With some walls and some fastening systems, it is possible to drive fasteners as soon as the cabinet is aligned and leveled. If the cabinetmaker is mounting to a masonry wall and elects to drive cut nails or screws which will thread directly into masonry, he or she can simply align the cabinet units properly and drive fasteners. In mounting to a stud wall, however, it is a very good idea to determine stud location before the cabinet is set against the wall.

There are several ways to determine stud location. Some installers use a magnetic stud-finding tool. (See Figure 12-17.) This tool is just a pivot-mounted magnet surrounded by a plastic case. The magnet is attracted to nails or screws used to secure drywall to studs. This attraction causes the magnet to move on its pivot. The tool is simply

FIGURE 12-17 The magnet of a stud finder is attracted to nails or screws used to hold drywall onto studs. (Photograph courtesy of Stanley Tools, Division of The Stanley Works, New Britain, CT 06050.)

moved around on a wall until magnet movement indicates a stud. Another technique is tapping with a hammer. On stud walls covered with drywall board, tapping produces a hollow sound over most of the wall, but it yields a clearly more solid sound when we tap the wall directly over a stud. (Tapping is not an effective method for finding studs in thick plaster-covered walls, at least for most of us. Sound differences are difficult to detect in these walls.) To avoid damage to wall paint and texture, though, we should only tap in wall sections that are to be covered by cabinetry. Another indication of stud location is the presence of electrical boxes for outlets and switches, which are usually mounted directly to a stud. Whenever the installer thinks that a stud location is found, he or she should tack a nail through the wall to make sure. As soon as the nail is through the wallboard, we can tell whether or not we have hit a stud. It is sometimes necessary to move an inch to the right or left to hit the stud. In fact, when we are having trouble locating a stud, we can use the "machine-gun" approach. This is simply driving a nail, moving horizontally an inch or so to drive the nail again, over and over, until we find a stud. (See Figure 12-18.) It is important to take precau-

FIGURE 12-18 Sometimes it is necessary to use the "machine gun" approach to find a stud. The holes should be in a location that will be hidden by the cabinet.

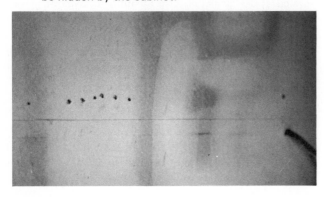

tions to avoid plumbing and electrical lines when looking for studs with a nail or when driving any fastener. Knowledge of local building practices is very valuable. Codes in a particular area may specify that stud centers are to be a certain distance apart (16-, 18-, and 24-in. separations are common), and framing carpenters have been following such standards for a long time anyway. When sure of the stud location, the installer should put small pencil marks on the wall to indicate where they are or measure and note their location from some reference point. This way, when cabinetry has been positioned exactly where it belongs on a stud wall, we can drive screws or nails without delay.

To use some fastening systems, particularly those involving screw anchors of any type, the installer actually has to align and level the cabinetry twice. The first positioning allows us to drill the clearance holes in nailers and mark the walls for drilling. Then the cabinetry is moved out of the way and holes are drilled in the wall for the female portion of the fastening system. After installing anchors, the installer has to realign and relevel cabinets to be exactly the same as they were in the first positioning. As an aid in repositioning the cabinets, it is a common practice to mark the floor, the wall, and the shims after the first leveling and alignment. This can be a help in getting units back in the same place. After all this, we can drive the fasteners, securing the woodwork in place. There is no wonder that so many cabinetmakers prefer cut nails, especially for securing base cabinetry, which rests directly on the floor.

CABINET LEVELING

Cabinet leveling is relatively simple, but we usually have to level cabinet units at the same time that we are aligning them to meet and to fit around appliances. The difficult part of high-quality installation is that we often have to synthesize several factors to achieve proper cabinet mounting location. In other words, we do not place cabinets and *then* level them; we have to consider these matters at the same time and determine how they affect each other.

When installation of a job is complete, all horizontal surfaces should be level, no matter how they are checked. The shelves and top of an upper cabinet are parallel with its bottom. Therefore, upper cabinets are checked for levelness by putting the level on its bottom or bottom rail. The shelves and bottom of a base cabinet are supposed to be parallel with its top edges, and we check base units by setting the level along its top rail, rear nailer, and ends. In theory, when we are done, a level set upon any horizontal cabinet surface will give a perfectly level reading. In practice, it is sometimes wise to sacrifice the perfectly level cabinet in favor of doors and drawers that operate properly on an untwisted frame. Slight irregularities in the cabinet, combined with more significant irregularities in a building, can twist a cabinet out of square. The installer should never try to twist a cabinet level by partly mounting it and then raising or lowering another portion.

Beginning Points

To begin an installation, the craftsman must remember several key principles for leveling. For one thing, individual cabinets are not leveled by themselves. The heights of many separate pieces in a roomful of cabinetry are interrelated. Bases and uppers that are physically connected, as in a return, must all be level with each other. Base sections on either side of a range or other appliance must also be level across the space. Upper sections must at least appear level across a window opening. In fact, they must be level when connected with a valance. In general, a single wall, an L-shape, or a U-shape of base or upper cabinetry is leveled as if it were a single piece. Therefore, we can help ourselves in two ways. First, we can determine the highest part of the floor and the lowest point of the soffit in a room before we attempt to do any leveling. We will want to keep cabinetry in contact with these points, and raise or lower elsewhere with shims, as needed. Second, if it is feasible to do so, we can join cabinet units together before moving into position. Particularly, short return sections are usually fastened to other pieces of cabinetry by drilling clearance and countersink holes and screwing face frames together. (See Figure 12-19.) In effect, this allows us to deal with more than one unit at the same time.

The decision to install cabinetry with or without molding may not be up to the installer, but the installer must achieve the desired results. Of course, cabinets built for trimless mounting will look slightly different from standard cabinetry. There is projecting scribe material wherever a primary surface contacts the building. Finished ends

will extend behind the back, for example. This really makes no difference, however, in techniques for aligning and leveling with shims. The main difference is in the procedures necessary after cabinetry has been put into position. On jobs that are to receive molding, we simply drive the necessary fasteners (unless we have to drill for anchors, of course). When scribing is necessary, we mark the positioned cabinetry with a scribing tool for cutting, demount the cabinet, trim it as required, and reposition it (this time without shims), before driving any fasteners. In either case, initial leveling procedures are the same.

Finally, an individual installer usually develops a preference for mounting bases or uppers first. Those who install base units first usually do so because they can use them as aids in holding uppers in position. They use short props, between base and upper sections, to align and level the upper cabinetry before mounting. The advantage of mounting upper cabinetry first is that the installer does not have to reach or lean over the bases to make adjustments or drive fasteners. Those who proceed this way use longer props which support the uppers from the floor. Tall cabinet units, such as pantries and ovens, must sometimes be positioned and mounted before adjacent pieces.

Leveling Upper or Wall Units

An installer should prepare props before lifting an upper cabinet into place. Props should be just long enough to raise the cabinet bottom to its location. They may be a bit (⅛ in.) longer, but excessive length will make them less stable. If a soffit is present, the props should be long enough to force the top of the cabinet against it. Most cabinetmakers make their own props by screwing together two overlapping strips of wood. These can be easily adjusted to any necessary length. (See Figure 12-20.) To avoid marring, the end of the prop that contacts the cabinet should be padded. It should also be positioned to contact the bottom of

FIGURE 12-19 Cabinet pieces joined with screws for a return. This makes it easy to treat several units as one.

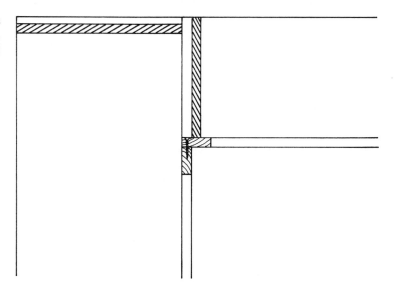

FIGURE 12-20 Props for mounting uppers may be two strips of wood held to a particular length with screws. Note the tapered MDF shims used for leveling adjustments.

the cabinet directly behind the face frame rather than the bottom of the face frame itself.

Tapered shims are also a necessity. The best shims are ones that the cabinetmaker makes specifically for cabinet installation. They should be dense and hard to compress, but they should be fairly easy to break or cut off once installed. The best material for shims is therefore probably medium-density fiberboard (⅝ or ¾ in.). Shims should be about 10 in. long; they should be tapered from approximately ⅝-in. thickness on one end to a virtual point on the other end.

If upper cabinets are to contact a furred-down soffit or ceiling, the installer simply lifts them into their approximate position, adjusts them laterally to equalize reveals or to align properly with other units, and then props them in place. This will usually require a helper. By holding a level against the bottom or bottom rail of the upper, we can tell whether or not a portion of the cabinet needs to be dropped away from the ceiling. If so, we support the cabinet by hand, loosen the prop, and drop the cabinet until the bubble of the level is where it should be. Then a shim may be placed as a spacer between the top of the cabinet and the ceiling.

When there is an open space above the upper cabinets, the leveling procedure is slightly different. Most installers draw a level line across the wall where the cabinet bottom will contact it. No shims are needed. We simply use the props to adjust the cabinet up or down so that the cabinet aligns properly with our level line. In a standard kitchen, the bottom of an upper cabinet will be located between 51 and 55 in. from the finished floor, depending on particular cabinet details and design. At this point, the installer usually drives fasteners. If scribing is necessary, however, there is still a good deal to be done.

Scribing

The first matter is to mark as perfect a scribe line as possible along the top of the cabinet on the face frame and finished ends. A compass or a set of wing dividers should be used as a marking tool. (See Figure 12-21.) The tool is used as follows:

1. Set the wing points so that they are exactly as far apart as the gap between the cabinet and the soffit *at its widest point*.

2. Draw the marking point along the surface of the cabinet while the other point guides firmly along the ceiling contour.

3. Keep the points even, without allowing one point to get ahead of the other.

4. Keep the tool as parallel as possible to the floor while marking.

After the scribe line is drawn, the cabinet should be taken off its props and cut. No attempt should be made to mark the finished ends or the bottom for scribe cuts until a nearly perfect fit is achieved along the top of the cabinet. What we desire here is a trimming cut that follows the contour of the ceiling. If the scribe line is fairly straight, it is possible to use a crosscut saw, but most installers use a saber saw with a fine or reverse-tooth blade. The cut should be on the waste side of the scribe line. Trimming exactly to the line may be accomplished with a plane, or rasp, or a belt sander. With the scribing cut accomplished, the installer puts the cabinet back in position against the ceiling. The props may have to be lengthened, but the cabinet should now be level and should contact the ceiling with no significant gaps. The installer may want to do some additional trimming for a more perfect fit. Once the upper has been scribed to fit the ceiling, we can scribe its bottom and finished ends to the wall, following the same marking and cutting procedures. It should be noted that when the scribe cuts are made on the rear edges of the cabinet, it will be moving closer to the wall a small amount. This may have

FIGURE 12-21 Set of wing dividers. (Photograph courtesy of Stanley Tools, Division of The Stanley Works, New Britain, CT 06050.)

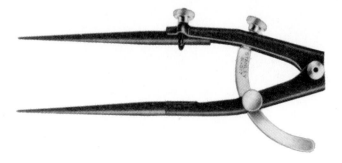

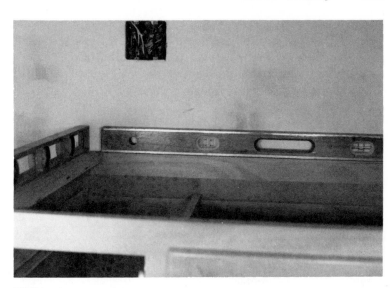

FIGURE 12-22 Leveling a single base unit. Note the use of two levels.

an effect on the first scribe job, along the top of the cabinet, and we may need to go back and give it some additional attention.

The procedures we have looked at here may be used in almost any scribing situation. There is little doubt that scribing of cabinet units can take a good deal of time, far more than the time it takes to apply molding, even when the molding itself requires scribing. The fact is that most modern customers are unwilling to pay the additional costs of a scribed installation. For this reason, most modern cabinetmakers usually plan for molding rather than scribing as a way of eliminating gaps.

Leveling Base Cabinetry

The cabinet installer begins the alignment and leveling of related base cabinetry at the floor's highest point. Occasionally, this high spot will be beneath an island base unit. If this is so, the proficient installer will locate and affix floor cleats for mounting the island first. This means that all the bases are aligned fairly carefully in order to find the exact floor positioning of the island. With the island resting

FIGURE 12-23 The rear of a base cabinet may be raised with shims behind the nailer, as long as the front of the toekick is not allowed to move outward.

in position, we draw lines on the floor where it is contacted by cabinet components. The island cabinet may then be moved aside, and we can attach cleats to the floor. It is important to fasten down the cleats in an arrangement that does not interfere with sleepers. The island may then be returned to its position. If an island is at the lowest part of the floor, we would follow this same procedure, but it would not be necessary to do so until other base units had been aligned, leveled, and mounted.

In leveling the base units, many installers use more than one level. It is quite common to employ a 2-ft level for checking sections front to back, while using a longer level along the back or front of the cabinetry. (See Figure 12-22.) In general, we keep the highest point of the base cabinetry exactly where it is and raise low spots to this level with shims. It is even all right to drive one fastener near the high point as an aid in holding this key position steady. We can raise cabinetry at the front or end by putting shims under the toekick, finished end, or sleeper. We do not have access to some sleepers, however. The rear of some cabinetry sections can be raised by putting shims between the nailer and the wall. (See Figure 12-23.) After all

the top surfaces of the base cabinetry have been brought level, we can drive fasteners (or drill for anchors or scribe to the floor if necessary). If there is a gap between the back of the cabinet and the wall in a location where a fastener is needed, we insert a shim here, too, to prevent twisting the cabinet or separation of cabinet members. It is also a good idea to insert shims snugly into gaps between the toekick and the floor, close to any sleepers. This assures good support.

If the base cabinets must be scribed, it is once again a time-consuming operation. The floor should be scribed first. With a decent floor fit, we can scribe finished ends. Sometimes the floor will be covered with tile of sufficient thickness to cover gaps between the floor and the cabinetry. This makes scribing to the floor unnecessary.

Leveling Other Cabinetry

Most installed cabinetry is leveled, scribed, and set in place in ways similar to conventional base and upper pieces, but references may be slightly different. With oven units, our primary concern should be to achieve a level surface on which to set the oven. With any upright unit, we are also interested in achieving a plumb finished end where the piece must be attached to adjacent cabinetry. Furthermore, it is sometimes necessary to raise an entire pantry or oven in order to align adjacent toekicks. To scribe such units, they must be forced against the ceiling and scribed like an upper unit.

A drawer cabinet, like the type mounted over a knee space, is leveled in the same way as base cabinetry, except that we cannot adjust its height with shims placed below, of course. The height of the finished top on such a unit, measured from the floor, is generally 27 to 28 in., a standard.

Furniture articles are generally delivered and set in place without much regard for leveling their tops. When we level a desk, a table, or a similar piece, we are most interested in keeping it from wobbling. While assembling a piece of furniture, we may want to mount levelers in its legs. These are simply T-nuts fitted into a predrilled hole on the bottom of each leg. The T-nut may be held in place by friction or with fasteners, and it will receive a nylon-headed bolt which may be used for raising or lowering a particular leg.

TRIMMING WITH MOLDINGS

Trimming with moldings has at least two purposes. As we have already noted, one purpose is to cover gaps between cabinetry and the floor, wall, or ceiling of a building. Molding can also have an appearance value of its own, however, or we would not see the variety of edge forms

that is currently available from suppliers who sell machined molding. (See Figure 12-24.) Furthermore, it is not uncommon to apply molding even when it is unnecessary to conceal a gap. For example, no molding is necessary along the top of an upper that does not fit against a ceiling, but we may judge such a piece to look better with molding applied here anyway.

Molding Edge Forms and Sizes

The most common type of molding for trimming cabinetry is flat molding or flat molding with one rounded-over edge. Its thickness is ¼ in., and its width is usually ¾ in., although wider moldings are often employed for covering wider gaps or scribing. Many jobs are trimmed out with this type of molding alone. Some cabinetmakers prefer to use molding of different dimensions and with different edge forms, particularly for top-edge trimming (along the tops of upper and floor-to-ceiling cabinets). What seems very sensible is for the installer to apply top-edge molding with a thickness and lower edge form identical or similar to door thickness (projection beyond the face frame) and outer-edge detail. Solid overlay doors with a cove detail around the outside edge suggest coved top moldings that are ¾ in. thick. The other moldings on a job may be flat.

Many cabinetmakers cut and mill their own moldings from scrap pieces left after cutting face frames and other solid pieces on a job. This utilizes the narrow scraps well, and we also achieve moldings that will match face frames. Craftsmen who generally work with surfaced four-quarter stock get most of their flat molding on the table saw by making rips just over ¼ in. wide. Board thickness (approximately ¾ in.) establishes the width of the molding. We gain wider molding stock by first ripping a solid board to the desired width and then edge ripping to ¼ in. Some shops may rip thicker stocks and then feed them through a thickness planer to arrive at final thickness. Round-overs and other edge forms are accomplished on the shaper or table router, of course, but the detailer should employ a feather board or similar device to hold materials down and against the fence. The visible face and edge of the molding strip should be sanded. Most shops sand molding once with a belt sander to remove mill marks, and again with a finishing sander and finer paper. Incidentally, moldings purchased from suppliers will often require some finish sanding.

Cutting and Affixing Molding

To achieve the most accurate fit, molding strips should be cut and mounted one piece at a time. If top-edge molding is different from other molding on the job, the installer should mount all top-edge pieces first. Top-edge molding strips should be butted into any walls which they contact.

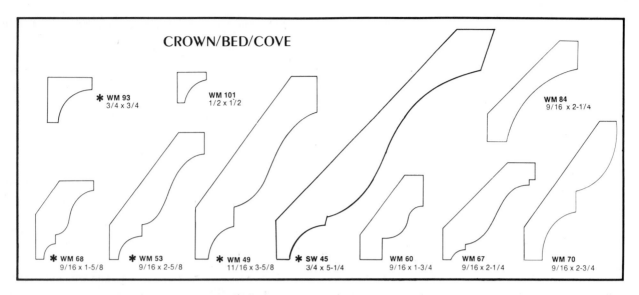

CROWN/BED/COVE

✱ WM 93
3/4 x 3/4

WM 101
1/2 x 1/2

WM 84
9/16 x 2-1/4

✱ WM 68
9/16 x 1-5/8

✱ WM 53
9/16 x 2-5/8

✱ WM 49
11/16 x 3-5/8

✱ SW 45
3/4 x 5-1/4

WM 60
9/16 x 1-3/4

WM 67
9/16 x 2-1/4

WM 70
9/16 x 2-3/4

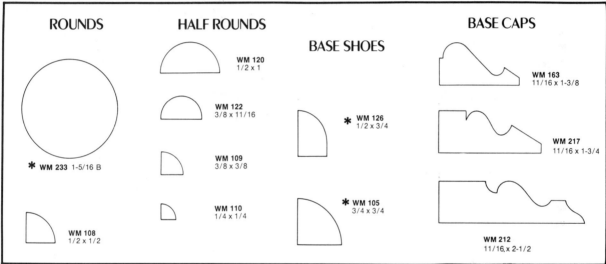

ROUNDS

HALF ROUNDS

BASE SHOES

BASE CAPS

WM 120
1/2 x 1

WM 122
3/8 x 11/16

WM 109
3/8 x 3/8

WM 110
1/4 x 1/4

✱ WM 233 1-5/16 B

WM 108
1/2 x 1/2

✱ WM 126
1/2 x 3/4

✱ WM 105
3/4 x 3/4

WM 163
11/16 x 1-3/8

WM 217
11/16 x 1-3/4

WM 212
11/16, x 2-1/2

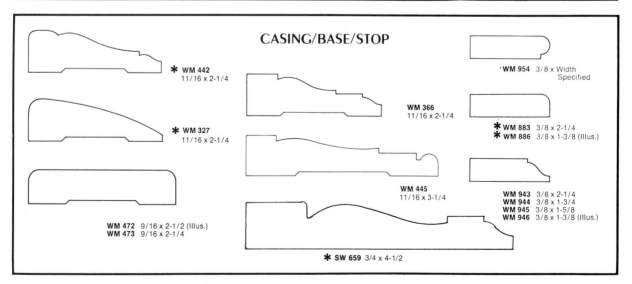

CASING/BASE/STOP

✱ WM 442
11/16 x 2-1/4

✱ WM 327
11/16 x 2-1/4

WM 472 9/16 x 2-1/2 (Illus.)
WM 473 9/16 x 2-1/4

WM 366
11/16 x 2-1/4

WM 445
11/16 x 3-1/4

✱ SW 659 3/4 x 4-1/2

·WM 954 3/8 x Width
Specified

✱ WM 883 3/8 x 2-1/4
✱ WM 886 3/8 x 1-3/8 (Illus.)

WM 943 3/8 x 2-1/4
WM 944 3/8 x 1-3/4
WM 945 3/8 x 1-5/8
WM 946 3/8 x 1-3/8 (Illus.)

FIGURE 12-24   Molding edge forms. (Courtesy of Southwest Hardwoods.)

Vertically mounted molding strips butt into these top-edge strips from below. Wherever molding pieces of the same size come together, they should be joined in a miter cut.

The trickiest part of trimming out a cabinet job is probably that of making accurate miter cuts. When pieces are too long or too short, the imperfection is obvious. However, there is no secret to learning good technique. All that we really need to do is be willing to take the time to get used to our tools. Naturally, until this skill is acquired, a novice trimmer will generally cut pieces a bit long, for fear of cutting them too short. But when trimming, long pieces are just as bad as short ones. If a piece is too long, it will buckle when mounted. Trimming a tiny amount off of a mitered end can be difficult, although such trimming can be reliably achieved with a high-quality miter box (electric or otherwise). On pieces that need mitering only at one end, it is a good habit to make the miter cut first, measure, and then make the straight cut. If these pieces are too long, they can be trimmed much more easily on the straight end than on the mitered end. Also, the trimmer soon learns to recognize that some joints do not need mitering at all—such as where horizontal and vertical strips meet behind a baseboard.

Probably, nothing is more important in good-quality trimming procedures than accurate measuring and marking. It is far better to mark a piece directly while holding it in position than it is to use a tape measure. We do this by making the necessary cut on one end, putting the piece exactly where it goes, and marking the other end as carefully as possible. (See Figure 12-25.)

Molding is usually attached only with brads (finishing nails for thick molding), spaced 5 to 10 in. apart, depending on location. Of course, pneumatic brad driving is a great help.

Scribing Moldings

On fairly straight walls, it is not usually necessary to scribe flat molding, because it flexes enough to adapt to most wall contours. When scribing is necessary, the procedure is virtually identical to that for scribing a cabinet surface. We cut the strip to length first, then tack it in its future location. It should contact the wall, ceiling, or floor at some point, but it should be held parallel to the cabinet edge that it will be covering. Let us say that we are scribing a piece of molding to an irregular wall where it contacts a finished end. The strip is tacked in place, marked with a scribing tool, demounted, and cut with a saber saw or coping saw. If possible, the installer will want to bevel the cut slightly so that only the thinnest possible molding edge will contact the wall. If unhappy with the cut, the woodworker can easily trim away small amounts of material with a sharp knife, a rasp, or even a belt sander.

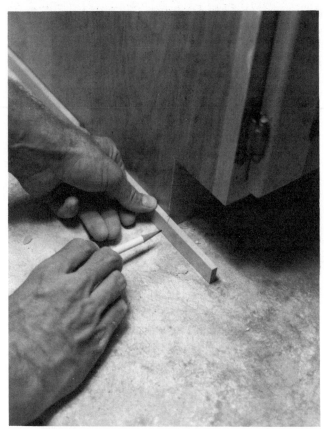

FIGURE 12-25 Marking for a miter. The molding is in its exact location. Note the line indicating the direction of the miter cut.

As a final molding consideration, the trimmer may look for opportunities to avoid trimming. If fairly thick tile or carpet is to be placed after the cabinets are installed, there is no need to trim next to the floor. Many installers apply no molding to the underside of an upper cabinet unless there is a substantial gap between it and the wall. Trimming is optional in situations such as these.

FITTING AND MOUNTING COUNTERTOPS

Fitting and mounting countertops will involve scribing. If only one edge must be scribed, this is fairly simple, as we have seen. The scribing of two edges on a top (most often at right angles to one another) is a bit more difficult. A situation that can be quite difficult, and one that presents itself fairly often, is when we must scribe the two ends and the rear edge of a wall-to-wall countertop. The focus of countertop installation, then, is on scribing procedures. Making joints and cutting for appliances are fairly simple operations. In our discussion we will emphasize plastic-laminate tops, but the same procedure can generally be used for plywood tops as well. The only important difference is that wood tops may have to be scribed more perfectly than plastic-laminate tops. This is because caulking is almost always applied around plastic laminate to achieve a watertight seal at contacted walls. Caulking may be applied at the edges of wood tops, too, of course, but it is usually laid on much less liberally since watertightness is not often a goal.

Scribing a Single Edge

Achieving a good seam between a single top edge and a wall is simple whether or not the top has a backsplash. When we remove material, the top will move back in relation to the cabinet below. But this is one-dimensional movement—straight back. Therefore, we can mark the plastic on the top and both self-edges of such a top at once. The key is accurate positioning in relation to the base unit. The installer should regard the following:

1. The front edge of the top (the self-edge) must be parallel to the front of the cabinet (the face frame).
2. The countertop should overhang both finished ends by the same amount (about 1 in.; see Figure 12-26).
3. Next to a free-standing range, the countertop should be flush with the face frame instead of overhanging it.
4. Plastic should contact the wall in at least one place.
5. Maximum rearward movement is no more than the space between the cabinet's facing and the self-edge backing strip (we should not remove more than this amount of material).

With the top sitting properly, the installer marks its rear for cutting. Here again, the two points of the marking tool must be kept even so that they are in a line perpendicular with the wall. (See Figure 12-27.) The tips must also be kept the same distance apart while they are drawn across the wall and the plastic. Remember that we are, in fact, projecting an image of the wall's surface on the top, and this projection must be a consistent depth from the wall.

With the scribe line drawn, we set up the top conveniently for cutting and trimming. Sawhorses are useful here. The scribe protection strip is now removed, and the plastic (or wood) may be cut. Tool applications differ quite widely here. Some cabinetmakers feel confident enough with a saber saw to use it for cutting almost to the line. This is a good choice for scribing to highly irregular surfaces such as adobe walls, but a reverse tooth should be used. Some installers feel that they have better control with

FIGURE 12-26 Positioning a small top for scribe marking its rear edge. Note the equalized overhang.

FIGURE 12-27 Marking a line for a single-edge scribe. The points must be kept in a line perpendicular to the wall.

a crosscut saw, or a coping saw for "bumpy" walls. Still others don their safety glasses and do their trimming with a router. With a trimming or straight bit, it is possible to freehand and follow the scribe line quite effectively. Some routers are specially designed for scribing. The base, coming almost to a point, will follow the wall as the bit cuts the same contour in the plastic. (See Figure 12-28.) For removal of small amounts of scribe, we can choose among a plane, a file, or a belt sander. A belt sander is tremen-

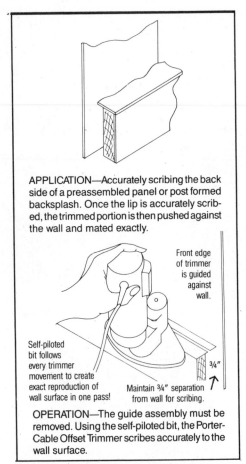

APPLICATION—Accurately scribing the back side of a preassembled panel or post formed backsplash. Once the lip is accurately scribed, the trimmed portion is then pushed against the wall and mated exactly.

Front edge of trimmer is guided against wall.

Self-piloted bit follows every trimmer movement to create exact reproduction of wall surface in one pass!

¾″

Maintain ¾″ separation from wall for scribing.

OPERATION—The guide assembly must be removed. Using the self-piloted bit, the Porter-Cable Offset Trimmer scribes accurately to the wall surface.

FIGURE 12-28 Scribing of a backsplash to the wall with a router. (Courtesy of Porter-Cable Corporation.)

FIGURE 12-29 Scribing with a belt sander.

dously valuable for this type of work. Held vertically, it allows good vision and control, even in following quite irregular surfaces. (See Figure 12-29.)

Scribing Two Edges

Countertops frequently contact walls in the rear and along one end. The countertop for a vanity unit with one wall end is an example. Returns and L-shaped countertops present a similar situation. We cannot scribe the edges one at a time because the removal of material allows movement, as we have seen, and this is two-dimensional movement. To understand the problem fully, let us consider an example.

Suppose that we have a plastic laminate top, finished on the left and with a wall end on the right. The walls are made of block, and we have to contour the plastic in such a way that it will fit into the mortar seams between block. It is 23 × 38 in. If we mark for scribing in the conventional way, the movement allowed by the second scribe job will destroy the alignment of the first scribe. (See Figure 12-30.) We obviously have to mark the scribe differently.

The solution is to hold the scribing tool differently, not with the points perpendicular to the wall. We make a two-dimensional projection of the wall by allowing the marking point of the compass to trail behind the point that is being guided along the wall. In our example, the marking point trails behind the guiding point by the same amount that we need to shift our top to the right after scribing the rear edge. This is about the depth of the recess where the mortar seam is at the wall end. This marking procedure requires a good deal of skill in keeping the projection depth even. If the top has a backsplash, it is probably wise to omit the plastic from its top edge. That way, the strip can be scribed to the wall independently and then cemented in place and trimmed even with the splash's finished face. Another approach is possible when we have mitered countertops that have to be joined at the job site. These can frequently be scribed one edge at a time and then put together, just as long as the T-shaped slots will still align well enough to allow insertion of tight joint fasteners.

Scribing Three Edges

Getting a good fit on a wall-to-wall top can be challenging. If such a top has a backsplash, plastic should be omitted from the top edge of the splash. This simplifies things a great deal because we can project one scribe at a time, as we have seen. Whenever possible, this is the best ap-

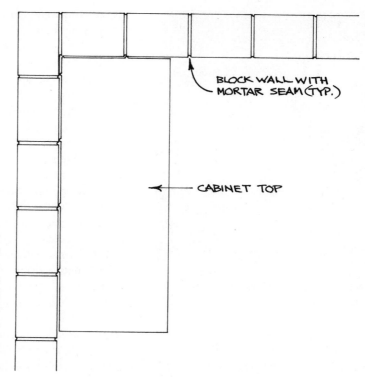

FIGURE 12-30 The result of one-dimensional scribing upon a top that has to move two directions. On this top, the rear edge was scribed first. When material was removed from the right end and the installer attempted to move the top to the right, projections in the rear edge no longer aligned with mortar seams.

proach. But with some tops, especially tops without splashes, this is not possible.

The most reliable way to achieve a matching cut on a splash-less, wall-to-wall top is not to scribe the top at all. Instead, the installer scribes other pieces, which can then be used as patterns. To do this, the installer puts a reference mark on the rear wall and a matching reference mark on the top. Placement of the marks can be fairly arbitrary, but they will have to match perfectly on the installed top. Next, we get two pieces to be used as patterns. They should be as deep as the top and long enough to overlap in the middle. The patterns are marked for scribing along the rear and wall end, as if we were marking a pair of two-edged tops. We must be careful to keep the front-edge overhang even, and can use a trailing marking point. After achieving a desirable fit, we transfer the wall reference point onto each pattern, align this mark with the mark on our countertop, and trace for the scribing cut.

A wall-to-wall top may also be scribed directly if the rear wall is fairly flat and straight, as well as square with the other two walls. Such a top is so long that we cannot get it in position for scribing without tilting one end up; and if we tilt it, it is impossible to get a reliable projection of the back wall. What we do is tilt the top and set it so that one of its ends is in contact with the wall. Before marking a line, however, we make sure that the countertop overhang will be even. We can do this by extending the plumb line of the cabinet's face frame upward with a level. (The rear edge of the top should be in full contact with the rear wall and the overhang should be even or this scribing pro-

cedure will not work.) Assured of full contact in the rear and a fairly even overhang, we mark for the scribe cut on this one end. Next, we repeat the procedure for the other end, but we use a wall-to-wall measurement as a reference to ensure that the two lines are the correct distance apart. Good results are achievable using this system, but it is almost impossible to use when the rear wall has a fairly irregular surface or is out of square with adjoining walls.

Cutting for Appliances

There are a number of appliances for which holes are necessary in the surface of a countertop. Most cutouts are for a sink, a cooktop, or a drop-in range. The top should be fitted into exact position before it is cut out. Most appliances that require a cutout will provide specific instructions for locating and dimensioning the cuts. However, a few general guidelines may be helpful, as follows;

1. Turn the top upside-down for marking and cutting; this allows us to avoid backsplashes that may be in the way of the cutting tools. (See Figure 12-31.)

2. Cooktops and most sinks are mounted with a metal ring, and the ring is used as a pattern for marking the cutout.

3. The cutout for a self-rimming sink may be marked by positioning the sink upside-down, marking around it, and then using a compass to "scribe" a smaller cutout hole.

FIGURE 12-31 Cutouts are usually made with the workpiece upside down. Note the sink used for marking.

4. Sinks are usually centered on a window, and cooktops are usually centered on a hood.

5. The placement of cabinet members may interfere with appliance position and should be considered.

6. The cutout for a drop-in range must usually match perfectly with stiles of the cabinet below.

With marking lines properly made, most cabinetmakers drill through from the rear and cut directly along the lines, using a saber saw and a standard-tooth (rather than reverse-tooth) blade. For making straight cuts such as those used for a drop-in range, some installers prefer to mark and cut from above, using a crosscut handsaw.

Assembling Countertop Joints

In an earlier chapter we looked at the specific procedures required to join sections of countertop. The installer has only to reassemble these joints. In a kitchen, bathroom, or other potentially wet location, the edges to be joined should receive a coating of moisture-resistant adhesive before being bolted together. Epoxy and hardener is a good choice for the adhesive in this application. When replacing and retightening the tight joint fasteners, the installer should take extra care to align decking, self-edging, and splashes to be even and flush.

After scribing the tops, cutting them out for appliances, and joining sections where necessary, the installer has only to fasten the tops down by driving screws from below, through the cabinet hold-downs. Since the total thickness of a hold-down and a countertop is usually 1½ in. we usually fasten the tops down with 1¼-in. drywall or wood screws. On each front-to-back hold-down, a screw should be driven near the front, near the back, and every 10 in. in between.

Some types of upper cabinetry, such as bookcases, actually contact and even rest on a countertop. (For an example, see Figure 3-3.) This changes installation procedures only a little. First, base units are almost always installed first. Second, if the upper cabinetry has a back, as it usually will, this upper will cover a substantial portion of the rear edge of the countertop where it joins the wall, and scribing the top becomes unnecessary. Last, it is usually best to attach the countertop to the bottom of the upper unit (the top may or may not be dadoed to receive the finished ends of the upper section, and it may or may not be rabbeted to receive a portion of the upper section's back), and then mount the entirety in place at once. If this is not possible, we usually do not fasten the top down to the base cabinet until the upper unit has been set. Then we drive shims between the hold-downs of the base cabinet and the underside of the countertop before driving hold-down screws, thus making sure of a tight fit above, where the upper contacts the countertop.

It should be noted that a cabinetmaker is not always asked to furnish a finished top. Ceramic and clay tiles remain popular and most cabinetmakers have nothing to do with tiling and grouting. Instead, we are often asked to provide subtops and mud bands for our own cabinetry.

A subtop is almost invariably ¾-in. plywood made with waterproof glue. Most commonly used grades are A-C and CDX. When the tile layer goes to work, he or she will usually cover the plywood with wire or fabric as well as mastic or other material for holding the tiles in place. There is no need whatsoever for tops to be scribed or very carefully fit. The edge of a subtop should not extend beyond a cabinet's face frame or finished end. Small gaps are acceptable where the sub-top meets a wall. Away from a cutout, seams may be made simply by laying pieces next to each other and fastening them both down. The pieces may be cut to size in the shop or at the job site. Some installers bring full sheets of plywood to the job, cut tops to size with a portable circular saw, provide cutouts, and fasten in place with screws or nails. (Here, we may drive fasteners from the top.) We are simply providing a rough decking for the laying of tile.

A mud band or edge band is a strip of wood applied as a facing to cover the raw edges of a subtop and tile. Quite frankly, it is a poor choice compared to bull-nosed tiles. Wood and grout simply do not adhere to each other very well. Look at the grout line along any mud band that has been in place for at least a month or two, and you will see a crack. If a mud band is called for, it can be measured and cut like molding. The cabinetmaker may also nail it in place with finishing nails, but to do so, we need to know how much depth to allow between the top of the mud band and the deck.

ADJUSTING DOORS AND DRAWERS

Adjusting doors and drawers requires an understanding of drawer guides and hinging systems (as we looked at in Chapter 9). Cabinetry that was properly fitted with doors and drawers and mounted at the job site without being twisted should really need very little adjusting, and the installer only has to mount hardware (if any is called for) and apply felt or rubber bumper pads (unless catches were applied). On the other hand, what should be is not always the reality of the situation, and adjustments are sometimes necessary. Approaching the completion of a cabinet installation, we should look for the following features to be proper:

1. Door and drawer front flatness on or in the frame (no raised corners)
2. Spacings between doors and drawer fronts along stiles, rails, and mullions
3. Spacings between edges of paired doors
4. Evenness of door and drawer lines (particularly, we should focus on the tops of doors and drawers for bases and the bottoms of doors on uppers)
5. Nonbinding drawer, door, and slide-out shelf movement

Improving Flatness

If a door or drawer front does not sit flat as it should, there are three possible causes. Most commonly, the door itself may be warped, or the cabinet facing may be twisted. It is also possible that there could be an error in the depth positioning of one or both hinges. A door with one of these problems is characterized by a raised corner. (See Figure 12-32.)

To improve the flat appearance of a door with a raised corner, we usually do nothing to the door itself. Instead, we alter the way that the door is mounted, in a way transferring the raised corner from the unhinged edge of the door to the hinged edge, where it is less noticeable. The way in which this is done depends partly on the type of hinge used, but in general, we work on the hinge–door relationship which is diagonal to the raised corner that we wish to adjust. If the lower-left corner of a door needs to be brought in toward the frame, we bring the upper right corner farther away from the facing. With some hinges, we withdraw the screws and reposition them to bring the corner of the door away from the face. With other hinges, we can insert a shim between the hinge and the rear surface of the door to make the adjustment. (See Figures 12-33 and 12-34.) Double demountable hinges are a favorite with the installer because they are so easy to adjust. In seconds, we can loosen the single screw that clamps the hinge into the face frame T-slot, adjust the door away from the frame, and retighten.

FIGURE 12-32   Door that needs flatness adjustment. Note the raised corner.

FIGURE 12-33   Inserting a shim between the hinge and the door surface.

FIGURE 12-34   Door from Figure 12-32 after adjustment.

If a door is seriously twisted, one of its corners will stand substantially away from the face frame, and neither shimming nor hinge repositioning will solve the problem. Such doors are often simply thrown in the trash and rebuilt, but there are also methods for twisting a door to conform to an individual cabinet facing. These methods are most effective on doors with no finish applied.

One possibility is to add moisture to a door or front and twist it as needed. The installer can choose to do this on-site, or the door may be brought back to the shop for this procedure. Moisture is added by sponging it on. Since we want fairly deep penetration of water into the wood fibers, we usually sponge the water on, allow some air drying, and then sponge again. With the door still wet, we twist it. On the job site, the twist is sometimes applied by nailing the raised corner down. For additional twist, we can put a shim between the cabinet facing and the adjacent door corner which already contacts the frame. We can twist a door in our shop without nails, by clamping its raised diagonal corners down. (See Figure 12-35.) After the door has fully dried, its contour will have changed, at least somewhat. Naturally, doors so altered will require substantial resanding. This procedure will work with many plank, doors, either plywood or solid.

Frame doors can be twisted to adapt to a cabinet contour also. However, rather than relying on absorption and loss of moisture to change the door permanently, it may be more effective to twist the door enough with clamps to break the seam between a stile and rail. Into the crack we insert a wedge from the front or rear to change the actual angle at which the two pieces meet. The wedge is knife thin and made of the same type of hardwood as the stile and rail. (See Figure 12-36.) It is glued in place, and as much glue as possible is worked into the joint. The door is clamped conventionally, across the stile-rail joint, and allowed to dry. Then it is resanded and rehung, with its changed contour.

Twists in doors can also be corrected with turnbuckles or shelving units that are mounted to the back of a door. Pantry doors can be quite large, and any warp in them is defined over a long diagonal. A twisted pantry door can thus be very noticeable. A rear-of-door shelving unit, if it is fairly deep and rigidly built with a flat back, will easily straighten a door when mounted. Most cabinetmakers avoid the use of turnbuckles except as a last resort. A turnbuckle consists of two eyelets that are screwed into the rear surface of a twisted door (near the raised corners), with rods or wires attached to the eyelets, and tightened.

A drawer front that does not sit flat on a face frame is usually this way because of misaligned guides rather than warpage. Of course, there are exceptions, but we can deal with warped drawer fronts just as we would doors. The misalignment that raises the corner of a drawer front is often the result of twisting a base cabinet during the leveling and

FIGURE 12-35   Twisting a door under clamp pressure.

mounting procedures, and the installer can avoid many problems by focusing on drawer alignment while leveling. Nevertheless, we can frequently improve the appearance of a drawer front's flatness by altering the guide position at the rear of the cabinet.

Drawer adjustment is actually the remounting of drawer guides in the rear of the cabinet. Some guides, such as three-roller guides, will involve removing some screws and repositioning the rear mounting bracket. Guides with wooden segments will often be tapped up, down, or sideways into a new position with a hammer. If this is necessary, the installer should glue new support blocks in place. If the raised (away from the facing) portion of the drawer

FIGURE 12-36   This frame door has been twisted enough to break the stile–rail joint, and now the cabinetmaker is preparing to insert a wedge that will change the angle at which the frame members meet. When reglued, with this wedge in place, this door will have a substantially different contour.

front is at the top, we need to drop the rear of the drawer box. If the side of the drawer front is raised up, we have to move the guides toward the other side of the cabinet. If it is only possible to get three corners of the drawer front to contact, obviously two of them should be top corners.

It should be stressed that the best door adjustments are not gained from door adjustment procedures at all, but rather from good care in all the prior operations that went into fabricating and installing the cabinet. It is far wiser to spend the time needed to make flat doors and square cabinets which need only minor adjustments after installation than it is to consume a good deal of time trying to make twisted doors and cabinetry look presentable. Many cabinetmakers would consider remedies such as adding moisture to a door or inserting shims at a broken joint to be signs of inferior workmanship. It is clear that precise machining and meticulous door and case assembly are of great importance.

Improving Space and Reveals

It is generally much easier to adjust doors for correct spacing than it is to adjust them for flatness. This is surface (up, down, and sideways) adjustment, not depth (in-out) adjustment.

Most doors require no major surface adjustments. The space between two paired doors will be a bit too narrow, or the bottom ends of a pair of upper doors will not quite line up. The required adjustments are often built into hinges. Demountable hinges are again among the easiest to adjust, with their single-screw mounting system. Many hinges have slotted screw holes for surface adjustment. Whenever possible, the installer uses these built-in adjustment features. When very minor sideways adjustments are required, certain types of hinges can be bent slightly to accomplish the repositioning. The installer uses a screwdriver to force pin position to the right or left. (See Figure 12-37.) If a door is badly misaligned, it will call for complete rehanging.

Drawer fronts, if mounted to subfronts, may be adjusted in one of two ways. One way is to remove the screws that hold the front in position on its subfront, reposition, and refasten. The other possibility is to adjust the entire drawer box. With side guides, we raise the box by lowering the position of the metal guide rails on the drawer sides. If there is sufficient clearance, we can make a side-to-side adjustment by putting a shim between the face frame and the metal guide member attached to it. (See Figure 12-38.)

It should be clear that an installer is actually using assembly skills when performing door and drawer adjustment. When reinstalling and adjusting other accessories, such as susans, the installer is again carrying out assembly tasks.

FIGURE 12-37 Bending the pin slightly as a door adjustment. Here, the bottom of the door is moved to the right.

FIGURE 12-38 Drawer position may be altered with a shim.

Mounting Hardware

Most pulls and knobs are attached to cabinetry with machine screws inserted from the rear. This system naturally requires drilling clearance holes for the machine screws. There are other methods of hardware attachment, but all require proper location of the hardware by accurate measuring. The hardware on doors is usually positioned a particular distance in from the edge and end. On frame doors, hardware is usually centered on the width of the door stile. For example, the center of a knob for a frame door on an upper cabinet may be 1 in. from the unhinged door edge and 4 in. up from its bottom end. Exact placement is a matter of convenience and individual preference.

A jig is often used for marking doors for hardware placement. The jig is simply a thin, square piece of wood with a hole in it and lips along one edge and one end. The lips contact door edges, and the hole is in appropriate position for door marking. (See Figure 12-39.) With lips that overhang both its faces, the jig is reversible for use on doors hinged on either the right or the left. It is possible to position holes wherever desired.

It is also possible to make a similar jig for marking drawer fronts, but many cabinetmakers simply measure them with a steel rule. Incidentally, most pulls or handles have threaded posts which are exactly 3 in. apart. On a drawer front that is 4 in. high and 13 in. long, a standard pull would require two drilled holes, each 2 in. down from the top edge and 5 in. in from either end.

Three-sixteenths of an inch is the most common diameter drilled as a clearance hole for hardware machine screws. The rear face of each door and drawer front should be backed up with scrap wood to prevent tear-out when drilling. The machine screws usually need to be ¼ in. longer than the depth of the door or drawer, and the ones provided

FIGURE 12-39 Jig for marking hardware location on doors. The awl starts the clearance hole, which can be completed with a drill.

by the manufacturer are sometimes not the correct length for the particular door or drawer design.

Finally, it is not a good idea to spin a piece of hardware onto a machine screw, not even a knob. Rather, the hardware item should be held steady while a screwdriver is used to tighten the machine screw from the rear side of the door or drawer. This prevents marring the finish on primary surfaces. With all the knobs or pulls in place, the installer should apply felt or rubber door bumpers wherever needed to soften operation noise. For the independent cabinetmaker, this is an excellent time to request final payment.

CHAPTER SUMMARY OF CABINETMAKING SKILLLS

Installation of cabinetry may require the application of a variety of tools and fasteners. The best installers are those who are prepared for any possibility—with the right fasteners and the right tools. Most important to the modern installer is a source of electricity to drive drills, saws, and other power tools which speed up installation procedures.

The proficient installer is aware of the many types of fasteners available for affixing cabinetry to the various types of walls and floors, and knows their advantages and disadvantages. For mounting to studs, the most popular system today is the use of drywall screws, driven by a screw gun or variable-speed drill. Some applications call for mounting screw anchors of various kinds, and this frequently requires positioning cabinetry twice—once for ac-

curate placement of screw anchors and once for affixing the cabinetry.

An installer needs to be able to recognize cabinet and appliance positioning, especially when no floor plan is available. This involves interpreting building features that signal particular cabinetry. For example, an installer knows that protruding pipes call for a sink, and that a base sink section usually has no top drawer and no fixed shelf. While identifying which pieces belong where, the installer is also cutting holes for pipes, ductwork, electrical access, and other features that may be incorporated into the cabinetry.

The cabinetmaker also evaluates walls and chooses appropriate fasteners at the very beginning of an installation job. If possible, we always choose fasteners that can be driven as soon as cabinetry has been positioned, avoiding those that require more than one accurate positioning.

Accurate cabinet positioning is a matter of alignment as well as leveling. There are certain keys that must be observed in order to align cabinets properly. Reveals around windows and doors should be kept consistent and equal, and the ends of some bases and uppers must be plumb in relation to each other. The height of upper cabinetry above the floor should be based on required appliance heights, soffit placement, or architectural standards.

The installer should consider all bases to be a unit that have to be leveled together, if they are connected or related. The same principle is also true for connected upper cabinetry. Upper cabinetry should be leveled with the lowest point of the soffit or ceiling as a reference point. The reference point for cabinetry that rests on the floor is the floor's highest point. If a cabinet must be scribed to the wall, ceiling, or floor, it is usually necessary to align it and level it two or more times. Most cabinetmakers install cabinetry with shims in place, however, and cover gaps with hardwood trim or molding. Irregular wall surfaces may require that molding strips be scribed, and it is frequently necessary to scribe countertops. The installer should therefore have good skill with a compass or set of wing dividers as a marking tool in scribing, as well as an ability with tools for trimming away material on the scribe job.

Cutting holes in a countertop and attaching it is a simple job, but fitting it in place can be tricky when the top must contact two or three walls. The installer learns a "trailing" technique which can be used with effectiveness to mark accurate scribe lines in some situations. In other cases, it may be necessary to make a scribed pattern or template that can be used to transfer a wall's contour into the edge of a top.

A thorough cabinet installer makes it a habit to inspect an installed job for proper door and drawer fit and operation, possessing knowledge of techniques that allow both surface and depth adjustments of doors and drawers.

THIRTEEN

FURNITURE MAKING

DIFFERENCES BETWEEN FURNITURE AND OTHER CABINETRY

Designing and constructing wooden furniture requires the skills possessed by a cabinetmaker. Throughout this book we have made references to differences between building furniture and building other forms of cabinetry. These differences may have seemed very slight—so slight, in fact, that we might be tempted to think of a furniture maker as a cabinetmaker who prefers to build movable items rather than fixed pieces to be installed into a house or other building. Readers with this idea are absolutely correct. For several centuries, cabinetmaking has referred to the finest joinery trades and has always included the building of fine furniture.

The finest furniture is actually the finest cabinetry. The chief difference is that furniture can be moved easily from one location to another because it is free-standing, whereas most modern conventional cabinets are fastened securely to a building. Of course, this difference suggests some more specific differences as well. Because a furniture piece must be free-standing, it must be stronger and more rigid than installed cabinetry. There are no walls or other building structures to add strength. Another difference is that furniture articles do not have wall ends. All exterior portions of a furniture piece are finished, primary surfaces except perhaps the back. These are "prescriptive" differences. That is, cabinetry is furniture only if it has no wall ends and if it is capable of being set up without external support. We may be able to point out some other major differences between furniture and other cabinetry as well (and we will look at these), but they will be "descriptive" differences. We can say, for example, that most drawers in a furniture piece are assembled with dovetails, and most drawers in installed cabinetry are assembled in other ways. But the presence of dovetail joints does not turn an installed piece of furniture into furniture, and the absence of dovetails cannot turn a piece of furniture into anything else. Here are several other descriptive characteristics of furniture:

- Although some furniture pieces have a true face frame, many (perhaps most) do not.
- Wooden drawer guides are still very common, although this may be something of an affectation (many of us are willing to bet that tomorrow's hand-made antique chests will have steel guides).

254

- Solid materials are preferred over plywood for certain secondary pieces such as drawer parts.
- Nails are usually avoided on primary surfaces.
- Most furniture is supported by feet, legs, or protruding toe pieces rather than toekicks and sleepers.
- Veneers are used primarily to extend the effects of a particular grain figure.

Naturally, our list is by no means complete. Furthermore, individual cabinetmakers develop very strong preferences in their own furniture-building procedures. Some will avoid certain modern materials and procedures, for example, for no other reason than that they are modern. Others do not hesitate to use vinyl-coated drawer guides and drywall screws. In general, the cabinetmaker must be his or her own judge in these matters. It is always possible to find someone who thinks we are too old-fashioned and another person who thinks we are too modern. In choosing furniture features, the best justifications are fulfillment of function (as always), beauty (to ourselves or to the receiver of our creation), and tendency to improve strength.

It probably makes a great deal of sense for capable cabinetmakers to design and build furniture items for their own use, for gifts to special people, and for sale. There is no better way to assure the acquisition of a piece that fulfills our own needs than to build it ourselves. Handmade furniture gifts are practical and highly valued, and well-made custom furniture can command a respectable price. Cabinetmakers should not hesitate, then, to initiate furniture projects. As we have seen, the only requirements are to build in one or two more finished surfaces and additional strength. We may employ conventional or other methods.

FRAMELESS DESIGN

Frameless design may be the wrong term to use in conjunction with furniture. As we have observed, furniture should be strong, and frame designs yield strength. Yet many desks and drawer chests are built without a face frame. How are these pieces given the strength and rigidity that comes with frames?

Horizontal Framework

One answer to our question is to build pieces with horizontal framework. We can look at this as shelf placement. We stop-dado each finished end for shelving, and we plan for a shelf below each drawer. What we actually build in, of course, is not a single-piece "shelf" but a frame below each drawer. (See Figure 13-1.) The front piece in the frame is made of the primary wood, and the other three pieces of the frame are made of secondary or tertiary woods. The frame should be joined with a dowel joint or a mortise-and-tenon joint. With notched ends, the frame will fit into the stop dado of finished ends, yielding a flush facing. The fit should be fairly tight, to promote rigidity. We can support the joint with screws driven through the frame from the inside, by toenailing, or with glue blocks. This sort of construction yields strength and has several other virtues as well. The front edge of each frame serves as a rail between drawers. The frame is lighter than a solid "shelf" below drawers, contributing to the mobility of the piece. If the cabinetmaker chooses wooden drawer guides, the frames will serve in this capacity also. A horizontal frame is frequently installed above the top drawer and used as a hold-down to secure the top. Many older and antique drawer units have the horizontal frame design—testimony

FIGURE 13-1 Furniture detail for horizontal framework used below drawers.

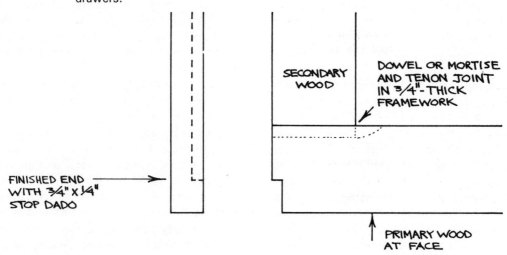

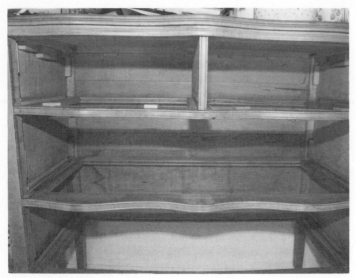

FIGURE 13-2   Drawer unit built with horizontal frame work.

to lasting strength. The furniture builders should realize, however, that employing a horizontal framework does not by itself provide the strength and rigidity of a face frame. (See Figure 13-2.)

Backs and Rear Frames

We have already observed at several points in the text that one thing which establishes strength in a cabinet is the installation of a back. With installed cabinetry, a back may be affixed mainly for the purpose of covering a wall, and it may be as thin as an ⅛ in. Further, backs are not usually received into a rabbet on the rear edge of an installed finished end unless scribing is planned. With furniture, finished ends are almost always rabbeted to receive the back. We obviously do not want molding along the rear edge of a furniture finished end, but mounting the back in a rabbet is only partly for the sake of appearance. A rabbet-fitted back also establishes more rigidity than does an overlaid back. A back fit snugly between ends simply restricts twisting and flexing of the cabinet much more than an overlaid back.

Sometimes, the rear edge of a finished end is actually a leg. (See Figure 13-3.) The leg may be rabbeted or dadoed to receive a back. A dadoed or slotted leg used to be very common because it gave the cabinetmaker a way of concealing thick ends of some back parts. Before plywood and other sheet goods were readily available, most cabinet backs consisted of several pieces. Rather than being edge glued, the backs were fabricated with interlocking details. For example, a back might consist of a series of slats, some of them ¼ in. thick and fairly wide, others ¾ in. thick, narrow, and slotted along the edge to receive the thinner

FIGURE 13-3   This rear leg was slotted or dadoed for placement of the back. Note that the back consists of more than one piece.

slats. The thinner slats are received at their ends by the dado in the leg; their edges are received by the slots cut in the thicker pieces. (Again, see Figure 13-3.)

Backs made of one piece have to be considered stronger than those made of slats or other interlocking or overlapping boards. The most common applications for a multipiece back today are to restore an old piece or to copy an old design.

Another rigidity option is to build a rear frame into a cabinet. This is simply a matter of building a frame like a face frame and attaching it inside the furniture piece's finished ends, top, and bottom. Using a rear frame allows easy mounting of many types of drawer guides. Only a thin back is needed behind the frame to keep out dust. This is an especially good strength option in cabinetry where drawers are to be mounted with no brace or rail in between. Rather than building a frame for the rear, some cabinetmakers simply install an ''X-brace'' or some other type of bracing in the rear of the box. (See Figure 13-4.)

FIGURE 13-4 Rear cabinet bracing, especially important in this piece because drawers are mounted flush with only a tiny space between.

Corner Bracing

The attachment of braces is not generally considered to be an alternative to frameless cabinetry. Rather, it is a method for achieving frame rigidity and strength. We often find corner braces in tables and chairs, used to stiffen the joints between legs and frame or apron members. (See Figure 13-5.) Braces may be metal or wood.

European-style assembly fittings may be classified loosely as corner braces. We have already discussed the use of these fittings, but it should be noted that the use of

FIGURE 13-5 Corner brace. This one is screwed into a dining room table leg, and its flanges fit into slots cut into the table apron.

assembly fittings in furniture production may grow more common. Shops that specialize in European cabinetry can naturally build furniture with the same assembly system. It will be interesting to witness the progression of this trend and to evaluate its effects on the mainstream of modern cabinetmaking.

DRAWERS

Drawers in furniture items are still storage boxes that slide in and out of a cabinet opening. We can, however, note some descriptive differences between furniture drawers and the drawers that are used in installed cabinetry.

The Furniture Drawer Box

Generally speaking, a furniture drawer box has four characteristics that make it different from the drawers in other cabinetry. First, it seldom has a subfront. The sides are joined directly to the drawer front. Second, the back and sides are usually made of solid secondary material rather than plywood. Before sheet goods became common, the bottoms were also made of solid stock. Third, backs are not generally slotted to receive the drawer bottom. Instead, the back is cut narrower than the drawer sides. Its edge sits on the top surface of the drawer bottom. Fourth, the joints are usually interlocking. Specifically, side-to-front joints are commonly dovetail joints, while sides may be joined to backs in a dovetail, a dado, or another joint. (See Figure 13-6.)

The reason for not employing drawer subfronts on

FIGURE 13-6 Furniture drawer box. Note the dovetails, the absence of a subfront, and the solid parts. This is a fairly modern design because the back is slotted to receive a plywood bottom.

FIGURE 13-7 This furniture drawer box has hand-cut dovetails, but it employs a subfront.

furniture probably has more to do with history and aesthetics than it does with function. A subfront does shrink the depth of a drawer, though. It is also superfluous in a way. Its only value is to simplify machining, assembly, and adjustment of the drawer box. Subfronts are employed on some modern custom furniture pieces, however. (See Figure 13-7.)

When a subfront is not used, a dovetail dado (a French dovetail) can be used easily with an overlay drawer front. We can also detail the ends of the front with "pins" to receive dovetailed sides.

The reason for making furniture drawers with solid materials is purely a matter of aesthetics. People continue to expect solid stock in secondary locations on furniture, and they naturally expect to pay for this feature. Since solid woods are generally unavailable in thicknesses that most cabinetmakers prefer for drawer sides (½ or ⅝ in.), stocks have to be milled down with a thickness planer. The plan-

ing takes a little time and results in some waste, but most customers prefer to pay these costs for the sake of beautiful solid drawer components. Naturally, shop owners without a planer are at a disadvantage here.

In the modern trade, there is really no reason not to allow the drawer bottom to be received into a machined slot in the drawer back. Before cabinetmakers began to use plywoods for drawer bottoms, there was a purpose for attaching the back with nails from below. The old-fashioned solid drawer bottoms were subject to cracking, splitting, and warping. There was a good chance that a drawer bottom would have to be repaired or replaced before the drawer showed any other signs of wear. Of course, a bottom held into dadoes on all four sides could not be removed without tearing apart the rest of the box. Therefore, it was wise to allow easy removal of the bottom, and a slip-in back was a good idea. Nowadays, there is no reason for a back that is easily removed. A plywood bottom may even outlive the glue bonds on the rest of the drawer box. Of course, the cabinetmaker may want to build his or her drawer boxes in the old way. There is nothing wrong with the technique (although a slotted back is stronger), but there is no longer any real need to build this way.

Dovetail joints are among the strongest joints that can be incorporated into a drawer box. Probably more important, dovetail joints are beautiful—and creating beauty is one of our goals.

The details necessary for a dovetail joint may be cut by hand or with the aid of a router and special jig. The interlocking portions of wood are referred to as tails and pins. On handmade dovetail joints, tails are usually wider than pins. In fact, it is most usual for the tails to be exactly twice as wide as the pins. The half-tails, at the top and bottom of the drawer side, should naturally be half the width of the other tails. This terminology refers to the visible parts of the joint after it has been assembled. (See Figure 13-8.)

FIGURE 13-8 Structure of a dovetail joint.

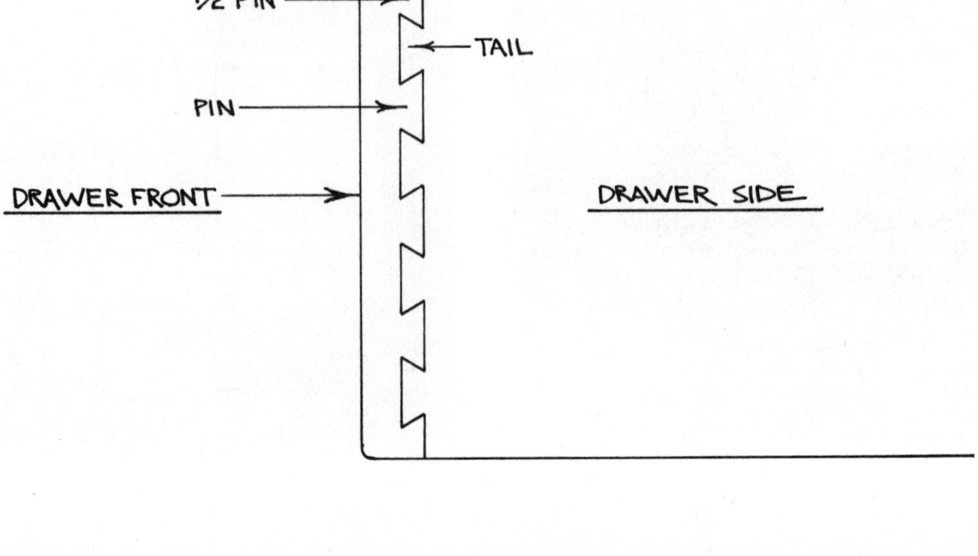

½ PIN

TAIL

PIN

DRAWER FRONT

DRAWER SIDE

FIGURE 13-9 Marking the end of a drawer side for cut depth. (Line has been darkened for visibility in the photograph.)

FIGURE 13-10 Marking lines for the angled cuts. (Lines have been darkened for visibility in the photograph.)

The tapered projections on ends of the side are the tails. If we are cutting the dovetails by hand, we shape the tails first. Cutting by hand requires the sharpest of tools, including a pointed marking tool, a dovetail saw, and wood chisels. A T-bevel and a conventional square are also useful.

The first matter is to determine the tail length. This will establish how deep the entry cuts need to be. If we are using a subfront, we will naturally make the tails to be exactly as long as the depth of the subfront. More commonly, we fit the tails directly into sockets cut in the actual drawer front, and we do not want the ends of the tails to project all the way through and be visible on the face of the drawer. When drawer fronts are approximately ¾ in. thick, it is common to give the attaching tails a length of ⅜ in. or slightly more. We mark a line across the face of each side at this dimension from the end. For this, it is considered best to score the line rather than to mark it with a pencil. We may use a marking gauge for this purpose, or we can mark with the sharpened point of an awl, using a conventional square as a guide. Most important is an accurate and narrow line. (See Figure 13-9.) All sides should be marked at once, of course.

The craftsman may need to spend some time in dimensioning the tails. Remember that the most common practice is to make each tail twice as wide as each pin, measured at their widest points. Thus ½-in. pins in the drawer front would suggest 1-in. tails in the matching side. Also, the angle of the cuts should be between 78 and 83°. Softer woods call for the more severe angles (75 to 80°). With this information, we can mark the face of each drawer side for its angled cuts. We do this with the aid of the T-bevel set to the desired angle. (See Figure 13-10.) Then we hold each side firmly in place and cut along the waste side of each angled line, being careful not to saw through the depth of cut line. The side may be held in a wood vise or

with hand screws. It is desirable to make each cut straight across the end of the stock, and it can therefore be helpful to guide the start of each cut with a square. (See Figure 13-11.) When all the angled cuts have been made, we can finish removing material between the tails in any convenient way, as long as we do not cross any lines. A coping saw is frequently used to cut away most of the material. A sharp chisel is used to remove the rest.

With tails properly cut into the sides, the cabinetmaker next turns attention to the front (and back, too, if dovetailing is planned for these joints). Each side is used to mark the end stock where it will actually be going. We hold the front firmly in a hand screw or wood vise, end up. The side is positioned over the end of the front *exactly* as will be required when we assemble the drawer. Then we

FIGURE 13-11 Guiding the start of a tail cut with a square.

FIGURE 13-12 Marking the depth of cut on the inner face of the drawer front. Note the markings to indicate a socket.

use a sharp point to mark the outline of the tails onto the end of the front. At this point in the procedure, it is imperative to mark the pieces that come together at each corner with a number or letter. We are fitting a unique side to a unique end, and getting pieces mixed up can result in very sloppy joints.

We also need to mark a depth of cut line across the inside face of the drawer front. Marked with an awl again, this line should define a depth of cut exactly equal to the thickness of the drawer side, as measured from the end of the front. (See Figure 13-12.) The depth of cut has to be deeper, naturally, if the drawer front must also receive a rabbet on its end. Finally, we mark lines perpendicular to the end, dividing the width of the front into socket and pin segments.

Next, we cut sockets into the end of the drawer front to allow insertion of the tails. This can be time consuming, because not even the entry cuts are through cuts unless we are using a subfront. (See Figure 13-13.) Finally, we take the time to remove all the socket material with sharp chisels. It is important to be patient here. If we try to remove too much material at once, we run a risk of splitting a pin. Patience also aids us in staying on the waste sides of each line, and this gives us the perfect fit we desire whenever we make this joint.

After accomplishing a proper fit at each corner, the box is ready for final machining and assembly. If rabbeting is necessary on the front, this is the time for it. This is also the time for cutting slots to hold the bottom. It is not difficult to lose orientation and accidentally cut the slots in the wrong place, especially on sides. After all the careful

fitting, nothing would be more annoying. It helps for the cabinetmaker to dry assemble each box, and mark slot location clearly.

Some cabinetmakers have developed a few power shortcuts for "handmade" dovetails, as well. The table saw can be used for making the tails, for example, For the entry cuts, we use a top-beveled blade, like one of the outside blades in a dado head set. The angle of cut is controlled by tilting the blade while blade height determines the length of tails (depth of cut). Sides are fed on end with an extended face miter gauge. After entry cuts are made, waste material is easy to remove with a coping saw, or we can use a series of feeds on the table saw. A subfront design allows similar machining for the pin stocks. A flat-topped blade is used in its upright position. Blade height controls socket depth. We feed pieces on end, with the extended-face miter gauge, but we change the angle of feed to achieve the tapered pins. This procedure allows us to "handmake" and yet produce identical details, if we machine every piece exactly the same before changing setups. This is a good system when we have to dovetail many drawer parts, but we still desire a hand-cut look. There are at least two drawbacks, however. First, it is easy to get mixed up on pieces, locate them wrong somehow, and wind up with angles cut on the wrong sides of lines or even cut backwards. Thus we usually wind up marking pieces by hand anyway, and merely removing material with the aid of a machine. Second, this is not really cutting by hand at all. If we are committed to handmade dovetails, it may be better to cut them by hand. Besides, the time spent in changing and perfecting setups might just as well be spent with a chisel in one hand and a mallet in the other.

There is no doubt that precision, hand-cut dovetails have an exquisite appearance. For the appreciative, they

FIGURE 13-13 The socket entry cuts must be made carefully. We must stay within all limiting lines. Note the perpendicular lines that separate pin and socket (waste) sections.

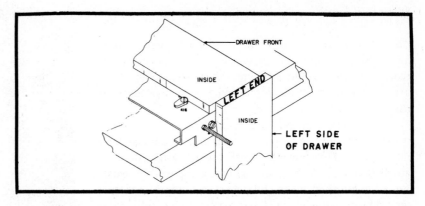

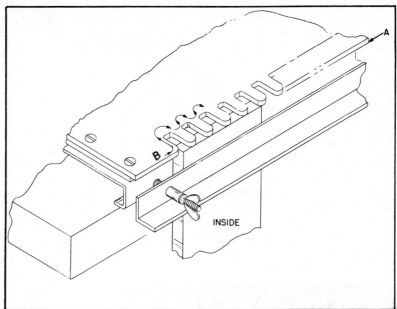

FIGURE 13-14 Matching pieces are clamped into the dovetailing jig and milled at the same time. (Courtesy of Porter-Cable Corporation.)

truly are worth the trouble. Few modern customers are willing to pay for the time required to build drawers in this way, but when price is not an issue, they are also a pleasure to construct.

Cutting dovetails with a router and special dovetailing template is also an option. Most dovetailed drawers found on modern factory-made furniture are cut by machine.

Dovetailing with a router is relatively simple. It is certainly much simpler than hand-cutting the same details. The router is fitted with a dovetailing bit and collar to follow the contours of the template. Each manufacturer of templates will specify particular instructions for use, but these tools are nearly all used in approximately the same way. Two pieces, a matching front and side, for example, are clamped in place and detailed at the same time. Since perfect positioning of the pieces is so important, the template is equipped with knobs or other controls for fine adjustment and stops which can be used for repetitious cuts. With the pieces clamped correctly in position, it is a fairly simple matter to follow the "fingers" of the template with

the router to achieve matching detail cuts. (See Figure 13-14.)

Routing dovetails with a template will produce tails that fit around pins quite well. There are some obvious differences between these and hand-cut dovetails, however. In the first place, the cuts are rounded where they meet. Tails are rounded on the inside, and sockets are round as well. We cannot see this on the assembled drawer. Also, the widths of routed tails and pins are exactly the same size. This helps make it easier, when browsing through an antique store, to tell the difference between older hand-made furniture pieces and newer ones. The depth-of-cut line, cut fairly deeply into the sides, may also be an indication of handcrafting.

Regardless of how the details are cut, components should fit together rather snugly. When all the cuts have been made for the dovetailed drawer, the pieces are then glued and clamped together. As in assembling any drawer, we should take care to ensure a square box, checking with a reliable, rigid square and adjusting the clamp position as necessary.

Mounting Furniture Accessories

The cabinetmaker who is proficient with the common door and drawer mounting procedures is already prepared to mount accessories into furniture. The systems employed are familiar ones, employing techniques we looked at in earlier chapters.

It is very common for a cabinetmaker to use some type of butt hinge in mounting doors to a traditional furniture piece. Pivot hinges, actually recessed into the top and bottom ends of the door, are also an option. On most furniture, hinges should be fully mortised into surfaces that they contact. Growing much more prevalent are fully concealed European style hinges. In most cases, then, a cabinetmaker will choose a hinge system for furniture which lends itself to concealment. As we have observed, though, hinge choice is a matter of taste, and some cabinetmakers will want to use hinges that have high visibility. Most people still prefer to avoid the spring-loaded, self-closing hinges, however. Doors may be kept closed with conventional friction or magnetic catches, but on furniture it is more common to see bullet catches (Figure 13-15) or surface latches (Figure 13-16).

There are a number of specialty hinges that a cabinetmaker buys and uses in specific applications. Gate-leg tables and some types of folding card table may require the

FIGURE 13-16   Surface latches on the doors of a "hoosier" cabinet.

use of special hinges, for example. Cabinetmakers who plan to build a good deal of furniture should familiarize themselves with the most common of these specialty hinges.

Drawer guiding systems, too, are those we have already looked at. The vinyl-coated guides and steel side guides are becoming more prevalent, but many furniture drawers are still guided with wood. We looked closely at techniques for mounting with side guides in Chapter 4.

When installing drawers and wooden guides in furniture, the cabinetmaker should focus on several keys in order to gain good results. Most important is beginning with a square drawer box and an equally square cabinet opening in which to fit it. Perfect squareness is vital when the drawer guides themselves are dadoed into the sides of the box (as in Figure 13-1), because we cannot make adjustments very easily.

To mount wood guides for the drawer sides to slide on is a simple process. The first matter is to set the wooden strips at the desired height. If the facing has rails below each drawer, we simply align the top of each wooden guide with the top of one of the rails. The rails should be wide enough to reach from their support position beneath the drawer sides to a fastening position on the interior or the finished end or another vertical member. (See Figure 13-17.) Of course, this strip should be perfectly perpendicular with the face of the cabinet, but if we are at all uncertain about the drawer front conforming properly to the face frame, we can raise or lower the rear of the guide as necessary for adjustment. Therefore, it is wise to surface mount the wooden guides with screws and no glue. This allows us to withdraw screws and change position of the guide as needed. After we are absolutely certain that we have positioned the wood guide in the right place, we can add glue blocks. Since it is usually necessary to change screw position only minimally, we should fill up undesirable screw

FIGURE 13-15   Bullet catch mounted in the top end of a door. The "bullet" is spring loaded and moves in and out.

FIGURE 13-17 Wood drawer guide fastened directly to the finished end.

holes with toothpicks or similar materials. This allows us to punch a new starting hole quite close to the old one.

The cabinetmaker adjusts side-to-side spacing of the drawer next. A drawer box is generally built approximately $\frac{1}{8}$ in. narrower than its intended opening. The spacing is necessary because solid stocks can swell a good deal, and the swelling can be enough to prohibit a drawer from opening. On the other hand, we do not want a sloppy fit, and we cannot simply allow a drawer box to bounce along on its guides. Therefore, we position strips to prohibit the sideways movement of each box. The strips must be narrow enough so that swelling of the wood fibers will not present a problem. The strips are seldom more than $\frac{3}{4}$ in. wide, often thinner. The thickness of the strips is whatever is needed to keep the drawer moving in and out in a straight

FIGURE 13-18 L-shaped wooden drawer guide. This type is milled to allow minimal friction with the face of the drawer side.

line. Sometimes this means only a shim; sometimes it means a thicker piece.

Naturally, it is possible to fabricate L-shaped pieces as wooden guides. These will both support the weight of the drawer and limit side-to-side movement. (See Figure 13-18.) As with anything made of wood, many variations are achievable. Still, the wooden guides we find in furniture are generally based on the same principles—hardwood strips to carry the weight of the drawer and pieces used as spacers on the sides. Antitip rails may be needed, but the wood guides can be made to serve in this way also, for the drawer below.

FURNITURE TOE PIECES

Furniture toe pieces are often different from those on installed cabinets. Installed cabinetry toekicks are almost always recessed. This arrangement allows a space for toes when we need to stand right next to a cabinet. A recessed kick is also more effective at hiding its own nicks and scratches. Furniture kicks often project. The effect is often a beautiful decoration, but projecting kicks may also have a primary function of contributing to stability. Since furniture is not installed, it can tend to tip forward when its doors or drawers are opened, especially if doors and drawers are fairly heavy. (See Figure 13-19.) Toe space is possible with a projecting toe piece, too. To achieve this, we simply cut away material on the bottom of the toe piece in a scalloped or decorative cut before mounting it on the cabinet. (See Figure 13-20.) Toe pieces such as this are generally mitered to meet in each corner. It is usually quite simple to conceal fasteners by driving them from the rear.

FIGURE 13-19   Note the projecting toe piece on this armoire. It adds stability to a piece with very heavy doors and drawer fronts.

FIGURE 13-20   Projecting toe piece cut for decoration and for toe space.

FIGURE 13-21   This chest has feet planted on its bottom to keep the sides, the front, and the rear of the chest off the floor.

However, on some of the finest of furniture, a separate toe piece (a plinth) is assembled and then attached to the bottom of the cabinetry with screws and glue blocks.

On some pieces, we need no toe piece whatsoever. Most tables are like this, obviously, and so are many other pieces with shaped legs. On a cedar chest, we may desire to raise the cabinetry off the floor by an inch or so. In this situation, we can attach blocks or "feet" to the chest's bottom. Held back far enough from the front, rear, and sides of the chest, the feet are hardly visible. (See Figure 13-21.)

FURNITURE JOINTS AND FASTENING SYSTEMS

Furniture joints and fastening systems are a necessity in some types of furniture construction. Earlier, we looked at several methods for concealing or avoiding fasteners, and these approaches are of value to custom furniture makers because we usually desire nothing to show on a wood furniture surface except for wood. In addition to using one of these systems, it is frequently necessary to create other special joints, especially in mounting tops to their cases.

Overhanging Tops

There are several systems that the maker of furniture can use to attach an overhanging top. Each system is easy to use, but in using any of them, we should remind ourselves to allow for shrinking and expansion. In much fine furniture, tops are made of solid materials.

An excellent way to attach a solid top is with conventional hold-downs. We make a shrinkage allowance with slotted screw holes. For screws at the front of the piece, we would drill standard clearance holes. For positions farther toward the back, we make slotted holes and drive the screw in the center of the slot. This keeps the

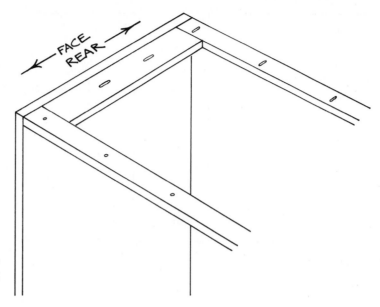

FIGURE 13-22 Hold-down for solid tops should possess slotted screw holes except in front.

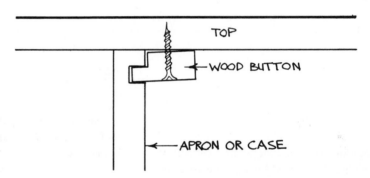

FIGURE 13-23 "Wood buttons" have a lip that fits into a slot in the case. Note spacings allowed for movement.

front overhang consistent but allows a solid top to shrink and to expand in width. (See Figure 13-22.)

A second attachment system that makes use of slotted holes for screws involves mounting an L-shaped metal bracket, called a shrinkage plate. One leg of the L has conventional screw clearance holes and is mounted to the case. The other leg possesses the slotted holes, allowing for expansion and contraction of the top. There are often two slots on the bracket, arranged at a right angle to one another. We insert the screw through the slot that is perpendicular to grain direction.

Wood buttons are another possibility. These are small blocks of wood with a protrusion or lip at the end. The lip fits into a slot cut into the vertical members of the case, and the button is screwed to the top. (See Figure 13-23.)

Maybe the most common fastening system for overhanging furniture tops is a type of toe-screwing called pocket screwing. The wood worker drills an angled pocket and clearance hole through the rear surface of the apron or case and attaches the top directly with screws. (See Figure 13-24.)

FIGURE 13-24 Tilted pocket screws were used to attach this top and apron.

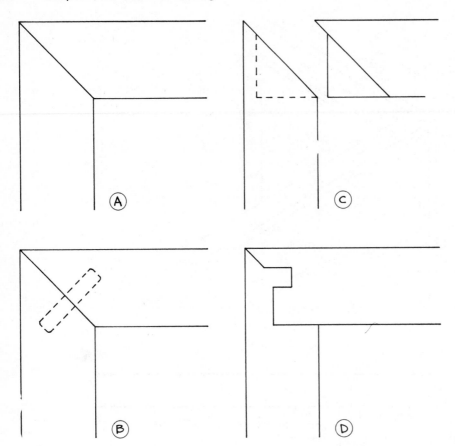

FIGURE 13-25 Four methods of attaching a flush furniture top.

Flush Tops

To attach a top that must be flush with the finished ends of a furniture piece, we need a worked joint. There are many such joints that cabinetmakers have developed over the centuries, and we will not try to look at them all. An individual cabinetmaker will often experiment and find his or her own system.

Mitering may be the most obvious solution. The setup is easy, and we can make simple through cuts on the ends of boards where they meet. (See Figure 13-25A.) However, a simple miter, with no reinforcement, is usually not considered strong enough to be used on furniture. If it can be concealed, a square strip of wood can be screwed to the top and finished end from inside, to serve as a corner brace. It is more common to strengthen the miter with further machining.

A rather simple solution to achieve is to make the conventional miter cuts all the way across the top and finished ends, and then to join the pieces with a blind spline. (See Figure 13-25B.)

Another possibility is to utilize blind rabbets in conjunction with mitering cuts. (See Figure 13-25C.) This looks like a through miter, but it is a much stronger joint. On the end of the top we first cut the required bevel-topped rabbet. The material can be cut away with two through cuts

on the table saw. Then we simply extend the miter across its face, to the desired depth. On the finished end, the rabbet is stop-cut first. Then it is mitered with a through cut.

An excellent choice is a combination of the miter and a tongue and groove. (See Figure 13-25D.) This type of joint is usually made with router bits or shaper knives, in through cuts. (See Figure 13-26.) Of course, it is possible to perform stop cuts in this detail, and to show only a conventional miter joint in front, but most cabinetmakers prefer to show their own abilities and allow the shape of this precision joint to show on the front edge.

Through dovetails and straight finger joints are other joining systems that require precise machining, and the cabinetmaker does not hestitate to use these for joining a top to finished ends, allowing the end grains to show.

A further possibility is to use veneers or skins (⅛-in. plywood) over a case made entirely of secondary woods. In following this procedure, the cabinetmaker must think about the ways in which the wood will shrink and expand. In particular, if solid stock is used as secondary or tertiary material to build the case, its tendency to shrink and swell in width and thickness can adversely affect the work done in veneers and skins. For example, we could build a cabinet with a flush top by laying a board over the piece used for the finished end and sand it flush. To cover the end grain of the top which shows at the top of the finished end,

FIGURE 13-26 Shaper knife for cutting a lock miter—the combination of a tongue and groove and a miter. (Courtesy of Delta International Machinery Corp.)

we could simply cover the ends with veneer. The trouble is that the solid pieces in the cabinet will change in width and thickness so much that the veneer job will be ruined. It will not take long for the seam line to be projected through the veneer. In the type of joint we are looking at here, veneers and skins can be attached over cases made of MDF and plywood more reliably than those made of solid stocks, and joints with exposed end grain should be avoided in the substrate behind veneer.

In choosing among the several designs for attachment of tops, the first determining factor is whether the top is flush or overhanging. For the overhanging top, any of the fastening systems is fairly easy to apply, but wood buttons may require a bit more time than the others. Other than a straight miter, none of the flush attachment systems can really be called easy to do. The key is again patience. The woodworker must be willing to spend time in achieving setups that are as precise as possible. In the sort of machining required, stocks should be as straight and flat as possible. With warped pieces, good results are nearly impossible to achieve. Naturally, it is important for the woodworker to use sample and practice pieces as much like the furniture components as possible.

TURNINGS

Turnings are pieces created by milling stocks as they are rotated. Turnings are frequently used as legs for chairs, tables and other furniture. They are also used as decor elements on some furniture pieces. We see these as finials on antique highboys. It is also possible to split a turning and mount it to the surface of a flat piece for decoration. (See Figure 13-27.)

In factory operations, and even in a few specialty shops, turning is a repetitious procedure. If hundreds of turnings have to be prepared, large-scale manufacturers use automated lathes that will produce exactly the same pattern over and over again. The cutters are set to achieve a desired shape, and the cutters themselves turn on a spindle. In fact, they turn at quite high speeds while the wood

FIGURE 13-27 Drawer chest with split spindles mounted to the face.

stock turns rather slowly. With cutters set up and stock in place, the turning of a single piece takes only seconds.

On the other hand, many cabinetmakers still use conventional wood lathes to accomplish beautiful turnings. Factory turnings are obviously not unique creations. Thus, for the builder of custom furniture, a wood lathe may be indispensable.

A wood lathe is simply a tool for holding wood securely and turning it while the craftsman uses a hand tool to create a shape by cutting or shaving away material. Each workpiece is held between the tool components called the headstock and the tailstock. (See Figure 13-28.) The headstock is connected to a motor and actually turns the workpieces. It is therefore stationary on the bed and has a spur center that will not allow stock ends to slip. The tailstock can be moved along the bed and locked in place according to the length of turning stocks being used, and it possesses a "cup center" which allows the stock to turn. When certain types of turnings are done on the lathe (such as bowls), we mount the workpiece only to the headstock, using a screw-in type of center or a face plate. Also mounted to the bed of the lathe is a component called a tool rest. The

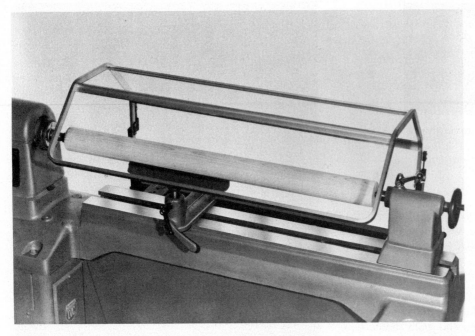

FIGURE 13-28 Wood lathe. Headstock is at left of bed; tailstock is at right. Between the two is the tool rest. Also note the safety shield. (Courtesy of Delta International Machinery Corp.)

tool rest is used for support of all the lathe hand tools. These, together with the clear shield that is used for a guard, are the principal parts of a lathe.

Designing the Turning

The first step in creating a turned article is designing. Of course, it is possible to go ahead and mount a wood stock and just "design as you go." In fact, this is probably a very good way for the novice turner to gain familiarity with lathe tools and achievable shapes. Experienced lathe operators will frequently proceed like this if they are making one-of-a-kind turnings. For example, only one turning was necessary to create the half-spindles in Figure 13-27.

On the other hand, drawing out the design is usually beneficial and sometimes necessary, especially if the wood worker has to make two or more turnings to be exactly the same. An example here would be the duplicate turnings needed for table legs. In fact, the wood turner who is making duplicates should make a full-scale line drawing of the piece on thin, rigid material (such as a piece of plastic laminate). We can then cut and sand to the line on the drawing and use this piece as a pattern or template. Each turning that we do can be checked for desired shape simply by holding the template along its edge. To arrive at a design, the turner will need to know what shapes are achievable with a standard lathe and a set of turning tools. These are as follows (Figure 13-29):

- *Bead:* convex section
- *Cove:* concave section
- *Taper:* (Probably self-explanatory) cone section
- *Rectangle:* (Self-explanatory) squared section

- *Shoulder:* rounded transition section (partial bead), usually connecting a rectangle to another section
- *Fillet:* transition section such as part of a cove

In addition to these are combination sections, such as vase-type shapes.

Using the Lathe

In general, we begin work on the lathe by mounting a square piece of stock into it. It is important to find the exact center on each end of the workpiece. By mounting the piece at its exact center, we keep vibrations to a minimum and keep rectangular sections on the finished piece properly centered. The easiest way to find the exact center is to draw two diagonal lines across each end. If we are careful to derive the lines from the exact corner, they will cross exactly in the center of the piece. (See Figure 13-30.) We punch a hole here with an awl for centering the spur or cup. It is probably best to remove the spur center from the headstock and tap it into the center on one end of the stock because there must be no slippage. When we tap the spur center in, we can use a block to protect it from a hammer or we can tap with a wooden mallet. A bit of paraffin should be applied to the cup center to reduce friction. Then we insert the spur back into the headstock (wood still attached), slide the tailstock along the bed until the point of the cup center is in firm contact with the workpiece, and lock the tailstock in position.

There are some safety concerns that must be dealt with in operating a lathe. As with all power tools, it is important to avoid loose clothing and jewelry. A matter that relates specifically to lathe use is proper placement of

FIGURE 13-29 This spindle consists mostly of bead sections. At the top is a rectangle with beveled edges. Its transition to the top bead section is a combination fillet and shoulder. Note the cove section and the ''vase'' directly below.

FIGURE 13-30 We can find the exact center of the stock by drawing diagonal lines. Where they cross, we punch a hole in which to position the spur or cup center.

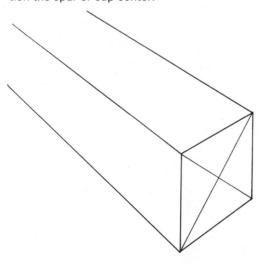

the tool rest. There should never be more than a ¼-in. space between the tool rest and the spinning wood stock.

One of the dangers of lathe operation is the potential for the wood stock to loosen and fly out of the machine. There are several misadjustments that can cause this, and the operator needs to take precautions before beginning any actual turning. First, the turner should make sure that the wood being worked on is held securely in both the headstock and tailstock. The spur center should be well embedded in the headstock end. At the tailstock end, the cup center should be embedded deep enough for its rim to penetrate the wood, and the locks that secure both the tailstock and the spindle in place should be secure. The turning speed must not be too high. The larger the diameter of the workpiece, the lower the speed setting must be. The type of shaping to be done is also a factor in speed settings. Rough shaping should be done at lower rpm ratings than finer-shaping cuts and sanding. If the tool has a clear plastic shield, this should be kept in place.

Lathe tools should be held securely. Most right-handed operators grip the rear of the tool's wooden handle with the right hand, in a firm but comfortable way. Far from the tool rest, this hand exerts most of the control over cutting and scraping. The left hand maintains fine control, near the tool rest. On many rough cuts, the left hand wraps palm down over the tool, like a fist. On finer cutting and scraping operations, we use the left thumb on top of the tool, fingers beneath.

The first cutting on the wood lathe is usually a roughing cut, turning the square stock into essentially round stock. It is important for two reasons. In the first place, we can raise the turning speed, once the square corners have been removed, and lathe tools work more smoothly at higher rpm ratings. In the second place, the square corners will result in a good deal of vibration as well as chipped and torn wood fibers. If planning a rectangular section in the turning, we have to mark the limits of this section so that we remember not to do any rounding in this section of the wood. With our workpiece now a cylinder, we can raise the speed of the tool and begin cutting in our chosen details.

For most turning, we generally proceed in this order:

1. With the stock turning, mark the limits of an individual shape (cove, bead, etc.) with a pencil.
2. If the shape is symmetrical and fairly long, mark the center of the shape as a reference. It may be a help to transfer this centering line to the tool rest.
3. Make entry cuts at the limiting lines. These are V-grooves for coves and beads; they are flat bottomed kerfs or parting cuts for tapers.
4. If particular diameters are required (as is often

the case, especially with duplicate pieces), reference depth cuts should be made. An example is the deepest part of a cove.

5. Reference diameters should be checked with outside calipers.

6. Remove material until the desired shape is achieved.

7. Smooth surfaces with appropriate tools and sandpaper.

Lathe Tools

For cutting wood stocks mounted in the lathe, we have three types of tools: gouges, skew chisels, and parting tools. (See Figure 13-31.)

A parting tool is used to separate or "part" sections from each other. It is used for making deep, narrow cuts such as the limiting cuts at the end of a taper and the depth reference cuts in the center of a cove.

A skew chisel is very versatile. It has a beveled cutting edge. The portion that projects farthest from the handle is called the point; the other end of the bevel is called the heel. The midsection of the cutting edge may be used for smooth cutting on straight and coved sections, as well as shoulder cuts. The point and the heel will cut V-grooves, as when making entries for coves, beads, and shoulders.

Gouges generally remove more material than that removed by any other lathe tool. They are used for turning the stock into a cylinder, for tapering, and cove cutting.

The gouge, the parting tool, and the skew chisel most often do their cutting just above the center of the stock.

FIGURE 13-31 Lathe tools.

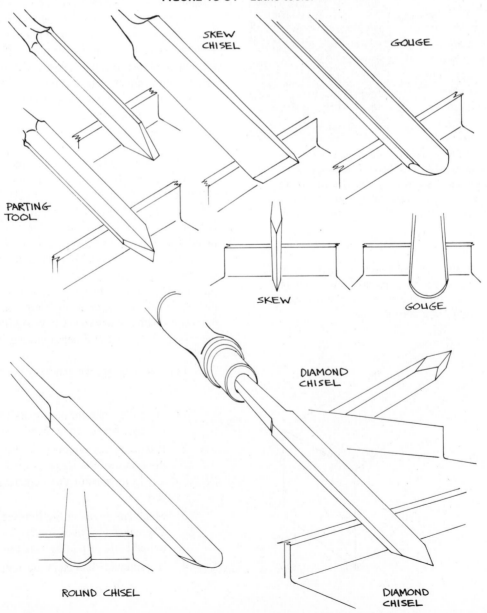

That is, the handle of the tool is held so that it is a bit lower than the cutting edge.

The lathe tools called roundnose, squarenose, and diamond-pointed chisels are held similarly, but they are used bevel down. They remove material more slowly than the first three lathe tools we looked at, and they are therefore employed for slower-speed turning and turning of thick stocks. It is common to use these tools for turning wood bowls and in other applications where we do not use the tailstock, but rather, mount our workpiece to the headstock only, by means of screwing it onto a faceplate.

As suggested earlier, the best way of learning to use lathe tools is to initiate a project that requires a few turnings. Some cabinetmakers who are confident in other projects will sometimes feel some hesitation about doing turnings, but there is no reason to feel this way. We should look at the use of the lathe simply as another problem-solving task in the field of cabinetmaking. The owner or worker in a small shop, who is most likely to use a lathe, will want to spend some time learning to manipulate the machine and the tools to produce specific designs. This prepares him or her for achieving particular turnings.

CHAPTER SUMMARY OF CABINETMAKING SKILLS

Furniture making is simply cabinetmaking which results in products that are movable instead of fixed to a wall or floor. Furniture must therefore be stronger and more rigid than installed cabinetry, and all its exterior surfaces are primary surfaces (except the back). Dovetailed drawer joints, wooden drawer guides, concealed fastening, plinths, and rigidity without a face frame are systems that a furniture builder will often employ.

The cabinetmaker who builds furniture must develop skills and methods for building strength into a furniture piece, especially if the piece is to have no face frame. Techniques that are important for this are the use of horizontal framework, rabbeted backs, rear frames, and braces.

Furniture drawer boxes are frequently dovetailed. Dovetails may be cut with a router aided by a special jig, or they may be cut by hand. In hand cutting, tails are made to be twice as wide as pins. Important tools for this are a dovetail and coping saw, a combination square, and a T-bevel, together with a sharp marking instrument.

Furniture building also calls for ability in using certain hinges—butt hinges and European hinges, primarily, in addition to some specialty hinge options.

Furniture drawer guiding is still by means of wood guides, although there is no functional reason for this. Side guides, especially the vinyl-coated ones, are being used more frequently. A variety of techniques may be employed to affix the wood guides.

Furniture toe pieces often protrude. This lends stability and decor. Special fastening methods are also employed to affix furniture tops to the rest of the unit—methods as simple as slotted-screw clearance holes and those as tricky to make as a combination miter–tongue-and-groove worked joint.

Turnings often make up furniture components. In high-production environments, thousands of identical spindles may be turned out by machine. Small shop operators learn mastery of the lathe instead.

INDEX